FEARLESS CRITIC

PRAISE FOR THE RESTAURANT GUIDES

"Pulls no punches...even icons get goosed."
–Austin American-Statesman

"Deft, unblushing prose...good friends to the
honest diner, they call it as they see it."
–T. Susan Chang, Boston Globe

"Exceptionally experienced restaurantgoers...
knowledgeable and enthusiastic about eating well."
–Yale Daily News

"Immensely useful, written with panache, as
respectful of 'Roadfood' as of 'fine-dining'... one of
the most compelling restaurant guides we've seen."
–Jane and Michael Stern, columnists, Gourmet

"Not just a useful book—a pleasure to read. The
only people who won't find it a pleasure are the
owners of some of the really bad restaurants it
warns us away from."
–David Ball, Professor Emeritus of
Comparative Literature, Smith College

"Scathing and scintillating."
–New Haven Register

THIRD EDITION, 2011/2012

Printed in the United States of America

10 9 8 7 6 5 4 3 2 1

ISBN 978-1-60816-041-9

FEARLESS CRITIC

HOUSTON RESTAURANT GUIDE

THIRD EDITION, REVISED & UPDATED

FEARLESSCRITIC.COM/HOUSTON

CONTENTS

HOUSTON CRITICS

Erin McReynolds, Houston Editor and Chief Critic

Panelists: Collier Chin, Robert Dubose, Jodie Eisenhardt, Willet Feng, Michael Fulmer, Misha Govshteyn, Huan Le, Judy Le, Ruthie Johnson Miller, Jody Stevens, Hannah Siegel-Gardner, Victoria Rittinger, Theo Shu, Richard Sucgang, Jenny Wang, Justin Yu

FEARLESS CRITICS

Robin Goldstein, Founder and Editor-in-Chief
Alexis Herschkowitsch, Managing Editor and Associate Publisher
Erin McReynolds, Editor and Chief Houston Critic
Kent Wang, Chief Technology Officer
Seamus Campbell, iPhone App Developer
Colleen Owens, Associate Editor and Social Media Director
Andrea Armeni, Contributing Editor
Justin Yu, Executive Chef
Dolly Li, Summer Intern
Tim Palin, Graphic Designer
Evan O'Neil, Graphic Designer
Hanami Sutton, Graphic Designer

FOUNDING EDITORS

Barry Goldstein, David Menschel, Clare Murumba, Susan Stubbs, Hal Stubbs, Lu Stubbs

SPECIAL THANKS

Fearless Critic Media would like to thank Ed Cavazos, Leslie Doherty, Julian Faulkner, Andrea Fleck-Nisbet, Andrew Gajkowski, Rosie Goldstein, Shannon Kelly, Kurtis Lowe, Jenny Mandel, David Matt, Colleen Owens, Jill Owens, Steven Pace, Judy Peck, Michael Powell, Marci Saunders, April Savard, Walter Schmamp, Giuliano Stiglitz, Frank Tasty, Heather Tietgens, Chris Tudor, Katie Tudor, Mike Vago, Sara Vielma-Bay, Tyce Walters, Walter Weintz, Peter Workman, the Yale Entrepreneurial Society, and the staff at Workman Publishing.

ABOUT THE HOUSTON EDITOR

ERIN MCREYNOLDS has written and edited for the Fearless Critic restaurant guides to Austin, Houston, Portland, Washington DC, and New Haven, making her one of few people in the country successfully using her MFA in creative writing. Her dream is to design a course that uses a combination of erotica and Malcolm Gladwell to produce better food and wine writers. She thinks the answer to America's problems is making everyone work in the restaurant industry for a while—many people will become better for it; the rest will be too jaded to muck things up. Also? More penguin-hugging.

ABOUT THE SERIES EDITORS

ROBIN GOLDSTEIN is the founder and editor-in-chief of the Fearless Critic series, a contributing writer to the New York Times "Freakonomics" blog, and the co-author of The Wine Trials, the world's bestselling guide to wine under $15. He has been a visiting scholar in behavioral economics at the University of California, Berkeley; authored six books of restaurant reviews; and written for more than 30 Fodor's travel guides, from Italy to Mexico, Argentina to Hong Kong. Robin is a graduate of Harvard University and the Yale Law School, and has a certificate in cooking from the French Culinary Institute in New York and a WSET advanced wine and spirits certificate. He is also a co-author of the watershed academic paper "Can People Tell Apart Pâté from Dog Food?", which inspired Stephen Colbert to eat a can of Fancy Feast cat food on national TV.

ALEXIS HERSCHKOWITSCH has written and edited for The Wine Trials, five Fearless Critic guides, and five Fodor's travel guides, from El Salvador to Thailand. Alexis is a graduate of the University of Texas at Austin and has a WSET advanced wine and spirits certificate. She consumes implausible quantities of crickets, horsemeat, and congealed goat's blood cubes at Gastronauts Society dinners, and later burns off the calories pole dancing.

ABOUT THE PANEL OF CRITICS

BLAIR COLLIER CHIN is known around town as "that fussy gay Asian." A Houston native who needlepoints in his spare time, he loves foie gras, gummy bears, and pool parties. Collier would never mix plaid with stripes. Don't ask him a question unless you want the honest answer. You'll generally find him drinking Champagne or extolling the virtues of the 1980s, the decade in which he was born...barely.

ROBERT DUBOSE is a lawyer and the creator of one of Houston's first food blogs, the now-defunct Food in Houston. He's also the author of the book Legal Writing for the Rewired Brain: Persuading Readers in a Paperless World, as well as a contributor to Houston It's Worth It: Ike, a book about Hurricane Ike. Robert's obsessions include mole, avant-garde jazz, type fonts, dumplings, web design, and greens. His greatest achievement is raising a daughter with a near-perfect palate.

JODIE EISENHARDT (@foodiehouston) loves rescue dogs, pastry chefs, food trucks, ginger beer, dark chocolate, and for her house to smell like just-cooked bacon. She craves food and music-related travel and firmly believes that no meal should ever be wasted, which is why she travels with her own Bunsen burner and s'mores kit. Jodie blogs at foodiehouston.blogspot.com.

WILLET FENG has the best name on the Houston panel. Don't call him "Wiley," although he certainly is, using his bad-ass chef magic to win the ladies. When he's not cooking for pro athletes, he's playing basketball or watching Dexter. Willet loves shellfish and fried eggs, and hates Subway commercials. He has a hidden birthmark, a love of all things Japanese, and a superhuman sense of smell.

MICHAEL FULMER, a Texas transplant originally from Washington, DC, was raised on his grandmother's Hungarian recipes and his father's infatuation with French cuisine. Once, he blind-tasted a sushi bar's entire menu, sparking his obsession with rare cuisines and ingredients. He has worked in the restaurant industry for more than 20 years and continues to engage in the dialectic of all things gastronomic. He also blogs about film at thebadandthebeautiful.net.

MISHA GOVSHTEYN is a professional megalomaniac by day and one of this city's surliest critics by night. However, his tough exterior conceals a puerile love of furry animals, Astroturf, and processed cheese. Misha has eaten at every Michelin-starred restaurant in the world. (Almost.) He's known for globetrotting, cherrypicking, and starting massive Twitter fights which result in civil misdemeanors. Ask him about sushi, Manresa, or his infant son. Misha blogs at tasty-bits.com.

HUAN LE is an Internet dinosaur who blogged about stocks and food long before "blog" was in the Oxford Dictionary of English. When not starting projects he can't finish, you can find him searching for the "oh damn!" moments that happen when the perfect morsel lands on the tongue. He compensates for his filial guilt about pursuing gustatory bliss by being a corporate lawyer on the side—forgive him his trespasses.

JUDY LE is the Houston panel's only mom, making her the group's disciplinarian. She previously served as food editor of Houstonist, but is taking a break from blogging to teach her baby the proper way to slurp jellyfish salad. She'll tell you where to find the greatest dumplings, ca phe sua da, and banh mi in Houston. When Judy isn't dunking on strangers in pickup basketball at the Y, she's cooking, traveling, or hunting for the perfect kimchi.

RUTHIE JOHNSON MILLER (@ruthiejsf) is a native Houstonian and former San Franciscan who loves avocado, butter, flip-flops, and every word that John Steinbeck ever wrote. Please do bring her breakfast tacos, tres leches, and puppies, but do not ever bring up eggplant, snakes, or the designated hitter. You can find her writing at greatfoodhouston.blogspot.com and culturemap.com.

VICTORIA RITTINGER loves kolaches, kittens, and shirtless soccer players. The only places she hasn't been are Antarctica, Xanadu, and the original Soviet Union. In fierce opposition to her German heritage, she hates potatoes in any form. Victoria is famous for having a dedicated drawer of animal fats in her refrigerator, and she's a staunch supporter of the theory that pie>cake.

THEO SHU (@theoShu) likes oysters. A lot. His love of Houston sports teams has resulted in anguish, self-loathing, and an unfortunate case of IBS. He numbs the pain with barbecue, old-fashioned hamburgers, and long walks on moonlit beaches. When he's not lamenting the lack of good pizza in town, he's petitioning state lawmakers to open a passable grocery store in his neighborhood.

HANNAH SIEGEL-GARDNER is a world traveler and professional writer who enjoys karaoke, latex, and the occasional Bourbon. Her love of doughnuts is legendary across Texas, as is her award-winning smile. Hannah also likes to dabble in sushi, fancypants burgers, and nasturtium. She snorts when she laughs.

JODY "CAKES" STEVENS (@jodycakes) is the chef/owner of jodycakes, which works tirelessly to sow the vegan/gluten-free seed in Houston. Few broads are as well versed in Indian food as this one, though she's known to enjoy a good burger and a whiskey. She cries when given a perfect pastry. Her favorite vacation spots all start with "I": Iceland, Ireland, Indonesia. She's the panel's ass-kicker, having served in the Air Force during Desert Storm.

RICHARD "DR. RICKY" SUCGANG is a molecular biologist and genomics scientist with a keen interest in food and cooking. He blogs at http://food.drricky.net.

JENNY WANG does her part to live up to her Twitter handle, @ImNeverFull. She's short on space, and tall on laughs, and she's been known to eat 10 pounds of crawfish in one sitting, and then follow it up with a burger crawl. In fact, If Jenny were a superhero, her name would be "The Hunger Buster," and she would keep the world safe from criminal appetites. Jenny's passions are soup dumplings, men with mustaches, and her two cats, Hello and Kitty.

JUSTIN YU—you may recognize him as a traveling member of Alice in Chains, but it is his love of Korean food and ramps that makes him an invaluable member of Houston's panel. When he's not riding bulls or skydiving, he trains snails. Also? He's a graduate of the Culinary Insitute of America, and he cooks. For money.

FOLLOW @FEARLESSCRITIC on twitter for new and revised reviews, updates, and more from the editors and critics.

THE FEARLESS CRITIC SYSTEM

If you're not familiar with the Fearless Critic style and philosophy, then welcome to a new kind of restaurant guide. Within these pages are 250 relentlessly opinionated full-page reviews of places to eat in the greater Houston area. We do not accept advertising from dining establishments, chefs, or restaurateurs.

We evaluate restaurants incognito, and we pay for our own meals. Most reviews are informed by years of repeat visits by our Fearless Critic panel, a team of local food nerds, chefs, critics, and writers who have been dining intensively in Houston for years.

In order to qualify for inclusion in this book, an establishment must serve food and be relevant to readers, whether for positive or negative reasons. Some restaurants that didn't make the cut for this book will have online reviews posted at www.fearlesscritic.com/houston. We encourage you to let us know about places we might have missed by emailing us at fearless@fearlesscritic.com, so that they might be included in the next edition.

BRUTALLY HONEST

As you might guess from the name of the book, Fearless Critic is brutally honest. We tell you exactly what we'd tell a good friend if she called us up and asked what we really thought of a place. Although some have called us "scathing," it is not our goal to stir controversy or insult restaurants.

We do believe, however, that in a world of advertorials and user-generated review websites, restaurant consumers deserve a hard-nosed advocate that can deliver the unapologetic, unvarnished truth. We hope to help you decide where to eat, and also where not to eat.

Therein, we believe, lies much of the usefulness of food criticism. For how is one to choose between two places if both are portrayed in dizzying, worshipful prose? Or if you don't know if the review you're reading is written by a real critic, or by the restaurant owner's brother?

And how frustrating is it when you spend a lot of your hard-earned money on a restaurant for a special occasion or date on the strength of what turns out to have been a sugar-coated review?

We aim for a punchy evaluation of a restaurant's strengths and weaknesses that ends with a clear judgment and recommendation. We hope that the money you've spent on this book will save you from wasting hundreds of dollars on boring meals. In short, our duty is to our readers, not to the restaurants. We don't expect you to agree with everything we say, but we do hope that you will give us the chance to earn your trust over the course of its 250 reviews. Whether you concur or dissent, we would love to hear from you. Engaging feedback makes our jobs worthwhile. Visit us at fearlesscritic.com to post your own opinions, or your thoughts on ours.

THE RATING SCALE

Two or more numerical ratings are assigned to most establishments. Ratings are not assigned to bakeries, groceries, markets, sweets shops, or other establishments that don't serve full meals.

Food rating (1 to 10 in increments of 0.1): This is a measure of the pure deliciousness of the food on offer. We close our eyes to reputation, price, and puffery when we taste, so don't be surprised to find a greasy spoon outscoring a historic, upscale, sit-down establishment, for one simple reason: the food just tastes better. Ambition and creativity are rewarded, but only if they also translate to deliciousness. A food score above 8 constitutes a recommendation; a 9 or above is a high recommendation. Don't expect grade inflation here.

Feel rating (1 to 10 in increments of 0.1): Rather than counting the number of pieces of silverware on the table or the number of minutes and seconds before the food arrives, we ask ourselves a simple question: does being here make us happy? Does the staff make us feel good? The most emphatic "yes" inspires the highest rating. We don't give out points for tablecloths or tuxedos. We reward warm lighting, comfortable seating, a finely realized theme, a strong sense of place or tradition, and a staff that's welcoming, professional, and contagiously enthusiastic about the food they're serving.

Wine, beer, and cocktail ratings (1 to 10 in increments of 0.5): Breadth, care of selection, and price are included in these ratings. More points are not necessarily awarded for the sheer number of wines, beers, or drinks served. The criteria used for these ratings are explained more fully in the "lists" section, where our rankings appear.

NEIGHBORHOODS

We have divided the city of Houston into the neighborhoods delineated below. We've listed a neighborhood more than once if it overlaps more than one of the broad subdivisions below. Outside the Houston city limits, the municipality name is listed in lieu of a neighborhood name.

OUTSIDE THE LOOP

North Houston: north of Loop 610 and east of N. Shepherd Dr. **Northwest Houston:** west of N. Shepherd Dr. and Durham Dr. and north of I-10, but not including Spring Branch. **Town & Country:** north of Memorial Dr., south of I-10, east of Sam Houston Pkwy. North, and west of Gessner Rd. **Memorial:** north of San Felipe St. and Forest Dr., south of I-10, east of Gessner Rd., west of and including Memorial Park. **Spring Branch:** north of I-10, south of Hammerly Blvd., east of Beltway 8, and west of Loop 610 and I-290. **West Houston:** north and west of Rt. 59 (Southwest Fwy.), south of I-10, but not including Chinatown, Westchase, Hillcroft, Galleria, Memorial, or Town & Country. **Westchase:** north of Westpark Tollway, south of Briar Forest Dr. and San Felipe Dr., east of Wilcrest Dr., and west of (but not including) Hillcroft Ave. and Voss Rd. **Galleria:** north of Rt. 59 (Southwest Fwy.), south of San Felipe St., east of (but not including) Hillcroft Ave. and Voss Rd., and west of Loop 610. **Hillcroft Area:** along Hillcroft Ave., north of Rt. 59 (Southwest Fwy.), and south of Westheimer. **Bellaire Chinatown:** north of Beechnut St., south of Westpark Tollway, east of Kirkwood Dr., west of Rt. 59 (Southwest Fwy.). **Bellaire:** within Bellaire municipality; or north of Beechnut St., south and east of Rt. 59 (Southwest Fwy.), and west of West University Place. **Meyerland:** north of W. Bellfort Ave., south of Holcombe Blvd., east of Chimney Rock Rd., southeast of the Bellaire municipality, and west of Buffalo Speedway. **South Houston:** South of W. Bellfort Ave., south of Loop 610 but not including Meyerland, east of S. Post Oak Rd., and west of Rt. 288. **Southeast Houston:** East of Rt. 288 and south of Loop 610. **Southwest Houston:** south of Beechnut St., south and west of Meyerland, and west of S. Post Oak Rd.

INSIDE THE LOOP, NORTH OF I-10

Northwest Houston: west of N. Shepherd Dr. and Durham Dr., north of I-10, but not including the area delineated by Spring Branch. **Heights:** north of I-10, south of Loop 610, east of N. Shepherd Dr., west of I-45. **Northeast Houston:** north of I-10 and east of I-45.

INSIDE THE LOOP, BETWEEN I-10 AND RT. 59

River Oaks: north of Rt. 59, south of Memorial Park and Memorial Dr., east of Loop 610, and west of Waugh Dr., but not including Greenway Plaza, Upper Kirby, or Montrose. **Greenway Plaza:** north of Bissonet St., south of Westheimer Rd., east of and including Weslayan St., and west of and including Buffalo Speedway. **Upper Kirby:** north of I-59, south of Inwood Dr., east of (but not including) Buffalo Speedway, and west of and including S. Shepherd Dr. **Washington:** north of Memorial Dr., south of I-10, east of Memorial Park, and west of I-45. **Montrose:** north of I-59, south of W. Gray St. and Inwood Dr., east of (but not including) S. Shepherd Dr., and west of and including Montrose Blvd. **Midtown:** northwest of Rt. 59, southwest of I-45, and east of (but not including) Montrose. **Downtown:** northeast of I-45, northwest of Rt. 59, and south of I-10. **East Houston:** inside Loop 610, east of Rt. 59, and east of Rt. 288.

INSIDE THE LOOP, SOUTH OF RT. 59

Bellaire: within Bellaire municipality; or north of Beechnut St., south and east of Rt. 59 (Southwest Fwy.), and west of West University Place. **Meyerland:** north of W. Bellfort Ave., south of Holcombe Blvd., east of Chimney Rock Rd., southeast of the Bellaire municipality, and west of Buffalo Speedway. **West U:** within the West University Place municipality; or north of Bellaire Blvd./Holcombe Blvd., south of but not including Westpark, and west of Kirby Dr. **Medical Center:** north of Loop 610, south of W. Holcombe Blvd., east of Buffalo Speedway, west of Rt. 288 PLUS the triangle north of Holcombe, east of Main St., and south of MacGregor Dr. **Rice Area:** north of the Medical Center, south of Rt. 59 (Southwest Fwy.), east of Buffalo Speedway, and west of Main St., Sunset Blvd., and Mandell St. **Hermann Park:** north of MacGregor Dr., south of Rt. 59 (Southwest Fwy.), east of the Rice area, and west of Rt. 288 (South Fwy.). **East Houston:** inside Loop 610, east of Rt. 59, east of Rt. 288.

THE OTHER STUFF ON THE PAGE

Average dinner price: This dollar value is a guide to how much, on average, you should expect to spend per person on a full dinner at the restaurant, including one alcoholic beverage and a 20% tip (for table-service establishments; we encourage you to tip at coffeeshops and take-out joints too, but we don't figure it into the meal price). At simple take-out places, this might be just a sandwich and a soda; at more elaborate sit-down restaurants, we usually figure in the cost of an appetizer (one for every person) and dessert (one for every two people). If the restaurant pushes bottled water or side dishes on you, we figure that in, too. For alcoholic drinks, too, we are guided by what people generally tend to order—from a beer to a third of a bottle of low-to-midpriced wine. Only restaurants that serve full meals and have ratings are eligible for price estimates.

Genre: Every establishment in the Fearless Critic book is associated with one or more culinary genres. Our "Lists" section includes a cross-referenced guide to all restaurants by genre. Most genres—e.g. **Indian** or **pizza**—are self-explanatory, but some require clarifiation: **American** covers traditional meat-and-potatoes fare, bar food, breakfast food, comfort food, greasy spoons, and so on. **Burgers** have their own category, as do **Steakhouses** and **Southern** cuisine, which includes soul food, fried chicken, Cajun, and Louisiana Creole cooking. We use the word **Modern** (not "New American") to describe the new wave of upmarket cuisine that draws upon diverse world ingredients and technique. This includes the market-to-table and haute nostalgic restaurants that have become fashionable lately. **Vegefusion** is world fusion cuisine aimed mainly at vegetarian and vegans. **Coffee** doesn't apply to any restaurant serving coffee—almost all of them do—but rather to an establishment where that's a particular focus.

Establishment type: We have divided eating establishments into several categories. The largest category is **casual restaurant**, which means a place with waiter service at tables but a generally laid-back atmosphere without much fuss. An **upmarket restaurant** is a place with more elegant, trendy, or special-occasion ambitions. The **counter service** category includes cafeterias, self-service places, and also establishments where you place an order at a counter but it is then brought out to your table. We see a **bar** as an establishment that's fundamentally about serving drinks at heart, but it must serve food to be included (although the kitchen often closes before the doors). Given the nature of **food carts**, their hours and locations may vary depending on weather, political events, faulty emergency brakes, and so on.

Reviews will come with a reminder to check their website or Twitter feed for the most current incormation. **Café** means a place whose primary business is the provision of coffee or tea, but it must serve food of some sort to be included in the book.

Address: We have included addresses and neighborhood designations for up to four locations, and where feasible, we have indexed additional locations in the Lists section of the book. For chains with more than four locations, consult www.fearlesscritic.com/houston for a listing of the others.

Special features: These appear in the middle column of information. By **date-friendly**, we mean establishments that we find particularly romantic in some way—and that doesn't necessarily mean tuxedoed waiters or high prices. We look for warm lighting, good vibes, and a sense of easy fun. **Kid-friendly** doesn't just mean a couple of high chairs in the corner; it means a place where the little ones will actually be happy, whether for culinary reasons or for the availability of special activities or play areas. The **live music** designation includes establishments that have it only on certain days or nights, so call ahead if it's atmospherically important to you. **Outdoor dining** can mean anything from a couple of sidewalk tables to a sprawling beer garden. **Wi-Fi** has to be free to qualify—this is the 21st century, after all. We are particularly careful when choosing which establishments to flag as **veg-friendly**. The designation is not limited to vegetarian-only places, but we look for menus where vegetarians will not just be accommodated—they'll actually have an ample selection.

FEARLESS FEEDBACK

The heart and soul of this endeavor is our belief that the world of restaurant reviewing can be improved by opening outspoken channels of communication between restaurants and their customers. If you have a bad meal, or a great one, tell the restaurant what was right and what was wrong. It can only help. And tell us too; we've set up comments at www.fearlesscritic.com/houston so that readers can express agreement or dissent. It doesn't require registration, and you can post anonymously. Our panelists will do their best to respond periodically.

THE FINE PRINT

This entire book is a work of opinion, and should be understood as such. Any and all judgments rendered upon restaurants within these pages, regardless of tense, are intended as statements of pure opinion. Facts have been thoroughly checked with the restaurants in person, via telephone, and on the restaurants' websites; we have gone to the utmost lengths to ensure that every fact is correct, and that every ingredient in every dish is properly referenced. Any factual errors that nonetheless remain are purely unintentional. That said, menus and plates (not to mention hours of operation) change so frequently at restaurants that any printed book, however new, cannot help but be a bit behind the times. Check in at www.fearlesscritic.com/houston for new reviews, updates, discussion boards, and more.

ABOUT FEARLESS CRITIC MEDIA

Fearless Critic Media is a lean, fiercely independent publishing house founded by Robin Goldstein in 2006 and dedicated to providing useful information in an engaging format. In conjunction with its partner, Workman Publishing Company, Fearless Critic Media publishes relentlessly opinionated, irreverent food and wine books. Look for The Wine Trials, The Beer Trials, and our restaurant guides to other cities, including Austin, Dallas, San Antonio, Washington DC, Portland, Seattle, and more, in bookstores, gift stores, and food and wine shops nationwide and on powells.com, barnesandnoble.com, and amazon.com. For more information, see **www.fearlesscritic.com** and follow **@fearlesscritic** on twitter. Fearless Critic books are distributed by Workman Publishing Company (workman.com).

PREFACE

You may have noticed that we've lost some weight. We're trying this new diet where we only include the top 250 restaurants that we feel are worth knowing about for whatever reason—not necessarily the food. This means that we still take the piss out of bloated icons now and then, but we also recommend some places that are worth going to just for the event of it, if not particularly for their kitchens.

Last Concert Café, for instance, gets its funkadelic groove on like no one else, while Hobbit Café is so adorably and sincerely fanatic (of the '70s as much as the Tolkein books) that you don't mind the mediocre and outdated vegetarian food. The underperforming barbecue at Goode Co. is still comforting, central, and indelible to the Houston landscape, and so it's hard to exclude from our top 250. And so forth.

We've also included our favorite places to drink, regardless of the food—beer, wine, and cocktails are finally being afforded their due treatment as cuisines, and so we rate those accordingly. (It's not unusual to find a place in here with an average food rating and outstanding drinks.) Anything else—and anything that's opened since we went to press—will be on our website, fearlesscritic.com, which, we are thrilled to announce, now has its own iPhone app, which can be downloaded from the app store. You can also keep up with our new reviews on Twitter (@fearlesscritic).

Defining any city's dining culture is impossible without considering its demographic and geography, and Houston's is, well, vast. While we are rich in cultural diversity, the inevitable segregation into dining neighborhoods—in a city this size—can result in an hour's drive from wherever you are to wherever you want to eat. It requires great commitment to branch out from the local and the familiar, and so the great irony of Houston is, perhaps, that while we enjoy more opportunities to eat Indian, Nigerian, authentic Chinese and Thai, Vietnamese, regional Mexican, and Central American street food, a relatively large percentage of the population doesn't. At least not with any regularity.

But as Misha Govshteyn pointed out in his Tasty Bits blog post recapping 2010, we're beginning to see the interest shift to the indigenous treasures of Houston's food scene (read: its ethnic holes in the wall), as the city's food writers grow increasingly bored of the homogenous clutch of newer restaurants whose interchangeable menus of "nouveau rustique" dishes are distinguishable only by the fonts they're printed in.

And the commentators aren't the only ones to take notice that "modern" has too often become mundane. A current of undiscovered culinary talent and ideas flows through the underground in the form of mobile kitchens, supper clubs, pop-up restaurants, on-the-farm dinners, and progressive tastings. While brick-and-mortar restaurants with high overhead can't afford to take risks on new techniques and ingredients, or overhaul their tired concepts, these free agents drive the scene forward, and their success has been critical to the project of improving the city's modern American dining scene and helping the city (and country) emerge from a cynical age in which food and wine was too often less about engaging the senses and imagination, and more about satisfying the accounting department.

Some of the best examples of this new genre require the time (and gas money) of a drive out to, say, Bootsie's Heritage Café in Tomball, or Chez Roux in Conroe, both of which purvey unforgettable meals that are more worthwhile than many of the ones at the more centrally located, pomped-up dinosaurs that draw considerably more visitors and their hard-earned dollars.

Restaurants will come and go. Trends will rise and fall. The noise and chatter about this movement or that, this chef or that, will crescendo and fade out over and over again. But what is indelible are those traditions born of what our own Dr. Ricky calls the city's unique juxtaposition of blue collar workers, Vietnamese, and old-school cowboy affluence, the enclaves of quasi-bohemian artists, Mexican day workers, working students, and rising professionals.

We are a major shipping nexus, an embryonic farmer's market destination, home to taquerías, refresquerías, ostionerías, churrascarias, and mega Asian markets. These are the embers that warm the hearts that adore the kolache, the boudin, the smoked brisket, the pho, the banh mi, the xiao long bao, the locally brewed beer, the telera, the bolillo, the loquat, the nopal, and the ca phe sua da. It is these pieces that define—with or without media championship—a vibrant Gulf Coast cuisine, and it is evolving.

–Erin McReynolds

PICTURE THESE ⟶ LISTS *IN* MOTION.

With the all-new, map-based **Fearless Critic Restaurant Guide iPhone app,** subscribers can read the full text of the book, see brand-new reviews every week, sort Fearless Critic ratings every which way, search for which restaurants are open *right now*, and subscribe to additional Fearless Critic cities. Now you can keep the book on your coffee table—and the app in your pocket.

FEARLESS CRITIC
THE APP

LISTS

AROUND TEXAS
FEARLESS CRITIC BOOKS & APPS

MOST DELICIOUS IN
AUSTIN

1. Uchi (9.8, Japanese)
2. Congress (9.7, Modern)
3. Franklin BBQ (9.5, Barbecue)
4. Uchiko (9.4, Japanese)
5. Jeffrey's (9.4, Modern)
6. Fino (9.3, Spanish)
7. Olivia (9.3, Modern)
8. Taco More (9.3, Mexican)
9. Justine's Brasserie (9.2, French)
10. A+A Sichuan Cuisine (9.2, Chinese)

From Fearless Critic Austin 2011/2012

MOST DELICIOUS IN
DALLAS

1. Tei An (9.8, Japanese)
2. The Mansion Restaurant (9.6, Modern)
3. Lucia (9.3, Italian)
4. Suze (9.3, Modern)
5. Charlie Palmer (9.2, Modern)
6. 2 The Second Floor (9.2, Modern)
7. The Grape (9.1, French)
8. Tei Tei Robata Bar (9.1, Japanese)
9. Samar by Stephan Pyles (9.1, Indian)
10. Al Biernat's (9.0, Steakhouse)

From Fearless Critic Dallas 2011/2012

MOST DELICIOUS IN
SAN ANTONIO

1. Sandbar (9.5, Seafood)
2. Dough (9.4, Italian)
3. Il Sogno (9.3, Italian)
4. The Lodge (9.1, Modern)
5. Biga (9.0, Modern)
6. Fig Tree (9.0, French)
7. Bin 555 (8.7, Modern)
8. Cascabel Mexican Patio (8.7, Mexican)
9. Jones Sausage & BBQ (8.6, Barbecue)
10. Gwendolyn (8.5, Modern)

From Fearless Critic San Antonio 2011/2012

Most delicious

These are Houston's **top 100 kitchens** judged from a **pure food** perspective. Ties are ordered by feel rating.

Rank		Food	Cuisine	Location	Type	Price
1	Chez Roux	9.6	French	Conroe	Upmarket	$95
2	Da Marco	9.6	Italian	Montrose	Upmarket	$90
3	Crawfish and Noodles	9.5	Southern	Bellaire Chinatown	Casual	$25
4	Himalaya	9.5	Pakistani	Southwest Houston	Casual	$15
5	Kata Robata	9.5	Japanese	Upper Kirby	Upmarket	$70
6	Bootsie's Heritage Café	9.4	Modern	Tomball	Casual	$75
7	Hugo's	9.3	Mexican	Montrose	Upmarket	$60
8	Vinoteca Poscol	9.3	Italian	Montrose	Wine bar	$40
9	Dolce Vita	9.2	Italian, Pizza	Multiple locations	Casual	$40
10	Feast	9.2	British	Midtown	Casual	$50
11	Stella Sola	9.2	Modern, Pizza	Heights	Upmarket	$55
12	Hubcap Grill	9.2	Burgers	Multiple locations	Counter	$10
13	Shanghai Restaurant	9.2	Chinese	Bellaire Chinatown	Casual	$15
14	Pho Binh	9.2	Vietnamese	Multiple locations	Casual	$10
15	Vic & Anthony's	9.1	Steakhouse	Downtown	Upmarket	$90
16	Korean Noodle House	9.1	Korean	Spring Branch	Casual	$10
17	Tony's	9.1	Italian	Greenway Plaza	Upmarket	$110
18	Udipi Café	9.1	Indian	Multiple locations	Casual	$10
19	Indika	9.0	Indian	Montrose	Upmarket	$60
20	Pho Danh II	9.0	Vietnamese	Bellaire Chinatown	Casual	$10
21	Que Huong	9.0	Vietnamese	Bellaire Chinatown	Casual	$10
22	Café Pita +	9.0	Bosnian	Westchase	Casual	$25
23	The Queen Vic Pub	8.9	Indian, British	Upper Kirby	Casual	$40
24	Zelko Bistro	8.9	American	Heights	Casual	$40
25	Teppay	8.9	Japanese	Galleria	Casual	$60
26	Gorditas Aguascalientes	8.9	Mexican	Bellaire Chinatown	Casual	$10
27	Killen's Steakhouse	8.9	Steakhouse	Pearland	Upmarket	$105
28	Shiv Sagar	8.9	Indian	Hillcroft Area	Counter	$10
29	Vieng Thai	8.9	Thai	Spring Branch	Casual	$25
30	Petrol Station	8.8	Burgers	Northwest Houston	Counter	$25
31	Great W'kana Café	8.8	Indian	Southwest Houston	Casual	$20
32	Bon Ga	8.8	Korean	Spring Branch	Casual	$20
33	Thien Thanh	8.8	Vietnamese	Bellaire Chinatown	Casual	$10
34	Bernie's Burger Bus	8.8	Burgers	Multiple locations	Food cart	$10
35	Eatsie Boys	8.8	Sandwiches	Multiple locations	Food cart	$10
36	Gatlin's Barbecue	8.8	Barbecue	Heights	Counter	$15
37	Pho Ga Dakao	8.8	Vietnamese	Bellaire Chinatown	Casual	$10
38	Gerardo's Drive-In	8.8	Mexican	North Houston	Counter	$10
39	Brasserie Max & Julie	8.7	French	Montrose	Upmarket	$65
40	Reef	8.7	Modern	Midtown	Upmarket	$65
41	Doña Tere	8.7	Mexican	Multiple locations	Counter	$5
42	Becks Prime	8.7	American	Multiple locations	Counter	$15
43	Samba Grille	8.6	Steakhouse	Downtown	Upmarket	$75
44	Taquería Del Sol	8.6	Mexican	Southeast Houston	Casual	$10
45	Tan Tan	8.6	Chinese	Multiple locations	Casual	$15
46	The Boiling Crab	8.6	Seafood	Bellaire Chinatown	Casual	$20

47	Saigon Pagolac	8.6	Vietnamese	Bellaire Chinatown	Casual	$25
48	Asia Market	8.6	Thai	Heights	Counter	$10
49	Burger Guys	8.6	Burgers	West Houston	Counter	$15
50	Kim Tai	8.6	Vietnamese	Midtown	Casual	$10
51	Dynasty/Willie's BBQ	8.6	Chinese	Multiple locations	Take-out	$5
52	Beaver's Ice House	8.5	American	Washington	Casual	$35
53	El Tiempo Cantina	8.5	Mexican	Multiple locations	Casual	$60
54	Huynh	8.5	Vietnamese	Downtown	Casual	$20
55	Hong Kong Food Street	8.5	Chinese	Bellaire Chinatown	Casual	$20
56	Pico's Mex-Mex	8.5	Mexican	Southwest Houston	Casual	$35
57	Pappas Bros.	8.5	Steakhouse	Galleria	Upmarket	$105
58	Sam's Deli Diner	8.5	Burgers	West Houston	Counter	$10
59	Frenchy's Chicken	8.5	Southern	Multiple locations	Counter	$10
60	Bombay Sweets	8.5	Indian	Hillcroft Area	Counter	$10
61	Pierson and Company	8.4	Barbecue	Northwest Houston	Counter	$15
62	Sweet n Namkin/Salaam	8.4	Indian	Southwest Houston	Counter	$15
63	Dim Sum King	8.4	Chinese	Bellaire Chinatown	Casual	$15
64	FuFu Café	8.4	Chinese	Bellaire Chinatown	Casual	$10
65	Thuan Kieu Com Tan	8.4	Vietnamese	Bellaire Chinatown	Casual	$15
66	Tandoori Nite	8.4	Indian	Sugar Land	Food cart	$20
67	Virgie's	8.4	Barbecue	Northwest Houston	Counter	$15
68	Taquería Tacambaro	8.4	Mexican	Heights	Food cart	$5
69	Hong Kong Dim Sum	8.4	Chinese	Bellaire Chinatown	Casual	$15
70	Mikki's Soul Food	8.4	Southern	Southwest Houston	Counter	$15
71	Le Mistral	8.3	French	West Houston	Upmarket	$75
72	Mockingbird Bistro	8.3	Modern	River Oaks	Upmarket	$70
73	El Hidalguense	8.3	Mexican	Spring Branch	Casual	$35
74	Giacomo's Cibo y Vino	8.3	Italian	Upper Kirby	Counter	$20
75	El Pupusodromo	8.3	Latin American	Multiple locations	Casual	$10
76	Teotihuacán	8.3	Mexican	Multiple locations	Casual	$10
77	Au Petit Paris	8.2	French	Upper Kirby	Casual	$70
78	Haven	8.2	Modern	Upper Kirby	Upmarket	$70
79	Pondicheri Café	8.2	Indian	Upper Kirby	Casual	$40
80	Perry's Steakhouse	8.2	Steakhouse	Multiple locations	Upmarket	$90
81	Piola	8.2	Pizza	Midtown	Casual	$30
82	Arco Seafood	8.2	Chinese	Bellaire Chinatown	Casual	$25
83	El Último	8.2	Mexican	Spring Branch	Food cart	$5
84	Peking Cuisine	8.2	Chinese	Bellaire Chinatown	Casual	$15
85	ToreOre	8.2	Korean	Memorial	Counter	$10
86	Anvil	8.1	Modern	Montrose	Cocktails	$20
87	Churrascos	8.1	Latin American	Multiple locations	Upmarket	$65
88	Captain Tom's	8.1	Seafood	Multiple locations	Counter	$15
89	Finger Licking Bukateria	8.1	Nigerian	West Houston	Casual	$15
90	Rioja	8.0	Spanish	West Houston	Upmarket	$65
91	London Sizzler	8.0	Indian	Southwest Houston	Casual	$30
92	The Tasting Room	8.0	Pizza	Multiple locations	Wine bar	$35
93	Ninfa's on Navigation	8.0	Mexican	Downtown	Casual	$30
94	Paulie's	8.0	Italian	Montrose	Counter	$20
95	Lucky Pot	8.0	Chinese	Bellaire Chinatown	Casual	$15
96	Sichuan Cuisine	8.0	Chinese	Bellaire Chinatown	Casual	$15
97	Sinh Sinh	8.0	Chinese	Bellaire Chinatown	Casual	$30
98	Goode Co. Taquería	8.0	Mexican	Rice Area	Counter	$25
99	Nga Restaurant	8.0	Vietnamese	Midtown	Casual	$10
100	La Pupusa Alegre	8.0	Latin American	Bellaire	Casual	$5

Good vibes

Fearless Critic's feel rating measures the enjoyment we get from the atmosphere and people. Here are the **top 45**. Ties are ordered by food rating.

Rank		Feel	Cuisine	Location	Type	Price
1	Américas	9.5	Latin American	Multiple locations	Upmarket	$70
2	Café Rabelais	9.5	French	Rice Area	Upmarket	$55
3	Hugo's	9.0	Mexican	Montrose	Upmarket	$60
4	Dolce Vita	9.0	Italian, Pizza	Multiple locations	Casual	$40
5	Feast	9.0	British	Midtown	Casual	$50
6	Beaver's Ice House	9.0	American	Washington	Casual	$35
7	El Tiempo Cantina	9.0	Mexican	Multiple locations	Casual	$60
8	Anvil	9.0	Modern	Montrose	Cocktails	$20
9	Rioja	9.0	Spanish	West Houston	Upmarket	$65
10	Brennan's of Houston	9.0	Southern	Midtown	Upmarket	$100
11	Backstreet Café	9.0	Modern	River Oaks	Upmarket	$65
12	Cyclone Anaya's	9.0	Mexican	Multiple locations	Casual	$35
13	t'afia	9.0	Modern	Midtown	Upmarket	$65
14	Benjy's	9.0	Modern	Multiple locations	Upmarket	$55
15	Ava Kitchen & Whiskey Bar	9.0	Modern	Upper Kirby	Upmarket	$55
16	Tiny Boxwood's	9.0	American	Greenway Plaza	Casual	$25
17	Ouisie's Table	9.0	Southern	River Oaks	Upmarket	$60
18	Last Concert Café	9.0	Mexican	Downtown	Casual	$35
19	The Ginger Man	9.0	American	Rice Area	Bar	$15
20	Chez Roux	8.5	French	Conroe	Upmarket	$95
21	Vic & Anthony's	8.5	Steakhouse	Downtown	Upmarket	$90
22	The Queen Vic Pub	8.5	Indian, British	Upper Kirby	Casual	$40
23	Zelko Bistro	8.5	American	Heights	Casual	$40
24	Brasserie Max & Julie	8.5	French	Montrose	Upmarket	$65
25	Reef	8.5	Modern	Midtown	Upmarket	$65
26	Samba Grille	8.5	Steakhouse	Downtown	Upmarket	$75
27	Huynh	8.5	Vietnamese	Downtown	Casual	$20
28	Le Mistral	8.5	French	West Houston	Upmarket	$75
29	Mockingbird Bistro	8.5	Modern	River Oaks	Upmarket	$70
30	Au Petit Paris	8.5	French	Upper Kirby	Casual	$70
31	Haven	8.5	Modern	Upper Kirby	Upmarket	$70
32	Pondicheri Café	8.5	Indian	Upper Kirby	Casual	$40
33	London Sizzler	8.5	Indian	Southwest Houston	Casual	$30
34	The Tasting Room	8.5	Pizza	Multiple locations	Wine bar	$35
35	Brenner's	8.5	Steakhouse	Multiple locations	Upmarket	$90
36	Garson	8.5	Middle Eastern	Hillcroft Area	Casual	$30
37	Mark's	8.5	Modern	Montrose	Upmarket	$110
38	Shade	8.5	Modern	Heights	Upmarket	$60
39	Canopy	8.5	Modern	Montrose	Upmarket	$70
40	Sushi Raku	8.5	Japanese	Midtown	Upmarket	$70
41	III Forks	8.5	Steakhouse	Downtown	Upmarket	$95
42	Branch Water Tavern	8.5	Modern	Heights	Upmarket	$45
43	Ibiza	8.5	Spanish	Midtown	Wine bar	$70
44	13 Celsius	8.5	Modern	Midtown	Wine bar	$20
45	Chuy's	8.5	Mexican	Multiple locations	Casual	$30

Wine

Fearless Critic's wine ratings, which include sake, consider quality, creativity, value, and depth—in that order. A small but interesting list that is carefully paired with the food might rank higher than a thick, overpriced volume of prestigious producers. We do, however, award extra points for older vintages. Establishments only receive a wine rating if we judge their wine programs to be ambitious or significant. Ties are ordered first by feel rating, then by food rating.

	Name	Cuisine	Location	Type	Price
9.5	Ibiza	Spanish, Modern	Midtown	Wine bar	$70
9.0	Café Rabelais	French	Rice Area	Upmarket	$55
9.0	Dolce Vita	Italian, Pizza	Multiple locations	Casual	$40
9.0	Reef	Modern, Seafood	Midtown	Upmarket	$65
9.0	Haven	Modern	Upper Kirby	Upmarket	$70
9.0	13 Celsius	Modern	Midtown	Wine bar	$20
9.0	Da Marco	Italian	Montrose	Upmarket	$90
9.0	Vinoteca Poscol	Italian	Montrose	Wine bar	$40
9.0	Stella Sola	Modern, Pizza	Heights	Upmarket	$55
8.5	Backstreet Café	Modern	River Oaks	Upmarket	$65
8.5	t'afia	Modern	Midtown	Upmarket	$65
8.5	Zelko Bistro	American, Modern	Heights	Casual	$40
8.5	Brasserie Max & Julie	French	Montrose	Upmarket	$65
8.5	Le Mistral	French	West Houston	Upmarket	$75
8.5	Au Petit Paris	French	Upper Kirby	Casual	$70
8.5	Branch Water Tavern	Modern, American	Heights	Upmarket	$45
8.5	Giacomo's Cibo y Vino	Italian	Upper Kirby	Counter	$20
8.5	Phillippe	Modern	Galleria	Upmarket	$80
8.5	Divino	Italian	Montrose	Casual	$50
8.5	Pappas Bros.	Steakhouse	Galleria	Upmarket	$105
8.5	Tintos	Spanish	River Oaks	Upmarket	$55
8.0	Feast	British	Midtown	Casual	$50
8.0	Rioja	Spanish	West Houston	Upmarket	$65
8.0	Samba Grille	Steakhouse	Downtown	Upmarket	$75
8.0	The Tasting Room	Pizza	Multiple locations	Wine bar	$35
8.0	Brenner's	Steakhouse	Multiple locations	Upmarket	$90
8.0	Shade	Modern	Heights	Upmarket	$60
8.0	Canopy	Modern	Montrose	Upmarket	$70
8.0	Paulie's	Italian, Sandwiches	Montrose	Counter	$20
8.0	Nelore Churrascaria	Steakhouse	Montrose	Upmarket	$75
8.0	Tony's	Italian	Greenway Plaza	Upmarket	$110
8.0	Voice	Modern	Downtown	Upmarket	$70
8.0	Oporto Café	Portuguese	Greenway Plaza	Wine bar	$50
7.5	Beaver's Ice House	American	Washington	Casual	$35
7.5	Brennan's of Houston	Southern, Modern	Midtown	Upmarket	$100
7.5	Chez Roux	French, Modern	Conroe	Upmarket	$95
7.5	Vic & Anthony's	Steakhouse	Downtown	Upmarket	$90
7.5	Mockingbird Bistro	Modern	River Oaks	Upmarket	$70
7.5	The Grove	Modern	Downtown	Upmarket	$65
7.5	Soma	Japanese, Modern	Washington	Casual	$75
7.5	RDG	Modern	Galleria	Upmarket	$100

7.5	Laurier Café	Modern, French	Greenway Plaza	Upmarket	$65
7.5	BRC	American	Heights	Casual	$40
7.0	Américas	Latin American	Multiple locations	Upmarket	$70
7.0	Hugo's	Mexican	Montrose	Upmarket	$60
7.0	Indika	Indian	Montrose	Upmarket	$60
7.0	Perry's Steakhouse	Steakhouse	Multiple locations	Upmarket	$90
7.0	Churrascos	Latin American	Multiple locations	Upmarket	$65
7.0	Masraff's	Modern	Memorial	Upmarket	$85
7.0	Max's Wine Dive	Modern	Washington	Wine bar	$50
7.0	Smith & Wollensky	Steakhouse	River Oaks	Upmarket	$105
7.0	Danton's	Seafood, Southern	Montrose	Casual	$50
7.0	Alexander the Great	Greek	Galleria	Upmarket	$65
6.5	Benjy's	Modern	Multiple locations	Upmarket	$55
6.5	III Forks	Steakhouse	Downtown	Upmarket	$95
6.5	Frank's Chop House	Steakhouse	River Oaks	Upmarket	$70
6.5	Del Frisco's	Steakhouse	Galleria	Upmarket	$100
6.0	Tiny Boxwood's	American, Pizza	Greenway Plaza	Casual	$25
6.0	Ouisie's Table	Southern	River Oaks	Upmarket	$60
6.0	Houston's	American	Multiple locations	Upmarket	$60
6.0	Tony Mandola's	Seafood, Southern	Multiple locations	Upmarket	$70
6.0	Brasil	Sandwiches, Pizza	Montrose	Café	$15
6.0	Killen's Steakhouse	Steakhouse	Pearland	Upmarket	$105
6.0	Fratelli's	Italian	Multiple locations	Casual	$40
5.0	Sushi Raku	Japanese	Midtown	Upmarket	$70
5.0	Kubo's	Japanese	Rice Area	Casual	$45
4.5	Mark's	Modern	Montrose	Upmarket	$110
4.0	Eddie V's	Seafood	Multiple locations	Upmarket	$90
4.0	Little Big's	Burgers	Multiple locations	Counter	$15

Beer

Fearless Critic's beer ratings consider the quality and depth of a restaurant's beer program. Establishments only receive a beer rating if we judge their beer programs to be ambitious or significant. Ties are ordered first by feel rating, then by food rating.

	Name	Cuisine	Location	Type	Price
9.5	The Ginger Man	American	Rice Area	Bar	$15
9.0	Anvil	Modern	Montrose	Cocktails	$20
9.0	13 Celsius	Modern	Midtown	Wine bar	$20
9.0	Petrol Station	Burgers	Northwest Houston	Counter	$25
8.5	Feast	British	Midtown	Casual	$50
8.5	The Queen Vic Pub	Indian, British	Upper Kirby	Casual	$40
8.5	Rudi Lechner's	German	Southwest Houston	Casual	$30
8.5	The Black Labrador Pub	American, British	Montrose	Bar	$30
8.5	Red Lion	American, British	Upper Kirby	Bar	$25
8.5	Hobbit Café	Vegefusion	Upper Kirby	Casual	$20
8.5	BRC	American	Heights	Casual	$40
8.0	Beaver's Ice House	American	Washington	Casual	$35
8.0	Backstreet Café	Modern	River Oaks	Upmarket	$65
8.0	Zelko Bistro	American, Modern	Heights	Casual	$40
8.0	Mockingbird Bistro	Modern	River Oaks	Upmarket	$70
8.0	The Flying Saucer	American	Downtown	Bar	$25
7.5	Ava Kitchen & Whiskey Bar	Modern	Upper Kirby	Upmarket	$55
7.5	London Sizzler	Indian	Southwest Houston	Casual	$30
7.5	The Grove	Modern	Downtown	Upmarket	$65
7.5	Baker St. (Sherlock's)	British, American	Multiple locations	Bar	$25
7.5	Guadalajara Hacienda	Mexican	Multiple locations	Casual	$35
6.0	Indika	Indian	Montrose	Upmarket	$60

Cocktails

Fearless Critic's cocktail ratings value creativity, balance, and complexity. Prestigious name-brand liquors are useless without a staff that knows how to mix them. Our tastes are aligned with the classic cocktail renaissance that's gradually taking hold all over the country. If you like sugary, vodka-based 'tinis, then you'll probably hate our cocktail recommendations. Establishments only receive a cocktails rating if we judge their cocktail programs to be ambitious or significant. Ties are ordered first by feel rating, then by food rating.

	Name	Cuisine	Location	Type	Price
10	Anvil	Modern	Montrose	Cocktails	$20
9.5	Beaver's Ice House	American	Washington	Casual	$35
9.0	Haven	Modern	Upper Kirby	Upmarket	$70
9.0	Branch Water Tavern	Modern, American	Heights	Upmarket	$45
9.0	Stella Sola	Modern, Pizza	Heights	Upmarket	$55
9.0	Ninfa's on Navigation	Mexican	Downtown	Casual	$30
8.5	Hugo's	Mexican	Montrose	Upmarket	$60
8.5	t'afia	Modern	Midtown	Upmarket	$65
8.5	Reef	Modern, Seafood	Midtown	Upmarket	$65
8.5	Indika	Indian	Montrose	Upmarket	$60
8.0	Backstreet Café	Modern	River Oaks	Upmarket	$65
8.0	The Queen Vic Pub	Indian, British	Upper Kirby	Casual	$40
8.0	Mockingbird Bistro	Modern	River Oaks	Upmarket	$70
8.0	The Grove	Modern	Downtown	Upmarket	$65
8.0	RDG	Modern	Galleria	Upmarket	$100
7.5	Américas	Latin American	Multiple locations	Upmarket	$70
7.5	Ava Kitchen & Whiskey Bar	Modern	Upper Kirby	Upmarket	$55
7.5	Danton's	Seafood, Southern	Montrose	Casual	$50
7.5	Pappas Seafood	Seafood	Multiple locations	Casual	$50
7.0	Shade	Modern	Heights	Upmarket	$60
7.0	Canopy	Modern	Montrose	Upmarket	$70
7.0	Houston's	American	Multiple locations	Upmarket	$60
7.0	Tony Mandola's	Seafood, Southern	Multiple locations	Upmarket	$70
6.5	Benjy's	Modern	Multiple locations	Upmarket	$55
6.5	Eddie V's	Seafood	Multiple locations	Upmarket	$90
5.5	Sushi Raku	Japanese	Midtown	Upmarket	$70
5.5	III Forks	Steakhouse	Downtown	Upmarket	$95
5.0	Kubo's	Japanese	Rice Area	Casual	$45

Margaritas

We judge margaritas separately from other cocktails, because restaurants and bars that do the former well do not always do the latter well, and vice versa. Whether margaritas are creative or classic, we rate them on their overall deliciousness and balance. Establishments only receive a margaritas rating if we judge their margarita programs to be ambitious or significant. Ties are ordered first by feel rating, then by food rating.

	Name	Cuisine	Location	Type	Price
9.5	Ninfa's on Navigation	Mexican	Downtown	Casual	$30
8.5	Cyclone Anaya's	Mexican	Multiple locations	Casual	$35
8.5	Pico's Mex-Mex	Mexican	Southwest Houston	Casual	$35
8.0	El Tiempo Cantina	Mexican	Multiple locations	Casual	$60
8.0	Chuy's	Mexican	Multiple locations	Casual	$30
8.0	Guadalajara Hacienda	Mexican	Multiple locations	Casual	$35
7.5	El Real	Mexican	Montrose	Casual	$35
7.5	Pappasito's	Mexican	Multiple locations	Casual	$35
7.5	Goode Co. Taquería	Mexican, Burgers	Rice Area	Counter	$25
7.0	Sylvia's Enchilada Kitchen	Mexican	Multiple locations	Casual	$20
7.0	100% Taquito	Mexican	Greenway Plaza	Counter	$10
6.5	Doneraki	Mexican	Multiple locations	Casual	$30
5.5	Lupe Tortilla	Mexican	Multiple locations	Casual	$35
3.0	El Hidalguense	Mexican	Spring Branch	Casual	$35
2.0	Taco Cabana	Mexican	Multiple locations	Counter	$10

By genre

Places to eat **listed by culinary concept, ranked by food rating**. Establishments that don't serve full meals (e.g. cafés, bakeries, grocery stores) appear as "NR" at the bottom of the list.

American *includes traditional American food, bar food, greasy-spoon fare, and breakfast food. For creative American or market-to-table cuisine, see "Modern." For steakhouses, Southern cuisine, sandwiches, or burgers, see those genres.*

8.9	Zelko Bistro	Heights	Casual	$40
8.7	Becks Prime	Multiple locations	Counter	$15
8.5	Beaver's Ice House	Washington	Casual	$35
8.5	Sam's Deli Diner	West Houston	Counter	$10
7.8	Jonathan's the Rub	Memorial	Casual	$35
7.7	Houston's	Multiple locations	Upmarket	$60
7.5	Branch Water Tavern	Heights	Upmarket	$45
7.2	Stanton's City Bites	Washington	Take-out	$10
6.8	Frank's Chop House	River Oaks	Upmarket	$70
6.8	BRC	Heights	Casual	$40
6.7	Lankford Grocery	Midtown	Casual	$10
6.6	Bellaire Broiler Burger	Bellaire	Counter	$10
6.6	Little Bitty Burger Barn	Northwest Houston	Counter	$10
6.6	Tel-Wink Grill	Southeast Houston	Casual	$10
6.5	Five Guys	Multiple locations	Counter	$10
6.4	Tiny Boxwood's	Greenway Plaza	Casual	$25
6.4	Christian's Tailgate	Multiple locations	Bar	$15
6.0	Red Lion	Upper Kirby	Bar	$25
5.6	Hobbit Café	Upper Kirby	Casual	$20
5.2	Whataburger	Multiple locations	Counter	$10
5.1	The Flying Saucer	Downtown	Bar	$25
5.0	The Breakfast Klub	Midtown	Counter	$15
4.1	Baker St. (Sherlock's)	Multiple locations	Bar	$25
4.0	House of Pies	Multiple locations	Casual	$10
3.0	The Black Labrador Pub	Montrose	Bar	$30
NR	The Ginger Man	Rice Area	Bar	$15

Baked goods

NR	Abdallah's	Hillcroft Area	Counter
NR	Alpha Bakery	Bellaire Chinatown	Take-out
NR	Crave Cupcakes	Multiple locations	Counter
NR	ECK Bakery	Bellaire Chinatown	Counter
NR	Empire Café	Montrose	Counter
NR	Hot Breads Bakery	Bellaire Chinatown	Counter
NR	Jungle Café	Bellaire Chinatown	Counter
NR	La Guadalupana	Montrose	Casual
NR	The Chocolate Bar	Multiple locations	Counter
NR	The Dessert Gallery	Multiple locations	Counter

Barbecue

8.8	Gatlin's Barbecue	Heights	Counter	$15
8.4	Pierson and Company	Northwest Houston	Counter	$15
8.4	Virgie's	Northwest Houston	Counter	$15
8.0	Burns Bar-B-Q	North Houston	Counter	$20
7.8	Guy's Meat Market	Medical Center	Counter	$5
6.1	Barbecue Inn	North Houston	Casual	$20
4.1	Goode Co. Texas Bar-B-Q	Multiple locations	Counter	$20

Bosnian

9.0	Café Pita +	Westchase	Casual	$25

Brazilian

8.6	Samba Grille	Downtown	Upmarket	$75
7.0	Nelore Churrascaria	Montrose	Upmarket	$75

British

9.2	Feast	Midtown	Casual	$50
8.9	The Queen Vic Pub	Upper Kirby	Casual	$40
6.0	Red Lion	Upper Kirby	Bar	$25
4.1	Baker St. (Sherlock's)	Multiple locations	Bar	$25
3.0	The Black Labrador Pub	Montrose	Bar	$30

Burgers *Ratings based solely on a restaurant's burger, independent of the overall food rating*

9.5	Hubcap Grill	Multiple locations	Counter	$10
9.5	Bernie's Burger Bus	Multiple locations	Food cart	$10
9.0	Samba Grille	Downtown	Upmarket	$75
9.0	Ninfa's on Navigation	Downtown	Casual	$30
9.0	Petrol Station	Northwest Houston	Counter	$25
9.0	Tornado Burger	Stafford	Counter	$10
9.0	Sam's Deli Diner	West Houston	Counter	$10
9.0	Burger Guys	West Houston	Counter	$15
9.0	Becks Prime	Multiple locations	Counter	$15
8.5	Guy's Meat Market	Medical Center	Counter	$5
8.5	Christian's Tailgate	Multiple locations	Bar	$15
8.5	Little Bitty Burger Barn	Northwest Houston	Counter	$10
8.5	Stanton's City Bites	Washington	Take-out	$10
8.0	Clay's	Northwest Houston	Counter	$25
8.0	Lankford Grocery	Midtown	Casual	$10
8.0	RDG	Galleria	Upmarket	$100
8.0	Jonathan's the Rub	Memorial	Casual	$35
8.0	Five Guys	Multiple locations	Counter	$10
6.0	Whataburger	Multiple locations	Counter	$10

Chinese

9.2	Shanghai Restaurant	Bellaire Chinatown	Casual	$15
8.6	Tan Tan	Multiple locations	Casual	$15
8.6	Dynasty/Willie's BBQ	Multiple locations	Take-out	$5
8.5	Hong Kong Food Street	Bellaire Chinatown	Casual	$20
8.4	Dim Sum King	Bellaire Chinatown	Casual	$15
8.4	FuFu Café	Bellaire Chinatown	Casual	$10
8.4	Hong Kong Dim Sum	Bellaire Chinatown	Casual	$15

Chinese *continued*

8.2	Arco Seafood	Bellaire Chinatown	Casual	$25
8.2	Peking Cuisine	Bellaire Chinatown	Casual	$15
8.0	Lucky Pot	Bellaire Chinatown	Casual	$15
8.0	Sichuan Cuisine	Bellaire Chinatown	Casual	$15
8.0	Sinh Sinh	Bellaire Chinatown	Casual	$30
7.8	San Dong Noodle House	Bellaire Chinatown	Counter	$10
7.6	East Wall	Bellaire Chinatown	Casual	$15
7.6	Viet Hoa	Southwest Houston	Counter	$10
7.6	Mandarin Café	Spring Branch	Casual	$15
7.0	Fung's Kitchen	Bellaire Chinatown	Upmarket	$45
6.8	Vinh Hoa	Bellaire Chinatown	Casual	$10
6.5	QQ Cuisine	Bellaire Chinatown	Casual	$10
4.5	Ocean Palace	Bellaire Chinatown	Casual	$30

Dim Sum

8.4	Dim Sum King	Bellaire Chinatown	Casual	$15
8.4	Hong Kong Dim Sum	Bellaire Chinatown	Casual	$15
8.2	Arco Seafood	Bellaire Chinatown	Casual	$25
7.0	Fung's Kitchen	Bellaire Chinatown	Upmarket	$45
4.5	Ocean Palace	Bellaire Chinatown	Casual	$30

Ethiopian

6.5	Blue Nile	Westchase	Casual	$25

French

9.6	Chez Roux	Conroe	Upmarket	$95
8.7	Brasserie Max & Julie	Montrose	Upmarket	$65
8.3	Le Mistral	West Houston	Upmarket	$75
8.2	Au Petit Paris	Upper Kirby	Casual	$70
7.3	Mélange Crêperie	Montrose	Food cart	$10
7.2	Café Rabelais	Rice Area	Upmarket	$55
7.0	Laurier Café	Greenway Plaza	Upmarket	$65

German

5.7	Rudi Lechner's	Southwest Houston	Casual	$30

Greek

7.6	Al's Quick Stop	Montrose	Counter	$10
6.8	Fadi's Mediterranean	Multiple locations	Counter	$15
6.7	Alexander the Great	Galleria	Upmarket	$65
6.4	Zabak's	Galleria	Counter	$15
6.3	Niko Niko's	Multiple locations	Counter	$20
6.2	Shawarma King	Hillcroft Area	Counter	$10

Ice cream

NR	Amy's Ice Cream	Upper Kirby	Counter	
NR	Hank's Ice Cream	Medical Center	Counter	
NR	The Chocolate Bar	Multiple locations	Counter	

Indian

9.5	Himalaya	Southwest Houston	Casual	$15
9.1	Udipi Café	Multiple locations	Casual	$10
9.0	Indika	Montrose	Upmarket	$60
8.9	The Queen Vic Pub	Upper Kirby	Casual	$40
8.9	Shiv Sagar	Hillcroft Area	Counter	$10
8.8	Great W'kana Café	Southwest Houston	Casual	$20
8.5	Bombay Sweets	Hillcroft Area	Counter	$10
8.4	Sweet n Namkin/Salaam	Southwest Houston	Counter	$15
8.4	Tandoori Nite	Sugar Land	Food cart	$20
8.2	Pondicheri Café	Upper Kirby	Casual	$40
8.0	London Sizzler	Southwest Houston	Casual	$30
6.5	Madras Pavilion	Multiple locations	Casual	$20
NR	Hot Breads Bakery	Bellaire Chinatown	Counter	

Italian

9.6	Da Marco	Montrose	Upmarket	$90
9.3	Vinoteca Poscol	Montrose	Wine bar	$40
9.2	Dolce Vita	Multiple locations	Casual	$40
9.1	Tony's	Greenway Plaza	Upmarket	$110
8.3	Giacomo's Cibo y Vino	Upper Kirby	Counter	$20
8.0	Paulie's	Montrose	Counter	$20
7.6	Fratelli's	Multiple locations	Casual	$40
6.9	Divino	Montrose	Casual	$50
3.5	Empire Café	Montrose	Counter	$15

Japanese

9.5	Kata Robata	Upper Kirby	Upmarket	$70
8.9	Teppay	Galleria	Casual	$60
7.7	Sushi Raku	Midtown	Upmarket	$70
7.6	Sushi Jin	West Houston	Casual	$45
7.3	Sushi Miyagi	Bellaire Chinatown	Casual	$35
7.2	Soma	Washington	Casual	$75
7.1	Nippon	Montrose	Casual	$45
6.8	Kaneyama	Westchase	Casual	$35
6.7	Kubo's	Rice Area	Casual	$45
6.4	Osaka	Montrose	Casual	$35

Jewish-style Deli

6.1	Kenny & Ziggy's	Galleria	Casual	$25

Korean

9.1	Korean Noodle House	Spring Branch	Casual	$10
8.8	Bon Ga	Spring Branch	Casual	$20
8.2	ToreOre	Memorial	Counter	$10
7.6	Nam Gang	Spring Branch	Casual	$30
7.6	Da Da Mi Sushi Bistro	Spring Branch	Casual	$35
7.6	Mandarin Café	Spring Branch	Casual	$15
6.8	Tofu Village	Bellaire Chinatown	Casual	$20

Latin American

8.3	El Pupusodromo	Multiple locations	Casual	$10
8.1	Churrascos	Multiple locations	Upmarket	$65

Latin American *continued*

8.0	La Pupusa Alegre	Bellaire	Casual	$5
7.7	Américas	Multiple locations	Upmarket	$70
7.4	Los Guanacos	Northwest Houston	Casual	$10
6.0	El Rey Taquería	Multiple locations	Counter	$10

Malaysian

6.5	Banana Leaf	Bellaire Chinatown	Casual	$25

Mexican

9.3	Hugo's	Montrose	Upmarket	$60
8.9	Gorditas Aguascalientes	Bellaire Chinatown	Casual	$10
8.8	Gerardo's Drive-In	North Houston	Counter	$10
8.7	Doña Tere	Multiple locations	Counter	$5
8.6	Taquería Del Sol	Southeast Houston	Casual	$10
8.5	El Tiempo Cantina	Multiple locations	Casual	$60
8.5	Pico's Mex-Mex	Southwest Houston	Casual	$35
8.4	Taquería Tacambaro	Heights	Food cart	$5
8.3	El Hidalguense	Spring Branch	Casual	$35
8.3	Teotihuacán	Multiple locations	Casual	$10
8.2	El Último	Spring Branch	Food cart	$5
8.0	Ninfa's on Navigation	Downtown	Casual	$30
8.0	Goode Co. Taquería	Rice Area	Counter	$25
8.0	La Moreliana	Multiple locations	Counter	$5
7.9	Doneraki	Multiple locations	Casual	$30
7.8	100% Taquito	Greenway Plaza	Counter	$10
7.8	Seco's Latin Cuisine	Rice Area	Casual	$30
7.7	Lupe Tortilla	Multiple locations	Casual	$35
7.5	Cyclone Anaya's	Multiple locations	Casual	$35
7.5	Tampico Seafood	Multiple locations	Casual	$20
7.4	Tacos Tierra Caliente	Montrose	Food cart	$10
7.3	Sylvia's Enchilada Kitchen	Multiple locations	Casual	$20
7.1	Guadalajara Hacienda	Multiple locations	Casual	$35
7.0	Jarro Café and Trailer	Spring Branch	Counter	$10
7.0	La Guadalupana	Montrose	Casual	$10
6.3	El Real	Montrose	Casual	$35
6.1	Chuy's	Multiple locations	Casual	$30
6.0	El Rey Taquería	Multiple locations	Counter	$10
5.4	Pappasito's	Multiple locations	Casual	$35
3.9	Taco Cabana	Multiple locations	Counter	$10
3.7	Last Concert Café	Downtown	Casual	$35

Middle Eastern

7.9	Garson	Hillcroft Area	Casual	$30
7.6	Al's Quick Stop	Montrose	Counter	$10
7.3	Abdallah's	Hillcroft Area	Counter	$15
6.8	Fadi's Mediterranean	Multiple locations	Counter	$15
6.4	Zabak's	Galleria	Counter	$15
6.4	Jerusalem Halal Deli	Hillcroft Area	Counter	$10
6.2	Shawarma King	Hillcroft Area	Counter	$10

Modern

9.6	Chez Roux	Conroe	Upmarket	$95

Modern *continued*

9.5	Kata Robata	Upper Kirby	Upmarket	$70
9.4	Bootsie's Heritage Café	Tomball	Casual	$75
9.2	Stella Sola	Heights	Upmarket	$55
8.9	Zelko Bistro	Heights	Casual	$40
8.7	Reef	Midtown	Upmarket	$65
8.3	Mockingbird Bistro	River Oaks	Upmarket	$70
8.2	Haven	Upper Kirby	Upmarket	$70
8.1	Anvil	Montrose	Cocktails	$20
7.9	Mark's	Montrose	Upmarket	$110
7.9	Shade	Heights	Upmarket	$60
7.9	RDG	Galleria	Upmarket	$100
7.8	Canopy	Montrose	Upmarket	$70
7.8	Phillippe	Galleria	Upmarket	$80
7.7	Brennan's of Houston	Midtown	Upmarket	$100
7.5	Backstreet Café	River Oaks	Upmarket	$65
7.5	Branch Water Tavern	Heights	Upmarket	$45
7.3	Voice	Downtown	Upmarket	$70
7.2	Soma	Washington	Casual	$75
7.1	t'afia	Midtown	Upmarket	$65
7.1	Ibiza	Midtown	Wine bar	$70
7.1	Masraff's	Memorial	Upmarket	$85
7.1	Oporto Café	Greenway Plaza	Wine bar	$50
7.0	Laurier Café	Greenway Plaza	Upmarket	$65
6.9	Benjy's	Multiple locations	Upmarket	$55
6.9	13 Celsius	Midtown	Wine bar	$20
6.9	Max's Wine Dive	Washington	Wine bar	$50
6.8	Ava Kitchen & Whiskey Bar	Upper Kirby	Upmarket	$55
6.1	The Grove	Downtown	Upmarket	$65

Nigerian

8.1	Finger Licking Bukateria	West Houston	Casual	$15

Pakistani

9.5	Himalaya	Southwest Houston	Casual	$15
7.8	La Sani	Southwest Houston	Casual	$30

Pizza *Ratings based solely on a restaurant's pizza, independent of the overall food rating*

9.0	Dolce Vita	Multiple locations	Casual	$40
9.0	Da Marco	Montrose	Upmarket	$90
8.5	Piola	Midtown	Casual	$30
8.0	The Tasting Room	Multiple locations	Wine bar	$35
8.0	Stella Sola	Heights	Upmarket	$55
6.0	Tiny Boxwood's	Greenway Plaza	Casual	$25
5.0	Brasil	Montrose	Café	$15

Polish

7.0	Polonia	Spring Branch	Casual	$30

Portuguese

7.1	Oporto Café	Greenway Plaza	Wine bar	$50

Sandwiches

8.8	Eatsie Boys	Multiple locations	Food cart	$10
8.0	Paulie's	Montrose	Counter	$20
7.8	Nguyen Ngo	Bellaire Chinatown	Counter	$5
7.4	Calliope's Po-Boy	East Houston	Casual	$15
7.2	Les Givral's	Midtown	Counter	$10
7.1	Alpha Bakery	Bellaire Chinatown	Take-out	$10
6.5	Thien An Sandwiches	Midtown	Counter	$10
6.1	Kenny & Ziggy's	Galleria	Casual	$25
6.0	Les Givral's Kahve	Multiple locations	Counter	$10
4.7	Brasil	Montrose	Café	$15

Seafood

8.7	Reef	Midtown	Upmarket	$65
8.6	The Boiling Crab	Bellaire Chinatown	Casual	$20
8.2	Arco Seafood	Bellaire Chinatown	Casual	$25
8.1	Captain Tom's	Multiple locations	Counter	$15
8.0	Sinh Sinh	Bellaire Chinatown	Casual	$30
7.5	Tampico Seafood	Multiple locations	Casual	$20
7.2	Eddie V's	Multiple locations	Upmarket	$90
7.1	Pappadeaux	Multiple locations	Casual	$45
7.1	Tony Mandola's	Upper Kirby	Upmarket	$70
7.0	Fung's Kitchen	Bellaire Chinatown	Upmarket	$45
6.9	Danton's	Montrose	Casual	$50
6.8	Vinh Hoa	Bellaire Chinatown	Casual	$10
6.2	Pappas Seafood	Multiple locations	Casual	$50
4.5	Ocean Palace	Bellaire Chinatown	Casual	$30

Southern *includes soul food, Cajun, Creole*

9.5	Crawfish and Noodles	Bellaire Chinatown	Casual	$25
8.6	The Boiling Crab	Bellaire Chinatown	Casual	$20
8.5	Frenchy's Chicken	Multiple locations	Counter	$10
8.4	Mikki's Soul Food	Southwest Houston	Counter	$15
8.1	Captain Tom's	Multiple locations	Counter	$15
7.7	Brennan's of Houston	Midtown	Upmarket	$100
7.4	Calliope's Po-Boy	East Houston	Casual	$15
7.1	Pappadeaux	Multiple locations	Casual	$45
7.1	Tony Mandola's	Upper Kirby	Upmarket	$70
6.9	Danton's	Montrose	Casual	$50
6.8	Clay's	Northwest Houston	Counter	$25
6.6	Alfreda's Cafeteria	Hermann Park	Counter	$15
6.2	Avenue Grill	Washington	Casual	$15
6.1	Barbecue Inn	North Houston	Casual	$20
5.6	Ouisie's Table	River Oaks	Upmarket	$60
5.0	The Breakfast Klub	Midtown	Counter	$15

Spanish

8.0	Rioja	West Houston	Upmarket	$65
7.6	Tintos	River Oaks	Upmarket	$55
7.1	Ibiza	Midtown	Wine bar	$70

Steakhouse

9.1	Vic & Anthony's	Downtown	Upmarket	$90

Steakhouse *continued*

8.9	Killen's Steakhouse	Pearland	Upmarket	$105
8.6	Samba Grille	Downtown	Upmarket	$75
8.5	Pappas Bros.	Galleria	Upmarket	$105
8.2	Perry's Steakhouse	Multiple locations	Upmarket	$90
7.9	Brenner's	Multiple locations	Upmarket	$90
7.9	Del Frisco's	Galleria	Upmarket	$100
7.7	III Forks	Downtown	Upmarket	$95
7.2	Eddie V's	Multiple locations	Upmarket	$90
7.1	Smith & Wollensky	River Oaks	Upmarket	$105
7.0	Nelore Churrascaria	Montrose	Upmarket	$75
6.8	Frank's Chop House	River Oaks	Upmarket	$70

Thai

8.9	Vieng Thai	Spring Branch	Casual	$25
8.6	Asia Market	Heights	Counter	$10
7.0	Kanomwan	East Houston	Casual	$20
6.9	Thai Gourmet	Galleria	Casual	$25
6.9	Thai Spice	Multiple locations	Casual	$10
5.9	Tony Thai	Multiple locations	Casual	$30

Turkish

7.5	Pasha	Rice Area	Casual	$35
7.1	Turquoise Grill	Upper Kirby	Casual	$35
6.3	Istanbul Grill	Rice Area	Casual	$30

Vegefusion

5.6	Hobbit Café	Upper Kirby	Casual	$20
3.7	Last Concert Café	Downtown	Casual	$35

Vietnamese

9.5	Crawfish and Noodles	Bellaire Chinatown	Casual	$25
9.2	Pho Binh	Multiple locations	Casual	$10
9.0	Pho Danh II	Bellaire Chinatown	Casual	$10
9.0	Que Huong	Bellaire Chinatown	Casual	$10
8.8	Thien Thanh	Bellaire Chinatown	Casual	$10
8.8	Pho Ga Dakao	Bellaire Chinatown	Casual	$10
8.6	Tan Tan	Multiple locations	Casual	$15
8.6	Saigon Pagolac	Bellaire Chinatown	Casual	$25
8.6	Kim Tai	Midtown	Casual	$10
8.5	Huynh	Downtown	Casual	$20
8.4	Thuan Kieu Com Tan	Bellaire Chinatown	Casual	$15
8.0	Nga Restaurant	Midtown	Casual	$10
7.8	Don Café	Bellaire Chinatown	Counter	$10
7.8	Nguyen Ngo	Bellaire Chinatown	Counter	$5
7.6	Café TH	Downtown	Counter	$10
7.2	Pho Saigon	Multiple locations	Casual	$15
7.2	Les Givral's	Midtown	Counter	$10
7.0	Kim Chau	Multiple locations	Casual	$10
6.8	Vinh Hoa	Bellaire Chinatown	Casual	$10
6.8	Tau Bay	Multiple locations	Casual	$10
6.5	Thien An Sandwiches	Midtown	Counter	$10
6.0	Les Givral's Kahve	Multiple locations	Counter	$10

Wine bar *Ratings based on food only. For wine ratings, see Best drinks.*

9.3	Vinoteca Poscol	Montrose	Wine bar	$40
8.0	The Tasting Room	Multiple locations	Wine bar	$35
7.1	Ibiza	Midtown	Wine bar	$70
7.1	Oporto Café	Greenway Plaza	Wine bar	$50
6.9	13 Celsius	Midtown	Wine bar	$20
6.9	Max's Wine Dive	Washington	Wine bar	$50

By location

Places to eat **listed by neighborhood, suburb, or town, ranked by food rating**. Establishments that don't serve full meals (e.g. cafés, bakeries, grocery stores) appear as "NR" at the bottom of the list.

Bellaire

		Cuisine	Type	Price
8.0	La Pupusa Alegre	Latin American	Casual	$5
8.0	La Moreliana	Mexican	Counter	$5
6.9	Thai Spice	Thai	Casual	$10
6.6	Bellaire Broiler Burger	Burgers, American	Counter	$10

Bellaire Chinatown

9.5	Crawfish and Noodles	Southern, Vietnamese	Casual	$25
9.2	Shanghai Restaurant	Chinese	Casual	$15
9.2	Pho Binh	Vietnamese	Casual	$10
9.0	Pho Danh II	Vietnamese	Casual	$10
9.0	Que Huong	Vietnamese	Casual	$10
8.9	Gorditas Aguascalientes	Mexican	Casual	$10
8.8	Thien Thanh	Vietnamese	Casual	$10
8.8	Pho Ga Dakao	Vietnamese	Casual	$10
8.7	Doña Tere	Mexican	Counter	$5
8.6	Tan Tan	Chinese, Vietnamese	Casual	$15
8.6	The Boiling Crab	Seafood, Southern	Casual	$20
8.6	Saigon Pagolac	Vietnamese	Casual	$25
8.6	Dynasty/Willie's BBQ	Chinese	Take-out	$5
8.5	Hong Kong Food Street	Chinese	Casual	$20
8.4	Dim Sum King	Chinese, Dim Sum	Casual	$15
8.4	FuFu Café	Chinese	Casual	$10
8.4	Thuan Kieu Com Tan	Vietnamese	Casual	$15
8.4	Hong Kong Dim Sum	Chinese, Dim Sum	Casual	$15
8.2	Arco Seafood	Chinese, Seafood	Casual	$25
8.2	Peking Cuisine	Chinese	Casual	$15
8.0	Lucky Pot	Chinese	Casual	$15
8.0	Sichuan Cuisine	Chinese	Casual	$15
8.0	Sinh Sinh	Chinese, Seafood	Casual	$30
7.8	San Dong Noodle House	Chinese	Counter	$10
7.8	Don Café	Vietnamese	Counter	$10
7.8	Nguyen Ngo	Sandwiches, Vietnamese	Counter	$5
7.6	East Wall	Chinese	Casual	$15
7.3	Sushi Miyagi	Japanese	Casual	$35
7.2	Pho Saigon	Vietnamese	Casual	$15
7.1	Alpha Bakery	Baked goods, Sandwiches	Take-out	$10
7.0	Fung's Kitchen	Chinese, Seafood	Upmarket	$45
7.0	Kim Chau	Vietnamese	Casual	$10
6.8	Tofu Village	Korean	Casual	$20
6.8	Vinh Hoa	Chinese, Vietnamese	Casual	$10
6.8	Tau Bay	Vietnamese	Casual	$10
6.5	Banana Leaf	Malaysian	Casual	$25
6.5	QQ Cuisine	Chinese	Casual	$10
5.9	Tony Thai	Thai	Casual	$30
4.5	Ocean Palace	Chinese, Dim Sum	Casual	$30

Bellaire Chinatown *continued*

3.9	Taco Cabana	Mexican	Counter	$10
NR	ECK Bakery	Baked goods	Counter	
NR	Hot Breads Bakery	Baked goods, Indian	Counter	
NR	Jungle Café	Baked goods	Counter	

Clear Lake

8.2	Perry's Steakhouse	Steakhouse	Upmarket	$90
7.7	Lupe Tortilla	Mexican	Casual	$35
6.9	Thai Spice	Thai	Casual	$10
4.1	Baker St. (Sherlock's)	British, American	Bar	$25

Conroe

9.6	Chez Roux	French, Modern	Upmarket	$95
7.1	Pappadeaux	Seafood, Southern	Casual	$45

Downtown

9.2	Hubcap Grill	Burgers	Counter	$10
9.1	Vic & Anthony's	Steakhouse	Upmarket	$90
8.8	Eatsie Boys	Sandwiches	Food cart	$10
8.7	Becks Prime	American, Burgers	Counter	$15
8.6	Samba Grille	Steakhouse, Brazilian	Upmarket	$75
8.5	Huynh	Vietnamese	Casual	$20
8.5	Frenchy's Chicken	Southern	Counter	$10
8.0	Ninfa's on Navigation	Mexican	Casual	$30
7.7	Ill Forks	Steakhouse	Upmarket	$95
7.6	Café TH	Vietnamese	Counter	$10
7.3	Voice	Modern	Upmarket	$70
7.1	Guadalajara Hacienda	Mexican	Casual	$35
6.9	Thai Spice	Thai	Casual	$10
6.3	Niko Niko's	Greek	Counter	$20
6.1	The Grove	Modern	Upmarket	$65
6.0	Les Givral's Kahve	Vietnamese, Sandwiches	Counter	$10
6.0	El Rey Taquería	Latin American, Mexican	Counter	$10
5.4	Pappasito's	Mexican	Casual	$35
5.2	Whataburger	Burgers, American	Counter	$10
5.1	The Flying Saucer	American	Bar	$25
3.7	Last Concert Café	Mexican, Vegefusion	Casual	$35

East Houston

8.5	Frenchy's Chicken	Southern	Counter	$10
8.1	Captain Tom's	Seafood, Southern	Counter	$15
7.9	Doneraki	Mexican	Casual	$30
7.4	Calliope's Po-Boy	Southern, Sandwiches	Casual	$15
7.0	Kanomwan	Thai	Casual	$20
6.2	Pappas Seafood	Seafood	Casual	$50
5.4	Pappasito's	Mexican	Casual	$35

Galleria

8.9	Teppay	Japanese	Casual	$60
8.7	Becks Prime	American, Burgers	Counter	$15
8.5	Pappas Bros.	Steakhouse	Upmarket	$105
7.9	Del Frisco's	Steakhouse	Upmarket	$100

Galleria *continued*

7.9	RDG	Modern	Upmarket	$100
7.8	Phillippe	Modern	Upmarket	$80
7.7	Américas	Latin American	Upmarket	$70
7.7	Houston's	American	Upmarket	$60
7.1	Pappadeaux	Seafood, Southern	Casual	$45
7.1	Pappas Burger	Burgers	Counter	$15
6.9	Thai Gourmet	Thai	Casual	$25
6.7	Alexander the Great	Greek	Upmarket	$65
6.5	Five Guys	Burgers, American	Counter	$10
6.4	Zabak's	Middle Eastern, Greek	Counter	$15
6.1	Kenny & Ziggy's	Jewish-style Deli	Casual	$25
5.4	Pappasito's	Mexican	Casual	$35
4.0	House of Pies	American	Casual	$10
3.9	Taco Cabana	Mexican	Counter	$10
NR	The Dessert Gallery	Baked goods	Counter	

Greenway Plaza

9.1	Tony's	Italian	Upmarket	$110
8.5	El Tiempo Cantina	Mexican	Casual	$60
7.8	100% Taquito	Mexican	Counter	$10
7.7	Lupe Tortilla	Mexican	Casual	$35
7.1	Guadalajara Hacienda	Mexican	Casual	$35
7.1	Oporto Café	Portuguese, Modern	Wine bar	$50
7.0	Laurier Café	Modern, French	Upmarket	$65
6.4	Tiny Boxwood's	American, Pizza	Casual	$25
3.9	Taco Cabana	Mexican	Counter	$10

Heights

9.2	Stella Sola	Modern, Pizza	Upmarket	$55
8.9	Zelko Bistro	American, Modern	Casual	$40
8.8	Gatlin's Barbecue	Barbecue	Counter	$15
8.6	Asia Market	Thai	Counter	$10
8.4	Taquería Tacambaro	Mexican	Food cart	$5
8.3	Teotihuacán	Mexican	Casual	$10
7.9	Shade	Modern	Upmarket	$60
7.7	Lupe Tortilla	Mexican	Casual	$35
7.5	Cyclone Anaya's	Mexican	Casual	$35
7.5	Branch Water Tavern	Modern, American	Upmarket	$45
7.5	Tampico Seafood	Seafood, Mexican	Casual	$20
6.9	Benjy's	Modern	Upmarket	$55
6.9	Thai Spice	Thai	Casual	$10
6.8	BRC	American	Casual	$40
6.4	Christian's Tailgate	Burgers, American	Bar	$15
6.2	Pink's Pizza	Pizza	Counter	$20
6.0	Les Givral's Kahve	Vietnamese, Sandwiches	Counter	$10
5.2	Whataburger	Burgers, American	Counter	$10

Hermann Park

6.6	Alfreda's Cafeteria	Southern	Counter	$15

Hillcroft Area

9.1	Udipi Café	Indian	Casual	$10

Hillcroft Area *continued*

8.9	Shiv Sagar	Indian	Counter	$10
8.5	Bombay Sweets	Indian	Counter	$10
8.3	El Pupusodromo	Latin American	Casual	$10
7.9	Garson	Middle Eastern	Casual	$30
7.3	Abdallah's	Middle Eastern	Counter	$15
6.4	Jerusalem Halal Deli	Middle Eastern	Counter	$10
6.2	Shawarma King	Middle Eastern, Greek	Counter	$10

Humble

6.2	Pappas Seafood	Seafood	Casual	$50
6.1	Chuy's	Mexican	Casual	$30

Katy

9.1	Udipi Café	Indian	Casual	$10
8.7	Doña Tere	Mexican	Counter	$5
8.2	Perry's Steakhouse	Steakhouse	Upmarket	$90
8.1	Captain Tom's	Seafood, Southern	Counter	$15
7.7	Lupe Tortilla	Mexican	Casual	$35
7.2	Pho Saigon	Vietnamese	Casual	$15
6.9	Thai Spice	Thai	Casual	$10
4.1	Baker St. (Sherlock's)	British, American	Bar	$25

Medical Center

8.5	Frenchy's Chicken	Southern	Counter	$10
7.8	Guy's Meat Market	Barbecue, Burgers	Counter	$5
6.5	Five Guys	Burgers, American	Counter	$10
3.9	Taco Cabana	Mexican	Counter	$10
NR	Hank's Ice Cream	Ice cream	Counter	

Memorial

8.2	Perry's Steakhouse	Steakhouse	Upmarket	$90
8.2	ToreOre	Korean	Counter	$10
8.0	The Tasting Room	Pizza	Wine bar	$35
7.9	Brenner's	Steakhouse	Upmarket	$90
7.8	Jonathan's the Rub	Burgers, American	Casual	$35
7.5	Cyclone Anaya's	Mexican	Casual	$35
7.3	Sylvia's Enchilada Kitchen	Mexican	Casual	$20
7.1	Masraff's	Modern	Upmarket	$85
7.1	Guadalajara Hacienda	Mexican	Casual	$35
NR	Crave Cupcakes	Baked goods	Counter	

Meyerland

3.9	Taco Cabana	Mexican	Counter	$10

Midtown

9.2	Feast	British	Casual	$50
8.7	Reef	Modern, Seafood	Upmarket	$65
8.6	Kim Tai	Vietnamese	Casual	$10
8.2	Piola	Pizza	Casual	$30
8.0	Nga Restaurant	Vietnamese	Casual	$10
7.7	Brennan's of Houston	Southern, Modern	Upmarket	$100

Midtown *continued*

7.7	Sushi Raku	Japanese	Upmarket	$70
7.5	Cyclone Anaya's	Mexican	Casual	$35
7.2	Pho Saigon	Vietnamese	Casual	$15
7.2	Les Givral's	Vietnamese, Sandwiches	Counter	$10
7.1	t'afia	Modern	Upmarket	$65
7.1	Ibiza	Spanish, Modern	Wine bar	$70
6.9	13 Celsius	Modern	Wine bar	$20
6.7	Lankford Grocery	Burgers, American	Casual	$10
6.5	Thien An Sandwiches	Vietnamese, Sandwiches	Counter	$10
6.4	Christian's Tailgate	Burgers, American	Bar	$15
5.2	Whataburger	Burgers, American	Counter	$10
5.0	The Breakfast Klub	American, Southern	Counter	$15

Montrose

9.6	Da Marco	Italian	Upmarket	$90
9.3	Hugo's	Mexican	Upmarket	$60
9.3	Vinoteca Poscol	Italian	Wine bar	$40
9.2	Dolce Vita	Italian, Pizza	Casual	$40
9.0	Indika	Indian	Upmarket	$60
8.9	Barcelona	Spanish	Upmarket	$65
8.8	Bernie's Burger Bus	Burgers	Food cart	$10
8.8	Eatsie Boys	Sandwiches	Food cart	$10
8.7	Brasserie Max & Julie	French	Upmarket	$65
8.5	El Tiempo Cantina	Mexican	Casual	$60
8.1	Anvil	Modern	Cocktails	$20
8.0	Paulie's	Italian, Sandwiches	Counter	$20
7.9	Mark's	Modern	Upmarket	$110
7.8	Canopy	Modern	Upmarket	$70
7.6	Al's Quick Stop	Middle Eastern, Greek	Counter	$10
7.4	Tacos Tierra Caliente	Mexican	Food cart	$10
7.3	Sylvia's Enchilada Kitchen	Mexican	Casual	$20
7.3	Mélange Crêperie	French	Food cart	$10
7.1	Nippon	Japanese	Casual	$45
7.0	Nelore Churrascaria	Steakhouse, Brazilian	Upmarket	$75
7.0	La Guadalupana	Mexican, Baked goods	Casual	$10
6.9	Divino	Italian	Casual	$50
6.9	Danton's	Seafood, Southern	Casual	$50
6.4	Osaka	Japanese	Casual	$35
6.3	El Real	Mexican	Casual	$35
6.3	Niko Niko's	Greek	Counter	$20
6.2	Pink's Pizza	Pizza	Counter	$20
6.0	Little Big's	Burgers	Counter	$15
4.7	Brasil	Sandwiches, Pizza	Café	$15
3.9	Taco Cabana	Mexican	Counter	$10
3.5	Empire Café	Baked goods, Italian	Counter	$15
3.0	The Black Labrador Pub	American, British	Bar	$30
NR	The Chocolate Bar	Ice cream, Baked goods	Counter	

North Houston

8.8	Gerardo's Drive-In	Mexican	Counter	$10
8.5	Frenchy's Chicken	Southern	Counter	$10
8.3	El Pupusodromo	Latin American	Casual	$10
8.3	Teotihuacán	Mexican	Casual	$10

North Houston *continued*

8.0	Burns Bar-B-Q	Barbecue	Counter	$20
7.9	Doneraki	Mexican	Casual	$30
7.7	Lupe Tortilla	Mexican	Casual	$35
7.5	Tampico Seafood	Seafood, Mexican	Casual	$20
7.2	Pho Saigon	Vietnamese	Casual	$15
7.1	Guadalajara Hacienda	Mexican	Casual	$35
6.2	Pappas Seafood	Seafood	Casual	$50
6.2	Pink's Pizza	Pizza	Counter	$20
6.1	Barbecue Inn	Southern, Barbecue	Casual	$20
6.0	El Rey Taquería	Latin American, Mexican	Counter	$10
5.4	Pappasito's	Mexican	Casual	$35
4.1	Baker St. (Sherlock's)	British, American	Bar	$25
3.9	Taco Cabana	Mexican	Counter	$10

Northwest Houston

8.8	Petrol Station	Burgers	Counter	$25
8.4	Pierson and Company	Barbecue	Counter	$15
8.4	Virgie's	Barbecue	Counter	$15
8.2	Perry's Steakhouse	Steakhouse	Upmarket	$90
8.1	Captain Tom's	Seafood, Southern	Counter	$15
8.0	La Moreliana	Mexican	Counter	$5
7.4	Los Guanacos	Latin American	Casual	$10
7.2	Pho Saigon	Vietnamese	Casual	$15
7.1	Pappadeaux	Seafood, Southern	Casual	$45
6.8	Clay's	Southern, Burgers	Counter	$25
6.6	Little Bitty Burger Barn	Burgers, American	Counter	$10
6.1	Chuy's	Mexican	Casual	$30
5.9	Tony Thai	Thai	Casual	$30
5.4	Pappasito's	Mexican	Casual	$35
4.1	Goode Co. Texas Bar-B-Q	Barbecue	Counter	$20

Pearland

8.9	Killen's Steakhouse	Steakhouse	Upmarket	$105
6.9	Thai Spice	Thai	Casual	$10

Rice Area

8.0	Goode Co. Taquería	Mexican, Burgers	Counter	$25
7.8	Seco's Latin Cuisine	Mexican	Casual	$30
7.5	Pasha	Turkish	Casual	$35
7.2	Café Rabelais	French	Upmarket	$55
6.9	Benjy's	Modern	Upmarket	$55
6.9	Thai Spice	Thai	Casual	$10
6.7	Kubo's	Japanese	Casual	$45
6.3	Istanbul Grill	Turkish	Casual	$30
4.1	Baker St. (Sherlock's)	British, American	Bar	$25
4.1	Goode Co. Texas Bar-B-Q	Barbecue	Counter	$20
NR	The Ginger Man	American	Bar	$15
NR	The Chocolate Bar	Ice cream, Baked goods	Counter	

River Oaks

8.3	Mockingbird Bistro	Modern	Upmarket	$70
7.9	Brenner's	Steakhouse	Upmarket	$90

River Oaks *continued*

7.7	Américas	Latin American	Upmarket	$70
7.6	Tintos	Spanish	Upmarket	$55
7.5	Backstreet Café	Modern	Upmarket	$65
7.1	Pappadeaux	Seafood, Southern	Casual	$45
7.1	Smith & Wollensky	Steakhouse	Upmarket	$105
6.8	Frank's Chop House	Steakhouse, American	Upmarket	$70
6.5	Five Guys	Burgers, American	Counter	$10
6.1	Chuy's	Mexican	Casual	$30
5.6	Ouisie's Table	Southern	Upmarket	$60
4.1	Baker St. (Sherlock's)	British, American	Bar	$25

Southeast Houston

9.2	Pho Binh	Vietnamese	Casual	$10
8.7	Doña Tere	Mexican	Counter	$5
8.6	Taquería Del Sol	Mexican	Casual	$10
8.0	La Moreliana	Mexican	Counter	$5
7.2	Pho Saigon	Vietnamese	Casual	$15
7.1	Pappas Burger	Burgers	Counter	$15
6.6	Tel-Wink Grill	American	Casual	$10
6.2	Pappas Seafood	Seafood	Casual	$50

Southwest Houston

9.5	Himalaya	Pakistani, Indian	Casual	$15
8.8	Great W'kana Café	Indian	Casual	$20
8.5	Pico's Mex-Mex	Mexican	Casual	$35
8.5	Frenchy's Chicken	Southern	Counter	$10
8.4	Sweet n Namkin/Salaam	Indian	Counter	$15
8.4	Mikki's Soul Food	Southern	Counter	$15
8.3	El Pupusodromo	Latin American	Casual	$10
8.3	Teotihuacán	Mexican	Casual	$10
8.0	London Sizzler	Indian	Casual	$30
7.8	La Sani	Pakistani	Casual	$30
7.6	Viet Hoa	Chinese	Counter	$10
7.1	Pappadeaux	Seafood, Southern	Casual	$45
6.8	Fadi's Mediterranean	Middle Eastern, Greek	Counter	$15
5.7	Rudi Lechner's	German	Casual	$30

Spring Branch

9.2	Pho Binh	Vietnamese	Casual	$10
9.1	Korean Noodle House	Korean	Casual	$10
8.9	Vieng Thai	Thai	Casual	$25
8.8	Bon Ga	Korean	Casual	$20
8.7	Becks Prime	American, Burgers	Counter	$15
8.3	El Hidalguense	Mexican	Casual	$35
8.2	El Último	Mexican	Food cart	$5
7.7	Lupe Tortilla	Mexican	Casual	$35
7.6	Nam Gang	Korean	Casual	$30
7.6	Da Da Mi Sushi Bistro	Korean	Casual	$35
7.6	Fratelli's	Italian	Casual	$40
7.6	Mandarin Café	Chinese, Korean	Casual	$15
7.0	Polonia	Polish	Casual	$30
7.0	Jarro Café and Trailer	Mexican	Counter	$10
7.0	Kim Chau	Vietnamese	Casual	$10

Spring Branch *continued*

6.5	Five Guys	Burgers, American	Counter	$10
6.0	El Rey Taquería	Latin American, Mexican	Counter	$10
5.2	Whataburger	Burgers, American	Counter	$10
4.1	Goode Co. Texas Bar-B-Q	Barbecue	Counter	$20

Stafford

7.4	Tornado Burger	Burgers	Counter	$10

Sugar Land

9.1	Udipi Café	Indian	Casual	$10
8.7	Becks Prime	American, Burgers	Counter	$15
8.4	Tandoori Nite	Indian	Food cart	$20
8.2	Perry's Steakhouse	Steakhouse	Upmarket	$90
7.7	Lupe Tortilla	Mexican	Casual	$35
7.2	Pho Saigon	Vietnamese	Casual	$15
6.5	Madras Pavilion	Indian	Casual	$20
5.4	Pappasito's	Mexican	Casual	$35
4.1	Baker St. (Sherlock's)	British, American	Bar	$25

Tomball

9.4	Bootsie's Heritage Café	Modern	Casual	$75
7.7	Lupe Tortilla	Mexican	Casual	$35

Town and Country

8.0	The Tasting Room	Pizza	Wine bar	$35
7.2	Eddie V's	Seafood, Steakhouse	Upmarket	$90

Upper Kirby

9.5	Kata Robata	Japanese, Modern	Upmarket	$70
8.9	The Queen Vic Pub	Indian, British	Casual	$40
8.8	Bernie's Burger Bus	Burgers	Food cart	$10
8.7	Becks Prime	American, Burgers	Counter	$15
8.3	Giacomo's Cibo y Vino	Italian	Counter	$20
8.2	Au Petit Paris	French	Casual	$70
8.2	Haven	Modern	Upmarket	$70
8.2	Pondicheri Café	Indian	Casual	$40
8.1	Churrascos	Latin American	Upmarket	$65
8.0	The Tasting Room	Pizza	Wine bar	$35
7.7	Houston's	American	Upmarket	$60
7.2	Eddie V's	Seafood, Steakhouse	Upmarket	$90
7.1	Pappadeaux	Seafood, Southern	Casual	$45
7.1	Tony Mandola's	Seafood, Southern	Upmarket	$70
7.1	Turquoise Grill	Turkish	Casual	$35
6.8	Ava Kitchen & Whiskey Bar	Modern	Upmarket	$55
6.5	Madras Pavilion	Indian	Casual	$20
6.2	Pappas Seafood	Seafood	Casual	$50
6.0	Red Lion	American, British	Bar	$25
5.6	Hobbit Café	Vegefusion, American	Casual	$20
5.4	Pappasito's	Mexican	Casual	$35
5.2	Whataburger	Burgers, American	Counter	$10
4.0	House of Pies	American	Casual	$10
3.9	Taco Cabana	Mexican	Counter	$10

Upper Kirby *continued*

NR	Amy's Ice Cream	Ice cream	Counter	
NR	The Dessert Gallery	Baked goods	Counter	

Washington

9.2	Hubcap Grill	Burgers	Counter	$10
8.5	Beaver's Ice House	American	Casual	$35
8.5	El Tiempo Cantina	Mexican	Casual	$60
7.2	Soma	Japanese, Modern	Casual	$75
7.2	Stanton's City Bites	Burgers, American	Take-out	$10
6.9	Max's Wine Dive	Modern	Wine bar	$50
6.5	Five Guys	Burgers, American	Counter	$10
6.2	Avenue Grill	Southern	Casual	$15
6.0	El Rey Taquería	Latin American, Mexican	Counter	$10

Webster

6.2	Pappas Seafood	Seafood	Casual	$50

West Houston

9.1	Udipi Café	Indian	Casual	$10
8.7	Doña Tere	Mexican	Counter	$5
8.7	Becks Prime	American, Burgers	Counter	$15
8.6	Burger Guys	Burgers	Counter	$15
8.5	Sam's Deli Diner	Burgers, American	Counter	$10
8.3	Le Mistral	French	Upmarket	$75
8.1	Churrascos	Latin American	Upmarket	$65
8.1	Finger Licking Bukateria	Nigerian	Casual	$15
8.0	Rioja	Spanish	Upmarket	$65
7.7	Lupe Tortilla	Mexican	Casual	$35
7.6	Sushi Jin	Japanese	Casual	$45
7.5	Cyclone Anaya's	Mexican	Casual	$35
7.3	Sylvia's Enchilada Kitchen	Mexican	Casual	$20
6.9	Thai Spice	Thai	Casual	$10
6.8	Fadi's Mediterranean	Middle Eastern, Greek	Counter	$15
6.5	Five Guys	Burgers, American	Counter	$10

West U

6.2	Pink's Pizza	Pizza	Counter	$20
NR	Crave Cupcakes	Baked goods	Counter	

Westchase

9.0	Café Pita +	Bosnian	Casual	$25
8.7	Becks Prime	American, Burgers	Counter	$15
8.6	Tan Tan	Chinese, Vietnamese	Casual	$15
7.9	Doneraki	Mexican	Casual	$30
7.2	Pho Saigon	Vietnamese	Casual	$15
6.9	Thai Spice	Thai	Casual	$10
6.8	Kaneyama	Japanese	Casual	$35
6.5	Blue Nile	Ethiopian	Casual	$25
4.1	Baker St. (Sherlock's)	British, American	Bar	$25

The Woodlands

9.2	Dolce Vita	Italian, Pizza	Casual	$40
8.7	Becks Prime	American, Burgers	Counter	$15
8.2	Perry's Steakhouse	Steakhouse	Upmarket	$90
7.7	Américas	Latin American	Upmarket	$70
7.7	Lupe Tortilla	Mexican	Casual	$35
4.1	Baker St. (Sherlock's)	British, American	Bar	$25

By special feature

Ranked by food rating. Establishments that don't serve full meals (e.g. cafés, bakeries, grocery stores) appear as "NR" at the bottom of the list.

Breakfast

		Cuisine	Location	Type	Price
8.9	Gorditas Aguascalientes	Mexican	Bellaire Chinatown	Casual	$10
8.8	Great W'kana Café	Indian	Southwest Houston	Casual	$20
8.8	Thien Thanh	Vietnamese	Bellaire Chinatown	Casual	$10
8.8	Pho Ga Dakao	Vietnamese	Bellaire Chinatown	Casual	$10
8.8	Gerardo's Drive-In	Mexican	North Houston	Counter	$10
8.7	Doña Tere	Mexican	Multiple locations	Counter	$5
8.6	Taquería Del Sol	Mexican	Southeast Houston	Casual	$10
8.5	El Tiempo Cantina	Mexican	Multiple locations	Casual	$60
8.5	Pico's Mex-Mex	Mexican	Southwest Houston	Casual	$35
8.5	Sam's Deli Diner	Burgers, American	West Houston	Counter	$10
8.4	Thuan Kieu Com Tan	Vietnamese	Bellaire Chinatown	Casual	$15
8.4	Taquería Tacambaro	Mexican	Heights	Food cart	$5
8.3	El Hidalguense	Mexican	Spring Branch	Casual	$35
8.3	El Pupusodromo	Latin American	Multiple locations	Casual	$10
8.3	Teotihuacán	Mexican	Multiple locations	Casual	$10
8.2	Pondicheri Café	Indian	Upper Kirby	Casual	$40
8.2	El Último	Mexican	Spring Branch	Food cart	$5
7.9	Doneraki	Mexican	Multiple locations	Casual	$30
7.8	Canopy	Modern	Montrose	Upmarket	$70
7.3	Voice	Modern	Downtown	Upmarket	$70
7.3	Abdallah's	Middle Eastern	Hillcroft Area	Counter	$15
7.3	Mélange Crêperie	French	Montrose	Food cart	$10
7.2	Stanton's City Bites	Burgers, American	Washington	Take-out	$10
7.1	Turquoise Grill	Turkish	Upper Kirby	Casual	$35
7.0	Jarro Café and Trailer	Mexican	Spring Branch	Counter	$10
7.0	La Guadalupana	Mexican	Montrose	Casual	$10
6.7	Lankford Grocery	Burgers, American	Midtown	Casual	$10
6.6	Tel-Wink Grill	American	Southeast Houston	Casual	$10
6.6	Alfreda's Cafeteria	Southern	Hermann Park	Counter	$15
6.5	Thien An Sandwiches	Vietnamese	Midtown	Counter	$10
6.4	Tiny Boxwood's	American, Pizza	Greenway Plaza	Casual	$25
6.3	Niko Niko's	Greek	Multiple locations	Counter	$20
6.2	Avenue Grill	Southern	Washington	Casual	$15
6.1	Kenny & Ziggy's	Jewish-style Deli	Galleria	Casual	$25
6.0	El Rey Taquería	Latin American	Multiple locations	Counter	$10
5.6	Ouisie's Table	Southern	River Oaks	Upmarket	$60
5.2	Whataburger	Burgers, American	Multiple locations	Counter	$10
5.0	The Breakfast Klub	American, Southern	Midtown	Counter	$15
4.7	Brasil	Sandwiches, Pizza	Montrose	Café	$15
4.0	House of Pies	American	Multiple locations	Casual	$10
3.9	Taco Cabana	Mexican	Multiple locations	Counter	$10

Breakfast *continued*

3.5	Empire Café	Baked goods	Montrose	Counter	$15
NR	Hot Breads Bakery	Baked goods	Bellaire Chinatown	Counter	

Brunch

9.4	Bootsie's Heritage Café	Modern	Tomball	Casual	$75
9.3	Hugo's	Mexican	Montrose	Upmarket	$60
9.2	Stella Sola	Modern, Pizza	Heights	Upmarket	$55
9.0	Indika	Indian	Montrose	Upmarket	$60
8.9	Zelko Bistro	American, Modern	Heights	Casual	$40
8.9	Gorditas Aguascalientes	Mexican	Bellaire Chinatown	Casual	$10
8.8	Great W'kana Café	Indian	Southwest Houston	Casual	$20
8.8	Pho Ga Dakao	Vietnamese	Bellaire Chinatown	Casual	$10
8.7	Brasserie Max & Julie	French	Montrose	Upmarket	$65
8.5	Beaver's Ice House	American	Washington	Casual	$35
8.5	El Tiempo Cantina	Mexican	Multiple locations	Casual	$60
8.4	Dim Sum King	Chinese, Dim Sum	Bellaire Chinatown	Casual	$15
8.4	Taquería Tacambaro	Mexican	Heights	Food cart	$5
8.4	Hong Kong Dim Sum	Chinese, Dim Sum	Bellaire Chinatown	Casual	$15
8.3	Le Mistral	French	West Houston	Upmarket	$75
8.3	Mockingbird Bistro	Modern	River Oaks	Upmarket	$70
8.3	El Hidalguense	Mexican	Spring Branch	Casual	$35
8.3	Teotihuacán	Mexican	Multiple locations	Casual	$10
8.2	Pondicheri Café	Indian	Upper Kirby	Casual	$40
8.2	Perry's Steakhouse	Steakhouse	Multiple locations	Upmarket	$90
8.1	Anvil	Modern	Montrose	Cocktails	$20
8.1	Churrascos	Latin American	Multiple locations	Upmarket	$65
8.0	Rioja	Spanish	West Houston	Upmarket	$65
8.0	The Tasting Room	Pizza	Multiple locations	Wine bar	$35
8.0	Ninfa's on Navigation	Mexican	Downtown	Casual	$30
8.0	Goode Co. Taquería	Mexican, Burgers	Rice Area	Counter	$25
7.9	Shade	Modern	Heights	Upmarket	$60
7.9	Doneraki	Mexican	Multiple locations	Casual	$30
7.9	RDG	Modern	Galleria	Upmarket	$100
7.8	Canopy	Modern	Montrose	Upmarket	$70
7.8	Seco's Latin Cuisine	Mexican	Rice Area	Casual	$30
7.7	Américas	Latin American	Multiple locations	Upmarket	$70
7.7	Brennan's of Houston	Southern, Modern	Midtown	Upmarket	$100
7.6	Tintos	Spanish	River Oaks	Upmarket	$55
7.5	Backstreet Café	Modern	River Oaks	Upmarket	$65
7.5	Cyclone Anaya's	Mexican	Multiple locations	Casual	$35
7.5	Branch Water Tavern	Modern, American	Heights	Upmarket	$45
7.3	Voice	Modern	Downtown	Upmarket	$70
7.1	Masraff's	Modern	Memorial	Upmarket	$85
7.1	Guadalajara Hacienda	Mexican	Multiple locations	Casual	$35
7.1	Turquoise Grill	Turkish	Upper Kirby	Casual	$35
7.0	Nelore Churrascaria	Steakhouse	Montrose	Upmarket	$75
7.0	Fung's Kitchen	Chinese, Seafood	Bellaire Chinatown	Upmarket	$45
7.0	Jarro Café and Trailer	Mexican	Spring Branch	Counter	$10
7.0	La Guadalupana	Mexican	Montrose	Casual	$10
6.9	Benjy's	Modern	Multiple locations	Upmarket	$55
6.9	Max's Wine Dive	Modern	Washington	Wine bar	$50
6.9	Danton's	Seafood, Southern	Montrose	Casual	$50
6.8	BRC	American	Heights	Casual	$40
6.6	Tel-Wink Grill	American	Southeast Houston	Casual	$10

Brunch *continued*

6.4	Tiny Boxwood's	American, Pizza	Greenway Plaza	Casual	$25
6.3	El Real	Mexican	Montrose	Casual	$35
6.3	Niko Niko's	Greek	Multiple locations	Counter	$20
6.1	Kenny & Ziggy's	Jewish-style Deli	Galleria	Casual	$25
6.0	El Rey Taquería	Latin American	Multiple locations	Counter	$10
5.6	Ouisie's Table	Southern	River Oaks	Upmarket	$60
5.6	Hobbit Café	Vegefusion	Upper Kirby	Casual	$20
5.0	The Breakfast Klub	American, Southern	Midtown	Counter	$15
4.7	Brasil	Sandwiches, Pizza	Montrose	Café	$15
4.5	Ocean Palace	Chinese, Dim Sum	Bellaire Chinatown	Casual	$30
4.0	House of Pies	American	Multiple locations	Casual	$10
3.7	Last Concert Café	Mexican	Downtown	Casual	$35
3.5	Empire Café	Baked goods	Montrose	Counter	$15
3.0	The Black Labrador Pub	American, British	Montrose	Bar	$30

BYO *We consider any restaurant with a corkage fee of $10 or under to be BYO. If there is a wine program, however, it is polite to tip on what you would have spent had you not brought your own. Offering a taste is optional.*

9.5	Himalaya	Pakistani, Indian	Southwest Houston	Casual	$15
9.2	Shanghai Restaurant	Chinese	Bellaire Chinatown	Casual	$15
9.0	Café Pita +	Bosnian	Westchase	Casual	$25
8.9	Vieng Thai	Thai	Spring Branch	Casual	$25
8.8	Great W'kana Café	Indian	Southwest Houston	Casual	$20
8.8	Thien Thanh	Vietnamese	Bellaire Chinatown	Casual	$10
8.6	Saigon Pagolac	Vietnamese	Bellaire Chinatown	Casual	$25
8.5	Huynh	Vietnamese	Downtown	Casual	$20
8.4	Thuan Kieu Com Tan	Vietnamese	Bellaire Chinatown	Casual	$15
8.4	Tandoori Nite	Indian	Sugar Land	Food cart	$20
8.0	Paulie's	Italian, Sandwiches	Montrose	Counter	$20
8.0	Lucky Pot	Chinese	Bellaire Chinatown	Casual	$15
8.0	Sichuan Cuisine	Chinese	Bellaire Chinatown	Casual	$15
7.9	Garson	Middle Eastern	Hillcroft Area	Casual	$30
7.8	Jonathan's the Rub	Burgers, American	Memorial	Casual	$35
7.5	Pasha	Turkish	Rice Area	Casual	$35
7.3	Sushi Miyagi	Japanese	Bellaire Chinatown	Casual	$35
7.1	Turquoise Grill	Turkish	Upper Kirby	Casual	$35
7.0	Kim Chau	Vietnamese	Multiple locations	Casual	$10
7.0	La Guadalupana	Mexican	Montrose	Casual	$10
7.0	Kanomwan	Thai	East Houston	Casual	$20
6.8	Fadi's Mediterranean	Middle Eastern	Multiple locations	Counter	$15
6.5	QQ Cuisine	Chinese	Bellaire Chinatown	Casual	$10
6.4	Zabak's	Middle Eastern	Galleria	Counter	$15
6.3	Istanbul Grill	Turkish	Rice Area	Casual	$30
6.0	Les Givral's Kahve	Vietnamese	Multiple locations	Counter	$10

Date-friendly

9.6	Chez Roux	French, Modern	Conroe	Upmarket	$95
9.6	Da Marco	Italian	Montrose	Upmarket	$90
9.5	Kata Robata	Japanese, Modern	Upper Kirby	Upmarket	$70
9.4	Bootsie's Heritage Café	Modern	Tomball	Casual	$75
9.3	Hugo's	Mexican	Montrose	Upmarket	$60
9.3	Vinoteca Poscol	Italian	Montrose	Wine bar	$40
9.2	Dolce Vita	Italian, Pizza	Multiple locations	Casual	$40

Date-friendly *continued*

9.2	Feast	British	Midtown	Casual	$50
9.2	Stella Sola	Modern, Pizza	Heights	Upmarket	$55
9.1	Vic & Anthony's	Steakhouse	Downtown	Upmarket	$90
9.1	Tony's	Italian	Greenway Plaza	Upmarket	$110
9.0	Indika	Indian	Montrose	Upmarket	$60
8.9	The Queen Vic Pub	Indian, British	Upper Kirby	Casual	$40
8.9	Zelko Bistro	American, Modern	Heights	Casual	$40
8.9	Teppay	Japanese	Galleria	Casual	$60
8.9	Killen's Steakhouse	Steakhouse	Pearland	Upmarket	$105
8.8	Great W'kana Café	Indian	Southwest Houston	Casual	$20
8.7	Brasserie Max & Julie	French	Montrose	Upmarket	$65
8.7	Reef	Modern, Seafood	Midtown	Upmarket	$65
8.6	Samba Grille	Steakhouse	Downtown	Upmarket	$75
8.6	Tan Tan	Chinese	Multiple locations	Casual	$15
8.5	Beaver's Ice House	American	Washington	Casual	$35
8.5	Huynh	Vietnamese	Downtown	Casual	$20
8.5	Pappas Bros.	Steakhouse	Galleria	Upmarket	$105
8.3	Le Mistral	French	West Houston	Upmarket	$75
8.3	Mockingbird Bistro	Modern	River Oaks	Upmarket	$70
8.2	Au Petit Paris	French	Upper Kirby	Casual	$70
8.2	Haven	Modern	Upper Kirby	Upmarket	$70
8.2	Pondicheri Café	Indian	Upper Kirby	Casual	$40
8.2	Perry's Steakhouse	Steakhouse	Multiple locations	Upmarket	$90
8.2	Piola	Pizza	Midtown	Casual	$30
8.1	Anvil	Modern	Montrose	Cocktails	$20
8.1	Churrascos	Latin American	Multiple locations	Upmarket	$65
8.0	Rioja	Spanish	West Houston	Upmarket	$65
8.0	London Sizzler	Indian	Southwest Houston	Casual	$30
8.0	The Tasting Room	Pizza	Multiple locations	Wine bar	$35
7.9	Brenner's	Steakhouse	Multiple locations	Upmarket	$90
7.9	Garson	Middle Eastern	Hillcroft Area	Casual	$30
7.9	Mark's	Modern	Montrose	Upmarket	$110
7.9	Shade	Modern	Heights	Upmarket	$60
7.9	Del Frisco's	Steakhouse	Galleria	Upmarket	$100
7.9	RDG	Modern	Galleria	Upmarket	$100
7.8	Canopy	Modern	Montrose	Upmarket	$70
7.8	Phillippe	Modern	Galleria	Upmarket	$80
7.7	Américas	Latin American	Multiple locations	Upmarket	$70
7.7	Brennan's of Houston	Southern, Modern	Midtown	Upmarket	$100
7.7	Sushi Raku	Japanese	Midtown	Upmarket	$70
7.7	III Forks	Steakhouse	Downtown	Upmarket	$95
7.6	Sushi Jin	Japanese	West Houston	Casual	$45
7.6	Tintos	Spanish	River Oaks	Upmarket	$55
7.6	Fratelli's	Italian	Multiple locations	Casual	$40
7.5	Backstreet Café	Modern	River Oaks	Upmarket	$65
7.5	Cyclone Anaya's	Mexican	Multiple locations	Casual	$35
7.5	Branch Water Tavern	Modern, American	Heights	Upmarket	$45
7.5	Pasha	Turkish	Rice Area	Casual	$35
7.3	Voice	Modern	Downtown	Upmarket	$70
7.2	Café Rabelais	French	Rice Area	Upmarket	$55
7.2	Eddie V's	Seafood	Multiple locations	Upmarket	$90
7.1	t'afia	Modern	Midtown	Upmarket	$65
7.1	Ibiza	Spanish, Modern	Midtown	Wine bar	$70
7.1	Masraff's	Modern	Memorial	Upmarket	$85

Date-friendly *continued*

7.1	Tony Mandola's	Seafood, Southern	Multiple locations	Upmarket	$70
7.1	Oporto Café	Portuguese	Greenway Plaza	Wine bar	$50
7.1	Smith & Wollensky	Steakhouse	River Oaks	Upmarket	$105
7.1	Turquoise Grill	Turkish	Upper Kirby	Casual	$35
7.0	Nelore Churrascaria	Steakhouse	Montrose	Upmarket	$75
7.0	Fung's Kitchen	Chinese, Seafood	Bellaire Chinatown	Upmarket	$45
7.0	Laurier Café	Modern, French	Greenway Plaza	Upmarket	$65
7.0	Polonia	Polish	Spring Branch	Casual	$30
6.9	Benjy's	Modern	Multiple locations	Upmarket	$55
6.9	13 Celsius	Modern	Midtown	Wine bar	$20
6.9	Divino	Italian	Montrose	Casual	$50
6.9	Max's Wine Dive	Modern	Washington	Wine bar	$50
6.9	Danton's	Seafood, Southern	Montrose	Casual	$50
6.9	Thai Gourmet	Thai	Galleria	Casual	$25
6.8	Ava Kitchen & Whiskey Bar	Modern	Upper Kirby	Upmarket	$55
6.8	Frank's Chop House	Steakhouse	River Oaks	Upmarket	$70
6.5	Blue Nile	Ethiopian	Westchase	Casual	$25
6.4	Osaka	Japanese	Montrose	Casual	$35
6.1	The Grove	Modern	Downtown	Upmarket	$65
6.0	Red Lion	American, British	Upper Kirby	Bar	$25
5.7	Rudi Lechner's	German	Southwest Houston	Casual	$30
5.6	Hobbit Café	Vegefusion	Upper Kirby	Casual	$20
4.7	Brasil	Sandwiches, Pizza	Montrose	Café	$15
3.5	Empire Café	Baked goods	Montrose	Counter	$15
3.0	The Black Labrador Pub	American, British	Montrose	Bar	$30
NR	The Ginger Man	American	Rice Area	Bar	$15
NR	Amy's Ice Cream	Ice cream	Upper Kirby	Counter	
NR	The Chocolate Bar	Ice cream	Multiple locations	Counter	
NR	Crave Cupcakes	Baked goods	Multiple locations	Counter	
NR	The Dessert Gallery	Baked goods	Multiple locations	Counter	
NR	Jungle Café	Baked goods	Bellaire Chinatown	Counter	

Kid-friendly

9.5	Crawfish and Noodles	Southern	Bellaire Chinatown	Casual	$25
9.2	Shanghai Restaurant	Chinese	Bellaire Chinatown	Casual	$15
9.1	Udipi Café	Indian	Multiple locations	Casual	$10
8.8	Bon Ga	Korean	Spring Branch	Casual	$20
8.8	Thien Thanh	Vietnamese	Bellaire Chinatown	Casual	$10
8.8	Bernie's Burger Bus	Burgers	Multiple locations	Food cart	$10
8.8	Gatlin's Barbecue	Barbecue	Heights	Counter	$15
8.8	Gerardo's Drive-In	Mexican	North Houston	Counter	$10
8.7	Becks Prime	American, Burgers	Multiple locations	Counter	$15
8.6	Taquería Del Sol	Mexican	Southeast Houston	Casual	$10
8.6	Tan Tan	Chinese	Multiple locations	Casual	$15
8.6	The Boiling Crab	Seafood, Southern	Bellaire Chinatown	Casual	$20
8.6	Burger Guys	Burgers	West Houston	Counter	$15
8.5	Hong Kong Food Street	Chinese	Bellaire Chinatown	Casual	$20
8.5	Sam's Deli Diner	Burgers, American	West Houston	Counter	$10
8.5	Frenchy's Chicken	Southern	Multiple locations	Counter	$10
8.5	Bombay Sweets	Indian	Hillcroft Area	Counter	$10
8.4	Dim Sum King	Chinese, Dim Sum	Bellaire Chinatown	Casual	$15
8.4	Thuan Kieu Com Tan	Vietnamese	Bellaire Chinatown	Casual	$15
8.4	Hong Kong Dim Sum	Chinese, Dim Sum	Bellaire Chinatown	Casual	$15
8.4	Mikki's Soul Food	Southern	Southwest Houston	Counter	$15

Kid-friendly *continued*

8.2	Piola	Pizza	Midtown	Casual	$30
8.2	Peking Cuisine	Chinese	Bellaire Chinatown	Casual	$15
8.2	ToreOre	Korean	Memorial	Counter	$10
8.1	Captain Tom's	Seafood, Southern	Multiple locations	Counter	$15
8.0	Ninfa's on Navigation	Mexican	Downtown	Casual	$30
8.0	Sinh Sinh	Chinese, Seafood	Bellaire Chinatown	Casual	$30
8.0	Goode Co. Taquería	Mexican, Burgers	Rice Area	Counter	$25
7.9	Doneraki	Mexican	Multiple locations	Casual	$30
7.8	100% Taquito	Mexican	Greenway Plaza	Counter	$10
7.8	San Dong Noodle House	Chinese	Bellaire Chinatown	Counter	$10
7.8	Don Café	Vietnamese	Bellaire Chinatown	Counter	$10
7.7	Lupe Tortilla	Mexican	Multiple locations	Casual	$35
7.6	East Wall	Chinese	Bellaire Chinatown	Casual	$15
7.5	Tampico Seafood	Seafood, Mexican	Multiple locations	Casual	$20
7.4	Calliope's Po-Boy	Southern	East Houston	Casual	$15
7.3	Mélange Crêperie	French	Montrose	Food cart	$10
7.2	Pho Saigon	Vietnamese	Multiple locations	Casual	$15
7.1	Pappadeaux	Seafood, Southern	Multiple locations	Casual	$45
7.1	Guadalajara Hacienda	Mexican	Multiple locations	Casual	$35
7.1	Nippon	Japanese	Montrose	Casual	$45
7.1	Pappas Burger	Burgers	Multiple locations	Counter	$15
7.0	Nelore Churrascaria	Steakhouse	Montrose	Upmarket	$75
7.0	Kim Chau	Vietnamese	Multiple locations	Casual	$10
7.0	Kanomwan	Thai	East Houston	Casual	$20
6.9	Thai Spice	Thai	Multiple locations	Casual	$10
6.8	Clay's	Southern, Burgers	Northwest Houston	Counter	$25
6.8	Kaneyama	Japanese	Westchase	Casual	$35
6.7	Lankford Grocery	Burgers, American	Midtown	Casual	$10
6.7	Alexander the Great	Greek	Galleria	Upmarket	$65
6.6	Bellaire Broiler Burger	Burgers, American	Bellaire	Counter	$10
6.6	Little Bitty Burger Barn	Burgers, American	Northwest Houston	Counter	$10
6.6	Tel-Wink Grill	American	Southeast Houston	Casual	$10
6.5	Five Guys	Burgers, American	Multiple locations	Counter	$10
6.3	Niko Niko's	Greek	Multiple locations	Counter	$20
6.2	Pappas Seafood	Seafood	Multiple locations	Casual	$50
6.1	Chuy's	Mexican	Multiple locations	Casual	$30
6.1	Barbecue Inn	Southern, Barbecue	North Houston	Casual	$20
6.1	Kenny & Ziggy's	Jewish-style Deli	Galleria	Casual	$25
6.0	Little Big's	Burgers	Multiple locations	Counter	$15
5.7	Rudi Lechner's	German	Southwest Houston	Casual	$30
5.6	Ouisie's Table	Southern	River Oaks	Upmarket	$60
5.6	Hobbit Café	Vegefusion	Upper Kirby	Casual	$20
5.4	Pappasito's	Mexican	Multiple locations	Casual	$35
5.2	Whataburger	Burgers, American	Multiple locations	Counter	$10
5.0	The Breakfast Klub	American, Southern	Midtown	Counter	$15
4.1	Goode Co. Texas Bar-B-Q	Barbecue	Multiple locations	Counter	$20
4.0	House of Pies	American	Multiple locations	Casual	$10
3.9	Taco Cabana	Mexican	Multiple locations	Counter	$10
NR	Amy's Ice Cream	Ice cream	Upper Kirby	Counter	
NR	The Chocolate Bar	Ice cream	Multiple locations	Counter	
NR	Crave Cupcakes	Baked goods	Multiple locations	Counter	
NR	The Dessert Gallery	Baked goods	Multiple locations	Counter	
NR	ECK Bakery	Baked goods	Bellaire Chinatown	Counter	
NR	Hank's Ice Cream	Ice cream	Medical Center	Counter	

Live music *of any kind, from jazz piano to rock, even occasionally*

9.3	Hugo's	Mexican	Montrose	Upmarket	$60
9.1	Vic & Anthony's	Steakhouse	Downtown	Upmarket	$90
9.1	Tony's	Italian	Greenway Plaza	Upmarket	$110
8.9	Gorditas Aguascalientes	Mexican	Bellaire Chinatown	Casual	$10
8.8	Petrol Station	Burgers	Northwest Houston	Counter	$25
8.5	Beaver's Ice House	American	Washington	Casual	$35
8.5	Pico's Mex-Mex	Mexican	Southwest Houston	Casual	$35
8.5	Sam's Deli Diner	Burgers, American	West Houston	Counter	$10
8.3	Le Mistral	French	West Houston	Upmarket	$75
8.3	El Hidalguense	Mexican	Spring Branch	Casual	$35
8.3	Teotihuacán	Mexican	Multiple locations	Casual	$10
8.2	Perry's Steakhouse	Steakhouse	Multiple locations	Upmarket	$90
8.0	Rioja	Spanish	West Houston	Upmarket	$65
8.0	The Tasting Room	Pizza	Multiple locations	Wine bar	$35
7.9	Garson	Middle Eastern	Hillcroft Area	Casual	$30
7.9	Doneraki	Mexican	Multiple locations	Casual	$30
7.8	La Sani	Pakistani	Southwest Houston	Casual	$30
7.7	Brennan's of Houston	Southern, Modern	Midtown	Upmarket	$100
7.6	Tintos	Spanish	River Oaks	Upmarket	$55
7.5	Backstreet Café	Modern	River Oaks	Upmarket	$65
7.2	Eddie V's	Seafood	Multiple locations	Upmarket	$90
7.1	t'afia	Modern	Midtown	Upmarket	$65
7.1	Masraff's	Modern	Memorial	Upmarket	$85
7.1	Pappadeaux	Seafood, Southern	Multiple locations	Casual	$45
6.9	13 Celsius	Modern	Midtown	Wine bar	$20
6.9	Danton's	Seafood, Southern	Montrose	Casual	$50
6.9	Thai Spice	Thai	Multiple locations	Casual	$10
6.7	Kubo's	Japanese	Rice Area	Casual	$45
6.7	Alexander the Great	Greek	Galleria	Upmarket	$65
6.4	Christian's Tailgate	Burgers, American	Multiple locations	Bar	$15
5.7	Rudi Lechner's	German	Southwest Houston	Casual	$30
5.6	Ouisie's Table	Southern	River Oaks	Upmarket	$60
5.1	The Flying Saucer	American	Downtown	Bar	$25
5.0	The Breakfast Klub	American, Southern	Midtown	Counter	$15
4.7	Brasil	Sandwiches, Pizza	Montrose	Café	$15
4.1	Baker St. (Sherlock's)	British, American	Multiple locations	Bar	$25
3.7	Last Concert Café	Mexican	Downtown	Casual	$35

Outdoor dining *of any kind, from sidewalk tables to a big backyard patio*

9.6	Chez Roux	French, Modern	Conroe	Upmarket	$95
9.5	Kata Robata	Japanese, Modern	Upper Kirby	Upmarket	$70
9.3	Hugo's	Mexican	Montrose	Upmarket	$60
9.2	Dolce Vita	Italian, Pizza	Multiple locations	Casual	$40
9.2	Feast	British	Midtown	Casual	$50
9.2	Stella Sola	Modern, Pizza	Heights	Upmarket	$55
9.2	Hubcap Grill	Burgers	Multiple locations	Counter	$10
9.1	Korean Noodle House	Korean	Spring Branch	Casual	$10
9.0	Indika	Indian	Montrose	Upmarket	$60
8.9	The Queen Vic Pub	Indian, British	Upper Kirby	Casual	$40
8.9	Zelko Bistro	American, Modern	Heights	Casual	$40
8.8	Petrol Station	Burgers	Northwest Houston	Counter	$25
8.8	Thien Thanh	Vietnamese	Bellaire Chinatown	Casual	$10
8.8	Bernie's Burger Bus	Burgers	Multiple locations	Food cart	$10
8.8	Eatsie Boys	Sandwiches	Multiple locations	Food cart	$10

Outdoor dining *continued*

8.8	Gatlin's Barbecue	Barbecue	Heights	Counter	$15
8.7	Brasserie Max & Julie	French	Montrose	Upmarket	$65
8.7	Reef	Modern, Seafood	Midtown	Upmarket	$65
8.7	Becks Prime	American, Burgers	Multiple locations	Counter	$15
8.6	Samba Grille	Steakhouse	Downtown	Upmarket	$75
8.5	Beaver's Ice House	American	Washington	Casual	$35
8.5	El Tiempo Cantina	Mexican	Multiple locations	Casual	$60
8.5	Pico's Mex-Mex	Mexican	Southwest Houston	Casual	$35
8.5	Frenchy's Chicken	Southern	Multiple locations	Counter	$10
8.4	Tandoori Nite	Indian	Sugar Land	Food cart	$20
8.4	Taquería Tacambaro	Mexican	Heights	Food cart	$5
8.3	Le Mistral	French	West Houston	Upmarket	$75
8.3	Mockingbird Bistro	Modern	River Oaks	Upmarket	$70
8.3	Giacomo's Cibo y Vino	Italian	Upper Kirby	Counter	$20
8.3	Teotihuacán	Mexican	Multiple locations	Casual	$10
8.2	Au Petit Paris	French	Upper Kirby	Casual	$70
8.2	Haven	Modern	Upper Kirby	Upmarket	$70
8.2	Perry's Steakhouse	Steakhouse	Multiple locations	Upmarket	$90
8.2	Piola	Pizza	Midtown	Casual	$30
8.2	El Último	Mexican	Spring Branch	Food cart	$5
8.1	Churrascos	Latin American	Multiple locations	Upmarket	$65
8.0	Rioja	Spanish	West Houston	Upmarket	$65
8.0	The Tasting Room	Pizza	Multiple locations	Wine bar	$35
8.0	Ninfa's on Navigation	Mexican	Downtown	Casual	$30
8.0	Paulie's	Italian, Sandwiches	Montrose	Counter	$20
8.0	Goode Co. Taquería	Mexican, Burgers	Rice Area	Counter	$25
7.9	Brenner's	Steakhouse	Multiple locations	Upmarket	$90
7.9	Garson	Middle Eastern	Hillcroft Area	Casual	$30
7.9	Shade	Modern	Heights	Upmarket	$60
7.9	Del Frisco's	Steakhouse	Galleria	Upmarket	$100
7.8	Canopy	Modern	Montrose	Upmarket	$70
7.8	Phillippe	Modern	Galleria	Upmarket	$80
7.8	100% Taquito	Mexican	Greenway Plaza	Counter	$10
7.8	Seco's Latin Cuisine	Mexican	Rice Area	Casual	$30
7.8	Jonathan's the Rub	Burgers, American	Memorial	Casual	$35
7.7	Américas	Latin American	Multiple locations	Upmarket	$70
7.7	Brennan's of Houston	Southern, Modern	Midtown	Upmarket	$100
7.7	Lupe Tortilla	Mexican	Multiple locations	Casual	$35
7.6	Tintos	Spanish	River Oaks	Upmarket	$55
7.6	Fratelli's	Italian	Multiple locations	Casual	$40
7.5	Backstreet Café	Modern	River Oaks	Upmarket	$65
7.5	Cyclone Anaya's	Mexican	Multiple locations	Casual	$35
7.5	Branch Water Tavern	Modern, American	Heights	Upmarket	$45
7.5	Pasha	Turkish	Rice Area	Casual	$35
7.5	Tampico Seafood	Seafood, Mexican	Multiple locations	Casual	$20
7.4	Tacos Tierra Caliente	Mexican	Montrose	Food cart	$10
7.3	Sylvia's Enchilada Kitchen	Mexican	Multiple locations	Casual	$20
7.3	Abdallah's	Middle Eastern	Hillcroft Area	Counter	$15
7.3	Mélange Crêperie	French	Montrose	Food cart	$10
7.2	Soma	Japanese, Modern	Washington	Casual	$75
7.1	t'afia	Modern	Midtown	Upmarket	$65
7.1	Ibiza	Spanish, Modern	Midtown	Wine bar	$70
7.1	Masraff's	Modern	Memorial	Upmarket	$85
7.1	Pappadeaux	Seafood, Southern	Multiple locations	Casual	$45

Outdoor dining *continued*

7.1	Guadalajara Hacienda	Mexican	Multiple locations	Casual	$35
7.1	Nippon	Japanese	Montrose	Casual	$45
7.1	Oporto Café	Portuguese	Greenway Plaza	Wine bar	$50
7.1	Smith & Wollensky	Steakhouse	River Oaks	Upmarket	$105
7.1	Turquoise Grill	Turkish	Upper Kirby	Casual	$35
7.0	Nelore Churrascaria	Steakhouse	Montrose	Upmarket	$75
7.0	Laurier Café	Modern, French	Greenway Plaza	Upmarket	$65
7.0	Jarro Café and Trailer	Mexican	Spring Branch	Counter	$10
7.0	La Guadalupana	Mexican	Montrose	Casual	$10
6.9	13 Celsius	Modern	Midtown	Wine bar	$20
6.9	Max's Wine Dive	Modern	Washington	Wine bar	$50
6.9	Danton's	Seafood, Southern	Montrose	Casual	$50
6.8	Clay's	Southern, Burgers	Northwest Houston	Counter	$25
6.8	BRC	American	Heights	Casual	$40
6.8	Fadi's Mediterranean	Middle Eastern	Multiple locations	Counter	$15
6.7	Lankford Grocery	Burgers, American	Midtown	Casual	$10
6.7	Kubo's	Japanese	Rice Area	Casual	$45
6.7	Alexander the Great	Greek	Galleria	Upmarket	$65
6.6	Little Bitty Burger Barn	Burgers, American	Northwest Houston	Counter	$10
6.4	Tiny Boxwood's	American, Pizza	Greenway Plaza	Casual	$25
6.4	Christian's Tailgate	Burgers, American	Multiple locations	Bar	$15
6.3	Istanbul Grill	Turkish	Rice Area	Casual	$30
6.3	Niko Niko's	Greek	Multiple locations	Counter	$20
6.2	Shawarma King	Middle Eastern	Hillcroft Area	Counter	$10
6.1	The Grove	Modern	Downtown	Upmarket	$65
6.0	Red Lion	American, British	Upper Kirby	Bar	$25
6.0	Little Big's	Burgers	Multiple locations	Counter	$15
5.6	Ouisie's Table	Southern	River Oaks	Upmarket	$60
5.6	Hobbit Café	Vegefusion	Upper Kirby	Casual	$20
5.4	Pappasito's	Mexican	Multiple locations	Casual	$35
5.1	The Flying Saucer	American	Downtown	Bar	$25
5.0	The Breakfast Klub	American, Southern	Midtown	Counter	$15
4.7	Brasil	Sandwiches, Pizza	Montrose	Café	$15
4.1	Baker St. (Sherlock's)	British, American	Multiple locations	Bar	$25
4.1	Goode Co. Texas Bar-B-Q	Barbecue	Multiple locations	Counter	$20
3.9	Taco Cabana	Mexican	Multiple locations	Counter	$10
3.7	Last Concert Café	Mexican	Downtown	Casual	$35
3.5	Empire Café	Baked goods	Montrose	Counter	$15
3.0	The Black Labrador Pub	American, British	Montrose	Bar	$30
NR	The Ginger Man	American	Rice Area	Bar	$15
NR	Amy's Ice Cream	Ice cream	Upper Kirby	Counter	
NR	The Dessert Gallery	Baked goods	Multiple locations	Counter	

Wi-Fi

9.6	Chez Roux	French, Modern	Conroe	Upmarket	$95
9.5	Kata Robata	Japanese, Modern	Upper Kirby	Upmarket	$70
9.3	Hugo's	Mexican	Montrose	Upmarket	$60
8.8	Petrol Station	Burgers	Northwest Houston	Counter	$25
8.5	Beaver's Ice House	American	Washington	Casual	$35
8.5	Pico's Mex-Mex	Mexican	Southwest Houston	Casual	$35
8.3	Le Mistral	French	West Houston	Upmarket	$75
8.3	Giacomo's Cibo y Vino	Italian	Upper Kirby	Counter	$20
8.2	Haven	Modern	Upper Kirby	Upmarket	$70
8.2	Peking Cuisine	Chinese	Bellaire Chinatown	Casual	$15

8.0	Rioja	Spanish	West Houston	Upmarket	$65
8.0	London Sizzler	Indian	Southwest Houston	Casual	$30
8.0	The Tasting Room	Pizza	Multiple locations	Wine bar	$35
7.8	Canopy	Modern	Montrose	Upmarket	$70
7.5	Branch Water Tavern	Modern, American	Heights	Upmarket	$45
7.4	Calliope's Po-Boy	Southern	East Houston	Casual	$15
7.3	Voice	Modern	Downtown	Upmarket	$70
7.1	Ibiza	Spanish, Modern	Midtown	Wine bar	$70
7.1	Masraff's	Modern	Memorial	Upmarket	$85
7.1	Oporto Café	Portuguese	Greenway Plaza	Wine bar	$50
7.1	Turquoise Grill	Turkish	Upper Kirby	Casual	$35
6.9	Benjy's	Modern	Multiple locations	Upmarket	$55
6.9	13 Celsius	Modern	Midtown	Wine bar	$20
6.9	Max's Wine Dive	Modern	Washington	Wine bar	$50
6.9	Thai Spice	Thai	Multiple locations	Casual	$10
6.8	BRC	American	Heights	Casual	$40
6.5	Madras Pavilion	Indian	Multiple locations	Casual	$20
6.4	Christian's Tailgate	Burgers, American	Multiple locations	Bar	$15
6.0	Red Lion	American, British	Upper Kirby	Bar	$25
6.0	Little Big's	Burgers	Multiple locations	Counter	$15
6.0	Les Givral's Kahve	Vietnamese	Multiple locations	Counter	$10
5.7	Rudi Lechner's	German	Southwest Houston	Casual	$30
5.1	The Flying Saucer	American	Downtown	Bar	$25
5.0	The Breakfast Klub	American, Southern	Midtown	Counter	$15
4.7	Brasil	Sandwiches, Pizza	Montrose	Café	$15
4.1	Baker St. (Sherlock's)	British, American	Multiple locations	Bar	$25
3.7	Last Concert Café	Mexican	Downtown	Casual	$35
3.5	Empire Café	Baked goods	Montrose	Counter	$15
3.0	The Black Labrador Pub	American, British	Montrose	Bar	$30
NR	The Ginger Man	American	Rice Area	Bar	$15
NR	The Chocolate Bar	Ice cream	Multiple locations	Counter	
NR	The Dessert Gallery	Baked goods	Multiple locations	Counter	

Vegetarian-friendly guide

Places to eat that are **unusually strong in vegetarian options.** This doesn't just mean that there are salads or veggie pastas available; it means that vegetarians will really be happy with the selection at these places. Ranked by **food rating** unless otherwise noted. Establishments that don't serve full meals (e.g. cafés, bakeries, grocery stores) appear as "NR" at the bottom of the list.

All vegetarian-friendly establishments

9.5	Himalaya	Pakistani, Indian	Southwest Houston	Casual	$15
9.4	Bootsie's Heritage Café	Modern	Tomball	Casual	$75
9.2	Dolce Vita	Italian, Pizza	Multiple locations	Casual	$40
9.2	Stella Sola	Modern, Pizza	Heights	Upmarket	$55
9.1	Udipi Café	Indian	Multiple locations	Casual	$10
9.0	Indika	Indian	Montrose	Upmarket	$60
8.9	Shiv Sagar	Indian	Hillcroft Area	Counter	$10
8.9	Vieng Thai	Thai	Spring Branch	Casual	$25
8.8	Great W'kana Café	Indian	Southwest Houston	Casual	$20
8.8	Thien Thanh	Vietnamese	Bellaire Chinatown	Casual	$10
8.6	Asia Market	Thai	Heights	Counter	$10
8.5	Beaver's Ice House	American	Washington	Casual	$35
8.5	Hong Kong Food Street	Chinese	Bellaire Chinatown	Casual	$20
8.5	Bombay Sweets	Indian	Hillcroft Area	Counter	$10
8.4	Sweet n Namkin/Salaam	Indian	Southwest Houston	Counter	$15
8.4	FuFu Café	Chinese	Bellaire Chinatown	Casual	$10
8.4	Thuan Kieu Com Tan	Vietnamese	Bellaire Chinatown	Casual	$15
8.4	Tandoori Nite	Indian	Sugar Land	Food cart	$20
8.4	Taquería Tacambaro	Mexican	Heights	Food cart	$5
8.3	Giacomo's Cibo y Vino	Italian	Upper Kirby	Counter	$20
8.2	Haven	Modern	Upper Kirby	Upmarket	$70
8.2	Pondicheri Café	Indian	Upper Kirby	Casual	$40
8.2	Piola	Pizza	Midtown	Casual	$30
8.2	Peking Cuisine	Chinese	Bellaire Chinatown	Casual	$15
8.1	Anvil	Modern	Montrose	Cocktails	$20
8.0	London Sizzler	Indian	Southwest Houston	Casual	$30
8.0	The Tasting Room	Pizza	Multiple locations	Wine bar	$35
8.0	Paulie's	Italian, Sandwiches	Montrose	Counter	$20
7.8	Canopy	Modern	Montrose	Upmarket	$70
7.8	San Dong Noodle House	Chinese	Bellaire Chinatown	Counter	$10
7.6	Nam Gang	Korean	Spring Branch	Casual	$30
7.6	Al's Quick Stop	Middle Eastern	Montrose	Counter	$10
7.6	Café TH	Vietnamese	Downtown	Counter	$10
7.5	Backstreet Café	Modern	River Oaks	Upmarket	$65
7.5	Pasha	Turkish	Rice Area	Casual	$35
7.3	Sushi Miyagi	Japanese	Bellaire Chinatown	Casual	$35
7.3	Abdallah's	Middle Eastern	Hillcroft Area	Counter	$15
7.3	Mélange Crêperie	French	Montrose	Food cart	$10

All vegetarian-friendly establishments *continued*

7.2	Les Givral's	Vietnamese	Midtown	Counter	$10
7.1	t'afia	Modern	Midtown	Upmarket	$65
7.1	Alpha Bakery	Baked goods	Bellaire Chinatown	Take-out	$10
7.0	Fung's Kitchen	Chinese, Seafood	Bellaire Chinatown	Upmarket	$45
7.0	Kim Chau	Vietnamese	Multiple locations	Casual	$10
6.9	Benjy's	Modern	Multiple locations	Upmarket	$55
6.9	13 Celsius	Modern	Midtown	Wine bar	$20
6.9	Divino	Italian	Montrose	Casual	$50
6.9	Thai Gourmet	Thai	Galleria	Casual	$25
6.9	Thai Spice	Thai	Multiple locations	Casual	$10
6.8	Fadi's Mediterranean	Middle Eastern	Multiple locations	Counter	$15
6.8	Tofu Village	Korean	Bellaire Chinatown	Casual	$20
6.6	Little Bitty Burger Barn	Burgers, American	Northwest Houston	Counter	$10
6.5	Blue Nile	Ethiopian	Westchase	Casual	$25
6.5	Madras Pavilion	Indian	Multiple locations	Casual	$20
6.4	Tiny Boxwood's	American, Pizza	Greenway Plaza	Casual	$25
6.4	Zabak's	Middle Eastern	Galleria	Counter	$15
6.4	Jerusalem Halal Deli	Middle Eastern	Hillcroft Area	Counter	$10
6.3	Niko Niko's	Greek	Multiple locations	Counter	$20
6.2	Shawarma King	Middle Eastern	Hillcroft Area	Counter	$10
6.2	Pink's Pizza	Pizza	Multiple locations	Counter	$20
6.1	Chuy's	Mexican	Multiple locations	Casual	$30
6.0	Little Big's	Burgers	Multiple locations	Counter	$15
5.9	Tony Thai	Thai	Multiple locations	Casual	$30
5.6	Hobbit Café	Vegefusion	Upper Kirby	Casual	$20
4.7	Brasil	Sandwiches, Pizza	Montrose	Café	$15
3.7	Last Concert Café	Mexican	Downtown	Casual	$35
3.5	Empire Café	Baked goods	Montrose	Counter	$15
NR	Amy's Ice Cream	Ice cream	Upper Kirby	Counter	
NR	The Chocolate Bar	Ice cream	Multiple locations	Counter	
NR	Crave Cupcakes	Baked goods	Multiple locations	Counter	
NR	The Dessert Gallery	Baked goods	Multiple locations	Counter	
NR	ECK Bakery	Baked goods	Bellaire Chinatown	Counter	
NR	Hank's Ice Cream	Ice cream	Medical Center	Counter	
NR	Hot Breads Bakery	Baked goods	Bellaire Chinatown	Counter	
NR	Jungle Café	Baked goods	Bellaire Chinatown	Counter	

Vegetarian-friendly with top feel ratings

9.0	Dolce Vita	Italian, Pizza	Multiple locations	Casual	$40
9.0	Beaver's Ice House	American	Washington	Casual	$35
9.0	Anvil	Modern	Montrose	Cocktails	$20
9.0	Backstreet Café	Modern	River Oaks	Upmarket	$65
9.0	t'afia	Modern	Midtown	Upmarket	$65
9.0	Benjy's	Modern	Multiple locations	Upmarket	$55
9.0	Tiny Boxwood's	American, Pizza	Greenway Plaza	Casual	$25
9.0	Last Concert Café	Mexican	Downtown	Casual	$35
8.5	Haven	Modern	Upper Kirby	Upmarket	$70
8.5	Pondicheri Café	Indian	Upper Kirby	Casual	$40
8.5	London Sizzler	Indian	Southwest Houston	Casual	$30
8.5	The Tasting Room	Pizza	Multiple locations	Wine bar	$35
8.5	Canopy	Modern	Montrose	Upmarket	$70
8.5	13 Celsius	Modern	Midtown	Wine bar	$20
8.5	Chuy's	Mexican	Multiple locations	Casual	$30
8.0	Himalaya	Pakistani, Indian	Southwest Houston	Casual	$15

Vegetarian-friendly with top feel ratings *continued*

8.0	Bootsie's Heritage Café	Modern	Tomball	Casual	$75
8.0	Stella Sola	Modern, Pizza	Heights	Upmarket	$55
8.0	Indika	Indian	Montrose	Upmarket	$60
8.0	Hong Kong Food Street	Chinese	Bellaire Chinatown	Casual	$20
8.0	Giacomo's Cibo y Vino	Italian	Upper Kirby	Counter	$20
8.0	Piola	Pizza	Midtown	Casual	$30
8.0	Paulie's	Italian, Sandwiches	Montrose	Counter	$20
8.0	Nam Gang	Korean	Spring Branch	Casual	$30
8.0	Pasha	Turkish	Rice Area	Casual	$35
8.0	Divino	Italian	Montrose	Casual	$50
8.0	Hobbit Café	Vegefusion	Upper Kirby	Casual	$20
8.0	Brasil	Sandwiches, Pizza	Montrose	Café	$15
8.0	Empire Café	Baked goods	Montrose	Counter	$15
7.5	Udipi Café	Indian	Multiple locations	Casual	$10
7.5	Great W'kana Café	Indian	Southwest Houston	Casual	$20
7.5	Sushi Miyagi	Japanese	Bellaire Chinatown	Casual	$35
7.5	Fung's Kitchen	Chinese, Seafood	Bellaire Chinatown	Upmarket	$45
7.5	Thai Gourmet	Thai	Galleria	Casual	$25
7.5	Fadi's Mediterranean	Middle Eastern	Multiple locations	Counter	$15
7.5	Blue Nile	Ethiopian	Westchase	Casual	$25
7.5	Little Big's	Burgers	Multiple locations	Counter	$15
7.0	Sweet n Namkin/Salaam	Indian	Southwest Houston	Counter	$15
7.0	Al's Quick Stop	Middle Eastern	Montrose	Counter	$10
7.0	Café TH	Vietnamese	Downtown	Counter	$10
7.0	Abdallah's	Middle Eastern	Hillcroft Area	Counter	$15
7.0	Tofu Village	Korean	Bellaire Chinatown	Casual	$20
7.0	Little Bitty Burger Barn	Burgers, American	Northwest Houston	Counter	$10
7.0	Zabak's	Middle Eastern	Galleria	Counter	$15
7.0	Tony Thai	Thai	Multiple locations	Casual	$30

Vegetarian-friendly and date-friendly

9.4	Bootsie's Heritage Café	Modern	Tomball	Casual	$75
9.2	Dolce Vita	Italian, Pizza	Multiple locations	Casual	$40
9.2	Stella Sola	Modern, Pizza	Heights	Upmarket	$55
9.0	Indika	Indian	Montrose	Upmarket	$60
8.8	Great W'kana Café	Indian	Southwest Houston	Casual	$20
8.5	Beaver's Ice House	American	Washington	Casual	$35
8.2	Haven	Modern	Upper Kirby	Upmarket	$70
8.2	Pondicheri Café	Indian	Upper Kirby	Casual	$40
8.2	Piola	Pizza	Midtown	Casual	$30
8.1	Anvil	Modern	Montrose	Cocktails	$20
8.0	London Sizzler	Indian	Southwest Houston	Casual	$30
8.0	The Tasting Room	Pizza	Multiple locations	Wine bar	$35
7.8	Canopy	Modern	Montrose	Upmarket	$70
7.5	Backstreet Café	Modern	River Oaks	Upmarket	$65
7.5	Pasha	Turkish	Rice Area	Casual	$35
7.1	t'afia	Modern	Midtown	Upmarket	$65
7.0	Fung's Kitchen	Chinese, Seafood	Bellaire Chinatown	Upmarket	$45
6.9	Benjy's	Modern	Multiple locations	Upmarket	$55
6.9	13 Celsius	Modern	Midtown	Wine bar	$20
6.9	Divino	Italian	Montrose	Casual	$50
6.9	Thai Gourmet	Thai	Galleria	Casual	$25
6.5	Blue Nile	Ethiopian	Westchase	Casual	$25
5.6	Hobbit Café	Vegefusion	Upper Kirby	Casual	$20

Vegetarian-friendly and date-friendly *continued*

4.7	Brasil	Sandwiches, Pizza	Montrose	Café	$15
3.5	Empire Café	Baked goods	Montrose	Counter	$15
NR	Amy's Ice Cream	Ice cream	Upper Kirby	Counter	
NR	The Chocolate Bar	Ice cream	Multiple locations	Counter	
NR	Crave Cupcakes	Baked goods	Multiple locations	Counter	
NR	The Dessert Gallery	Baked goods	Multiple locations	Counter	
NR	Jungle Café	Baked goods	Bellaire Chinatown	Counter	

Vegetarian-friendly and kid-friendly

9.1	Udipi Café	Indian	Multiple locations	Casual	$10
8.8	Thien Thanh	Vietnamese	Bellaire Chinatown	Casual	$10
8.5	Hong Kong Food Street	Chinese	Bellaire Chinatown	Casual	$20
8.5	Bombay Sweets	Indian	Hillcroft Area	Counter	$10
8.4	Thuan Kieu Com Tan	Vietnamese	Bellaire Chinatown	Casual	$15
8.2	Piola	Pizza	Midtown	Casual	$30
8.2	Peking Cuisine	Chinese	Bellaire Chinatown	Casual	$15
7.8	San Dong Noodle House	Chinese	Bellaire Chinatown	Counter	$10
7.3	Mélange Crêperie	French	Montrose	Food cart	$10
7.0	Kim Chau	Vietnamese	Multiple locations	Casual	$10
6.9	Thai Spice	Thai	Multiple locations	Casual	$10
6.6	Little Bitty Burger Barn	Burgers, American	Northwest Houston	Counter	$10
6.3	Niko Niko's	Greek	Multiple locations	Counter	$20
6.1	Chuy's	Mexican	Multiple locations	Casual	$30
6.0	Little Big's	Burgers	Multiple locations	Counter	$15
5.6	Hobbit Café	Vegefusion	Upper Kirby	Casual	$20
NR	Amy's Ice Cream	Ice cream	Upper Kirby	Counter	
NR	The Chocolate Bar	Ice cream	Multiple locations	Counter	
NR	Crave Cupcakes	Baked goods	Multiple locations	Counter	
NR	The Dessert Gallery	Baked goods	Multiple locations	Counter	
NR	ECK Bakery	Baked goods	Bellaire Chinatown	Counter	
NR	Hank's Ice Cream	Ice cream	Medical Center	Counter	

What's still open?

This is our late-night guide to Houston food. These places claim to stay open as follows; still, we recommend calling first, as the hours sometimes aren't honored on slow nights. Establishments that don't serve full meals (e.g. cafés, bakeries, grocery stores) appear as "NR" at the bottom of the list.

Weekday food after 10pm

9.5	Kata Robata	Japanese, Modern	Upper Kirby	Upmarket	$70
9.2	Shanghai Restaurant	Chinese	Bellaire Chinatown	Casual	$15
9.0	Indika	Indian	Montrose	Upmarket	$60
8.9	The Queen Vic Pub	Indian, British	Upper Kirby	Casual	$40
8.9	Teppay	Japanese	Galleria	Casual	$60
8.9	Gorditas Aguascalientes	Mexican	Bellaire Chinatown	Casual	$10
8.8	Petrol Station	Burgers	Northwest Houston	Counter	$25
8.6	Taquería Del Sol	Mexican	Southeast Houston	Casual	$10
8.6	Tan Tan	Chinese	Multiple locations	Casual	$15
8.6	Saigon Pagolac	Vietnamese	Bellaire Chinatown	Casual	$25
8.5	Hong Kong Food Street	Chinese	Bellaire Chinatown	Casual	$20
8.5	Frenchy's Chicken	Southern	Multiple locations	Counter	$10
8.4	Sweet n Namkin/Salaam	Indian	Southwest Houston	Counter	$15
8.4	FuFu Café	Chinese	Bellaire Chinatown	Casual	$10
8.4	Tandoori Nite	Indian	Sugar Land	Food cart	$20
8.2	Piola	Pizza	Midtown	Casual	$30
8.1	Anvil	Modern	Montrose	Cocktails	$20
8.1	Captain Tom's	Seafood, Southern	Multiple locations	Counter	$15
8.0	Rioja	Spanish	West Houston	Upmarket	$65
8.0	London Sizzler	Indian	Southwest Houston	Casual	$30
8.0	Sinh Sinh	Chinese, Seafood	Bellaire Chinatown	Casual	$30
7.9	Mark's	Modern	Montrose	Upmarket	$110
7.9	Doneraki	Mexican	Multiple locations	Casual	$30
7.9	Del Frisco's	Steakhouse	Galleria	Upmarket	$100
7.8	Phillippe	Modern	Galleria	Upmarket	$80
7.6	Da Da Mi Sushi Bistro	Korean	Spring Branch	Casual	$35
7.6	East Wall	Chinese	Bellaire Chinatown	Casual	$15
7.5	Branch Water Tavern	Modern, American	Heights	Upmarket	$45
7.3	Voice	Modern	Downtown	Upmarket	$70
7.2	Soma	Japanese, Modern	Washington	Casual	$75
7.1	Nippon	Japanese	Montrose	Casual	$45
7.1	Oporto Café	Portuguese	Greenway Plaza	Wine bar	$50
6.9	13 Celsius	Modern	Midtown	Wine bar	$20
6.9	Max's Wine Dive	Modern	Washington	Wine bar	$50
6.8	BRC	American	Heights	Casual	$40
6.5	Blue Nile	Ethiopian	Westchase	Casual	$25
6.4	Osaka	Japanese	Montrose	Casual	$35
6.4	Christian's Tailgate	Burgers, American	Multiple locations	Bar	$15
6.3	El Real	Mexican	Montrose	Casual	$35

6.0	Red Lion	American, British	Upper Kirby	Bar	$25
5.9	Tony Thai	Thai	Multiple locations	Casual	$30
5.2	Whataburger	Burgers, American	Multiple locations	Counter	$10
5.1	The Flying Saucer	American	Downtown	Bar	$25
4.7	Brasil	Sandwiches, Pizza	Montrose	Café	$15
4.1	Baker St. (Sherlock's)	British, American	Multiple locations	Bar	$25
4.0	House of Pies	American	Multiple locations	Casual	$10
3.9	Taco Cabana	Mexican	Multiple locations	Counter	$10
3.7	Last Concert Café	Mexican	Downtown	Casual	$35
3.0	The Black Labrador Pub	American, British	Montrose	Bar	$30
NR	The Ginger Man	American	Rice Area	Bar	$15
NR	Amy's Ice Cream	Ice cream	Upper Kirby	Counter	

Weekday food after 11pm

9.2	Shanghai Restaurant	Chinese	Bellaire Chinatown	Casual	$15
8.9	The Queen Vic Pub	Indian, British	Upper Kirby	Casual	$40
8.9	Gorditas Aguascalientes	Mexican	Bellaire Chinatown	Casual	$10
8.8	Petrol Station	Burgers	Northwest Houston	Counter	$25
8.6	Taquería Del Sol	Mexican	Southeast Houston	Casual	$10
8.6	Tan Tan	Chinese	Multiple locations	Casual	$15
8.5	Hong Kong Food Street	Chinese	Bellaire Chinatown	Casual	$20
8.5	Frenchy's Chicken	Southern	Multiple locations	Counter	$10
8.4	Sweet n Namkin/Salaam	Indian	Southwest Houston	Counter	$15
8.4	FuFu Café	Chinese	Bellaire Chinatown	Casual	$10
8.4	Tandoori Nite	Indian	Sugar Land	Food cart	$20
8.1	Anvil	Modern	Montrose	Cocktails	$20
8.0	Sinh Sinh	Chinese, Seafood	Bellaire Chinatown	Casual	$30
7.9	Doneraki	Mexican	Multiple locations	Casual	$30
7.6	Da Da Mi Sushi Bistro	Korean	Spring Branch	Casual	$35
7.6	East Wall	Chinese	Bellaire Chinatown	Casual	$15
7.5	Branch Water Tavern	Modern, American	Heights	Upmarket	$45
7.3	Voice	Modern	Downtown	Upmarket	$70
6.9	13 Celsius	Modern	Midtown	Wine bar	$20
6.9	Max's Wine Dive	Modern	Washington	Wine bar	$50
6.8	BRC	American	Heights	Casual	$40
6.4	Christian's Tailgate	Burgers, American	Multiple locations	Bar	$15
5.2	Whataburger	Burgers, American	Multiple locations	Counter	$10
5.1	The Flying Saucer	American	Downtown	Bar	$25
4.7	Brasil	Sandwiches, Pizza	Montrose	Café	$15
4.1	Baker St. (Sherlock's)	British, American	Multiple locations	Bar	$25
4.0	House of Pies	American	Multiple locations	Casual	$10
3.9	Taco Cabana	Mexican	Multiple locations	Counter	$10
NR	The Ginger Man	American	Rice Area	Bar	$15
NR	Amy's Ice Cream	Ice cream	Upper Kirby	Counter	

Weekday food after midnight

8.9	Gorditas Aguascalientes	Mexican	Bellaire Chinatown	Casual	$10
8.5	Hong Kong Food Street	Chinese	Bellaire Chinatown	Casual	$20
8.5	Frenchy's Chicken	Southern	Multiple locations	Counter	$10
8.4	Sweet n Namkin/Salaam	Indian	Southwest Houston	Counter	$15
8.4	FuFu Café	Chinese	Bellaire Chinatown	Casual	$10
8.1	Anvil	Modern	Montrose	Cocktails	$20
8.0	Sinh Sinh	Chinese, Seafood	Bellaire Chinatown	Casual	$30

Weekday food after midnight *continued*

7.6	Da Da Mi Sushi Bistro	Korean	Spring Branch	Casual	$35
6.8	BRC	American	Heights	Casual	$40
6.4	Christian's Tailgate	Burgers, American	Multiple locations	Bar	$15
5.2	Whataburger	Burgers, American	Multiple locations	Counter	$10
5.1	The Flying Saucer	American	Downtown	Bar	$25
4.1	Baker St. (Sherlock's)	British, American	Multiple locations	Bar	$25
4.0	House of Pies	American	Multiple locations	Casual	$10
3.9	Taco Cabana	Mexican	Multiple locations	Counter	$10
NR	The Ginger Man	American	Rice Area	Bar	$15

Weekday food after 1am

8.9	Gorditas Aguascalientes	Mexican	Bellaire Chinatown	Casual	$10
8.5	Hong Kong Food Street	Chinese	Bellaire Chinatown	Casual	$20
8.4	Sweet n Namkin/Salaam	Indian	Southwest Houston	Counter	$15
8.4	FuFu Café	Chinese	Bellaire Chinatown	Casual	$10
8.1	Anvil	Modern	Montrose	Cocktails	$20
8.0	Sinh Sinh	Chinese, Seafood	Bellaire Chinatown	Casual	$30
6.4	Christian's Tailgate	Burgers, American	Multiple locations	Bar	$15
5.2	Whataburger	Burgers, American	Multiple locations	Counter	$10
4.1	Baker St. (Sherlock's)	British, American	Multiple locations	Bar	$25
4.0	House of Pies	American	Multiple locations	Casual	$10
3.9	Taco Cabana	Mexican	Multiple locations	Counter	$10
NR	The Ginger Man	American	Rice Area	Bar	$15

Weekday food after 2am

8.9	Gorditas Aguascalientes	Mexican	Bellaire Chinatown	Casual	$10
5.2	Whataburger	Burgers, American	Multiple locations	Counter	$10
4.0	House of Pies	American	Multiple locations	Casual	$10
3.9	Taco Cabana	Mexican	Multiple locations	Counter	$10

Weekend food after 10pm

9.6	Da Marco	Italian	Montrose	Upmarket	$90
9.5	Crawfish and Noodles	Southern	Bellaire Chinatown	Casual	$25
9.5	Himalaya	Pakistani, Indian	Southwest Houston	Casual	$15
9.5	Kata Robata	Japanese, Modern	Upper Kirby	Upmarket	$70
9.3	Hugo's	Mexican	Montrose	Upmarket	$60
9.3	Vinoteca Poscol	Italian	Montrose	Wine bar	$40
9.2	Dolce Vita	Italian, Pizza	Multiple locations	Casual	$40
9.2	Stella Sola	Modern, Pizza	Heights	Upmarket	$55
9.2	Shanghai Restaurant	Chinese	Bellaire Chinatown	Casual	$15
9.1	Vic & Anthony's	Steakhouse	Downtown	Upmarket	$90
9.1	Tony's	Italian	Greenway Plaza	Upmarket	$110
9.1	Udipi Café	Indian	Multiple locations	Casual	$10
9.0	Indika	Indian	Montrose	Upmarket	$60
8.9	The Queen Vic Pub	Indian, British	Upper Kirby	Casual	$40
8.9	Teppay	Japanese	Galleria	Casual	$60
8.9	Gorditas Aguascalientes	Mexican	Bellaire Chinatown	Casual	$10
8.8	Petrol Station	Burgers	Northwest Houston	Counter	$25
8.8	Great W'kana Café	Indian	Southwest Houston	Casual	$20
8.7	Brasserie Max & Julie	French	Montrose	Upmarket	$65
8.7	Reef	Modern, Seafood	Midtown	Upmarket	$65
8.7	Becks Prime	American, Burgers	Multiple locations	Counter	$15
8.6	Samba Grille	Steakhouse	Downtown	Upmarket	$75

Weekend food after 10pm *continued*

8.6	Taquería Del Sol	Mexican	Southeast Houston	Casual	$10
8.6	Tan Tan	Chinese	Multiple locations	Casual	$15
8.6	Saigon Pagolac	Vietnamese	Bellaire Chinatown	Casual	$25
8.5	Beaver's Ice House	American	Washington	Casual	$35
8.5	El Tiempo Cantina	Mexican	Multiple locations	Casual	$60
8.5	Hong Kong Food Street	Chinese	Bellaire Chinatown	Casual	$20
8.5	Pico's Mex-Mex	Mexican	Southwest Houston	Casual	$35
8.5	Pappas Bros.	Steakhouse	Galleria	Upmarket	$105
8.5	Frenchy's Chicken	Southern	Multiple locations	Counter	$10
8.4	Sweet n Namkin/Salaam	Indian	Southwest Houston	Counter	$15
8.4	FuFu Café	Chinese	Bellaire Chinatown	Casual	$10
8.4	Tandoori Nite	Indian	Sugar Land	Food cart	$20
8.3	Le Mistral	French	West Houston	Upmarket	$75
8.3	El Hidalguense	Mexican	Spring Branch	Casual	$35
8.2	Au Petit Paris	French	Upper Kirby	Casual	$70
8.2	Haven	Modern	Upper Kirby	Upmarket	$70
8.2	Perry's Steakhouse	Steakhouse	Multiple locations	Upmarket	$90
8.2	Piola	Pizza	Midtown	Casual	$30
8.2	Arco Seafood	Chinese, Seafood	Bellaire Chinatown	Casual	$25
8.2	El Último	Mexican	Spring Branch	Food cart	$5
8.1	Anvil	Modern	Montrose	Cocktails	$20
8.1	Churrascos	Latin American	Multiple locations	Upmarket	$65
8.1	Captain Tom's	Seafood, Southern	Multiple locations	Counter	$15
8.1	Finger Licking Bukateria	Nigerian	West Houston	Casual	$15
8.0	Rioja	Spanish	West Houston	Upmarket	$65
8.0	London Sizzler	Indian	Southwest Houston	Casual	$30
8.0	Ninfa's on Navigation	Mexican	Downtown	Casual	$30
8.0	Sinh Sinh	Chinese, Seafood	Bellaire Chinatown	Casual	$30
7.9	Garson	Middle Eastern	Hillcroft Area	Casual	$30
7.9	Mark's	Modern	Montrose	Upmarket	$110
7.9	Shade	Modern	Heights	Upmarket	$60
7.9	Doneraki	Mexican	Multiple locations	Casual	$30
7.9	Del Frisco's	Steakhouse	Galleria	Upmarket	$100
7.8	Canopy	Modern	Montrose	Upmarket	$70
7.8	Phillippe	Modern	Galleria	Upmarket	$80
7.8	La Sani	Pakistani	Southwest Houston	Casual	$30
7.8	100% Taquito	Mexican	Greenway Plaza	Counter	$10
7.8	Seco's Latin Cuisine	Mexican	Rice Area	Casual	$30
7.7	Américas	Latin American	Multiple locations	Upmarket	$70
7.7	Sushi Raku	Japanese	Midtown	Upmarket	$70
7.7	III Forks	Steakhouse	Downtown	Upmarket	$95
7.7	Houston's	American	Multiple locations	Upmarket	$60
7.6	Sushi Jin	Japanese	West Houston	Casual	$45
7.6	Tintos	Spanish	River Oaks	Upmarket	$55
7.6	Da Da Mi Sushi Bistro	Korean	Spring Branch	Casual	$35
7.6	East Wall	Chinese	Bellaire Chinatown	Casual	$15
7.5	Backstreet Café	Modern	River Oaks	Upmarket	$65
7.5	Cyclone Anaya's	Mexican	Multiple locations	Casual	$35
7.5	Branch Water Tavern	Modern, American	Heights	Upmarket	$45
7.5	Pasha	Turkish	Rice Area	Casual	$35
7.5	Tampico Seafood	Seafood, Mexican	Multiple locations	Casual	$20
7.4	Calliope's Po-Boy	Southern	East Houston	Casual	$15
7.3	Voice	Modern	Downtown	Upmarket	$70
7.2	Soma	Japanese, Modern	Washington	Casual	$75

7.2	Eddie V's	Seafood	Multiple locations	Upmarket	$90
7.1	t'afia	Modern	Midtown	Upmarket	$65
7.1	Ibiza	Spanish, Modern	Midtown	Wine bar	$70
7.1	Masraff's	Modern	Memorial	Upmarket	$85
7.1	Pappadeaux	Seafood, Southern	Multiple locations	Casual	$45
7.1	Tony Mandola's	Seafood, Southern	Multiple locations	Upmarket	$70
7.1	Guadalajara Hacienda	Mexican	Multiple locations	Casual	$35
7.1	Nippon	Japanese	Montrose	Casual	$45
7.1	Oporto Café	Portuguese	Greenway Plaza	Wine bar	$50
7.1	Pappas Burger	Burgers	Multiple locations	Counter	$15
7.0	Fung's Kitchen	Chinese, Seafood	Bellaire Chinatown	Upmarket	$45
7.0	Jarro Café and Trailer	Mexican	Spring Branch	Counter	$10
6.9	Benjy's	Modern	Multiple locations	Upmarket	$55
6.9	13 Celsius	Modern	Midtown	Wine bar	$20
6.9	Divino	Italian	Montrose	Casual	$50
6.9	Max's Wine Dive	Modern	Washington	Wine bar	$50
6.9	Thai Gourmet	Thai	Galleria	Casual	$25
6.8	Ava Kitchen & Whiskey Bar	Modern	Upper Kirby	Upmarket	$55
6.8	Frank's Chop House	Steakhouse	River Oaks	Upmarket	$70
6.8	BRC	American	Heights	Casual	$40
6.8	Kaneyama	Japanese	Westchase	Casual	$35
6.8	Tofu Village	Korean	Bellaire Chinatown	Casual	$20
6.8	Vinh Hoa	Chinese	Bellaire Chinatown	Casual	$10
6.7	Kubo's	Japanese	Rice Area	Casual	$45
6.7	Alexander the Great	Greek	Galleria	Upmarket	$65
6.5	Blue Nile	Ethiopian	Westchase	Casual	$25
6.5	Banana Leaf	Malaysian	Bellaire Chinatown	Casual	$25
6.4	Osaka	Japanese	Montrose	Casual	$35
6.4	Christian's Tailgate	Burgers, American	Multiple locations	Bar	$15
6.3	El Real	Mexican	Montrose	Casual	$35
6.3	Niko Niko's	Greek	Multiple locations	Counter	$20
6.2	Pappas Seafood	Seafood	Multiple locations	Casual	$50
6.2	Shawarma King	Middle Eastern	Hillcroft Area	Counter	$10
6.2	Pink's Pizza	Pizza	Multiple locations	Counter	$20
6.1	Chuy's	Mexican	Multiple locations	Casual	$30
6.1	The Grove	Modern	Downtown	Upmarket	$65
6.0	Red Lion	American, British	Upper Kirby	Bar	$25
6.0	Little Big's	Burgers	Multiple locations	Counter	$15
5.9	Tony Thai	Thai	Multiple locations	Casual	$30
5.6	Ouisie's Table	Southern	River Oaks	Upmarket	$60
5.6	Hobbit Café	Vegefusion	Upper Kirby	Casual	$20
5.4	Pappasito's	Mexican	Multiple locations	Casual	$35
5.2	Whataburger	Burgers, American	Multiple locations	Counter	$10
5.1	The Flying Saucer	American	Downtown	Bar	$25
4.7	Brasil	Sandwiches, Pizza	Montrose	Café	$15
4.5	Ocean Palace	Chinese, Dim Sum	Bellaire Chinatown	Casual	$30
4.1	Baker St. (Sherlock's)	British, American	Multiple locations	Bar	$25
4.0	House of Pies	American	Multiple locations	Casual	$10
3.9	Taco Cabana	Mexican	Multiple locations	Counter	$10
3.7	Last Concert Café	Mexican	Downtown	Casual	$35
3.5	Empire Café	Baked goods	Montrose	Counter	$15
3.0	The Black Labrador Pub	American, British	Montrose	Bar	$30
NR	The Ginger Man	American	Rice Area	Bar	$15
NR	Amy's Ice Cream	Ice cream	Upper Kirby	Counter	

Weekend food after 10pm *continued*

NR	The Chocolate Bar	Ice cream	Multiple locations	Counter	
NR	The Dessert Gallery	Baked goods	Multiple locations	Counter	

Weekend food after 11pm

9.2	Shanghai Restaurant	Chinese	Bellaire Chinatown	Casual	$15
9.1	Tony's	Italian	Greenway Plaza	Upmarket	$110
8.9	The Queen Vic Pub	Indian, British	Upper Kirby	Casual	$40
8.9	Gorditas Aguascalientes	Mexican	Bellaire Chinatown	Casual	$10
8.8	Petrol Station	Burgers	Northwest Houston	Counter	$25
8.6	Samba Grille	Steakhouse	Downtown	Upmarket	$75
8.6	Taquería Del Sol	Mexican	Southeast Houston	Casual	$10
8.6	Tan Tan	Chinese	Multiple locations	Casual	$15
8.5	Hong Kong Food Street	Chinese	Bellaire Chinatown	Casual	$20
8.5	Frenchy's Chicken	Southern	Multiple locations	Counter	$10
8.4	Sweet n Namkin/Salaam	Indian	Southwest Houston	Counter	$15
8.4	FuFu Café	Chinese	Bellaire Chinatown	Casual	$10
8.4	Tandoori Nite	Indian	Sugar Land	Food cart	$20
8.3	El Hidalguense	Mexican	Spring Branch	Casual	$35
8.2	Piola	Pizza	Midtown	Casual	$30
8.2	El Último	Mexican	Spring Branch	Food cart	$5
8.1	Anvil	Modern	Montrose	Cocktails	$20
8.1	Captain Tom's	Seafood, Southern	Multiple locations	Counter	$15
8.0	Sinh Sinh	Chinese, Seafood	Bellaire Chinatown	Casual	$30
7.9	Mark's	Modern	Montrose	Upmarket	$110
7.9	Doneraki	Mexican	Multiple locations	Casual	$30
7.8	Phillippe	Modern	Galleria	Upmarket	$80
7.7	Sushi Raku	Japanese	Midtown	Upmarket	$70
7.6	Tintos	Spanish	River Oaks	Upmarket	$55
7.6	Da Da Mi Sushi Bistro	Korean	Spring Branch	Casual	$35
7.6	East Wall	Chinese	Bellaire Chinatown	Casual	$15
7.5	Branch Water Tavern	Modern, American	Heights	Upmarket	$45
7.5	Tampico Seafood	Seafood, Mexican	Multiple locations	Casual	$20
7.4	Calliope's Po-Boy	Southern	East Houston	Casual	$15
7.3	Voice	Modern	Downtown	Upmarket	$70
7.2	Soma	Japanese, Modern	Washington	Casual	$75
7.1	Oporto Café	Portuguese	Greenway Plaza	Wine bar	$50
6.9	13 Celsius	Modern	Midtown	Wine bar	$20
6.9	Max's Wine Dive	Modern	Washington	Wine bar	$50
6.8	BRC	American	Heights	Casual	$40
6.5	Blue Nile	Ethiopian	Westchase	Casual	$25
6.4	Osaka	Japanese	Montrose	Casual	$35
6.4	Christian's Tailgate	Burgers, American	Multiple locations	Bar	$15
6.3	El Real	Mexican	Montrose	Casual	$35
6.0	Red Lion	American, British	Upper Kirby	Bar	$25
6.0	Little Big's	Burgers	Multiple locations	Counter	$15
5.2	Whataburger	Burgers, American	Multiple locations	Counter	$10
5.1	The Flying Saucer	American	Downtown	Bar	$25
4.7	Brasil	Sandwiches, Pizza	Montrose	Café	$15
4.1	Baker St. (Sherlock's)	British, American	Multiple locations	Bar	$25
4.0	House of Pies	American	Multiple locations	Casual	$10
3.9	Taco Cabana	Mexican	Multiple locations	Counter	$10
3.7	Last Concert Café	Mexican	Downtown	Casual	$35
3.0	The Black Labrador Pub	American, British	Montrose	Bar	$30
NR	The Ginger Man	American	Rice Area	Bar	$15

Weekend food after 11pm *continued*

NR	Amy's Ice Cream	Ice cream	Upper Kirby	Counter	
NR	The Chocolate Bar	Ice cream	Multiple locations	Counter	
NR	The Dessert Gallery	Baked goods	Multiple locations	Counter	

Weekend food after midnight

9.2	Shanghai Restaurant	Chinese	Bellaire Chinatown	Casual	$15
8.9	Gorditas Aguascalientes	Mexican	Bellaire Chinatown	Casual	$10
8.8	Petrol Station	Burgers	Northwest Houston	Counter	$25
8.6	Taquería Del Sol	Mexican	Southeast Houston	Casual	$10
8.6	Tan Tan	Chinese	Multiple locations	Casual	$15
8.5	Hong Kong Food Street	Chinese	Bellaire Chinatown	Casual	$20
8.5	Frenchy's Chicken	Southern	Multiple locations	Counter	$10
8.4	Sweet n Namkin/Salaam	Indian	Southwest Houston	Counter	$15
8.4	FuFu Café	Chinese	Bellaire Chinatown	Casual	$10
8.2	Piola	Pizza	Midtown	Casual	$30
8.1	Anvil	Modern	Montrose	Cocktails	$20
8.0	Sinh Sinh	Chinese, Seafood	Bellaire Chinatown	Casual	$30
7.9	Doneraki	Mexican	Multiple locations	Casual	$30
7.6	Da Da Mi Sushi Bistro	Korean	Spring Branch	Casual	$35
7.5	Branch Water Tavern	Modern, American	Heights	Upmarket	$45
7.3	Voice	Modern	Downtown	Upmarket	$70
6.9	13 Celsius	Modern	Midtown	Wine bar	$20
6.9	Max's Wine Dive	Modern	Washington	Wine bar	$50
6.8	BRC	American	Heights	Casual	$40
6.5	Blue Nile	Ethiopian	Westchase	Casual	$25
6.4	Osaka	Japanese	Montrose	Casual	$35
6.4	Christian's Tailgate	Burgers, American	Multiple locations	Bar	$15
6.3	El Real	Mexican	Montrose	Casual	$35
6.0	Red Lion	American, British	Upper Kirby	Bar	$25
6.0	Little Big's	Burgers	Multiple locations	Counter	$15
5.2	Whataburger	Burgers, American	Multiple locations	Counter	$10
5.1	The Flying Saucer	American	Downtown	Bar	$25
4.1	Baker St. (Sherlock's)	British, American	Multiple locations	Bar	$25
4.0	House of Pies	American	Multiple locations	Casual	$10
3.9	Taco Cabana	Mexican	Multiple locations	Counter	$10
NR	The Ginger Man	American	Rice Area	Bar	$15
NR	Amy's Ice Cream	Ice cream	Upper Kirby	Counter	

Weekend food after 1am

8.9	Gorditas Aguascalientes	Mexican	Bellaire Chinatown	Casual	$10
8.6	Taquería Del Sol	Mexican	Southeast Houston	Casual	$10
8.6	Tan Tan	Chinese	Multiple locations	Casual	$15
8.5	Hong Kong Food Street	Chinese	Bellaire Chinatown	Casual	$20
8.5	Frenchy's Chicken	Southern	Multiple locations	Counter	$10
8.4	Sweet n Namkin/Salaam	Indian	Southwest Houston	Counter	$15
8.4	FuFu Café	Chinese	Bellaire Chinatown	Casual	$10
8.1	Anvil	Modern	Montrose	Cocktails	$20
8.0	Sinh Sinh	Chinese, Seafood	Bellaire Chinatown	Casual	$30
7.9	Doneraki	Mexican	Multiple locations	Casual	$30
7.5	Branch Water Tavern	Modern, American	Heights	Upmarket	$45
6.9	13 Celsius	Modern	Midtown	Wine bar	$20
6.9	Max's Wine Dive	Modern	Washington	Wine bar	$50
6.8	BRC	American	Heights	Casual	$40

Weekend food after 1am *continued*

6.5	Blue Nile	Ethiopian	Westchase	Casual	$25
6.4	Christian's Tailgate	Burgers, American	Multiple locations	Bar	$15
6.3	El Real	Mexican	Montrose	Casual	$35
6.0	Little Big's	Burgers	Multiple locations	Counter	$15
5.2	Whataburger	Burgers, American	Multiple locations	Counter	$10
5.1	The Flying Saucer	American	Downtown	Bar	$25
4.1	Baker St. (Sherlock's)	British, American	Multiple locations	Bar	$25
4.0	House of Pies	American	Multiple locations	Casual	$10
3.9	Taco Cabana	Mexican	Multiple locations	Counter	$10
NR	The Ginger Man	American	Rice Area	Bar	$15

Weekend food after 2am

8.9	Gorditas Aguascalientes	Mexican	Bellaire Chinatown	Casual	$10
8.6	Taquería Del Sol	Mexican	Southeast Houston	Casual	$10
8.6	Tan Tan	Chinese	Multiple locations	Casual	$15
8.5	Frenchy's Chicken	Southern	Multiple locations	Counter	$10
8.0	Sinh Sinh	Chinese, Seafood	Bellaire Chinatown	Casual	$30
7.9	Doneraki	Mexican	Multiple locations	Casual	$30
6.3	El Real	Mexican	Montrose	Casual	$35
6.0	Little Big's	Burgers	Multiple locations	Counter	$15
5.2	Whataburger	Burgers, American	Multiple locations	Counter	$10
4.0	House of Pies	American	Multiple locations	Casual	$10
3.9	Taco Cabana	Mexican	Multiple locations	Counter	$10

Top tastes

3rd Coast Menu, Bootsie's Heritage Café
Aji sashimi, Teppay
Asada and cheese torta, 100% Taquito
Ask Bobby, Anvil
Bacon mushroom Swiss burger, Sam's Deli Diner
Banh bot chien, Tan Tan
Banh uot thit nuong, Huynh
Beef brisket, Virgie's
Beef fajitas, El Tiempo Cantina
Biscuits, Tel-Wink Grill
Black Forest cake, Jungle Café
Brisket, Gatlin's Barbecue
Bun bo Hue, Pho Danh II
Caldo Tlalpeño, Pico's Mex-Mex
Cevapi sandwich, Café Pita +
Cheese enchiladas with chile gravy, Sylvia's Enchilada Kitchen
Chicken tikka masala, Himalaya
Chicken wings nuoc mam, Crawfish and Noodles
Chilaquiles al carbon, Jarro Café and Trailer
Chinese spaghetti with seafood, Mandarin Café
Chocolate éclair, Hot Breads Bakery
Chopped beef sandwich, Burns Bar-B-Q
Contained Decadence (snicker), Phillippe Restaurant & Lounge
Corndog shrimp with Tabasco rémoulade, Haven
Crab cake, Vic & Anthony's
Crème brûlée bread pudding, Killen's Steakhouse
Crispy-skin snapper, Reef
Dahi puri, Sweet n Namkin/Salaam Namaste
Dan tat, Dim Sum King
Deviled chicken bones, Feast
Dungeness crab rice, Arco Seafood Restaurant
Fajita burger, Ninfa's on Navigation
Frank the Pretzel, Eatsie Boys
Fried chicken, Frenchy's Chicken
Fried shrimp, Barbecue Inn
Fried sole, Vinh Hoa
Frito Pie Burger, Hubcap Grill
Goi ngo sen tom thit, Que Huong
Gyro, Al's Quick Stop
Haemul pajeon, Bon Ga
Hot pot, Sichuan Cuisine

Ice cream, The Chocolate Bar
Kinutamaki, Sushi Miyagi
Live spotted prawns, Sinh Sinh
Margherita at CityCentre, The Tasting Room
Masala bhindi, London Sizzler
Mexican martini, Chuy's
Mushroom-apricot biryani, Great W'kana Café
New York strip, Samba Grille
Oxtail, Mikki's Soul Food
Pad kee mao, Asia Market
Pan de cazón, Hugo's
Pan-fried dumplings, San Dong Noodle House
Parrillada, Teotihuacán
Pastry plate, Canopy
Pho #6 (rare steak and crispy fat), Pho Binh
Pho ga with everything, Pho Ga Dakao
Pork chop, Perry's Steakhouse
Salt-toasted ribs, Shanghai Restaurant
Shiner Bock ice cream, Amy's Ice Cream
Shrimp BLT, Paulie's
Sliders, Little Bitty Burger Barn
Smoked boudin, Pierson and Company
Smoked salmon appetizer, Houston's
Snapper Martha, Tony Mandola's
Spicy double cheeseburger, Tornado Burger
Spinach enchiladas, Seco's Latin Cuisine
Tacos de mollejas, Taquería Tacambaro
Tacos tripas, El Último
Taleggio pizza, Dolce Vita
The Rancor, Petrol Station
The Substitute, Bernie's Burger Bus
Tres leches, La Guadalupana
Whole grilled red snapper, Tampico Seafood
Whole roasted branzino, Da Marco
Xiao long bao, FuFu Café

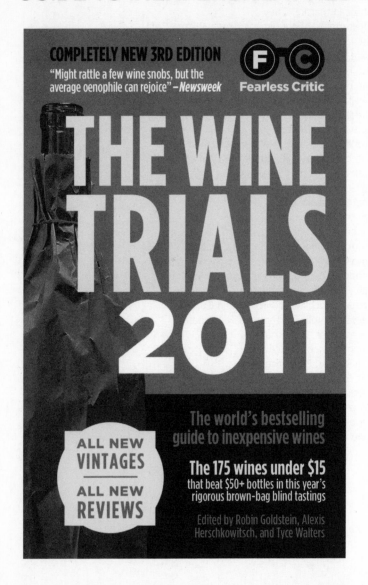

REVIEWS

OUR WRITING CAN SOMETIMES GET CROTCHETY.

BUT NOT OUR FORMAT.

With the all-new, map-based **Fearless Critic Restaurant Guide iPhone app,** subscribers can read the full text of the book, see brand-new reviews every week, sort Fearless Critic ratings every which way, search for which restaurants are open *right now*, and subscribe to additional Fearless Critic cities. Now you can keep the book on your coffee table—and the app in your pocket.

FEARLESS CRITIC
THE APP

Abdallah's

This friendly grocery and bakery also serves legit Lebanese at low, low prices

7.3 Food
7.0 Feel

$15 Price

Middle Eastern
Baked goods
Counter service

Hillcroft Area
3939 Hillcroft Ave.
(713) 952-4747

Hours
Mon–Sat
8:00am–9:00pm
Sun
8:00am–6:00pm

Bar
None

Credit cards
Visa, MC, AmEx

Features
Outdoor dining
Veg-friendly

Locals in the know love this happy hidden gem in the back of a general store. The huge buffet spread opens daily around 11:30, and it goes fast; get there early to enjoy the fresh dishes like whole grilled fish or tabbouleh. Braised lamb shanks, on the other hand, get better as the day goes on, so perhaps risk them running out and wait a while if this is what you crave. You can also get some made-to-order items until about half an hour before closing.

The building could use some work, but upbeat Middle Eastern pop music adds to the experience, and while you wait, you can pick through bulghur wheat, tahini, myriad pickled vegetables, and of course freshly baked pita bread and pastries. There are also all the necessary ingredients to light up your hookah, including the pipes themselves.

At $4.99, the beef shawarma is one of the cheapest—and best—in Houston. Tender and hearty lamb kebab is also a sound order, with a choice of two sides and rice or lentils. To finish, have a little flaky, almost-too-dry baklava with some Arabic coffee. Every once in a while, the store sells bottles of the family's first-press olive oil from their orchards in the old country. Unfiltered and cloudy, it's a steal at $20 a bottle, especially compared to American-made rip-offs that lurk in certain "specialty" stores.

Alexander the Great

Authentic Greek cuisine whose cost is most
palatable on fun weekend nights

www.alexanderthegreat.cc

Greek
Upmarket restaurant

Galleria
3055 Sage Rd.
(713) 622-2778

Hours
Mon–Thu
11:00am–10:00pm
Fri
11:00am–11:00pm
Sat
noon–11:00pm
Sun
noon–9:00pm

Bar
Beer, wine, liquor

Credit cards
Visa, MC, AmEx

Reservations
Accepted

Features
Kid-friendly
Live music
Outdoor dining

Alexander the Great is just about the only real upmarket Greek restaurant left in Houston, even if the restaurant's sign looks as downmarket as they come, with that comic-Greek Disneyesque font. The strip mall doesn't help appearances either, nor does the enormously tacky Greek statue that visually assaults you the moment you step into the restaurant.

In this case, upmarket Greek translates to pricey fishes and meats, prepared on big platters, and served in a festive weekend atmosphere, with live music and belly dancers. (Weekends are just about the only time people come here—come on a weekday and be prepared for a lonely room.) The food will be much more convincing during those times as well; saganaki cheese is flambéed to ideal squeaky resilience at the table; moussaka is silky, with an addictive balance of flavors from potatoes, eggplant, and beef. Grape leaves and kofta are correctly seasoned and moist; lemony oven-roasted potatoes glisten with olive oil and are unusually good. Don't miss juicy grilled shrimp and quail, nor tender rack of lamb. We love seeing whole fish like charcoal-broiled snapper on the menu, but we'd be even happier if they cooked it a touch less.

The prices are a bit unjustifiable, unless you figure in entertainment, and the rarity of authentic Greek menus in town.

Alfreda's Cafeteria

6.6 Food   **5.0** Feel

Humble settings and humble food from and for the soul

$15 Price

Comfort food usually translates to (or tastes best in) sloppy downmarket digs. And while Alfreda's Cafeteria makes an effort, with cherry bright white-and-yellow walls, the paint job's just sloppy enough to fit the genre. The restroom signs are in Magic Marker; the booths come in bright orange, brown, and faded peach; and the mismatched chairs are decidedly secondhand.

The beauty's all behind the counter—namely, the women working behind it who seem to know everyone: "Hey Al, what can I get for you today?" "Good to see you, James—want chicken again?" They dish up the greatest hits of East Texas soul food from a steam table that changes daily, and the longer the food sits and stews in it, the better it gets. Plates come with a meat and three sides; we recommend the superlative fried catfish with its thin, golden crunch. Generous-sized oxtails simmered in a light stew taste like a really good pot roast. Smothered steak is tender and covered with thick, flavorful gravy. Sides benefit from long cooking, too: pulverized sweet potatoes receive a little dose of extra sugar that is complemented perfectly by earthy, metallic cabbage accented by a smoky bacon flavor. Is there anything better, really, than food that's blissfully oblivious to culinary trends?

Southern
Counter service

Hermann Park
5101 Almeda Rd.
(713) 523-6462

Hours
Daily
6:00am–7:00pm

Bar
None

Credit cards
Visa, MC, AmEx

7.1
Food

4.5
Feel

$10
Price

Alpha Bakery

Fresh-baked baguette and to-go sandwiches
fly around this crowded indoor-mall staple

**Baked goods
Sandwiches**
Take-out

Bellaire Chinatown
11209 Bellaire Blvd.
(281) 988-5222

Hours
Daily
7:00am–8:00pm

Bar
None

Credit cards
None

Features
Veg-friendly

This no-frills Vietnamese bakery has some stiff
competition in the banh mi arena from the
excellent Nguyen Ngo across the street. But if
you come to the Hong Kong 4 shopping center,
you might as well swing by here to pick up
some sandwiches to go. You'll have to elbow
your way past the pushy customers that pack
the place, and compete for the attention of the
busy, curt staff...but isn't that part of the joy of
metropolitan living?

The standout here is the bread, made on-site
and warmed in the toaster before each
sandwich is made. The combination meat's our
favorite order, with a little gamey pâté and
fresh-tasting, crunchy pickled vegetables—ask
for a little extra mayo and pâté for the most
indulgent treat; chicken can be good or a little
dry and stringy, depending upon what time you
get it. Still, it's hardly a bust. Make sure to grab
some of the great pre-packaged items like
vegetarian stir-fry and banh cam (fried sesame
balls with sweet bean filling). And it's not
unusual to see older ladies grabbing 10
sandwiches to take home and feed people with
later—they reheat in the toaster oven pretty
nicely; or take some baguette home for that
simple, traditional French breakfast of
champions.

Al's Quick Stop

About the best and cheapest gyros in town, alongside carne and cigarettes

7.6 Food

7.0 Feel

$10 Price

**Middle Eastern
Greek**
Counter service

Montrose
2002 Waugh Dr.
(713) 522-5170

Hours
Sun–Thu
11:00am–9:00pm
Fri–Sat
11:00am–10:00pm

Bar
Beer, wine

Credit cards
Visa, MC, AmEx

Features
Veg-friendly

This place, besides being a standard quickie mart, also conceals a quality Middle Eastern restaurant and a carnicería within its walls. You wouldn't know any of this at first glance—nor is the place even easy to spot, given its lack of a sign (look next to Rudyard's)—but then you'll notice pictures of dishes on the wall; and then you'll notice their incredibly low prices. And look behind you at the above-average wine selection. Of course, you can't consume it here, but you should take it all to go anyway.

The Middle Eastern fare includes gyros, kebab plates, and hummus. A falafel sandwich with yogurt sauce, lettuce, tomato, and pickled vegetables runs a remarkable $3.99 ($2.99 on Tuesdays). The crispy, hot falafel mingles nicely with the acidic vegetables and yogurt, even if it is a little dry. But the gyro here is fantastic—easily on par with Chicago's Greektown versions. Tender marinated meat gets lightly crisped and caramelized on the grill, and then tucked into a soft, warm pita with grilled onions and tomato. It's heaven.

Although the Mexican's not as best-in-class, the carnicería purveys decent homemade chorizo and fajita meat, marinated in a garlicky mix. Fajita meat, cat food, toilet paper, and gyros. Now there's a mix for you.

7.7 Food	**9.5** Feel
$70 Price	**7.5** Drinks

Américas

Cordúa-patented good times that aren't always just for show

www.cordua.com

Latin American
Upmarket restaurant

River Oaks
2040 West Gray
(832) 200-1492

Galleria
1800 Post Oak Blvd.
(713) 961-1492

The Woodlands
21 Waterway Ave.
(281) 367-1492

Hours
Mon–Thu
11:00am–10:00pm
Fri
11:00am–11:00pm
Sat
noon–11:00pm
Sun
10:30am–9:00pm
Hours vary by location

Bar
Beer, wine, liquor

Credit cards
Visa, MC, AmEx

Reservations
Accepted

Features
Brunch
Date-friendly
Outdoor dining

Américas is a lot of fun, especially the Galleria flagship: picture a Gaudí art-nouveau mansion transplanted into a South American rainforest, then repurposed as an Amsterdam coffeeshop. There's hardly a bad table amid these rock tunnels and archways of cascading colors, psychedelic glass lamps, and, of course, the tree standing in the middle of the restaurant; service, however can be charmlessly chainy.

The platings are as bold as the décor. Irrepressibly smoky, but otherwise unremarkable, are "marineros" (crab claws), surrounding a deliciously sticky, starchy yuca cake. A seafood tower starter is a meal unto itself. Ceviche is inoffensive but not great, tackily served in a carved-out pineapple, and even more tackily served with those same smoky crab claws. Still, these are fun entries to something solidly enjoyable like tender churrasco steak, well seasoned and carefully cooked, and not a half-bad deal. We also like the grilled quail, with great texture and crispy skin, available in a mixed grill on some nights or bacon-wrapped as a "taquito" side. Fish mains have come medium-dry and uninteresting. And then there's that famous Cordúa tres leches: lots of hype, lots of sugar, and not much condensed-milk flavor. Cachaça cocktails are decent, as is the Argentine Malbec selection— mostly, they make great excuses to gawk at the surroundings.

Amy's Ice Cream

This worthy Austin dessert empire cuts a
silky, creamy swath through Texas

www.amysicecream.com

Amy's exuberant brand of ice cream shops is
making its funky, cow-printed way throughout
Texas, providing some much-needed levity
against the serious and icy face of the healthier
(depending on your toppings, of course) frozen
yogurt legion. At 14% butterfat, Amy's ice
cream is unapologetically rich, and the rotating
flavors are pure and intense. Another of the
main attractions is the friendly "scoopers" with
eclectic headgear and behind-the-counter
antics. They perform circus-like feats with
"crush-ins"—candy, fruit, cookie dough, and
dozens of other treats that are ruthlessly
whacked and beaten into submission (and into
your ice cream) in a spectacular scoop-flipping
display that rivals the knife-throwing chefs at
those Japanese teppanyaki steakhouses.

The technique was invented in 1970s
Massachusetts, by Steve Herrell (of Steve's,
where Amy once worked). But it's been since
co-opted by sterile, cost-analysis-obsessed
chains; Amy's quality and "weird" vibe, on the
other hand, inspire a possessive pride,
particularly in the shop's native Austin. You'll
find her sweetly cinnamony "Mexican Vanilla"
in shakes and desserts all over town. Sweet
cream is more ideal as a simpler base for crush-
ins. Fruit ice creams taste like actual fruit.
Kahlua, rum, Shiner, and Guinness show up
frequently as buttery, decadent flavors with a
grown-up fermented edge to them. Because
adults, too, scream for ice cream.

Ice cream
Counter service

Upper Kirby
3816 Farnham St.
(713) 526-2697

Hours
Mon–Thu
11:30am–11:00pm
Fri–Sat
11:30am–midnight

Bar
None

Credit cards
Visa, MC

Features
Date-friendly
Kid-friendly
Outdoor dining
Veg-friendly

Anvil

A place where new and old legends are
forged with skill and devotion

www.anvilhouston.com

Modern
Cocktail bar

Montrose
1424 Westheimer Rd.
(713) 523-1622

Hours
Mon–Sat
5:00pm–2:00am

Sun
11:00am–2:00am

Bar
Beer, liquor

Credit cards
Visa, MC, AmEx

Reservations
Accepted

Features
Brunch
Date-friendly
Good beers
Good cocktails
Veg-friendly

The cocktail is emerging from its Dark Age; an
age in which corporate restaurant groups
saturated neon -tinis with candy-sweet mixers
for a quick buck. Mixologists' names now
appear on menus alongside those of chefs, and
the artisan-bartenders, no longer content to mix
for the lowest common denominator, seek out
the best small-production spirits, make their
own bitters, and muddle anything that grows, in
search of new flavors and legacies.

Anvil stands among the nationally revered
few, for its unflagging commitment to anything
potable, for its attention to the finicky needs of
each spirit—it knows when to gently stir and
when to feverishly whip, when to use large,
unmelting ice cubes and when to use crushed
(or none at all). The list of cocktails changes
somewhat seasonally, but on any given day, you
can try a new concoction devised from rows of
bitters, house-made beers, and obscure spirits
from exotic lands: Oaxaca, Alsace, Tennessee.
Confidently order classics, as well: their
recreations go beyond faithful to enlightened.

Greenway coffee is treated with almost equal
care, as is beer. In bottle, there are local micros
and several Belgians, and a dozen ever-changing
taps—check the chalkboard. The small array of
foods to support your drinking is quite good:
panini bursting with flavor, playful pizzas
(including a brunchy version), and cheeses from
Texas farms. A refuge, indeed. For us as well as
the cocktail.

Arco Seafood

8.2 Food   **6.0** Feel

$25 Price

A Chinese banquet hall that does it equally well from the land, the sky, and the sea

Like most Chinese seafood places, Arco's big, banquety, and brightly lit. Come with a large group and sample what's in the tanks, easily the most alluring design element here. You may have to stave off your server's persuasive efforts to get you to order the most expensive fish swimming that day (one time, a $90 grouper). And the $15 per bottle corkage fee is too high for this genre, but you really should bring your own anyway; this selection's full of grossly overproduced bottles that can afford to advertise on billboards.

If prestige is your thing, you'll find shark fin here, a silly, overpriced ingredient that basically tastes like glass noodles, whatever your ethical stance. But there's an otherwise lovely seafood stew with it, as well as delicious abalone and a bounty of fun, bobbing creatures. Greens are lovely and über-garlicky. Twice-cooked pork has come shimmering with real chili flavor. Best of all is a fresh-from-the-tank Dungeness crab dish with beautifully textured rice. We've also been pleasantly surprised by those usually rubbery and bland denizens, lobster and chicken. Peking duck has great crispy skin (you've got to love fat), and it's wrapped in fluffy rice-flour buns that remind us a bit of Momofuku's. Sweet and sour fish is, happily, not of the neon-gloop variety, and the tilapia's more striped-bass-like than it is muddy. Good news, if you can't afford the grouper.

Chinese
Seafood
Dim Sum
Casual restaurant

Bellaire Chinatown
9896 Bellaire Blvd.
(713) 774-2888

Hours
Mon–Thu
10:30am–10:00pm
Fri
10:30am–11:00pm
Sat
10:00am–11:00pm
Sun
10:00am–10:00pm

Bar
Beer, wine

Credit cards
Visa, MC, AmEx

Reservations
Accepted

Asia Market

For authentic Thai, look—where else?—in the back of this shabby little grocery

www.asiamarket-hou.com

Thai
Counter service

Heights
1010 W. Cavalcade St.
(713) 863-7074

Hours
Tue–Fri
11:00am–8:00pm
Sat
10:00am–8:00pm
Sun
10:00am–7:00pm

Bar
None

Credit cards
Visa, MC

Features
Veg-friendly

Nothing excites us quite like a grocery that serves food out of the back. (Especially when it's called "Asia Market," which we've found, in several cities, to be like secret code for "authentic, amazing Southeast Asian food within.") The place looks condemned with its bars on the doors, but the aisles hold treats like Thai chilies, Thai basil, fresh galangal, mint, mung bean sprouts, fresh noodles, and three types of house-roasted chili pastes.

At the back of the store, where you'll be joined by Laotians, Cambodians, and Thai (and maybe a monk or two), som tam—the staple green papaya salad—is prepared to order. It's good, acidic, and spicy; if you're farang (Thai for Westerner), push to get it Thai-spicy. Pad Thai isn't common in Thailand, but if you must have it, Asia Market's is easily the best in town, piquant and tangy with dried shrimp, peanuts, lime, and fresh, resilient noodles. Pad see ew is also top notch. Sticky rice, that cheap Thai mainstay—pair it with the som tam—is better here than it is at Vieng, Asia Market's authentic-Thai competitor in town. (On the other hand, Vieng has better som tam.)

Desserts change daily but usually include homemade bean-paste cakes and pastries. Every visit here is an opportunity to dispense with farang tastes and discover new pleasures.

Au Petit Paris

A French bistro that tries to value quality
over quantity—as it should

www.aupetitparisrestaurant.com

8.2	8.5
Food	Feel

$70	8.5
Price	Wine

Au Petit Paris inhabits a converted bungalow
with Provençal-yellow walls that are filled with
black-and-white photos of Paris. The Guimard-
inspired Art Nouveau sign is convincing, as is the
menu of bistro classics. But on a busy night, the
tiny restaurant is so noisy with loud Americans
that the din can drown out all Gallic pretenses;
the lovely patio tries to sustain the illusion,
despite the telltale Houston climate.

But the first bite of foie gras terrine—now
there's your ticket: a creamy slice of fat mosaic
topped with a thick yellow layer of…more fat.
Somehow, the elements do not separate, and a
little balsamic vinegar balances the richness. *This*
feels like France. Regulars might find themselves
bored with the unchanging selection, and may
notice an inconsistency—sometimes it's stellar,
sometimes hardly appealing. At best, even banal
seared scallops, accented with a sliver of bacon
wedged in their flesh and served on a purée of
cauliflower, curry, and mustard, have exotic
depth. Roast chicken tartlet with leek and
caramelized onion, rack of lamb with Dijon
mustard sauce, and duck confit are winners;
equally accomplished are simple desserts, like a
fluffy chocolate mousse infused with Grand
Marnier. The wine list is small, serviceable, and
affordable, and you'd do well to stick close to
the Rhône, Alsace, or Languedoc. After all,
when in France…

French
Casual restaurant

Upper Kirby
2048 Colquitt St.
(713) 524-7070

Hours
Mon
5:30pm–9:30pm
Tue–Thu
11:00am–2:00pm
5:30pm–9:30pm
Fri
11:00am–2:00pm
5:30pm–10:30pm
Sat
5:30pm–10:30pm

Bar
Beer, wine

Credit cards
Visa, MC, AmEx

Reservations
Accepted

Features
Date-friendly
Outdoor dining

6.8	9.0
Food	Feel

$55	7.5
Price	Beer

Ava Kitchen & Whiskey Bar

An affordable Del Grande venture that
doesn't skimp on swagger and sex appeal

www.avaalto.com

Modern
Upmarket restaurant

Upper Kirby
2800 Kirby Dr.
(713) 386-6460

Hours
Mon–Wed
11:00am–3:00pm
5:00pm–10:00pm

Thu–Sat
11:00am–3:00pm
5:00pm–11:00pm

Bar
Beer, wine, liquor

Credit cards
Visa, MC, AmEx

Reservations
Accepted

Features
Date-friendly

Armed with primo real estate in the West Ave
luxury apartment complex, a website depicting
young couples in pre- and post-coital tableaus,
and all the interesting light fixtures the Schiller-
Del Grande group can afford, Ava Kitchen &
Whiskey Bar parades onto Houston's restaurant
scene like a braying, beleaguered peacock. The
implication that there's any sort of focus on
whiskey that warrants distinction is as guilty of
false advertising as the suggestion that hot sex
has anything to do with an evening here. Unless
you're dating someone who's turned on by a
"River Oaks Sparkling Cosmo."

It's not just that we're bored to tears by the
city's growing number of indistinct menus of
meat-and-veg-with-acidic-complement; it's that
when it isn't executed well, like overcooked
squid stuffed with otherwise tasty, fennelly
sausage, it's beyond tedious. Puréed white bean
and bacon soup is monotone and mealy;
pappardelle with wild mushrooms and mute
duck is boring, although the mushrooms are put
to good use in a salad vibrant with umami and
zest. Among the strongest orders is a good and
light Niçoise salad (ask for the tuna seared rare).

Of the desserts, a salted caramel tarte tartin
has been lovely, and sweetness is judiciously
restrained. The bar boasts a generous (but far
from geeky) spirit and bottled-beer selection,
and the décor is beguiling with its blend of Old
World (Parisian-blue walls, chandeliers, exposed
brick) and New (red suede banquettes and two-
toned wood floors). At least that coupling is
guaranteed and successful.

Avenue Grill

East Texas soul food from an unchanging courthouse diner

6.2 Food

8.0 Feel

$15 Price

Southern
Casual restaurant

Washington
1017 Houston Ave.
(713) 228-5138

Hours
Mon–Fri
5:30am–3:00pm
Sat–Sun
6:00am–2:00pm

Bar
None

Credit cards
Visa, MC, AmEx

Reservations
Not accepted

This quaint café is across the street from the courthouse, so its crowd includes police, court employees, jurors, and lawyers (the kind who don't wear expensive suits). If you've done anything wrong recently, don't let it show here. The décor's minimal; the tables and bar stools have an un-self-conscious '50s style that doesn't feel calculated—it's more like they never got around to buying or hiring anything or anyone new.

The standard diner breakfast is filling and cheap (and tastes like it), but better is the cafeteria-style lunch, where Southern food steams from buffet trays. (On weekends, the menu's just burgers, sandwiches, and breakfast.) These vary daily, but usually include chicken and gummy, biscuit-like dumplings, and a chicken-fried steak that's deep-fried, not pan-cooked. It's one of the better of its kind in Houston. Aside from these, the mains are not as good as the sides. Fortunately, each lunch plate comes with three. There are slow-cooked greens with the bite of earth and metal; pinto beans in a piggy broth; candy-ish sweet potatoes, and so on. Meals also come with a basket of yeast rolls and unsweetened cornbread, and the three sides can include dessert, the best being a peach cobbler in a thick sauce with a doughy crust. Now *that* wrong you can do 'round here.

7.5	9.0
Food	Feel

$65	8.5
Price	Wine

Backstreet Café

A lovely, high-society classic with Southern-meets-European tastes

www.backstreetcafe.net

Modern
Upmarket restaurant

River Oaks
1103 S. Shepherd Dr.
(713) 521-2239

Hours
Mon–Thu
11:00am–10:00pm
Fri–Sat
11:00am–11:00pm
Sun
10:00am–9:00pm

Bar
Beer, wine, liquor

Credit cards
Visa, MC, AmEx

Reservations
Accepted

Features
Brunch
Date-friendly
Good beers
Good cocktails
Live music
Outdoor dining
Veg-friendly

Backstreet Café has hardly changed in nearly thirty years—and we love it for that. While most unchanging relics of bygone food trends are left in the dust by kitchens craning their necks ever further towards molecular biology, unlikely fusions, and uncharted territory, this lovely River Oaks restaurant contents itself with being a haven of reliability. The one area where it refreshes itself, thankfully, is in its beverage program, which is earnest, experienced, and enthusiastic. You can here discover unmarketed wine-producing regions, as well as the unsung older styles of unfortunately overhyped regions—all astutely paired with your meal. Cocktails are carefully made and traverse the classic and creative (bet you wouldn't expect to find excellent German beers in bottle, either).

There's a surprising, fetching assortment of vegetarian dishes involving roasted and grilled preps of mostly seasonal vegetables, served with hearty and well-executed grains. Fish is also cooked and plated judiciously. Some classic Euro plates are solid, like butternut squash ravioli with sage brown butter, or mussels with chorizo. We bring visitors for the straight-ahead Southern stuff, like fried-green-tomato salad with blue cheese and pecans; crispy bacon-wrapped quail with jalapeño cheese grits; or spicy grilled shrimp over stone-ground cheese grits. We also recommend the delicious hashes and Benedicts at brunch, which, in the gracious garden with a brandy milk, is one of Houston's finest Sunday past times.

Baker St. (Sherlock's)

More "what's up, Homes" than Sherlock
Holmes, but the pub grub ain't half bad

4.1	8.0
Food	Feel

$25	7.5
Price	Beer

www.bakerstreetpub.com

Any time the word "pub" is involved, assume
that's where the focus lies. The grill's a mere
afterthought, for customers whose taste buds
after a few beers or sugary, strong cocktails
won't be the most discerning. Service is tanned,
lean, and vacant—not exactly Arthur Conan
Doyle material. The atmosphere makes more of
an attempt to evoke a British pub from the
Sherlock Holmes novels, but fails to emulate the
quiet congeniality of the genre. It's dark and
heavily wooded, but the effect is soundly
trounced by Guinness paraphernalia, Trivia
Night antics, and flat-screen TVs.

That said, the pub grub isn't all that bad.
Buffalo wings strike a delicate balance of
vinegary Buffalo sauce with rich blue cheese.
Burgers are basic and good, cooked to
temperature; we recommend adding bacon and
cheddar. Of course, Baker's take on British
classics—unevenly cooked shepherd's pie and
bangers and mash—are available at your own
risk. "Baja Tacos" have somehow managed to
find their way onto the menu as well, but you
should know better.

On weekends, it becomes quite the pick-up
scene, with crowds spilling onto the sidewalks;
during these times, it's next to impossible to get
a pint at the bar from the dozen-plus taps of
microbrews and British crowd-pleasers. Instead,
settle into a booth if you can, and let the pretty
people take care of you.

British
American
Bar

River Oaks
1952 W. Gray
(713) 521-1881

Rice Area
5510 Morningside Dr.
(713) 942-9900

Westchase
10001 Westheimer Rd.
(713) 977-1857

More locations
and features at
fearlesscritic.com

Hours
Daily
11:00am–2:00am
Hours vary by location

Bar
Beer, wine, liquor

Credit cards
Visa, MC, AmEx

Reservations
Accepted

Features
Good beers
Live music
Outdoor dining
Wi-Fi

Banana Leaf

Houston's seen better Malaysian, but this is still a delicious introduction

www.bananaleafhouston.com

Malaysian
Casual restaurant

Bellaire Chinatown
9889 Bellaire Blvd.
(713) 771-8118

Hours
Sun–Thu
11:00am–9:30pm
Fri–Sat
11:00am–10:30pm

Bar
None

Credit cards
Visa, MC

Reservations
Not accepted

We're not sure why Houston can't seem to hold onto a Malaysian restaurant for very long. And while we've lost much stronger Malaysian entries than Banana Leaf, this is the best we've got. For now.

Perhaps in a panic, it tries to make the cuisine accessible, but it shoots itself in the foot by doing so. It mutes the heat and spice of sambal shrimp and beef rendang, and the warm, welcoming staff pushes those of the Caucasian persuasion away from classics like nasi lemak or assam laksa because of their wonderful (but notoriously Anglo-repellant) fishy funk. Dishes with the most public appeal, like mango shrimp, are more expensive. Instead, insist upon tom yum fish head, and plump Hainan chicken served with rice cooked in its fat. Order the whole flounder—flounder flesh stands up best to wok cooking but is delicate enough to absorb its slightly sweet shrimp paste, and the larger bones impart moisture and flavor.

A point of great pride here is roti canai, which you can watch being shaped into large discs and tossed into the air, à la pizzeria. It's served warm with lightly crispy edges and a soft, doughy center, and an accompanying curry sauce that is not as spicy as you'd find in Southeast Asia. C'mon, we're *Texans*…we can handle spice, and a whole lot more.

Barbecue Inn

Chicken-fried nostalgia, Hon

6.1 Food

8.0 Feel

$20 Price

Southern Barbecue
Casual restaurant

North Houston
116 W. Crosstimbers St.
(713) 695-8112

Hours
Tue–Sat
10:30am–10:00pm

Bar
Beer, wine

Credit cards
Visa, MC, AmEx

Reservations
Not accepted

Features
Kid-friendly

Barbecue Inn has changed very little since 1946, and it's got the original menu on the wall to prove it (and from the looks of it, the original clientele, too). The carpet certainly hasn't changed since the '70s, and neither has the waitstaff, who will likely call you "Honey" and make you just so happy to be there.

So what do you order at the Barbecue Inn? Certainly not the barbecue. While it is decent, you can find better. What you're here for is this: jumbo, fresh, juicy shrimp, nicely battered and deep fried, and served with homemade tartar sauce. These fry cooks really know how to walk the crispy line between too hard and soggy. Fried chicken is another plate for the record books, served piping hot alongside some of Houston's best french fries, hand-cut and well seasoned, with a perfect texture for gravy-dipping. (Baked potatoes are also fun, if only because they come with three-cup serving carousels of cheese, sour cream, and bacon that seem to have disappeared everywhere else two decades ago.) And don't forget the third element in the holy trinity: chicken-fried steak. This one sits pretty under a blanket of artery-clogging cream gravy. Man, if only Elvis were still alive to see this place. (Check under the carpet.)

Beaver's Ice House

A fun, low-key place for Anvil cocktails and modernized Texas cuisine

www.beavershouston.com

American
Casual restaurant

Washington
2310 Decatur St.
(713) 864-2328

Hours
Tue–Wed
11:00am–10:00pm
Thu–Fri
11:00am–11:00pm
Sat
noon–11:00pm
Sun
11:00am–10:00pm

Bar
Beer, wine, liquor

Credit cards
Visa, MC, AmEx

Reservations
Accepted

Features
Brunch
Date-friendly
Good beers
Good cocktails
Live music
Outdoor dining
Veg-friendly
Wi-Fi

Beaver's Ice House is one of those places that's most successful when thought of as a great cocktail bar with decent food, rather than the other way around. Its bar, which was built by the Anvil folks, is the biggest draw for those in the know; yet gourmands will enjoy themselves so long as they keep expectations reasonable. Execution is pretty inconsistent, but when it's on, the chicken-fried New York strip is incredible, with an impressively nuanced white gravy. A wedge salad is an overpriced bummer, and smoked lamb shank has teetered on the verge of inedibly gamey and underseasoned. Then again, mac and cheese is reliably delicious, as are crisp-exteriored fried boudin balls. The odds are better on slower nights, when Gulf fish specials have been respectable, and at brunch, when classics like migas and French toast are gussied up with stuff like smoked queso and liquor marinades.

There are several decent Texan draft beers and more American micros in bottle; some of the wines, although all offered by the glass (check for freshness), are respectable and totally affordable. Equally modestly priced are the excellent cocktails, a mix of faithfully rendered classics and innovative seasonal mixes like a "Fairfield Sour," a Bourbon drink using Texas plums, lemon, and ginger. We love to sample the list in this minimal, modern setting of tree-trunk tables and environmentally friendly paints, or on the pleasant open, pebbly patio. And there's pretty good food, too? Well, bonus.

Becks Prime

Happily, delicious, beefy actions speak louder than self-aggrandizing words

www.becksprime.com

8.7 Food

4.0 Feel

$15 Price

A meal at Becks is a visual barrage of propaganda, from *Texas Monthly* kiss-ups to six-square-foot food-porn images of burgers, steaks, and chicken; even the sandwich-basket paper is striped with laudatory quotes from the *Houston Press* and *USA Today* absorbing the fry grease. Other than the occasional splash of red paint, self-promotion is this restaurant's sole interior-decorating motif.

Still, the hype is justified. The ground beef is not Prime, as suggests the name, but it's Choice, ground and formed in-house, well seasoned, and grilled over mesquite. Sweet buns, smeared with mayonnaise-based "Prime Sauce," absorb the juices well. The kitchen-sink-style "Bill's Burger" adds sautéed onions, jalapeños, bacon, cheddar, and lettuce along with that sauce, but the patty is good enough to warrant just a basic cheeseburger order.

The much-crowed-about fries are inconsistent; sometimes they're crispy and sometimes limp. Shakes are too thick, while grilled and butterflied hot dogs are good. Burgers, although enormous, are pricy; one with fries and an iced tea costs nearly $15—not prohibitive, but definitely toeing the line. Is all the self-promotion meant to reassure sticker-shocked customers that their money has been well spent? It has. But the proof is in the basket on the table, not in the writing on the wall.

American Burgers

Counter service

Upper Kirby
2902 Kirby Dr.
(713) 524-7085

Spring Branch
1001 E. Memorial Loop
(713) 863-8188

Downtown
919 Milam St.
(713) 659-6122

More locations
and features at
fearlesscritic.com

Hours
Sun–Thu
11:00am–10:00pm
Fri–Sat
11:00am–11:00pm
Hours vary by location

Bar
Beer, wine

Credit cards
Visa, MC, AmEx

Features
Kid-friendly
Outdoor dining

6.6 Food 7.5 Feel

$10 Price

Bellaire Broiler Burger

A mom-and-pop stand still making burgers the way they did 35 years ago

Burgers
American
Counter service

Bellaire
5216 Bellaire Blvd.
(713) 668-8171

Hours
Mon–Sat
11:00am–8:00pm

Bar
Beer, wine

Credit cards
Visa, MC, AmEx

Features
Kid-friendly

Bellaire Broiler Burger is one of those places where you know it's got to have looked exactly this way for decades (even the employees seem not to have changed). The brick walls, muted earth tones, and orange roof have a distinctive "Brady Bunch" feel that only swells as multiple generations of Bellaire families pile in to stake their claim at one of the booths.

We credit our love for these burgers with the gas-fired flame broiler, which provides plenty of flavor, plus that heady char you smell from the parking lot. The process cooks the burgers quickly, thus the juices remain—as much as they can for a rather thin quarter-inch patty. The house-made chili is spiked with cumin and plenty of onion (sublime). There are flame-broiled chicken sandwiches for the health-conscious, but with a generous heap of mayo. A fried fish sandwich with tartar sauce is greasy and heavy, and a dubious salad comes with "garden vegetables" (is the garden on a Sysco truck?). Shakes are old school, so thick you can just forget the straw. Opt for thick onion rings over the french fries, which are the mealy crinkle-cut variety—just like they were thirty years ago.

Benjy's

The Village hotspot is good for happy hour, but BOW down to chow down

www.benjys.com

6.9	9.0
Food	Feel

$55	6.5
Price	Wine

Both Benjy's locations are fun, trendy places to be (and interior-design wonderlands), places whose menus don't exactly struggle to keep up with the modern wave of farm-to-table kitchens serving upgraded comfort cuisine. If the Bohemian-Asian décor is any clue, you can expect a certain outdatedness to the food—or is it classic? Bypass ho-hum Asian fusion attempts like potstickers, blandly grilled calamari, and ingredient-laden pizzas. In fact, we get the most enjoyment from brunch, and a few happy hour specials that give us an excuse to hang out in the pretty bar and ogle the pretty people.

The cocktails attract the ladies like nectar—which is exactly what the drinks taste like. But if a mojito or decent beer on tap is all you need, both are quite cheap from 4–7pm every night. We prefer Rice Village's $5 menu, which includes addictively spicy beef arepas and delicious sesame-crusted agedashi tofu with orange-chili sauce. At dinner, salads full of nuts and fruits are also a strong suit. After happy hour, we find the Benjy's on Washington (BOW) kitchen just a notch better at execution and plating. Sauces and flavors show more grown-up restraint, and meats are more aptly cooked. Best of all is brunch at this location (if you don't mind the frequent wait), featuring tender shortrib enchiladas, expertly crisped chicken and waffles, and much-loved nut-crusted challah French toast.

Modern
Upmarket restaurant

Rice Area
2424 Dunstan Rd.
(713) 522-7602

Heights
5922 Washington Ave.
(713) 868-1131

Hours
Sun–Mon
11:00am–9:00pm
Tue–Thu
11:00am–10:00pm
Fri–Sat
11:00am–11:00pm
Hours vary by location

Bar
Beer, wine, liquor

Credit cards
Visa, MC, AmEx

Reservations
Accepted

Features
Brunch
Date-friendly
Veg-friendly
Wi-Fi

Bernie's Burger Bus

A bright yellow schoolbus that schools
Houston on the ideal burger

www.berniesburgerbus.com

Burgers
Food cart

Upper Kirby
Lizzards Pub: 2715
Sackett St.
(281) 386-2447

Montrose
Inversion: 1953
Montrose Blvd.
(281) 386-2447

Hours
Wed–Fri
5:00pm–9:00pm
Hours vary by location
Check website for
current hours and
location

Bar
None

Credit cards
Visa, MC, AmEx

Features
Kid-friendly
Outdoor dining

Some basic burger arithmetic:

Problem: Burger > mouth = irritation + mess
Solution: Bernie's burgers, while substantial, are
a manageable size and not super drippy.

Problem: "Medium-rare" = "Medium-well"
(FALSE)
Solution: Char-tasting burgers are actually
cooked to order.

Problem: Mobile food = impossible to grid
Solution: You can depend on two locations:
Lizzard's Pub (Wed-Fri nights, on whose patio
you can enjoy a dive-bar beer), and Inversion
Coffeehouse at lunchtime (Mon and Wed).
Check the website or Twitter (@berniesburgers)
for other appearances.

Problem: French fries + 10 minutes = suck
Solution: Bernie's actually stand up to time, and
homemade ketchup + chipotle aïoli =
awesomeness.

Problem: Mayo + mustard + ketchup + pickle +
thin-sliced onions + lettuce + slow-roasted garlic
tomatoes = "The Principal"
Solution: Actually, not a problem at all.

Problem: 2(Applewood smoked bacon grilled-
cheese sandwich) + 2(patty) + Texas cheddar +
caramelized onions = "Detention," or HEART
ATTACK.
Solution: None. But what a way to go.

The Black Labrador Pub

Follow the cobblestone path to beer and beware the cafeteria-era takes on pub grub

www.blacklabradorpub.com

3.0	8.5
Food	Feel

$30	8.5
Price	Beer

The Black Labrador's impossibly charming Old-World atmosphere makes it one of our favorite haunts in town. Ivy-covered buildings and cobblestones line the parking lot, transporting you, for a moment, to an old alley in Oxford. Inside are the cramped tables and low ceilings that are vital to a beautiful, classic British pub atmosphere, and there's occasional live music at the upstairs jazz club, Cezanne.

But eat elsewhere first. Great British traditions like fish and chips, and steak and kidney pie are massacred here beyond recognition. Add to this grave situation a thoughtless mix of Tex-Mex favorites at a hefty price, and it's enough to sour the great mood created by the surroundings. Bangers are dry, underseasoned, and won't spark your libido in the way that pig usually does; the mashed potatoes hint at that soulless taste of the school cafeteria. We don't even know where to begin with the steak and kidney pie, whose thick brown sauce tastes of nothing but flour. There's a decent black bean soup, and some pretty good desserts, but we'd rather just drink from the nice selection of British and domestic beers, poured into personalized silver tankards that hang over the bar for frequent customers. The servers wear short plaid skirts and knee-highs, but this appears to somehow have little effect on our enjoyment of the food.

American British

Bar

Montrose
4100 Montrose Blvd.
(713) 529-1199

Hours
Mon–Thu
11:00am–11:00pm
Fri–Sat
11:00am–midnight
Sun
11:00am–10:00pm

Bar
Beer, wine, liquor

Credit cards
Visa, MC, AmEx

Features
Brunch
Date-friendly
Good beers
Outdoor dining
Wi-Fi

Blue Nile

A nourishing and delicious take on a cuisine we'd like to see more of in Houston

www.bluenilerestaurant.com

Ethiopian
Casual restaurant

Westchase
9400 Richmond Ave.
(713) 782-6882

Hours
Sun–Thu
11:00am–11:00pm
Fri–Sat
11:00am–2:00am

Bar
Beer, wine

Credit cards
Visa, MC, AmEx

Reservations
Accepted

Features
Date-friendly
Veg-friendly

Despite the wealth of Ethiopian-Americans living out in Katy and Pearland, Houston only has a couple of Ethiopian restaurants (this one being the best). Few cuisines on Earth are so deeply satisfying, so complex, smoky, spicy, soulful, and healthy. Use the injera bread as an ersatz utensil—its citric sourness is a great complement to the food. But beware how quickly it expands in the stomach.

The African décor—brightly zig-zagging fabrics in orange, yellow, and turquoise—brightens up the otherwise dimly lit spot. The menu isn't dumbed down, using exact Ethiopian words for dishes, leaving the burden of explanation on the unbelievably patient staff. Service this caring translates across any barrier.

One meat and one vegetable combination is a great way to sample the cuisine. Kik alicha (split peas) are creamy but pebbly, with just enough onion flavor. Gomen (collard greens cooked with peppers and garlic) could have a place on any Southern table. Kitfo (a tartare in an enticing blend of spices) is delicious; anyone will love doro wot, tender chicken drumsticks in earthy, robust berbere sauce—or alicha wot, lamb in the same sauce.

Afterward, enjoy freshly brewed, tableside-prepared coffee, and that feeling of salubrious fullness that comes from eating food from the cradle of mankind.

The Boiling Crab

Chinatown on the outside, but all Louisiana on the inside

8.6 Food

7.0 Feel

$20 Price

www.theboilingcrab.com

For some of the best Louisiana-style, Gulf-fresh food around, you need only venture into…Chinatown. Tucked neatly into the same shopping center that houses seafood market giant Viet Hoa, The Boiling Crab stands heads and (ahem) tails above many other crawfish-centric eateries. Here, there's a liberal and complex spicing that eludes a lot of other places. There are several options in this territory: the one with the worst name, "The Whole Sha-bang," just so happens to be the best, with a kick of fresh citrus. And while most anyone can do a good crawfish/shrimp/crab boil, what distinguishes Boiling Crab is its performance with fried foods. Fried catfish has a light and crunchy cornmeal crust, and plump, fried oysters release a funky brininess when bitten into. Gumbo has that mysterious swampy flavor you only find along the Mississippi.

The restaurant's got all the usual charms of a place with "boil" in its name: fish netting and crab traps as décor, wax paper instead of tablecloths, dueling television sets, and an attentive, hospitable staff. You'll find your cold, cheap beer replaced quickly, and water refilled just as soon as you start fanning your fiery mouth. This place may be a chain, but take off the sign and we might as well be in an old Aransas Pass shanty…with bubble tea next door.

Seafood
Southern
Casual restaurant

Bellaire Chinatown
8300 W. Sam Houston
(281) 988-4750

Hours
Mon–Fri
3:00pm–10:00pm
Sat–Sun
noon–10:00pm

Bar
Beer

Credit cards
Visa, MC

Reservations
Not accepted

Features
Kid-friendly

8.5 Food | 4.5 Feel

$10 Price

Bombay Sweets

Have a decent vegetarian buffet, but better samosas, chaat, and sweet treats

Indian
Counter service

Hillcroft Area
5827 Hillcroft St.
(713) 780-4453

Hours
Daily
10:30am–9:30pm

Bar
None

Credit cards
Visa, MC, AmEx

Features
Kid-friendly
Veg-friendly

For South Asian and Middle Eastern food, Hillcroft reigns supreme. And of this area's Indian restaurants, only Himalaya and London Sizzler are more renowned than Bombay Sweets in the non-Indian-community oral legend. The lunchtime buffet, although appropriately cheap and well-stocked, has been known to harbor staling naan and sogging fried foods. Yet Bombay Sweets excels at samosas and puffed-ricey Bombay-style chaat, like bhelpuri. Vegetarians will be plenty happy here, but the à-la-carte menu can be bewildering and the staff behind the counter far from helpful (and dosai are much better at Udipi). Saag paneer is dark, less creamy and less rich (the purists prefer it this way) than the version at your average Indian buffet in a non-Indian neighborhood. We've had better-seasoned versions of chana masala, and better rice. The tamarind and coconut chutneys are as intense and fulfilling as they need to be.

Really, the best eating at Bombay Sweets is—hello—the sweets; rows and rows of glistening, powdered, plumped, and rainbow-colored baubles in the bakery cases. They do err on the sweet-sweet side, but we love the carrot halwa (like a carrot cake brownie), and several flavors of burfi, especially chocolate. Even though chocolate isn't really traditional in India, it makes for one happy assimilation.

Bon Ga

Bypass the barbecue for a garden of sweet-savory-spicy earthly delights

8.8 Food

7.0 Feel

$20 Price

Korean
Casual restaurant

Spring Branch
9861 Long Point Rd.
(713) 461-5265

Hours
Daily
10:00am–10:00pm

Bar
Beer, wine

Credit cards
Visa, MC

Reservations
Accepted

Features
Kid-friendly

It's not clear what Bon Ga "Garden Restaurant" means—it clearly isn't vegetarian, nor does it have a garden. Tucked away in an unassuming shopping center in an area with so many borderline-health-code-violation restaurants, it's refreshingly clean and tidy. Service is push-button—no joke, you actually have a call button at your table, allowing the whole place to run with only a couple of waitpeople, whom we suppose to be related, give that the restaurant's family-owned, with the chef a frail-looking, middle-aged woman with a warm smile and a deft hand at seasoning.

While the barbecue at Bon Ga isn't a bad way to go, it's the other dishes that really get your juices flowing. The banchan side dishes are one of the better sets in town. Bibimbap is flawless, with fresh and pickled vegetables and well-marinated meat coming together to form a sweet, savory, filling, but still light and perfectly sized for lunch. Get it in the super-heated stone bowl so you can mix in the crusty cooked rice, adding another dimension of texture. Tofu stews are another specialty, with fresh-cracked egg adding extra body to a haunting, spicy broth. The standout here is freshly rolled beef soup dumplings that taste hand-made and deeply meaty. After all that, you can go on ahead and have some barbecue, if you must.

9.4 Food

8.0 Feel

$75 Price

Bootsie's Heritage Café

A silencing, but hardly sobering answer to jokes about trendy locavore restaurants

www.bootsiescafe.wordpress.com

Modern
Casual restaurant

Tomball
112 Commerce St.
(281) 516-9699

Hours
Wed–Sat
11:00am–2:00pm
6:00pm–10:00pm
Sun
11:00am–2:00pm

Bar
Beer, wine

Credit cards
Visa, MC, AmEx

Reservations
Essential

Features
Brunch
Date-friendly
Veg-friendly

The rhapsodizing about Bootsie's Heritage Café out in the hinterlands of Tomball has reached a fevered pitch that's excited food editors even farther away in Manhattan's Condé Nast offices. But unlike so many of those contenders whose perverse inclusions in national magazines have more to do with PR firms than anything, Bootsie's is legit. Reservations are necessary for entry into this Elysian fantasy, where the "sole food" (sustainable, organic, local, ethical) movement is a refreshing ideal carried out with Mason-jar sincerity, and a sense of adventure.

The menu's nouvelle rustique conceits still manage to elicit a thrill from even the most jaded among us, like an exceptional preparation of raw meaty cobia (kingfish) with pickled peaches and grassy, lemony sorrel. Such delights are found in the terrifically affordable six- or nine-course "3rd coast menu," featuring such endeavors as a black-eyed pea risotto that deliciously outdoes itself. On Tuesdays, the place is open only for a ten-course "Heritage dinner," by reservation only. Each course is explained and paired with wine (competently, but their passion seems reserved for the food) for $75 per person.

Sure, there are missteps—hardly avoidable with such a freewheeling, changing menu, and you may tire of the un-ironic glut of references to "local." (Certain "Portlandia" sketches come to mind.) But give us this over an unmemorable, expensive meal in town—any town—any day.

Branch Water Tavern

A late-night whiskey refuge with some decent small bites

7.5	8.5
Food	Feel

$45	9.0
Price	Drinks

www.branchwatertavern.com

Branch Water Tavern's hedonistic selection of American whiskeys nods to the rusticity of a simpler era, while the geekiness it employs is thoroughly modern. The space previously belonged to a divey billiards club, and there's an unfussy romance to the restoration, with the vintage appeal of graphic wallpaper, lots of warm wood, and etched, properly sized glassware. The concept of serving artisanal and ancestral foods in a saloon-like setting has been wildly successful in bellwether dining scenes like Brooklyn and Portland, but is relatively new to Houston, and nearly unmatched.

While the resulting hype meant pre-opening rhapsodies about the beak-to-tail dishes employing locally raised duck, and chicken-fried oysters with Buffalo-style hot sauce, our experiences have been wildly inconsistent, peppered with overcooked meats, underseasoned and tough burgers, and stale-tasting duck fat popcorn. The small plates tend to be better, including well-made rillettes and pâtés, crispy fried olives, and plump, luscious mussels in Riesling with a garlicky bite and a whisper of harissa. The dessert program is even stronger.

The best way to approach Branch Water is as a great bar with better-than-usual bar food. Those merits are enough: these balanced Bourbon cocktails will introduce some to drinking Bourbon neat (then Irish whisky, Scotch, and so on), and the selection will excite those who already do.

Modern American
Upmarket restaurant

Heights
510 Shepherd Dr.
(713) 863-7777

Hours
Tue–Wed
11:00am–midnight
Thu
11:00am–1:00am
Fri
11:00am–2:00am
Sat
5:00pm–2:00am
Sun
11:00am–10:00pm

Bar
Beer, wine, liquor

Credit cards
Visa, MC, AmEx

Reservations
Accepted

Features
Brunch
Date-friendly
Good cocktails
Outdoor dining
Wi-Fi

4.7
Food

8.0
Feel

$15
Price

6.0
Wine

Brasil

Next door to our favorite bookstore, a culturally satisfying café

www.brasilcafe.net

Sandwiches
Pizza
Café

Montrose
2604 Dunlavy St.
(713) 528-1993

Hours
Daily
7:30am–midnight

Bar
Beer, wine

Credit cards
Visa, MC, AmEx

Features
Brunch
Date-friendly
Live music
Outdoor dining
Veg-friendly
Wi-Fi

Brasil makes a great hangout, if not such a strong ersatz office. Despite the draconian policies of the past, people are now welcome to work on their laptops here for a long while without harassment, but the Wi-Fi's spotty—skip this place if your work relies on it. The coffee's not so good, but if that's not a concern, you'll love being here. The numerous windows and exposed brick, as well as the industrial-chic exposed pipes and beams, lend an airiness to the place. You can sometimes watch movies on the brilliant outdoor patio amid an explosion of greenery.

Bread is made on site, but isn't necessarily good. Burger buns are quite dry, and pizza crusts (cooked in a regular convection oven) are thinnish but too doughy. And while there are some exotic-sounding items on the menu, it's best to go simple here. Vegetarian sandwiches are well constructed and full of natural and grilled flavor. Soups make a good effort, and salads are reliable and not overdressed. Whatever you do, avoid the Italian beef sausage—it's rubbery and tastes like overcooked taco meat, with none of the expected fennel or caraway flavors of Italian sausage. Be cautious with the cheap-but-decent wines, which are improperly stored and may be stale by the glass; beer's reliable, but best with a side of movie on that patio.

Brasserie Max & Julie

8.7 Food

8.5 Feel

A lovely French meal that goes easy on your senses and your pocketbook

$65 Price

8.5 Wine

www.maxandjulie.net

This hospitable and comfortable place, with its warm red fabrics and bright-brass railings, plays the French brasserie part exceedingly well. And its Francophile wine list is full of reputable producers from both popular and obscure regions; all are priced reasonably and chosen with care. But we're not sure how reliable that menu is; they're often out of our first choices.

The menu represents the food of France's countryside as well as its finer restaurants, and even the presentation of bone marrow is considerate. You spoon the rich, creamy marrow out of its giant bones, sprinkle on some salt, and spread it onto toast—or, better yet, crackly baguette slices from the table basket. Steak tartare is well seasoned and tender, and salade Landaise is lovely, with frisée, seared chicken liver, juicy lardons, an expertly poached egg, and impeccable vinaigrette. Steak au poivre gets a lot of kick from its coarse peppercorns, and comes with frites that approach earthly perfection, although we question the use of filet mignon, a notoriously flavorless cut.

Sometimes service can seem impatient, overpouring wines and coming across as eager for you to hurry along, which you must resist, if you want a truly French experience.

French
Upmarket restaurant

Montrose
4315 Montrose Blvd.
(713) 524-0070

Hours
Mon
5:30pm–10:00pm
Tue–Wed
11:00am–2:30pm
5:30pm–10:00pm
Thu–Fri
11:00am–2:30pm
5:30pm–11:00pm
Sat
11:00am–11:00pm
Sun
11:00am–9:00pm

Bar
Beer, wine

Credit cards
Visa, MC, AmEx

Reservations
Accepted

Features
Brunch
Date-friendly
Outdoor dining

BRC

It's not *big* but it is *red*-blooded, and with a burger to *cock*-a-doodle-do about

www.brcgastropub.com

American
Casual restaurant

Heights
519 Shepherd Dr.
(713) 861-2233

Hours

Mon–Tue
11:00am–2:00pm
5:00pm–midnight

Wed–Fri
11:00am–2:00pm
5:00pm–1:00am

Sat
10:00am–2:00pm
5:00pm–2:00am

Sun
10:00am–2:00pm
5:00pm–midnight

Bar
Beer, wine

Credit cards
Visa, MC, AmEx

Reservations
Not accepted

Features
Brunch
Good beers
Outdoor dining
Wi-Fi

BRC looks like something HGTV would build in a bachelor's basement on a $1,000 budget. (We mean that in a good way.) The vintage cream-and-white wallpaper is very chic, the billiards-green and beef-brown Naugahyde banquettes are old-school clubby, and the long bar evokes Grandpa's quartz-streaked bowling ball. Restrooms are unisex, the lighting is low, and at peak hours, it's as loud and crowded as a roadhouse.

The beer selection is better than a roadhouse's, with about two dozen taps pouring American microbrews (macros, too). Forget the wines—most here are in the Big, Oaky Motor-oil (BOM, or Fruit BOM) style—or try a homemade wine cooler (it tastes like sangría).

Pimento cheese dip, a staff favorite, is creamy, tangy, and addictive. There's a daily changing mac and cheese whose success varies: the blue cheese is salty but mild enough to really work; dryish chile con queso's perhaps *too* mild. Fish and chips (called "fries"…take that, Redcoats!) have a crisp pale ale batter and good, pickly tartar sauce; the fish within is tender and steamy. Daily changing mussels and fries (called "Coastal American versions"…take that, Belgians!) come with fun saucy accoutrements. But you really should be ordering a scrumptious burger with thick slices of maple-kissed bacon, aged cheddar, and "secret sauce," all smooshed into a Slow Dough pretzel bun. Late-night Americana at its best.

The Breakfast Klub

Just add maple syrup and Tabasco and stir

5.0 Food

8.0 Feel

$15 Price

www.thebreakfastklub.com

American Southern
Counter service

Midtown
3711 Travis St.
(713) 528-8561

Hours
Mon–Fri
7:00am–2:00pm
Sat
8:00am–2:00pm
Sun
9:00am–2:00pm

Bar
None

Credit cards
Visa, MC, AmEx

Features
Brunch
Kid-friendly
Live music
Outdoor dining
Wi-Fi

People love them some Breakfast Klub, as you can tell from the hour-long wait outside on weekends. The menu mostly comprises Southern classics like grits, fried catfish, and fried chicken and waffles; the trademark Southern hospitality extends to large tables full of groups and families, and the queue out the door is full of people from all walks of life—from post-church folks who grew up on their Southern grandma's cooking, to alcohol-marinated hipsters. The funky art on the deep red walls and the dark wood tones lend the place a somewhat surprising sophistication.

Of course, the food here is a cardiologist's worst nightmare. The specialties of "katfish," along with grits (excellent), sausage (greasy), and waffles (cardboard), all come in huge portions that are so heavy and monotonous that they all require a complement of both maple syrup and Tabasco. Krazy!

Aside from breakfast items, there are daily classic-Southern specials like étouffée, "Chikin Fried Chikin," and red beans and rice. The Breakfast Klub is a fun, culty tradition, but one with jacked-up prices brought about by overhyping. It seems to be one of those places that's well patronized mostly because the thought of it closing terrifies the city. And, hey, the soporific effects of the food will help make napping easier—that's never a bad thing.

Brennan's of Houston

Welcome back to an old-South class act

www.brennanshouston.com

Southern Modern
Upmarket restaurant

Midtown
3300 Smith St.
(713) 522-9711

Hours
Mon–Sat
11:00am–2:00pm
5:45pm–10:00pm
Sun
10:00am–2:00pm
5:45pm–10:00pm

Bar
Beer, wine, liquor

Credit cards
Visa, MC, AmEx

Reservations
Accepted

Features
Brunch
Date-friendly
Live music
Outdoor dining

When Brennan's—of the New Orleans nobility that owns Commander's Palace—was destroyed by a fire in 2008, Houston mourned one of its oldest traditions: paying exorbitant amounts of money to dine on classic Creole-influenced dishes pomped and served amid historic, exceedingly charming circumstances. Happily, the old building has been faithfully restored, right down to the oak that shades the garden patio, a French Quarter replica sans litter and graffiti. Inside, well-spaced tables and warm lighting fill the many large rooms, each tastefully and chicly decorated.

We find the food even better this time around, if their prices are still somewhat indefensible. Gumbo sports a superior dark roux and intoxicating filé; Gulf seafood is expertly cooked; sauces are aptly reduced and intense; and you may never have better-textured grits west of the Mississippi. The glut of butter and cream here is artfully balanced, often by the well-placed vegetable. Sometimes, however, the emperor wears no clothes; Brennan's bastion of opulence, turtle soup, is more about the copious cream and sherry-splashed sweetness than it is about the merits of that particular meat.

The wine list has swept some undeniable bottles into its grandiose net, but prepare to pay handsomely; service is professional and capable as ever. Since you're here, you must end with Brennan's infamous bananas Foster—the original tableside gimmick, but one we would have missed.

Brenner's

A reliably opulent and old-guard steakhouse with some surprise touches

7.9	8.5
Food	Feel

$90	8.0
Price	Wine

www.brennerssteakhouse.com

Although Landry's took over Brenner's from the family in '02, it is every bit the genteel aristocrat it always was—a fact that's avouched by comically pompous service (how coarse would you like your tableside pepper grind?) and over-the-top décor. In the older Memorial location, choose a windowside table for the best view of a melodramatic garden that clashes superbly with the stuffy Victorian mirrors, lamps, glassware, and chests of the interior. The River Oaks location's soaring, two-floor atrium has a surreally beautiful flow and a pandering, blue-lit rooftop lounge with a luxuriant view.

Brenner's has always made a mean steak, although we wish it would bring bone-in cuts back on the regular menu. They come medium-rare as ordered, with an appropriate char, and are gloriously simple in their salt-and-pepper coats. But the details aren't up to supporting-role status, beginning with embarrassingly supermarket-ish bread and continuing with a wedge salad whose "signature Roquefort" doesn't really come together well. Creamed spinach is gummy and clammy, with a taste that strongly evokes Knorr's onion soup packets, and the highly self-touted apple strudel is just okay.

Kudos to a wine list that goes beyond the usual steakhouse conceits with some truly respectable domestic producers and a handful of far-flung gems, all within a very hospitable price range. It's those touches—and the great steak—that best illustrate Brenner's enduring class.

Steakhouse
Upmarket restaurant

River Oaks
1 Birdsall St.
(713) 868-4444

Memorial
10911 Katy Fwy.
(713) 465-2901

Hours
Sun–Mon
5:00pm–9:00pm
Tue–Thu
11:00am–2:00pm
5:00pm–9:00pm
Fri
11:00am–2:00pm
5:00pm–10:00pm
Sat
5:00pm–10:00pm
Hours vary by location

Bar
Beer, wine, liquor

Credit cards
Visa, MC, AmEx

Reservations
Accepted

Features
Date-friendly
Outdoor dining

Burger Guys

The burger fiends bliss out over Akaushi, duck fat, and donuts

www.theburgerguys.com

Burgers
Counter service

West Houston
12225 Westheimer Rd
(281) 497-4897

Hours
Mon–Thu
11:00am–9:00pm
Fri–Sat
11:00am–10:00pm

Bar
None

Credit cards
Visa, MC, AmEx

Features
Kid-friendly

A lot of fuss is made over Akaushi, a breed of Japanese wagyu raised in Texas. Its muscle fibers are longer and thinner, resulting in more tender meat, and the fat's intramuscular, so you get a great composition of flavor and texture. It's full of monounsaturated fat, making it much healthier than the typical Choice—or even Prime—ground beef. Here, it makes for a good, juicy burger that's especially pleasing if you go in for complex constructions.

A Shipley's donut burger is just over the top completely, but somehow works; the caramelized onions tie it all together. A Vietnamese-inspired burger with pâté and pickled carrots is even more of a flavor stretch, as is an Aussie-inspired burger with beets and grilled pineapple. Better are the more classic approaches, like a "Houston" with bacon-onion jam and house-made pickled jalapeños; the maple-smoked cheddar's a crazy delicious flavor despite not having the melting capabilities of American.

There's a glut of other ecstasy-inducing items like epic milkshakes, cane-sugar soda fountain drinks, wonderful hot dogs (especially the one wrapped in crisp bacon), and duck fat french fries that manage an erotic hypnosis. Rack up a slew of the eleventy-jillion dipping sauces here, including a Lebanese aïoli and a wonderful jalapeño-cilantro, and try to undo all the good you just did by eating Akaushi beef.

Burns Bar-B-Q

Now and then, a taste of Hill Country
authenticity right outside the Loop

8.0	4.0
Food	Feel

$20
Price

Burns Bar-B-Q recently moved from one
dilapidated building sitting in the middle of a
rough neighborhood in North Houston to
another. As a result, it may suffer some
inconsistency, but so do the best Hill Country
smokehouses. This is the real deal, folks, so your
enjoyment requires patience: try to remember
their strict cash-only policy and short work
week; the wait tends to be interminably long
(especially on Saturdays); and the menu is a
confusing list of combinations (go with #1, it
easily feeds three to four). While the ordering
goes fairly quickly, the kitchen seems to be in no
hurry. We once waited an hour for our order—
with about 50 other people in the small front
room—only to learn that they were out of
brisket. A riot nearly ensued.

That extremely tender and super smoky
brisket could, on its best days, compete with the
hallowed pits of Central Texas. Pork spare ribs
are just as exemplary; they're aggressively smoky
and seasoned just right, with a pleasant
chewiness. The one weakness is the sausage—
it's ground super-fine, and the result is a
processed texture and flavor. The barbecue
sauce has a balance of tangy and sweet, with a
smoky complexity that not everyone will
appreciate. The same goes for the service, which
can be on the curt side—now *that's* unlike a Hill
Country experience.

Barbecue
Counter service

North Houston
7117 N. Shepherd Dr.
(713) 692-2800

Hours
Wed–Fri
10:30am–7:30pm
Sat
10:30am–7:00pm

Bar
None

Credit cards
None

9.0 Food

6.0 Feel

$25 Price

Café Pita +

You don't have to crave Balkan food—just incredible, homemade comfort food

Bosnian
Casual restaurant

Westchase
10890 Westheimer Rd.
(713) 953-7237

Hours
Mon–Thu
11:00am–9:00pm
Fri
11:00am–10:00pm
Sat–Sun
noon–10:00pm

Bar
Beer, wine, BYO

Credit cards
Visa, MC

Reservations
Not accepted

Houston's best purveyor of Bosnian cuisine is also its rare purveyor of an always-exciting menu of consistently delicious and spectacularly cheap dishes. The basis of a meal here is homemade lepinje, a doughy bread that makes excellent cevapi (sandwiches) with beef-and-lamb sausages. It's only one of many house-made wonders that define this devoted, disciplined, diminutive kitchen, which serves a stark, but somehow cozy room. The warm, genuine staff imports from Chicago such rarities as a Bosnian version of feta, which has a more sour, fermented flavor than the standard Greek stuff. There's also some of the deepest-flavored "pastrami" we've ever tasted, a cured beef cut that plays off like Italy's air-dried bresaola, only smokier. Don't miss the expertly fried cheese, homemade in the halloumi style and delicately battered. We've developed a curious obsession with its texture—which, surprisingly, becomes more irresistible as it cools off and congeals, revealing more of its sexy squeak.

Don't waste room on American familiars like chicken Caesar salad, and dry and relatively flavorless shish kebabs. But why would you, with fried anchovies and their delightfully forward marine flavor; comforting sarma (stuffed cabbage in a flavorful broth); and soft pirjan (meltingly braised lamb shank with potatoes and vegetables) to choose from?

Café Rabelais

The food's fine, but the overall evening here is even better

7.2	9.5
Food	Feel

$55	9.0
Price	Wine

www.caferabelais.com

Flickering votives, chalkboards, walls lined with bottles of wine. When done right, as it is here, there is hardly any atmosphere more romantic, more bewitching, than that of a low-key French bistro. You might even forget that you had to wrestle your car between huge SUVs in the parking-challenged neighborhood. And it really is one of the best date spots in the city; servers are attentive but not intrusive, and the hand-written menu board gives the feeling that the night has been crafted especially for you. The French wine list, which is refreshingly half-bottle heavy, is extensive and almost sacrificially well priced. As for the food, it's competent—even sometimes spectacular. Mussels come in a too-creamy broth with little oomph, but they're sensual and their frites excellent. The nightly specials are often some of the most amazing dishes, like a plum tart topped with boudin noir and melting foie gras, or rabbit moutarde. In general, meat dishes outshine fish, which, while cooked expertly, are less inspiring.

Where some complain that Rabelais underseasons its food now and then, others might find the restraint refreshing, and anyway, the excellence is in the details. A chocolate silk pie, for example, is made multi-dimensional in texture as well as flavor by a crunchy walnut crust. Like many dishes here, it's not mind-blowing, but combined with the atmosphere and wine list, it outdoes itself.

French
Upmarket restaurant

Rice Area
2442 Times Blvd.
(713) 520-8841

Hours
Mon
6:00pm–9:00pm
Tue–Wed
11:00am–2:30pm
6:00pm–9:00pm
Thu–Sat
11:00am–2:30pm
6:00pm–10:00pm

Bar
Beer, wine

Credit cards
Visa, MC, AmEx

Reservations
Not accepted

Features
Date-friendly

Café TH

A downtown-and-vegan-accessible café
with *both* great pho and banh mi

Vietnamese
Counter service

Downtown
2108 Pease St.
(713) 225-4766

Hours
Mon–Wed
11:00am–3:00pm
Thu–Fri
11:00am–3:00pm
6:00pm–9:00pm
Sat
11:00am–3:00pm

Bar
None

Credit cards
Visa, MC

Features
Veg-friendly

Café TH stands out among Houston's pho shops as a contemporary, attractive little thing. Its black-and-white-striped awning is appropriately Montmartre-ish, and a similar French influence is felt when the owner greets you at your table to ask how the food is—the food that he cooked for you. The brightly colored walls and above-average tea also communicate the point that this is a thoroughly modern take on traditional Vietnamese bistro classics.

In that vein, everything's prepared with more care than in your typical Vietnamese café, but the flavors are a bit more muted, particularly the acid and salt (seafood noodle soup's quite…mild). Banh mi comes on terrific baguette (available, too, in wheat—what would Julia Child say?) and made with fresh, wonderful ingredients. Beef pho is a standout, even—get this—vegan pho. It's surprisingly complex and hearty; we won't be trading in our marrowy versions anytime soon, but we're happy for the previously pho-less vegans out there. Green curry has a pleasant heat and lemongrassy, gingery flavor, but its ungainly chunks of overcooked potato make it a little mushy. Meatballs are tasty, and bahn bot chien is crisp and delicious, if not as good as that of Tan Tan or Kim Tai. But for a soup or sandwich near the office, it's awesome. (Particularly for vegans.)

Calliope's Po-Boy

Houston's never tasted so close to N'awlins

7.4 Food

6.5 Feel

$15 Price

www.calliopespoboy.com

New Orleans is a unique, seductive culture; America's mischievous wink. It's a culture kept alive by its people, and it fans out like a delta, nourishing Texans with an affluvial, muddy flavor that others can only weakly mimic. Calliope's Po'-Boy feeds Houston authentic New Orleans food from its modest strip-mall storefront. The friendly staff is rightfully proud of its food. Although the neighborhood is a little rundown, the interior of pleather chairs and red tablecloths over cheap tables feels safely sterile—even mundane, like some of the best po' boy shops in New Orleans. And like those, Calliope's French bread is custom-baked in the style of the traditional Leidenheimer recipe— crunchy on the outside and soft inside. Soft-shell crab, catfish, shrimp, and oysters are fried artfully, maintaining their moisture inside a crispy cornmeal breading. The whole thing is dressed with the traditional mayo, tomato, lettuce, and pickle, to which you add as much hot sauce as you can handle.

The best po' boy we ever had in New Orleans was dripping with salty roast beef and gravy, and this one is a fair comparison, if not quite as addictively salty. While the gumbo is thinnish, it has an excellent complexity of flavor and heat, one that is rarely produced with success outside of the Big Easy. Thankfully, we're within reach.

Southern Sandwiches
Casual restaurant

East Houston
2130 Jefferson St.
(713) 222-8333

Hours
Mon–Thu
10:00am–10:00pm
Fri
10:00am–midnight
Sat
11:00am–midnight
Sun
10:30am–5:00pm

Bar
None

Credit cards
Visa, MC, AmEx

Reservations
Not accepted

Features
Kid-friendly
Wi-Fi

Canopy

Pastries and a posh breakfast make good excuses to hang out in this pleasant space

www.canopyhouston.com

Modern
Upmarket restaurant

Montrose
3939 Montrose Blvd.
(713) 528-6848

Hours
Mon
7:00am–3:00pm
5:00pm–9:00pm
Tue–Thu
7:00am–3:00pm
5:00pm–10:00pm
Fri
7:00am–3:00pm
5:00pm–10:30pm
Sat
9:00am–3:00pm
5:00pm–10:30pm
Sun
9:00am–3:00pm
5:00pm–9:00pm

Bar
Beer, wine, liquor

Credit cards
Visa, MC, AmEx

Reservations
Accepted

Features
Brunch
Date-friendly
Outdoor dining
Veg-friendly
Wi-Fi

Whether or not we especially crave any of its food, we like being at Canopy. The inside's got an airy mid-century appeal to it, complete with Eames-style chairs, and the sidewalk seating is pleasant. Tables are free of linen and fuss, and the menu suffers from less globe-trotting jetlag than the one at sister restaurant Shade.

You have plenty of chances to go, considering there's the rare breakfast and lunch offered here in addition to dinner and brunch. Most items have the de rigueur Southern comfort bent to them, like fried chicken salad and buttermilk-crusted pork loin. Breads and pastries are pretty fantastic, though, and reason enough to hit it up on a weekend mid-morning. Burgers and French toast made with challah are always a selling point for us. At dinner, the more Latin American-influenced dishes fare less well, like overwrought lobster enchiladas and a chile relleno that can't compete with the authentic versions around town, but do trust in a grilled red snapper whose "Thai curry" beurre blanc works surprisingly well. Salads rely, as they should, on their components for flavor, not on the dressing; soups like French onion are satisfying and well made. Cocktails are fine but hardly noteworthy, while the mostly domestic and French wine list has a few glimmers of brilliance in the mid-range. That seems to be the general behavior here, overall.

Captain Tom's Seafood

8.1 Food   **7.5** Feel

The bounty of the Gulf and the swamp, served raw and fried

$15 Price

There are a few of these restaurants around town, each shaped like an old fishing boat; the landscaping even consists of discarded oyster shells. Inside, the only seating is a horseshoe of stools around the semi-open kitchen, making for some tight quarters (there are no tables), but it only adds to the experience. Whether at lunch or dinner, you might have to fight for a seat, and, although the capacity is around 70, don't even think about bringing large parties.

There are two preparations at Captain Tom's: fried and raw. Fried means it's dredged in cornmeal, done (usually) to a near-perfect crisp (sometimes it can be overfried), and served immediately. Fried seafood is what the Gulf Coast is known for, yet it's surprisingly hard to find in Houston—props to Tom's for its sense of place. There's stuffed crab (savory, moist), frog legs, fried shrimp (pungent), and some really good (if mushy) gumbo on the cheap. Whole flounder and catfish can be a little overcooked, but the bones do their job by keeping moisture in the meat. In a move we'd like to see more often, fried jalapeños come stuffed with succulent crabmeat. A visit here wouldn't be complete without a michelada—get them to throw an oyster on the bottom for the original oyster shooter. Be careful with these...it's easy to go overboard.

Seafood
Southern
Counter service

East Houston
13955 E. Fwy.
(713) 451-3700

Northwest Houston
9651 FM 1960 W.
(281) 890-8334

Katy
20525 Katy Fwy.
(281) 829-6407

Hours
Sun–Thu
11:00am–11:00pm
Fri–Sat
11:00am–midnight

Bar
Beer, wine

Credit cards
Visa, MC, AmEx

Features
Kid-friendly

Chez Roux

One of Houston's best restaurants is in...Conroe?

www.latorrettadellagoresortandspa.com

French Modern
Upmarket restaurant

Conroe
600 La Torretta Blvd.
(936) 448-4400

Hours
Tue–Sat
5:30pm–9:00pm

Bar
Beer, wine, liquor

Credit cards
Visa, MC, AmEx

Reservations
Essential

Features
Date-friendly
Outdoor dining
Wi-Fi

Drive through sterile suburban neighborhoods and a macabre procession of chain restaurants to the luxury resort La Torretta Del Lago. For running this gauntlet, you are rewarded with one of the finest meals in the state (and if you come at the right time, one hell of a sunset).

You'll be greeted with the finest modern-elegant dining room that money can buy, complete with stunning lake view. Both the menu and meticulous technique are true-blue French, right down to the insistence of using the finest local ingredients. We've had a soufflé made with Texas's own Veldhuizen Farm cheddar, an impossibly airy and rich cloud floating upon sweet creamed corn—all Lone Star and all Gaul. Turnip fondant has come caramelized to a near-toffee flavor, threaded with savory, salty bits of duck confit. Foie gras mousse with walnut bread is as texturally stirring and flawless as a Jean-Luc Godard film. We've enjoyed a cart of fully ripened French cheeses allowed to rest at room temperature; figs stuffed with whipped Fourme d'Ambert; and a foie gras terrine tickled with Muscat and pungent baby leeks.

The low points are few, but noticeable: sometimes-awkward service; and a wine list that mingles compulsory domestic clunkers with better, but overpriced, French bottles. Nevertheless, this is some of the most capable French cooking found in Texas, and with one of the loveliest views.

The Chocolate Bar

Gifts, indulgences, and perhaps even
endangered commodities worth hoarding

www.theoriginalchocolatebar.com

The Chocolate Bar has three distinct layers:
chocolates, ice cream, and baked goods. While
"chocolate" is baked right into the name, we
actually find the ice cream's the most bangin'
virtue here. There are inventive flavors like
"Root Beer Float" and "Chocolate Cape Cod"
(with cranberries and dark chocolate chips), and
they specialize in generally mixing chocolate ice
cream with any number of nuts, goo, and
candy. Next are the cakes, whose display is like
diabetic porn. Expensive porn, considering a
single slice is $10. But these are monster cakes.
"Aunt Etta's" four-layered chocolate cake is
dense, rich, and dark; the "Bayou City Mud Pie"
is a delightfully messy mix of mousse and
brownies. If you want something smaller and
cheaper, a mini cupcake or a brownie is a
superb and indulgent, but still totally
manageable, prospect.

Homemade chocolates come in all sorts of
cutesy shapes like calculators and tennis rackets
that are clearly intended as gifts—chocolate
toothbrushes could deliver a confusing message.
Chocolate-dipped fruits and pretzels behind the
counter are far better than your average candy,
and also far more expensive. But considering
that the world's chocolate comes from a scant
percentage of land—only within ten degrees of
the equator—the high prices make sense. It's a
rare commodity; cheap chocolate is hardly
chocolate, anyway.

Ice cream
Baked goods
Counter service

Montrose
1835 W. Alabama St.
(713) 520-8599

Rice Area
2521 University Blvd.
(713) 520-8888

Hours
Mon–Thu
10:00am–10:00pm
Fri–Sat
10:00am–midnight
Sun
noon–10:00pm

Bar
None

Credit cards
Visa, MC, AmEx

Features
Date-friendly
Kid-friendly
Veg-friendly
Wi-Fi

6.4 Food
7.0 Feel

$15
Price

Christian's Tailgate

A reliable divey burger that has its place—
among karaoke stars and $1 Bud Lights

www.christianstailgate.com

Burgers
American
Bar

Heights
7340 Washington Ave.
(713) 864-9744

Midtown
2000 Bagby St.
(713) 527-0261

Hours
Mon–Sat
11:00am–2:00am
Sun
11:00am–midnight

Bar
Beer, wine, liquor

Credit cards
Visa, MC, AmEx

Features
Live music
Outdoor dining
Wi-Fi

There are two Christian's locations: the original,
a soulful shack-like structure on Washington;
and the newer one, a commercialized, confused
place that's let its hip Midtown location go to its
head. Many people prefer the original because
of its comfortable outdoor patio and long-
storied history; perhaps that just makes the food
taste better. The draw is the burgers and simple
food, like fried chicken tenders and fried catfish
po' boys. However famous they are, the burgers
are just good and honest: a well-seasoned patty
piled with lettuce, tomato, pickles, onions,
mustard, and mayonnaise on a fluffy bun.
People go crazy for the meat, which is ground
and formed in house—but there are plenty of
places that just buy the frozen patties and still
make a better burger. Christian's claims to
honor rare orders, but it's never come less than
medium; on the bright side, at least they don't
overcook it, either.

This being, first and foremost, a bar, there are
theme parties weekly with karaoke and retro
videos—and some ridiculous specials, like $1
domestic drafts and well drinks. The regulars are
a scrappy bunch that don't take lightly to the
riff-raff walking in off the street, but the staff
are (for the most part) friendly—until the place
gets really packed, in which case, look out.

Churrascos

This first and most approachable Nuevo Latino restaurant isn't half bad

www.cordua.com

8.1	8.0
Food	Feel
$65	7.0
Price	Wine

The granddaddy of the Cordúa chain is still going strong at over twenty years old, pleasing the crowds with the same tender, if overpriced, marinated tenderloins. The décor still works, the service still works, and the whole package, however predictable it has become, still works. Sure, the food tastes like it's made—from ingredient procurement to preparation strategy—simply to satisfy a bottom line. And the many outposts of this restaurant group, in spite of their different branding strategies, visual themes, and target markets, do a lot of the same things. We're not just talking about the tres leches, or the fried plantain chips and chimichurri that greet you when you sit down (which are addictive). We're also talking about the marineros, those smoky crab claws—which aren't bad, but aren't exactly good either. We're also talking about the underperforming ceviche, or the mixed grill of overcooked seafood called "Opereta."

The ubiquitous maduros (sweet roasted plantains) and yuca fries are fun and blameless. There have opened, since Churrascos first spread its Latin American message of meat in Houston, several better and more authentic churrascarias, it's true—but we can't downplay Cordúa's enduring role as the first and still most approachable.

Latin American
Upmarket restaurant

Upper Kirby
2055 Westheimer Rd.
(713) 527-8300

West Houston
9705 Westheimer Rd.
(713) 952-1988

Hours
Mon–Thu
11:00am–9:30pm
Fri
11:00am–10:30pm
Sat
11:30am–10:30pm
Sun
11:00am–9:00pm
Hours vary by location

Bar
Beer, wine, liquor

Credit cards
Visa, MC, AmEx

Reservations
Accepted

Features
Brunch
Date-friendly
Outdoor dining

6.1	8.5
Food	Feel

$30	8.0
Price	Margs

Chuy's

Going statewide might dilute the food, but not the Mexican martinis

www.chuys.com

Mexican
Casual restaurant

River Oaks
2706 Westheimer Rd.
(713) 524-1700

Northwest Houston
19827 Northwest Fwy.
(281) 970-0341

Humble
20502 Hwy. 59 N.
(281) 540-7778

Hours
Sun–Thu
11:00am–10:00pm
Fri–Sat
11:00am–11:00pm
Hours vary by location

Bar
Beer, wine, liquor

Credit cards
Visa, MC, AmEx

Reservations
Accepted

Features
Good cocktails
Kid-friendly
Veg-friendly

Say what you will about this broadening enchilada empire, it feels like a fun night out, and it beats most other Tex-Mex happy hours by miles. Not that you'll remember, given how strong these margaritas and Mexican martinis are. The latter have better flavor than the margarita, which can be a little soapy-sweet.

The endless mid-century paraphernalia, which is oddly heavy with Elvis overtones, is carefully done up with Disney-esque detail, and visitors— even in Dallas and Houston—feel like they're being treated to that patented Austin "weird," without as much of the gross falseness of national chains like Buco di Beppo. Obviously, it feels more legit at the Zilker original. The food is also somehow best here, and then worsens with distance. The queso (which you can serve yourself for free out of a faux-'50s-car hood during happy hour) is the creamy, intense best of its kind, while Hatch green chile enchiladas (during Hatch season in fall) hit just the right balance of Tex and Mex. Sauces are a bit uneven from branch to branch—tomatillo can be insipid and watery, and the more suburban locations may be to blame for a creamy jalapeño that bears an uncanny resemblance to only slightly peppery ranch. Dry chicken seems to be a universal problem, but beef fajitas are usually well seasoned, remarkably tender, and come with tasty flour tortillas. Tastier with strong drinks.

Clay's

Burgers and chicken-fried steak with a side of petting zoo

www.claysrestaurant.com

6.8	8.0
Food	Feel

$25
Price

**Southern
Burgers**
Counter service

Northwest Houston
17717 Clay Rd.
(281) 859-3773

Hours
Mon–Thu
11:00am–9:00pm
Fri–Sat
11:00am–10:00pm
Sun
11:00am–8:00pm

Bar
Beer, wine

Credit cards
Visa, MC, AmEx

Features
Kid-friendly
Outdoor dining

What's better than eating one of the city's best chicken-fried steaks? Doing it in peace while your kids pet a goat. This woodsy family oasis hunkers between industrial garages and Northwest Houston's cookie-cutter subdivisions, and is seemingly always packed. Expect a wait during peak hours—at least they have that petting zoo, right? The back patio's often filled with parents sucking down cold beers while the young'uns run wild in the yard full of peacocks, mules, miniature horses, and chickens. Beware of the free-roaming restaurant cats; they fear no one and might jump up on the table to sniff what's in your basket.

Aside from the typical artery-clogging fried finger food, including (now and then) excellent fried okra, there are outstanding hand-formed burgers. They're juicy and beefy, with just enough char to make them unforgettable. But the pièce de résistance is the galactic-sized, tender chicken-fried steak, smothered in homemade cream gravy and served up with two sides (we like the garlic mashed potatoes and the cole slaw—"We chop all that cabbage into little slices by hand ever'day," they tell us). The gravy is awesome, with the right balance of pepper and creaminess, and no mealy starchiness. We've hardly had better, in or out of the Loop. Hey, the food may not be the healthiest, but for family-bonding time, it can't be beat.

Crave Cupcakes

Pricy treats that still make cheaper gifts
than precious jewelry

www.cravecupcakes.com

Cupcakes, although not the rage they once were, are maintaining their A-status enough to warrant interior design from places like the award-winning avroKO. The effect makes Crave look—with its abundance of glass and sunlight—every bit like a fine jewelry store. It's no accident that the colors within are brown and turquoise, bearing an uncanny resemblance to the famous palette of Tiffany's. Cupcakes arranged in precise lines are carefully iced in elegant shades of taupe, cocoa, and eggshell. While the cakes are uniformly moist, the intensity of flavor varies: key lime cake has more vanilla than tart lime, and red velvet doesn't taste enough like cocoa. Dark chocolate has the unmistakable taste of chocolate, but without the deep bitterness implied by the "dark." Frostings are more assertive and usually garnished well: a burst of tartness from key lime zest rounded out with finely crushed graham cracker, and cream cheese frosting with just the right blend of sweet and sour.

The $3.25 price tag is a bit hard to stomach. In many cases, it feels as though you're really paying for precious touches like the fondant seal that comes on some of the cakes, imprinted with the Crave logo. For that reason, they make popular gifts and wedding-cake substitutes. What, we wonder, will become the cupcake substitute?

Crawfish and Noodles

Every dish in this happy Cajun-Asian place is a point of Houston pride

9.5	8.0
Food	Feel

$25
Price

www.crawfishandnoodle.com

If we had to explain Houston to someone, we'd bring them here, to a menu that is the crossroads between Cajun frog legs and Vietnamese bo luc lac; between fried rice and nuoc mam-marinated crispy fried chicken wings. Where bowls of angry red crawfish face off against whole fried crabs, both bursting with garlic, luxurious butter, and spicy heat. Where the critters of the Gulf crawl up on the shore and get the salt-and-pepper treatment.

In fact, this happy, amphibious place has well surpassed our former East-meets-South favorite, The Boiling Crab. And the prices are all Bellaire: you can get three whole blue crabs for $14.95, and they'll be the best in the city. Awesomesauce! For that matter, the tender and butter-beefy bo luc lac is best in class, too, coming with a heap of shallots and garlic. It kind of makes us look forward to the end of crawfish season so we can focus on the Vietnamese dishes here.

The service couldn't be friendlier, or more helpful. Which is another perfect illustration of our hospitable city. And if they didn't get the point by then, we'd make them suck a crawfish head. Ain't no bunch of sissies in Houston.

Southern Vietnamese
Casual restaurant

Bellaire Chinatown
10613 Bellaire Blvd.
(281) 988-8098

Hours
Mon
3:00pm–10:00pm
Tue
5:00pm–10:00pm
Wed–Thu
3:00pm–10:00pm
Fri
3:00pm–11:00pm
Sat
noon–11:00pm
Sun
noon–10:00pm

Bar
Beer, wine

Credit cards
Visa, MC

Reservations
Accepted

Features
Kid-friendly

Cyclone Anaya's

Diners, not their wallets, get clobbered by potent margaritas and fresh Tex-Mex

www.cycloneanaya.com

Mexican
Casual restaurant

Heights
1710 Durham Dr.
(713) 862-3209

Midtown
309 Gray St.
(713) 520-6969

Memorial
5761 Woodway Dr.
(713) 339-4552

West Houston
800 Town and Country
(713) 461-1300

Hours
Mon–Thu
11:00am–10:00pm
Fri
11:00am–11:00pm
Sat
10:00am–10:00pm
Sun
8:30am–10:00pm
Hours vary by location

Bar
Beer, wine, liquor

Credit cards
Visa, MC, AmEx

Reservations
Accepted

It seems that about half of downtown's offices empty into the raucous Midtown Anaya's after work so everyone can unwind with huge, super-strong margaritas. (Send someone early, as getting a table outside is a Herculean feat.) The others branches are still quite lively, but calm by comparison.

Cyclone Anaya's is named for a former professional wrestler whose family owns and runs them all. And it's a fun scene—it feels like everyone's there, packed into large booths with chic lighting fixtures glinting off copious amounts of bling.

The food's all Tex-Mex comfort, and it's not spectacular, but everything manages to escape the usual problems that plague Tex-Mex kitchens: taco beef and tamales are aggressively seasoned and moist; cheese melts all the way and doesn't get that goopy wallpaper-paste consistency. It's best showcased on chicken enchiladas in red corn tortillas, topped with a lively tomatillo sauce; the chile con carne enchiladas are a little monotonous. Fajitas are fine, if not flaunting the smoky mesquite flavor of the best versions in town. Remarkably fresh-tasting salsa is just hot and chunky enough, whereas the creamy sauce on several platters is too thick and sweet, smothering whatever lies beneath. Much like, we guess, Cyclone Anaya did to his opponents.

Da Da Mi Sushi Bistro

7.6 Food

7.0 Feel

Even the jaded get a kick out of Korean-style sashimi straight from the tanks

$35 Price

Korean sashimi is different from the Japanese sort. For one thing, the size of cuts are bigger; for another, anything procured from a market may still be somewhat frozen in places—this is intentional. It's a texture preference. Anyway, these aren't the best orders here. See those tanks? That's where your dinner lives. Korean sashimi means having a wriggling octopus, crunchy abalone, sea cucumber (whose ammonia flavor has its fans), or ethereal flounder dispatched and served to you, sometimes still wriggling. Dip it in a sesame-oil-and-garlic sauce and gnaw it into submission, then take a shot of soju. Order a whole fish if you have three or more people—with all those free banchan sides, it'll be more than enough to satiate. Spicy fish stew is also good, as is a sultry egg casserole, and charred whole sardines. But for freshness that's memorable and exciting, you can't beat those tanks.

Though it's in a rough-and-tumble shopping center, Da Da Mi has a fun, boisterous sushi chef and grateful staff who make up for the lack of atmosphere. Odd-looking dividers give each table complete privacy and service only comes at the push of the button (literally). Drink up, have fun, and don't frown and poke at your food…lest it should poke back.

Korean
Casual restaurant

Spring Branch
1927 Gessner Dr.
(832) 657-0007

Hours
Daily
6:00pm–1:00am

Bar
Beer, wine, liquor

Credit cards
Visa, MC, AmEx

Reservations
Accepted

9.6 Food	**8.0** Feel
$90 Price	**9.0** Wine

Da Marco

Exemplary Italian served in a surprisingly casual and approachable atmosphere

www.damarcohouston.com

Italian
Upmarket restaurant

Montrose
1520 Westheimer Rd.
(713) 807-8857

Hours
Tue–Thu
11:30am–2:00pm
5:30pm–10:00pm
Fri
11:30am–2:00pm
5:30pm–11:00pm
Sat
5:30pm–11:00pm

Bar
Beer, wine, liquor

Credit cards
Visa, MC, AmEx

Reservations
Accepted

Features
Date-friendly

We continue to have the best culinary experiences in Houston at this world-class restaurant. The kitchen's often mislabeled as "northern Italian" because the virtuoso chef is from Friuli, but the menu spans the entirety of the Boot. Buffalo-milk burrata—a profound, cream-spiked version of mozzarella, paired with exceptionally ripe tomatoes—derives from Puglia. Campania is where you'd see the most wood-fired brick ovens of the sort Da Marco uses for its margherita pizza, whose balance of ripe, reduced tomato flavor with sharp, brick-seared ash approaches perfection. An old Jewish recipe from Rome is the basis for delicately fried artichoke alla giudea, dressed in olive oil with mint, lemon, and a touch of orange. And you'd find a whole roasted branzino—a sweet, firm white fish, here fired in the wood-burning oven—absolutely anywhere along the coastline.

There are periodic missteps: risotto has come gooey and dense, while sweet corn ravioli's been overcooked. But these flaws are more likely during the (still awesome) $25 three-course business lunch. The wine list could have been put together by any great Italian wine journalist, and it's spectacularly priced.

Even the atmosphere is authentically Italian in its simplicity: well-dressed (but not overdressed) tables; cozy, low ceilings; an airy porch-style room. But we've found service hurried and brusque, and even recently dined with children running rampant through the dining room. C'mon now, is that any way to treat Houston's best restaurant?

Danton's

A classy but easy seafood house with all the Bayou City favorites

6.9	7.5
Food	Feel

$50	7.5
Price	Drinks

www.dantonsseafood.com

The menu at Danton's reads like a favorite old book, full of characters you know well—namely Gulf seafood that's stuffed, grilled, grilled *and* stuffed, or deep fried. And while it's nice inside and the service is upmarket, it's not at all fussy. On Sundays, there's a great live blues brunch that makes the distance between here and New Orleans seem that much shorter. The seafood gumbo, on the other hand, although appropriately dark and thick, tastes too far from the muddy banks of the Mississippi. But on the upside, the kitchen does a great job of not drowning seafood mains in sauces; even a "Baked Crab Balinese" reaches true comfort-food level with a cheesy, creamy sauce that manages to stay just this side of extreme. Stuffed fish is even more restrained—whether it's redfish or the catch of the day—and cooked just fine.

The choice of sides is a mile-long list that includes five variations of rice. There's an equally lengthy cocktail list that makes some admirable attempts, like a gumbo'd-up Bloody Mary, but better is the improved wine list that now has a handful of classic seafood mates like Sancerre, Godello, and even the rare Old-World-style Chardonnay from California. When these are half-price, and oysters are just $.75 apiece (as they are at happy hour), the deal's as sweet as crabmeat.

Seafood
Southern
Casual restaurant

Montrose
4611 Montrose Blvd.
(713) 807-8889

Hours
Mon–Sat
11:00am–2:30pm
5:30pm–10:00pm
Sun
11:00am–4:00pm

Bar
Beer, wine, liquor

Credit cards
Visa, MC, AmEx

Reservations
Accepted

Features
Brunch
Date-friendly
Live music
Outdoor dining

7.9	7.5
Food	Feel

$100	6.5
Price	Wine

Del Frisco's

A luxurious setting for a luxurious and—
expertly handled—steak

www.delfriscos.com

Steakhouse
Upmarket restaurant

Galleria
5061 Westheimer Rd.
(713) 355-2600

Hours
Mon–Fri
11:00am–11:00pm
Sat–Sun
5:00pm–11:00pm

Bar
Beer, wine, liquor

Credit cards
Visa, MC, AmEx

Reservations
Accepted

Features
Date-friendly
Outdoor dining

This is the sort of opulent, over-the-top steakhouse chain that exemplifies old-school hospitality; the kind of place into which Dudley Moore's Arthur would have drunkenly stumbled, only to have the maître d' wordlessly slip a coat on his prostitute companion. And its improved service swishes and performs amid dramatic architecture, stuffy dark woods and wrought iron, and decorative bottles of terribly expensive wine.

Needless to say, the prices are in line with those at other high-end steakhouses, and the steak follows suit. A Prime New York strip with its trademark skirt of fat comes judiciously seasoned and broiled to a char on the outside, while maintaining maximum juiciness inside. These guys are grill ninjas: a rare-plus request, so often brushed off as medium-rare, comes expertly executed, with a bright-red, slightly warm center. Filet mignon, a challenge due to its inherent lack of marbling, still manages a supremely succulent tenderness, so you'd better believe the one-pound ribeye, with its liberal marbling, is worth the cardiologist's bill. Sides can't compete, with the potatoes au gratin merely a coagulated lump of potato and cheese, and onion rings neutered of flavor.

The wine list's a hefty tome of New World-style *Spectator* darlings, but with a pretty good range of price points. Cocktails are of the overpriced, oversized, and not very carefully executed variety. They're, in other words, appropriately over the top.

The Dessert Gallery

A turn-and-burn cake operation that's not at all short on shortening and sugar

www.dessertgallery.com

It must be that crackish aspect of sugar that leads clamoring crowds to pay such high prices for sticky-sweet cakes scarcely better than those your reasonably competent aunt could turn out. Or maybe it's the cushy couches. Or the city's singular obsession with sweets. Whatever the reasons for the Dessert Gallery's success, its bright interiors are consistently overpowered by herds of people. Couches are taken over by groups of friends, while rambunctious children, seemingly propelled by sugar-fueled jet engines that enable them to outrun their frantic parents, are everywhere. Staff members have a hard time keeping track of who has ordered which cake. It's a madhouse.

Although there's a huge variety, there's a shortening-and-sugar sameness to the many-layered cakes, whose frosting and art appears to be of the grocery-store variety. The popular "Chocolate Euphoria" is decadent, with textures of smooth and chunky dark chocolate dominating the palate for about three bites, at which point your euphoria turns to sloth. Cheesecake works in the same manner. Carrot cake holds out longer before its flavors becoming boring and overbearing; most of the tooth-numbingly-sweet cream-cheese icing winds up scraped off to the side. Nevertheless, the cakes are better than the cookies, which are often too hard and missing that critical salty component. But you know what? The kids don't seem to mind.

Baked goods
Counter service

Upper Kirby
3600 Kirby Dr.
(713) 522-9999

Galleria
1616 Post Oak Blvd.
(713) 622-0007

Hours
Mon–Thu
11:00am–10:00pm
Fri–Sat
11:00am–midnight
Sun
noon–10:00pm
Hours vary by location

Bar
None

Credit cards
Visa, MC, AmEx

Features
Date-friendly
Kid-friendly
Outdoor dining
Veg-friendly
Wi-Fi

8.4 Food
6.5 Feel

Dim Sum King

An almost pleasant atmosphere in which to eat made-to-order dim sum

$15
Price

**Chinese
Dim Sum**
Casual restaurant

Bellaire Chinatown
9160 Bellaire Blvd.
(713) 270-6788

Hours
Mon
10:00am–8:00pm
Wed–Fri
10:00am–8:00pm
Sat–Sun
10:00am–9:00pm

Bar
None

Credit cards
Visa, MC

Reservations
Not accepted

Features
Brunch
Kid-friendly

Dim Sum King is neck-and-neck with Hong Kong Dim Sum for best in show. Both places offer dim sum at all hours, and make it to order from your completed checklist. But where HK Dim Sum tends to feel like an unwelcoming human zoo, Dim Sum King (look for the small font beneath the looming "Police" sign) is cozier, and the service, comparatively speaking, is downright motherly. Parking is a real hassle, though; if there's a wait, it will move fast.

The picture guide to the dim sum is not only a good crutch, but an encouragement to branch out with confidence. Keep an open mind, and you'll find that the chicken feet (fung zau) here are tender, with a satisfying little gelatinous crunch; spare ribs (pai gwat) are worth the sticky fingers as you nibble your way around the well-spiced bits. Turnip cake (lo bak go) is good, if a bit flimsy, and sticky rice in lotus leaf (lo mai gai) gets that chewy exterior from steaming in metal, which we rather like (we have oral fixations, sue us). Dan tat (egg custard tarts) are better here than at HK Dim Sum, with doughy sesame-studded shells. Whatever you do, make sure you leave room for these.

Divino

A small, simple trattoria with pretty good food, reasonable prices, and great wines

www.divinohouston.com

6.9	8.0
Food	Feel
$50	8.5
Price	Wine

Italian
Casual restaurant

Montrose
1830 W. Alabama St.
(713) 807-1123

Hours
Mon–Thu
5:30pm–10:00pm
Fri–Sat
5:30pm–10:30pm

Bar
Beer, wine

Credit cards
Visa, MC, AmEx

Reservations
Accepted

Features
Date-friendly
Veg-friendly

Divino was always a fine neighborhood choice, if not much more. That is, unless you were coming for wine from their retail side—there are some outstanding Italian selections at a steal, even if the driving principle seems to be *Spectator* points. Occasional sales bring prices even lower, so it pays to sign up for email alerts. But it's also a romantic dinner place, too; the unassuming storefront belies an intimate, cozy hideaway full of dark woods and photographs of Italian landscapes. The menu isn't particular to one region, although it does claim a number of dishes from Emilia-Romagna, as the chef spent some time cooking there.

Lightly fried calamari has always been a standout, and pastas are competently al dente, and served in huge portions with simple sauces. Fettucine and risotto are fine, but the best work is house-made ravioli (especially goat cheese with pine nuts; the mushroom ravioli are served in a broth choking a bit on truffle oil). Meats are handled more deftly than they once were, like Texas quail that used to come overcooked, but are now grilled to a fine and tender consistency, served with a tart, not-too-sweet cherry reduction.

We'd still bypass the perfunctory, uninspired dessert menu and instead have an actually affordable Amarone and cheese board—a classic end to any Italian meal, just before the digestifs, of course.

Dolce Vita

Authentic, affordable Italian that's still some of the best

www.dolcevitahouston.com

Italian
Pizza
Casual restaurant

Montrose
500 Westheimer Rd.
(713) 520-8222

The Woodlands
1701 Lake Robbins Dr.
(281) 465-4420

Hours
Tue–Fri
5:00pm–10:00pm
Sat
noon–11:00pm
Sun
noon–10:00pm
Hours vary by location

Bar
Beer, wine, liquor

Credit cards
Visa, MC, AmEx

Reservations
Accepted

Features
Date-friendly
Outdoor dining
Veg-friendly

Sometimes the qualities that most attract you to lovers, or restaurants, are the same ones that irritate you. Maybe the service is spotty because they cram in so many tables. Maybe the kitchen is occasionally inconsistent because they're operating on a cost base that allows them to keep nearly every item on the menu under $15. And it's impossible not to forgive this place, with its principled devotion to preparing strictly authentic Italian dishes, serving them in a warm, bustling, effortlessly enjoyable two-story space with a patio.

As with any rocky relationship, drinks help. The wine list is exemplary; it's all Italian, all small-production, and more about terroir than about emulating big California styles. For under $30, you can have an evocative, balanced wine.

So we return again and again, on one visit enduring a limp, blond crust; on another, finding ourselves blessed with a crisp, lightly charred version that's rivaled only by that of Marco Wiles's other Houston restaurant, Da Marco (it's amazing with butternut squash and pancetta). We may be lucky enough to dine upon expertly fried rapini blanketed with snowflakes of grana padano, or we may suffer through leaden gnocchi that used to be pillowy soft. We'll dip crunchy fennel into bagna cauda, that glorious ambrosia of garlic, anchovies, and oil, and relive our best memories of Dolce Vita in the truffled-egg toast. We're done longing for it to change—we are wiser now, and simply accept it for what it is.

Don Café

Some of the best banh mi in town, plus a few rare soup alternatives

7.8 Food **5.0** Feel

$10 Price

Don Café is big and vibrant, and while relatively undecorated, it's comfortable and bright. The counter is normally manned with one of the friendly owning family members. Even if there's a long line—local office workers tend to bring huge to-go-order lists at lunchtime—food will come quickly, and you'll be in and out within 30 minutes.

The Vietnamese classics are all decent: bowls of hot noodle soup (including an alluring sour snail soup that's got the most satisfying texture for the orally fixated), crispy Vietnamese egg rolls, and rice plates with charcoal-grilled pork. But the star of the show is banh mi. It's an absolutely fresh, warm, and tasty creation that's worth triple its $2.50 price. The pièce de résistance is the crusty baguette with its velvety innards. The carrots aren't pickled, though, and the jalapeño's a little ungainly and seeded; but overall, with the cilantro, pâté, mayo, and great cold cuts or grilled meat, it's a happy symphony.

For a place this affordable, you wouldn't expect things to be so consistently terrific, but even the packaged spring rolls sitting on the counter are as moist and fresh as any. The coffee's not made to order; rather it's kept in a pot where it gets tinny. But your cheap, quick sandwich (and sour snail soup) needs? Covered.

Vietnamese
Counter service

Bellaire Chinatown
9300 Bellaire Blvd.
(713) 777-9500

Hours
Daily
8:00am–9:00pm

Bar
None

Credit cards
None

Features
Kid-friendly

Doña Tere

Best tamales in town—better, fresh from
the steamer

www.tamalesdonatere.net

Mexican
Counter service

West Houston
8607 Long Point Rd.
(713) 461-5683

Bellaire Chinatown
8331 Beechnut St.
(713) 270-8501

Southeast Houston
9335 Gulf Fwy.
(713) 947-0153

More locations
and features at
fearlesscritic.com

Hours
Mon–Sat
9:30am–8:30pm
Sun
9:30am–3:00pm

Bar
None

Credit cards
Visa, MC

Some claim Alamo has the best tamales, but we
find them a little dense and underwhelming.
Doña Tere's are the finest we've had in town,
especially when they're just out of the steamer.
They have a creamy texture that melds with the
filling to produce a gooiness close to godliness.
Wait too long, and the effect goes away,
leaving you with, still, one of the best things of
its kind in Houston.

There are about a dozen varieties, including a
few sweet tamales. Versions with green sauce
tend to be hotter than red, and have a creeping
chile flavor that lingers long after they're gone.
A green chile pork tamal is earthy and sweet,
hot and tart; cheese and jalapeño tamales are
kind of a waste of time. We've had quasi-
religious experiences with just-steamed tamales
oaxaqueños with chicken and complex, smoky
red chile sauce running through it like a vein
(oaxaqueños are larger and fluffier, and
steamed in banana leaves).

The dining rooms aren't much to look at;
take-out is the preferred option for most
customers, and tamales sell out fast. Breakfast is
pretty underwhelming, and you can't really
order any until around 10am. To drink, try atole,
a cornstarch-based hot beverage that's
traditionally paired with tamales, flavored with
cinnamon and vanilla, and then your choice of
fruit or chocolate.

Doneraki

Reliable Tex-Mex until the wee hours

7.9	8.0
Food	Feel

$30	6.5
Price	Margs

www.doneraki.com

The name doesn't exactly sound Mexican, but supposedly, it's named after a man called Eraki, who invented tacos al pastor. Putting aside all the coincidences and dubious stories, though, the Tex-Mex menu here, if predictable, is dead-on. That doesn't mean everything tastes ideal—the salsa is just okay, with little kick; queso's pleasant enough but similarly light on chile intrigue. But then grilled quail—which comes à la carte or on a pricey parrillada—scales the heights of char-grilled supremacy, its skin crisped without its juicy meat exposed to heat for a second too long. Beef and sirloin adobada also perform well, their marinades infusing the flavor but not dominating it. Chicken breast can be slightly dry, but you're not here for that, anyway. Various enchiladas perform with consummate skill: the cheese is not congealed, the salsa verde has the right degree of tang, that Tex-Mex chili gravy is rich and guiltily good. Margaritas aren't quite tart enough, but they're not absurdly sweet either, and they pack a good punch (especially at $2 a pop, all day on Monday through Wednesday).

Of the two locations, the one of Gulfgate is the original and most interesting, sporting an enormous, room-sized replica of a Diego Rivera mural. But if you're stuck at work, they'll deliver, so long as you order 10 items or more.

Mexican
Casual restaurant

North Houston
2836 Fulton St.
(713) 224-2509

Westchase
7705 Westheimer Rd.
(713) 975-9815

East Houston
300 Gulfgate Ctr.
(713) 645-6400

Hours
Sun–Thu
8:00am–midnight
Fri–Sat
8:00am–3:00am
Hours vary by location

Bar
Beer, wine, liquor

Credit cards
Visa, MC, AmEx

Reservations
Accepted

Features
Brunch
Kid-friendly
Live music

Dynasty/Willie's BBQ

In two Chinatown supermarkets, hidden worlds of glistening, crispy flesh

Chinese
Take-out

Bellaire Chinatown
9600 Bellaire Blvd.
(713) 995-4088

Bellaire Chinatown
9896 Bellaire Blvd.
(713) 772-7882

Hours
Daily
9:00am–9:30pm
Hours vary by location

Bar
None

Credit cards
Visa, MC, AmEx

Willie Lai is a man with one crazy talent for crisping up animal skins. He runs both the hidden Chinese barbecue joints in the backs of Dynasty Supermarket (where it's called Dynasty Chinese BBQ) and in the newer Golden Foods (where it's Willie's BBQ). Dynasty is one of the oldest Asian grocery stores on Bellaire. The sounds, smells, and yellow hue haven't changed much over the last couple of decades. Prepare to be serenaded by the high-pitched sound of whole flocks of animals being mechanically taken apart in the butcher shop. Push around your rickety cart, and you'll experience the briny spray and smell of fish being cleaned and gutted in the seafood department. Golden Foods is much cleaner and more sparkly…if you like that sort of thing.

In the backs of both, greasy, withering cooks chop up cheap, surpassingly delicious Chinese roast duck, barbecued pork, and crispy-skinned pigs. This is downmarket Cantonese meat at its finest, and anyone nostalgic for Hong Kong's Mong Kok neighborhood will fall in love. For less than $5, you can get a pile of char siu duck or pork with rice and a vegetable to go. The décor's not much beyond carcasses hanging medievally on hooks, and sometimes whole roasted pigs ($120-200, if you want to luau, but your HOA forbids digging pits in the backyard).

East Wall

Authentic and often-rustic Cantonese in a lovely space with a...stirring display

7.6 Food
6.5 Feel

$15 Price

This spruced-up and slightly elegant space is filled with large tables of mostly Chinese families drawn by authentic Cantonese cooking. On weekends, come early or be prepared to wait.

We like salted pork with dried shrimp, a rustic dish served on farms throughout China. Fish is a good bet here, especially deep fried in sweet corn sauce, or fried whole with a sauce that's sweet, sour, and spicy. Roast duck is dry, and hot pots aren't so stellar. Focus instead on salt-and-pepper squid; pork spare ribs, deep fried just right and topped with jalapeños, green onions, and garlic; and "house special chow mein," a basket of fried egg noodles topped with your choice of meat and vegetables and a salty brown sauce.

Of the legitimate Chinese restaurants in Houston, East Wall seems to be more concerned about appealing to Americans; much of its staff speaks English, and menus employ helpful pictures. We'd argue that the only lamentable wall between cultures is the display of plastic-wrapped pieces of dried shark's fin enclosed in a glass case. Perhaps the recently installed LCD display depicting a yellow bouncing smiley face is supposed to make us feel better.

Chinese
Casual restaurant

Bellaire Chinatown
9889 Bellaire Blvd.
(713) 981-8803

Hours
Daily
11:00am–midnight

Bar
Beer, wine

Credit cards
Visa, MC, AmEx

Reservations
Accepted

Features
Kid-friendly

Eatsie Boys

A colorful, busy little trailer of guys living the farm-to-sandwich dream

www.eatsieboys.com

Sandwiches
Food cart

Montrose
1712 Westheimer Rd.
(845) 430-8479

Downtown
901 Bagby St.
(845) 430-8479

Hours
Wed
11:00am–2:00pm
Thu–Sun
11:00am–6:00pm
Check website for
current hours and
location

Bar
None

Credit cards
Visa, MC, AmEx

Features
Outdoor dining

One of Houston's favorite kitchens on wheels, Eatsie Boys hums around the city at lunch, dinner, and late-night, usually between UrbanHarvest farmer's market and Agora Coffeehouse (just look for the trailer that looks kind of like Keith Haring's impression of a salad bowl). They pop up elsewhere now and then; follow them on Twitter (@eatsieboys) to keep up.

Most people first formed their addictions to "Frank the Pretzel" (chicken-poblano sausage with Chardonnay mustard on a pretzel bun from Slow Dough) at that farmer's market. Another market favorite, Grateful Bread (headed by one of the Boys' fathers), makes the sausage and some of the breads used here, like a crunchy baguette that admirably supports the "Sabotage's" roasted, juicy pork with local braised greens and sharp provolone cheese. It also works in "Da Bomb," which, overstuffed with pickled carrots, cilantro, jalapeño, and cucumber, reminds us just enough of a banh mi, but with chicken or tofu. We love "Pork Snuggies," with those doughy steamed buns that are becoming a favorite ingredient of the nation's mobile chefs. They're stuffed with pork belly, green onions, a judicious amount of hoisin, and a terrific house-pickled cucumber. Best of all, almost everything's locally raised and made.

ECK Bakery

The Egg Custard King—accept no substitutes

Houston's best-kept secret is ECK Bakery's Chinese egg custard tart, or dan tat ("dan ta" in Mandarin). They're usually unspectacular on the dessert carts at dim sum, but ECK stands for "Egg Custard King," so if you're going to judge its merits anywhere, let it be here.

Located in an otherwise deserted shopping center not too far from Bellaire, little about this pristine spot says "bakery," except for the display cases. The walls are decorated with T-shirts and useless knick-knacks that you might haphazardly buy on New York's Canal Street, and shelves stock baking items of indeterminate use. Even other baked goods seem like part of the irrelevant background: raisin bread is plump and fluffy, but seems to be missing its crucial raisins; small, mochi-like pastries covered in shredded coconut, called lo mai chi, are quite good (especially mango, when in season). There are tasty Chinese versions of sausage-stuffed kolaches—but these things are mere distractions. At all times of day, tarts are coming out of the oven and being snatched up by crazed customers. And it's no wonder: the crust flakes at the slightest nudge of the tongue, and the filling is rich while not heavy, sweet without being overbearing. For those freaks who hate guilty pleasures (and, okay, cholesterol), they have a yolk-less custard that's almost as good...almost.

Baked goods
Counter service

Bellaire Chinatown
6918 Wilcrest Dr.
(281) 933-6808

Hours
Daily
8:00am–9:00pm

Bar
None

Credit cards
None

Features
Kid-friendly
Veg-friendly

7.2	7.5
Food	Feel
$90	6.5
Price	Drinks

Eddie V's

An expense-account scene spreads across the Southwest

www.eddiev.com

Seafood Steakhouse
Upmarket restaurant

Upper Kirby
2800 Kirby Dr.
(713) 874-1800

Town and Country
12848 Queensbury Ln.
(832) 200-2380

Hours
Sun–Thu
4:30pm–10:00pm
Fri–Sat
4:30pm–11:00pm
Hours vary by location

Bar
Beer, wine, liquor

Credit cards
Visa, MC, AmEx

Reservations
Accepted

Features
Date-friendly
Live music

The Eddie V's group now has 14 branches of its three different restaurants (including Wildfish and Roaring Fork), and while its home office is in Arizona, it seems poised to take over Texas. The atmosphere is dark—overly so—and clubby, with curvy banquettes, live piano, and Jazz Age-style artwork, with a generic newness to it all. The slightly more informal bar area's more comfortable than the tricked-out and often comically fussy dining room, and sitting here with happy-hour-priced appetizers and decent $5 martinis is a guilty pleasure.

The menu, as well as the atmosphere, caters to a certain income bracket—one that perhaps doesn't mind that the $15 lump crab cakes are pretty unremarkable, or that a pound of broiled from-frozen lobster tail costs twice what it would if culled fresh from a Chinese seafood tank. Likewise, Chilean sea bass, steamed and served in a delicious soy and sherry broth, is much cheaper at Japanese and Chinese places serving it just as flaky, buttery, and sweet. Prime steaks are juicy and cooked appropriately to temperature (creamed spinach almondine is a good side), but if you want steak, why not choose the dry-aged version at a similarly pricey and clubby steakhouse?

The wine list's only discernible guiding principle is ripping off people who like wines with "cake" implications. There are simply better seafood, steak, wine, and upscale options in whatever city Eddie V's is in.

El Hidalguense

A vibrant Mexican goat-roasting party every weekend

8.3	8.0
Food	Feel

$35	3.0
Price	Margs

Mexican
Casual restaurant

Spring Branch
6917 Long Point Rd.
(713) 680-1071

Hours
Mon–Fri
7:00am–9:00pm
Sat–Sun
7:00am–midnight

Bar
Beer

Credit cards
Visa, MC, AmEx

Reservations
Not accepted

Features
Brunch
Live music

El Hidalguense feels more legit and neighborly than most Mexican restaurants in town. The food's authentic and the service attentive; you can duck in for take-out meat by the pound, or spend hours getting drunk on the cheap. Free tequila digestifs are always nice (El Hidalguense only has a license to sell beer, so the margaritas are made with faux-liquor mix).

The dressed-down bright room echoes with extended-family Spanish-language crosstalk, and it glows from an open fire roasting the dramatically hanging carcasses of goats, lambs, and cows. On weekends, you'll likely dine to mariachis, and instead of chips and salsa, you're brought complimentary, if dry, chicken flautas and a thick chile sauce. Charro beans, which come out before your mains, have enough pork backbone to eat them like soup. But the main event is the enormously overpriced cabrito asado (which three signs insist is the best in town). The grilled baby goat usually shows up tender and basted by its own juices, but in need of a liberal salting; the meat closest to the rib bones is best. Grilled lamb (borrego) is less impressive and fairly underseasoned. Better is the winning "mixteca" preparation, in which the meat is steamed with a chile-based sauce in a leaf, like cochinita pibil. What a way to treat a lamb! What a way to treat a neighbor!

8.3 Food | 7.5 Feel

$10 Price

El Pupusodromo

A salvadoreño street food to replace your puffy taco obsession

Latin American
Casual restaurant

Hillcroft Area
5902 Renwick Dr.
(713) 661-4334

Southwest Houston
6817 Bissonnet St.
(713) 270-5030

North Houston
13235 Veterans
Memorial Dr.
(281) 587-2800

Hours
Daily
10:00am–9:00pm

Bar
Beer

Credit cards
Visa, MC

Reservations
Not accepted

There are a few tiny El Pupusodromos dotting the cityscape, our favorite of these inhabiting a vintage Taco Bell. In this Salvadoran-flag-blue space, for some reason, we feel the masa's griddled just a little more softly, the flavors just a bit more vivid. The service is certainly warm and friendly wherever you go, although you will benefit from a basic command of Spanish. Each table has its own jar of curtido, the essential pickled cabbage condiment, although this one could stand to be a bit more acidic. Fresh juices like maracuyá (passion fruit) and pineapple contribute a sense of freshness to a soda-and-caffeine society. The natural juices also aid in digestion. Some Central American beers in can aren't a bad choice, either.

Salvadoran tamales are fluffier and lighter than their Mexican cousins, and here, tamales de elote are airy and corn-sweet, served with thick cream that really kicks your taste buds into overdrive. The same can be said for fried plantains with that crema; get it with some refried beans, and you've got a delicious Salvadoran breakfast. Pupusas are the star of the show, though, especially the classic revueltas (stuffed with bean, cheese, and chicharrones). They're not as greasy as other versions, yet they're still lardy-flavorful. Fortunately, there's probably one of these near you.

El Real

As good as any late-late-night Tex-Mex greasy spoon...why, what have you heard?

6.3	8.0
Food	Feel

$35	7.5
Price	Margs

www.elrealtexmex.com

Mexican
Casual restaurant

Montrose
1201 Westheimer Rd.
(713) 524-1201

Hours
Mon–Thu
11:00am–11:00pm
Fri
11:00am–3:00am
Sat
10:00am–3:00am
Sun
10:00am–11:00pm

Bar
Beer, wine, liquor

Credit cards
Visa, MC, AmEx

Reservations
Not accepted

Features
Brunch

One time, we teamed up with this hot-shot chef to start a restaurant that we thought would do justice to Tex-Mex. Never mind the name of the restaurant, or our chef partner. It was another city. You don't know it.

Anyway, despite our combined credentials, we got such sour feedback from everyone. Some said they could get better Tex-Mex from longstanding, humbler places; others said, "If it ain't broke, why'd you go and break it?" Ouch. Looking back, it was a mistake to make our margaritas too sweet, but we eventually limed them up enough; and maybe we did choke the chili con carne with too much cumin. But when you ordered our cheese enchiladas—our pride and joy—with that and sour cream, it totally worked. Yet despite our efforts to use ideally melting yellow cheese, everyone just shrugged.

Fajitas were a pain: sometimes we'd get the marinade just right but overcook the meat, and sometimes they were tender but underflavored. And the puffy tacos! Maybe we shouldn't have used as our paragon of this genre Crazy Pedro's Oil City. The shells would just melt into greasy puddles on the plate! Our chips and salsa were good—especially our secret guajillo salsa (you had to request it), and our refried beans lardy and awesome. Posole was rockin', too. But man, what a tough ride it was.

We hear another restaurant-critic-and-chef team did something similar here in Houston. Anyone know how that turned out?

6.0 5.5
Food Feel

$10
Price

El Rey Taquería

It's certainly the king of Cuban fast food joints

www.elreytaqueria.com

Latin American
Mexican
Counter service

Washington
910 Shepherd Dr.
(713) 802-9145

Downtown
233 Main St.
(713) 225-1895

North Houston
3330 Ella Blvd.
(713) 263-0659

Spring Branch
9742 Katy Fwy.
(832) 358-8100

Hours
Mon–Wed
7:00am–10:00pm
Thu–Sat
7:00am–3:00am
Sun
8:00am–10:00pm
Hours vary by location

Bar
None

Credit cards
Visa, MC, AmEx

Features
Brunch

This Cuban/Mexican fast food restaurant proves that you can actually get a good meal from a drive-thru. True, there are better Cuban places, better taquerías, and better rotisserie chicken. But for doing all at once, El Rey is a totally sound choice.

Stale, industrial-tasting corn and flour tortillas diminish the tacos, but their fillings are good, especially tempura shrimp with concentrated, pungent cilantro sauce. We also love a "Cuban Taco" with pork, sweet fried plantains, and smoky black beans. Cuban sandwich bread is too flimsy to stand up to the roasted pork, Swiss cheese, and pickles; it's better suited to the first-rate grilled fish torta, with ideal mayo and shredded-cabbage crunch. Ropa vieja ("old clothes"), the stewed and shredded beef standard of Cuban cuisine, is authentically stringy and tangy, although it needs more garlic. Another good choice is any variation of rotisserie chicken; chicken tortilla soup is some of the best around, with mild fat-slicked broth. A plate of tender, lemony-garlicky pork chunks is also excellent. Espresso-based coffee drinks are simple and strong.

The locations are small and can get cramped; only the one downtown—with its drink fountain, multiple registers, and pager system—seems up to the task of serving large crowds. Elsewhere, during lunch rushes, you might wait forever; at least you can do it in your car.

El Tiempo Cantina

8.5	9.0
Food	Feel

Pricey parrillas that are delicious and
plentiful precursors to the action next door

$60	8.0
Price	Margs

www.eltiempocantina.com

The first two tests of Tex-Mex are margaritas
and queso, and El Tiempo is one for two. The
former are excellent, even the cheaper versions,
although you should pass on the Mexican
martinis, which are missing the trademark three-
refill shaker. But queso is a big letdown,
basically just undersalted melted cheese with
practically no chile flavor, served with crumbly
baked flour tortillas.

Beyond that, the menu is completely
overwhelming. Pages upon pages of the same
meats arranged in different forms—tacos,
enchiladas, flautas, fajitas, parrilladas—leave
your head (and wallet) spinning. Although
we've gotten surprising pleasure from spinach
enchiladas, our advice is to stick to the fajitas
and parrilladas. Most of what's on the parrillada
is good: deeply flavored beef and sausage; juicy,
smoky pork tenderloin cubes; and tender quail.
Parrilladas for one actually feed four—as they
should, given that some cost up to $60.
Everything on the menu, in fact, is too
expensive, even given the gargantuan portions.
The deluxe filet parrillada for four (so, 16)
actually costs over $200. The lobster, though, is
rubbery, and shrimp wrapped in bacon are
disappointingly mealy. Stick to the terrific meats
and fowl.

At the Richmond location, a copy of your
receipt gains you free admission to next-door's
divey Diamond Cabaret, in case you didn't blow
enough money already.

Mexican
Casual restaurant

Greenway Plaza
3130 Richmond Ave.
(713) 807-1600

Montrose
1308 Montrose Blvd.
(713) 807-8996

Washington
5602 Washington Ave.
(713) 681-3645

Hours
Mon–Tue
11:00am–9:00pm
Wed–Thu
11:00am–10:00pm
Fri
11:00am–11:00pm
Sat
9:30am–11:00pm
Sun
9:30am–9:00pm
Hours vary by location

Bar
Beer, wine, liquor

Credit cards
Visa, MC, AmEx

Reservations
Accepted

Features
Brunch
Good cocktails
Outdoor dining

El Último

Beware the tripe path, forever will it dominate your destiny; consume you it will

Mexican
Food cart

Spring Branch
7403 Long Point Rd.
No phone

Hours
Mon–Fri
8:00am–10:00pm
Sat
8:00am–midnight
Check website for current hours and location

Bar
None

Credit cards
None

Features
Outdoor dining

You may find tripe off-putting, all fetid and spongy, but El Último's superlative rendering is such that you may actually change your mind. Who would have thought that this shiny taco truck (which, as of press time, had not a single health-code violation at its last inspection— something not even the top kitchens in town can boast) in front of a car wash would make tripe the way it ought to be—crunchy on the outside with a soft, chewy interior (a little like pork rinds)? While you're here, why not try the slow-cooked head meat, served shredded in its own broth with a salty queso fresco crumbled on top? Add a roasted jalapeño and you'll stop making that but-it's-head face. Now there's no going back—you've sullied yourself this much— go ahead and have tacos de orejas, with crisp and quite chewy sliced pig's ears.

Flour tortillas are handmade and green salsa is nuclear hot, so be careful. And while barbacoa is perfectly lovely, all unctuous and rich, you kind of have to admit these things fall a little flat compared to that tripe taco. You're kind of still thinking about it—it lingers in your memory like a cruel lover. This is how tripe fans are made.

Empire Café

A much-loved neighborhood icon best for its cake and company

3.5 Food | **8.0** Feel

$15 Price

www.empirecafe.com

A fool and his money are easily separated, but when they are separated over and over again, one has to tip a hat to somebody. In this case, to Empire Café and its innocent snare of plentiful shaded outdoor seating, a cozy Old-World interior combined with hip and moody music, familiar and friendly service, and the self-perpetuating crowd of pretty and lively people. There's a constant queue at the register, which is most frustrating if all you want is coffee (over-extracted and bitter, like a certain mermaid's brew). And, like its genre-mate Brasil, Empire has finally caved and now offers free Wi-Fi.

But keep in mind that food here is an afterthought. You'd have to assemble a crack squad of Jersey mafia food consultants to come up with a more pedestrian Italian-American menu than this, from minestrone to eggplant parmigiana. Bland chicken breast inhabits every corner of the menu. Pastas come dissociated from their sauces. There are also some ill-fated vegetarian attempts, like a $10 main of nothing but grilled vegetables and potatoes, or a doomed Portobello-and-goat-cheese panino. Even breakfast is a buzzkill: "Italian French toast" is like eating candied bread, and scrambles are routinely overdone. Do have a huge piece of cake—especially coconut and lemon. On Mondays, they're half price, and you shouldn't have a hard time convincing someone to come share it.

Baked goods
Italian
Counter service

Montrose
1732 Westheimer Rd.
(713) 528-5282

Hours
Sun–Thu
7:30am–10:00pm
Fri–Sat
7:30am–11:00pm

Bar
Beer, wine, liquor

Credit cards
Visa, MC, AmEx

Features
Brunch
Date-friendly
Outdoor dining
Veg-friendly
Wi-Fi

6.8 Food | 7.5 Feel

$15 Price

Fadi's Mediterranean

A trough-like buffet for the eyes, but a gourmet feast on the palate

www.fadiscuisine.com

Middle Eastern Greek
Counter service

Southwest Houston
4738 Beechnut St.
(713) 666-4644

Southwest Houston
8383 Westheimer Rd.
(713) 532-0666

West Houston
12360 Westheimer Rd.
(281) 556-8390

Hours
Sun–Thu
11:00am–9:00pm
Fri–Sat
11:00am–10:00pm

Bar
BYO

Credit cards
Visa, MC, AmEx

Features
Outdoor dining
Veg-friendly

Fadi's must be responsible for most Houstinites' introduction to Middle Eastern food, considering the law of averages (there are three around town). True, they each appear to have been decorated from a restaurant catalog's section on "Middle Eastern:" generic and vaguely regional art hangs on warmly painted walls, and interesting, but wholly inauthentic lighting fixtures dangle from the ceiling. Yet it feels familial, despite the cafeteria-style tray service.

As ever, start with an acidic, refreshing cold salad. Tabbouleh and dolmade have a great balance, but fattoush needs a heavy salting. While chicken tends to be dry and bland, kebabs are always fresh and incredibly well seasoned. Whenever succulent braised lamb shank's on the buffet, snatch it up fast. Avoid fish, whose flavors are muted by accoutrements like subpar tomatoes. Braised vegetables in a curry sauce are a great vegetarian option, as is smoky baba ghanoush. The lunch crowd can pack it in, so beware on weekdays. Dinner and weekends are a better option; they're just crowded enough to ensure that food doesn't sit on the buffet table too long.

The fresh juices offered at the end of the buffet are a nice touch. The baklava's a bit too sweet, but date cookies are an ideal marriage between pastry and fruit. Snag an extra one for the ride home—or better yet, an extra shank.

Feast

Go whole hog, head to tail

9.2	9.0
Food	Feel

$50	8.5
Price	Beer

sites.google.com/site/feasthouston

We love Feast with all our hearts—and guts, kidneys, and livers. This fearless English kitchen celebrates nose-to-tail eating of locally and naturally raised animals, a concept so deliciously responsible that it makes even staunch vegetarians light up in appreciation (before running for their lives). So despite the occasional inconsistencies of execution, the valet-only driveway, and having to drink a respectable, complex wine out of thick, minerally tumblers that destroy its nuances, we still give Feast three resounding cheers.

Timid diners have plenty to chew on, like braised pork finished simply with spinach and a crusty gratin of potatoes; white bean soup with tomatoes and kale; or garlicky, briny plump shrimp. But its best work is inspired by the Michelin-starred St. John in London (where one of the chef/owners of Feast worked), showcasing the guttural, primal delights that can only come from the usually discarded body bits: stuffed duck neck with lovely crunchy and charred bits; inky black pudding with a hint of mint; pan-fried beef tongue with onion gravy; lamb testicles fried to a crisp shell and gently firm, mushroomy center. It all begins with spectacular bread and softened butter, and is lovely with several of the Old World, affordable wines here. But this cuisine (and the simple décor of dark wooden beams and hearth fire) begs for something pubbier; something from the ample selection of English stouts and ales. Go on, drink your courage and be well-rewarded.

British
Casual restaurant

Midtown
219 Westheimer Rd.
(713) 529-7788

Hours
Mon–Thu
5:00pm–10:00pm
Fri–Sat
11:00am–2:30pm
5:00pm–10:00pm
Sun
5:00pm–9:00pm

Bar
Beer, wine, liquor

Credit cards
Visa, MC, AmEx

Reservations
Accepted

Features
Date-friendly
Good beers
Outdoor dining

Finger Licking Bukateria

One of Texas's only Nigerian restaurants—
and possible night clubs

Nigerian
Casual restaurant

West Houston
9811 Bissonnet St.
(713) 270-7070

Hours
Mon–Thu
11:00am–10:00pm
Fri–Sat
11:00am–11:00pm
Sun
11:00am–9:00pm

Bar
Beer, wine

Credit cards
Visa, MC, AmEx

Reservations
Not accepted

Finger Licking Bukateria ("bukateria" translates roughly to "informal restaurant") is flanked by Afghan and Middle Eastern eateries, and it utterly transports you to another country. If you're white, you'll probably get stares for being the only one. Everything is foreign; customs are different, the menu is totally disorienting. In other words, we love it.

But overly protective staff will inevitably push you towards boring chicken with rice, assuring you that you won't like the authentic meats on the menu. We caved once and had a plate of braised greens and sweet potatoes; it was nice enough, but not really worth its asking price. Fight the good fight! Getting goat will be an uphill battle, but it's worth it. We also like eggy egusi (a seed) and spinach, with undertones of dried shrimp. Tripe is soft and tender, and springy cubes of cow's knee are worth the fight, too. All of it comes with fufu, a gnocchi-ish starch made from white yam flour pounded into a tight ball, served in a plastic bag. This one, however, can be *too* starchy. Oxtails are overbraised, and therefore leeched of their beefy flavor.

Judging by the disco ball, dance floor, and large televisions showing African music videos, we suspect that on weekends after dinner the place turns into a Nigerian expat rager—if you *really* want to feel foreign, try coming then.

Five Guys

Meat haiku

Food Feel

$10
Price

www.fiveguys.com

**Burgers
American**
Counter service

To commune with flesh.
To feel it fall like pleasure
from your lips. Five Guys

strips your hunger raw.
Hedonistic animal
possessed. Get some now.

Five Guys gets you in
your gut. Feeds your empty with
hope and calories.

The whole room is bare.
Ordering is like high school.
It doesn't matter.

Get yours like we get
ours: Two plump patties, cheese, stuffed
between seeded buns.

The secret is the
better bread. Buttery sweet.
Changing everything.

Like a meat grilled cheese
Candies drip. And forbidden flesh
(bacon) taut and crisp.

You can never get
enough. You will never get
enough. Die happy.

(Guest review by Lil' G)

Washington
3939 Washington Ave.
(713) 426-5558

Galleria
1715 Post Oak Blvd.
(713) 960-1525

Medical Center
8505 S. Main St.
(713) 662-2075

More locations
and features at
fearlesscritic.com

Hours
Daily
11:00am–10:00pm

Bar
None

Credit cards
Visa, MC

Features
Kid-friendly

5.1	8.0
Food	Feel

$25	8.0
Price	Beer

The Flying Saucer

A huge, comprehensive beer selection with plenty of cheesy opportunities

www.beerknurd.com

American
Bar

Downtown
705 Main St.
(713) 228-7468

Hours
Mon–Wed
11:00am–1:00am

Thu–Fri
11:00am–2:00am

Sat
noon–2:00am

Sun
noon–midnight

Bar
Beer, wine, liquor

Credit cards
Visa, MC, AmEx

Features
Good beers
Live music
Outdoor dining
Wi-Fi

While there's something unbeatable about hanging out at a locally owned and operated pub, and while we're fortunate enough to have a few of those, we cannot deny the extensive selection at the Flying Saucer chain. It's thorough and comprehensive, where more local programs have narrowed down to focus mainly on micro-microbrews and a handful of Abbeys and Trappists. The wider range here will include lots of mass-produced beer as well, and so the crowd's more of a heterogeneous mix of highbrow and lowbrow. Daily specials are as agreeable as the fratty vibe, and trivia nights are emceed by a member of the mini-skirted waitstaff.

The large space has a nook and cranny for every person: comfortable couches, hard wooden tables, booths, and a festively lit patio. And while the attire of the beer goddesses (their official designation—Hooters doesn't edify its sex-symbol staff nearly as well) may exude vapidity, each possesses an impressive knowledge of beer.

The food's as predictably pub-grubbish as any, but it still beats the paltry choices at those more focused pubs. Serviceable pizzas are served by the slice; chili-cheese fries are a total reptilian-brain treat; and a gloppy burger with whiskey cheddar is never a bad thing. And a compulsory education in beer and cheese pairing is also available. That's not so lowbrow, after all.

Frank's Chop House

A good ol' American meal in a nice restaurant that's not *too* nice

6.8	8.0
Food	Feel

$70	6.5
Price	Wine

www.frankschophouse.com

This is the perfect place to take your grandpa for dinner. He won't be overstimulated by the beige stucco building, nor will his blood pressure rise at the underwhelming, knee-jerk wine list (though he may have a minor coronary over the mark-ups). He'll certainly appreciate the old-timey class of Frank #1 (there are two Franks—Crapitto and Butera) manning the front of house, chatting up guests as they dine at unadorned-yet-polished tables in a room warm with medium-brown woods. They've taken measures to make the place nice enough to warrant the price tag, but not stuffy.

Your grandfather will also appreciate Frank #2's expertly prepared, old-fashioned comfort food. Fried chicken is not at all greasy, with a crunchy, flavorful crust. Chicken-fried steak is tender, with a crisp outside that holds up to the creamy, peppery gravy; and the crust stays on, bite after bite. As for steaks, this one is just—as chop houses go—eh. Ribeye is thinly cut and saucy, with virtually no char. But the double-bone pork chop rocks—it's 16 ounces of correctly cooked pig. At the end of the meal, grandpa will declare it "very good," and you might sort of agree. It's just a safe, good meal that won't knock anyone dead.

Steakhouse
American
Upmarket restaurant

River Oaks
3736 Westheimer Rd.
(713) 572-8600

Hours
Mon–Fri
11:00am–10:00pm
Sat
5:00pm–11:00pm
Sun
5:00pm–9:00pm

Bar
Beer, wine, liquor

Credit cards
Visa, MC, AmEx

Reservations
Accepted

Features
Date-friendly

7.6	6.0
Food	Feel

$40	6.0
Price	Wine

Fratelli's

Navigate around the American touches for some authentic tastes of Emilia-Romagna

www.fratellishouston.com

Italian
Casual restaurant

Spring Branch
1330 Wirt Rd.
(713) 263-0022

Spring Branch
10989 NW Fwy.
(713) 957-1150

Hours
Mon–Thu
11:00am–2:30pm
5:00pm–9:30pm
Fri
11:00am–2:30pm
5:00pm–10:00pm
Sat
5:00pm–10:00pm

Bar
Beer, wine, liquor

Credit cards
Visa, MC, AmEx

Reservations
Accepted

Features
Date-friendly
Outdoor dining

These two pretty authentic Italian restaurants are in the oddest places: one's in a decaying strip mall just outside the Loop on 290, and the other's in a tonier strip mall near Hilshire Village. The atmosphere at the original Fratelli's is so sweetly downmarket-trying-for-upmarket that it can look cheap and depressing, especially in daylight. Butter-yellow walls are scattered with tacky prints, there's a weird island of houseplants in the center of the room, and the small, older crowd is quite subdued. But then, some of the city's worst food is served in high-dollar, high-concept restaurants.

Fratelli's makes a stab at concentrating on Emilia-Romagna, arguably the finest region for Italian food—and it often finds success. Saltimbocca alla romana, made properly with veal sautéed and rolled with prosciutto in a Marsala-butter sauce, explodes in the mouth with sage. Spinach gnocchi are large, ill-shaped balls; much more rustic—and texturally enjoyable—than the prissy pillows you find at higher-end restaurants. Cracker-thin pizzas extend the menu down to Naples, and are strong, particularly the "Neptune" loaded with anchovies, squid, shrimp, and basil. There are some pandering Americana influences, like adding disjointed, meaningless grilled shrimp or chicken to a dish for an upcharge; fettuccine Alfredo and carbonara are both made with cream, instead of relying on the melting together of cheese and butter over hot noodles. The wine list, too, is most serviceable without the Americana influences of its own.

Frenchy's Chicken

Whether in a divey branch or a nice one, this is one gorgeous, sassy bird

8.5	6.0
Food	Feel

$10
Price

www.frenchyschicken.com

Most of the time, Frenchy's serves up some of the best fried chicken we've ever had. The franchise has multiple locations around Houston, but the original one by the University of Houston on Scott Street is the best of them all (there's also one in the HEB down the street). Don't be scared away by this shack of a restaurant that looks like it could crumble at any minute; just place your order at the window, and hope the ladies are in a good mood that day. They're nice to you if you're nice to them.

The waits are sometimes long, but they pay off. Also, words to the wise: credit cards are only accepted for purchases of over $5. After you've successfully ordered and gotten your food, get ready for the best part: the crispy, pleasantly spicy batter is the kind of thing that dreams are made of, with a nice, salty kick from Cajun seasoning. Sides range from buttery biscuits to just-average french fries, which hardly do justice to the joint's name. Opt instead for collards with bacon or dirty rice.

The Medical Center branch is much tonier, with jazzy lighting and art. At that one you can even order (gross) frozen cocktails, but this chicken goes down best with a frosty beer.

Southern
Counter service

Medical Center
8110 Kirby Dr.
(713) 592-9115

Downtown
3919 Scott St.
(713) 748-2233

East Houston
6102 Scott St.
(713) 741-2700

More locations
and features at
fearlesscritic.com

Hours
Sun–Thu
10:30am–1:00am
Fri–Sat
10:30am–3:00am
Hours vary by location

Bar
None

Credit cards
Visa, MC, AmEx

Features
Kid-friendly
Outdoor dining

FuFu Café

It's worth the wait for good soup dumplings; seems that everyone else agrees

Chinese
Casual restaurant

Bellaire Chinatown
9889 Bellaire Blvd.
(713) 981-8818

Hours
Daily
10:00am–2:00am

Bar
Beer, wine

Credit cards
Visa, MC

Reservations
Not accepted

Features
Veg-friendly

Pint-sized FuFu Café wins admirers where perhaps its fussier, pricier restaurant does not, mostly because of its adept soup dumplings (the skins of which actually stay intact but aren't too gummy) and terrific congee. Sure, the service is often overwhelmed and slow, and there isn't much to look at while you're waiting to be acknowledged, but to be fair, the management probably never imagined it would come to be considered Houston's leading provider of xiao long bao (which the menu calls, confusingly, "steamed pork buns").

Once you finally do get your food, FuFu is easy to like. It's equally well suited to a simple lunch or a late-late-night alcohol-sopper. Ma po tofu is fiery and flavorful, and full of mouth-trippy Szechuan peppercorns. Noodle soups are also reliable: spicy beef noodle soup is bracing and redolent of a broth long simmered with bones and fat, served with generous helpings of pickled mustard greens and bok choy. Mushroom soup is not quite so complex in flavor, but it *is* mushroomy. Pan-fried pork dumplings are just right, salted liberally and with a crusty, seared underbelly. When in season, razor clams are delicious. Skip most of the lunch specials, as they're normally run-of-the-mill dishes that are only there for the looks. And no matter how busy it is, don't run for shelter to FuFu Restaurant.

Fung's Kitchen

As divided as we are about this old grande dame, we can't deny she's unique

7.0 Food | **7.5** Feel

$45 Price

www.fungskitchen.com

It's true that the more longstanding and generally beloved an institution, the more divided people are over how much it deserves its accolades (see anyone famous for an example of this). Depending upon whom you ask, Fung's has one of the top five dim sum carts in town; or it's completely overrated. Or the live seafood is the only thing to order; or the restaurant simply serves the best Chinese in town, period.

What's inarguable is that the décor—the glossy marble tiles and gleaming tanks—defies most stereotypes about dirtiness and dinginess. Don't get us wrong, it's still wonderfully tacky: the huge running waterfall, self-important awnings, and over-the-top regal interior seem more suited to a state banquet than a relaxing dinner. (Not so for the neglectful and sometimes rude service.)

Fittingly, sometimes tradition gives way to impressive techniques, things like lotus-leaf-wrapped kudzu starch and red beans. And presentation is not an afterthought: think warming bitter-melon-and-pork soup in a hollowed-out gourd with Chinese characters carved into its side. Tanks are full of wonderful, fresh Maine lobster and king crab, and their flavors are showcased, not muddied, with sauces.

The rough spots can be annoying, given the high price: oversteamed fish and whatnot. And we don't need to tell you, but don't order the gloppy, uniform Americanized stuff here. At least we all agree there.

Chinese
Seafood
Dim Sum
Upmarket restaurant

Bellaire Chinatown
7320 Southwest Fwy.
(713) 779-2288

Hours
Sun–Thu
11:00am–10:00pm
Fri–Sat
11:00am–11:00pm

Bar
Beer, wine

Credit cards
Visa, MC, AmEx

Reservations
Accepted

Features
Brunch
Date-friendly
Veg-friendly

Garson

Persian stews and lively flavors that are even better with a side of belly dancing

www.garsonhouston.com

Middle Eastern
Casual restaurant

Hillcroft Area
2926 Hillcroft St.
(713) 781-0400

Hours
Sun–Thu
11:00am–10:00pm
Fri–Sat
11:00am–11:00pm

Bar
Beer, wine, liquor, BYO

Credit cards
Visa, MC, AmEx

Reservations
Accepted

Features
Date-friendly
Live music
Outdoor dining

You can't miss Garson; there's a huge sign out front with the name of the place in big caps—and plenty of parking, for a change. The atmosphere, though white-tableclothed, is inviting and comfortable with a waitstaff that's eager to help you find something exciting for your palate, which shouldn't be a problem here. Flatbread with feta, basil, and radishes start your meal, which should definitely include a stew of some sort. These are treasure troves of meat, lentils, greens, and kidney beans, along with a few more unexpected treats that we'll leave you to discover for yourself. Braised lamb shank is tender, with a pleasant gaminess accented by cinnamon and coriander; don't forget to dig out the bone marrow—it's the best part. Pan-fried eggplant atop one stew is among the most stirring flavors in town. As for non-stewed meats, ground beef kebabs fare better than chicken, which can be dry. We also like the various versions of juicy ribeye with vegetables.

The succinct wine list is perfunctory and not terribly exciting; a modest $8-10 corkage fee invites some experimentation—this is a cuisine that makes magic with a wide range of wines. Come on a weekend night for some belly shakin'.

Gatlin's Barbecue

8.8 Food

6.0 Feel

$15 Price

Don't let the squeaky clean looks fool you—
this here's some dirty, smoky goodness

www.gatlinsbbq.com

Barbecue
Counter service

Heights
1221 1/2 W. 19th St.
(713) 869-4227

Hours
Tue–Sat
11:00am–7:00pm

Bar
None

Credit cards
Visa, MC, AmEx

Features
Kid-friendly
Outdoor dining

You needn't be Texan to be highly suspicious as you pull up to Gatlin's brand new, bland little taupe house with white trim and a shaded patio. Nothing about the look of the place says "serious barbecue;" not its deep-red curtains, nor its overproduced signage (although the Styrofoam containers are, we hate to say, legit). But the only thing that matters, where Texas barbecue is concerned, is the brisket—and this one tears down the house. Especially from the fattier ends, it falls apart in smoky chunks with peppery, salty charred bark; the fat's rendered so well into the meat that even leaner cuts are flavorful. No sauce is required (but it's of the thin and spicy variety, if you want it). So, Texas test #1: passed. Test #2 is ribs, which are wonderful, slipping easily from their bones with trace smokiness and a great rub. Ask Henry Gatlin if there are baby backs that day; for that matter, whatever he suggests, get it. Now, it's rare that anyone nails all three, but Test #3, the sausage, has just the right snap to the casing and lots of squirty action. After that, it's all gravy: sides like beans and potato salad are average, but dirty rice is spectacular; cobbler's inconsistent, but when it's good, it's maybe the best in town.

Prepare to sit outside, as the inside's only got a couple of small tables. But who wants to eat 'cue around curtains, anyway?

8.8 Food
5.0 Feel
$10 Price

Gerardo's Drive-In

And should you need a decorative cow skull, this is your place

Mexican
Counter service

North Houston
609 Patton St.
(713) 699-0820

Hours
Daily
6:00am–6:00pm

Bar
Beer

Credit cards
Visa, MC, AmEx

Features
Kid-friendly

It's known throughout the world's kitchens that nothing beats a face—the whole head, really. From fromage de tête to veal cheeks to barbacoa, head meat not only fed poor country folk for centuries, but continues to inspire chefs and gourmands ever in search of soul. In the back of this Mexican convenience store (with no discernable drive-thru anywhere), on Fridays through Sundays, giant pots rattle with the steaming of whole cow and lamb heads in chile-rich broth. Lines form not long after opening, and the friendly staff behind the counter will load you up with all the cilantro, onions, and tortillas you need to make delicious tacos from a heaping pile of barbacoa. Beef and lamb (borrego) are both tender and unctuous, but the lamb has a richer, slightly gamey flavor that is truly awe-inspiring. The three homemade salsas are all commendable, but bright, hot salsa verde is the stand-out.

Other items are all cheap and good: fajitas, enchiladas, flautas, mole, and more. Carnitas on the bone are great if still warm, but can dry out. (This is a phrase worth learning: Fueron cocinado recientemente [las carnitas]?) For the most part this is a take-out operation, but there are a few tables where you can sit and enjoy your excellent food in the company of its native, head-loving peoples.

Giacomo's Cibo y Vino

An outstanding Italian cafeteria that
encourages wine with lunch

8.3	8.0
Food	Feel
$20	8.5
Price	Wine

www.giacomosciboevino.com

It's hard for people Stateside to get used to the
idea that casual and excellent aren't mutually
exclusive (especially in this tony neighborhood),
but Giacomo's Cibo y Vino gives a crash course
in it. You'll move along a cafeteria line and
order from a counter (until 5pm, at which point
table service commences), and choose from
either prepared items like minestrone (delicious
and complex, with clean vegetal flavors), quick
made-to-order stuff (like terrific agnolotti
stuffed with Swiss chard, ricotta, and goat
cheese in sage butter), and dishes that require
slightly longer (fall-off-the-bone tender,
marinated chicken with incredible natural
flavor). Pappardelle al telefono is served not
with lobster and pink sauce as it so often is in
1980s-style Italian places, but with the flat
noodles dressed simply in olive oil, garlic, basil,
cherry tomatoes, and fresh mozzarella. The
result is a lighter post-prandial feeling—like how
you feel even after a large meal in Italy.

The squeaky clean and well-lit space is also
très European, with bare walls and tables, bright
red barstools, and a chalkboard of Italian wines.
There are non-Italian wines up there, too, and
these are well chosen, but you're in Rome (or
Venice or Lombardy), so do as Romans and
order Pieropan Soave or Statti Gaglioppo. The
prices are great and many bottles are offered as
3-oz., 6-oz., and 9-oz. carafe pours.

Italian
Counter service

Upper Kirby
3215 Westheimer Rd.
(713) 522-1934

Hours
Tue–Sat
11:00am–10:00pm
Sun
4:00pm–9:00pm

Bar
Wine

Credit cards
Visa, MC, AmEx

Features
Outdoor dining
Veg-friendly
Wi-Fi

9.0
Feel

$15
Price

9.5
Beer

The Ginger Man

Food, schmood—you're just here for the pubbish digs and 100 beers

www.gingermanpub.com

American
Bar

Rice Area
5607 Morningside Dr.
(713) 526-2770

Hours
Mon–Fri
2:00pm–2:00am
Sat–Sun
1:00pm–2:00am

Bar
Beer, wine

Credit cards
Visa, MC, AmEx

Features
Date-friendly
Good beers
Outdoor dining
Wi-Fi

The Ginger Man is just about the best beer bar in whatever city it inhabits. The locations are always cozy, handsome, and staffed by brilliant beertenders. Its biggest attraction is certainly the veritable universe of beer flowing from scores of taps at the smooth and gorgeous dark wood bar. Add the bottled selection, and you're up to around 100 brews available at any given time, chosen far more artfully than the similarly sized list at the competing Flying Saucer. Germans, Belgians, Czechs, Americans—if a nation makes a noteworthy beer, it's probably here. You might be able to work your way through the list, but the menu evolves somewhat seasonally. Be sure to ask what's new, or follow their Tweets for limited-edition tapping.

Think cocktails are only for liquors? Not so—there's a healthy list of beer blends that changes seasonally (just don't ask for the Dr. Pepper—it's apparently been overdone and makes the staff understandably cranky). Ask instead what the bartender's making. They won't steer you wrong. Think of the food as simply a means to keep drinking beer. The spinach-artichoke dip is fine, but we'd suggest the "Beer Companion," a nice-sized plate offering mediocre cheese, grapes, olives, salami, and bread. Or if you prefer, just order an oatmeal stout.

Goode Co. Taquería

A Goode-themed venture whose mesquite grill speaks louder than neon signs

8.0	6.0
Food	Feel

$25	7.5
Price	Margs

www.goodecompany.com

Goode Co. is as endemic to Houston as the Pappas empire, and its taquería deserves serious praise for keeping the menu to such a manageable number of options. The absolute best order here is anything mesquite-grilled: deliciously marinated, tender, but undersalted fajitas; chicken breast, dry and bland compared to other meats, but still wood-kissed; ribeye, pork chops, and even quail—a rare delicacy in the rest of the world but a mainstay 'round these parts.

Cheese enchiladas are great and gooey, but well-seasoned queso gets thick-skinned after only about fifteen seconds of neglect. Burgers take on the headiness of mesquite; at the toppings bar, you can pile on jalapeños, pico de gallo, and a delicious, dark roasted-tomato salsa, in addition to the standard lettuce, tomato, mayonnaise, and so on. It all makes for a burger well above average.

There's a terrific, full breakfast served on weekends, including a spectacular eggs with quail or venison sausage, but it shuts down at 12:30pm, excluding the party crowd for whom it might otherwise hold vast hangover-cure appeal. Frozen margaritas are strong and balanced, although the plastic-cup presentation takes away from the effect. No romantic cantina, this; the characteristic Goode Co. theming (neon signs and contrived hand-painted menus) gets lost in the cavernous, airy space—but still, it's a space filled with delicious mesquite-grill scents.

Mexican
Burgers
Counter service

Rice Area
4902 Kirby Dr.
(713) 520-9153

Hours
Mon–Thu
11:00am–10:00pm

Fri
10:30am–10:00pm

Sat–Sun
7:30am–10:00pm

Bar
Beer, wine

Credit cards
Visa, MC, AmEx

Features
Brunch
Kid-friendly
Outdoor dining

Goode Co. Texas Bar-B-Q

Good smoked duck and pecan pie, but this hyped chain's not as good as it thinks it is

www.goodecompany.com

Barbecue
Counter service

Rice Area
5109 Kirby Dr.
(713) 522-2530

Spring Branch
8911 Katy Fwy.
(713) 464-1901

Northwest Houston
20102 Northwest Fwy.
(832) 678-3562

Hours
Daily
11:00am–10:00pm

Bar
Beer, wine

Credit cards
Visa, MC, AmEx

Features
Kid-friendly
Outdoor dining

The barbecue entry from Houston's own Goode Co. is full of boasts, from the self-congratulatory wall paraphernalia to the overuse of the Copperplate Gothic font to the larger-than-life banner of long-bearded Jim Goode, "still at the reins" since 1977.

Perhaps unsurprisingly, it doesn't really live up to the hype. The best options are the moist smoked duck (if it's available) and jalapeño pork sausage, which is juicy and full flavored, if not the least bit spicy. But beef brisket—the pride of Texas barbecue—lacks flavor, even when ordered fatty. Nothing's particularly smoky, and the sauce tastes more like a jarred pasta sauce than an acidic balance for the meat. It's amazing that so many sides in one buffet could be undersalted, from overly eggy but okay potato salad to liquidy pinto beans to dry jambalaya to boring cole slaw. But pecan pie fans, rejoice: this one's better than most.

Don't expect basic politeness, or at least a willingness to tell you what is and is not available. We could dismiss this as quirky charm at a world-class destination joint, or at a dirt-cheap hole-in-the-wall, but not at a just-okay place whose marketing concessions include a line of (those same bland) barbecue sauces and a glossy catalog.

Gorditas Aguascalientes

8.9 Food
7.0 Feel

An ultra-traditional Mexican restaurant with a motherly touch

$10 Price

At lunch, large crowds descend on Gorditas Aguascalientes' budget-priced menu, and on weekends, entire families pack the dining room. Some days the entire restaurant will be consumed by a soccer match, while on others, you may come across an accordion-wielding mariachi and an albino singer who also plays washboard, a rare and entertaining sight. Once in a while you'll see the family that runs the restaurant assemble in the dining room as they take care of business, sometimes peeling a huge mound of garlic by hand. After midnight, you're likely to find the parking full of police cruisers, as the boys in blue meet regularly here to get their nightly fill of homemade Mexican food.

Order your meal to go and linger by the front door, so you can watch them prepare your meal, rolling out flour tortillas by hand, and cutting off slabs of masa and turning them into delicious huaraches, sopes, and gorditas (less than $2 a pop). Grilled quail is wonderfully tender and pink, served with onions and tortillas. Pitch-perfect Mexican breakfast plates are served any time of day and include some of the best chilaquiles in town.

Also, the kitchen's open late and serves great pozole and menudo, making it the next best thing to a 24-hour pharmacy.

Mexican
Casual restaurant

Bellaire Chinatown
6102 Bissonnet St.
(713) 541-4560

Hours
Daily
7:00am–3:00am

Bar
Beer

Credit cards
Visa, MC, AmEx

Reservations
Not accepted

Features
Brunch
Live music

Great W'kana Café

Let go and let this innovative, capable kitchen have its way with you

www.greatwkanacafe.com

Indian
Casual restaurant

Southwest Houston
11720 W. Airport Blvd.
(832) 886-4291

Hours
Sun–Fri
10:30am–3:00pm
5:30pm–10:00pm
Sat
10:30am–3:00pm
5:30pm–10:30pm

Bar
BYO

Credit cards
Visa, MC, AmEx

Reservations
Accepted

Features
Brunch
Date-friendly
Veg-friendly

While we wish great success for the restaurants we most love, we almost don't want to tell you about Great W'kana. As it is now, the kitchen gets overwhelmed with just two full booths; it's best to ask for dishes to come as they are prepared, not necessarily all at once. In this way, you can nibble on excellent house-made pickled vegetables to start (off the menu), take the time to sniff the saffron in the rice, identify each subtle spice as it unfolds in a dish with many layers—"W'kana" means "harmony," after all. The modernizations to the cuisine are careful and deliberate, with unique attention to detail standing in for the usual creative-kitchen conceit of "more is more" (despite what the "zany!" upholstery and tropical-colored walls might otherwise say). Goat biryani is wonderful, but so is the more unusual mushroom-apricot biryani. Also confidently order anything from the tandoor oven—even white-meat chicken, which comes intensely flavorful and moist. Flatbread kathi rolls filled with either meats or vegetables in warming spices are a great portable lunch.

Often, the innovations and elegant platings are successful, like a sprout salad garnish that's refreshing and texturally delightful; but some things are disorienting, such as avocado naan that calls to mind bad guacamole on ersatz tortillas. Still, to experience a rare form of Indian (and with your own wine, for a small corkage fee), come here—just please not on our nights.

The Grove

A dramatic and lovely scene on the Green
with approachable locavore leanings

6.1	8.5
Food	Feel

$65	8.0
Price	Drinks

www.thegrovehouston.com

The Grove is on the Discovery Green, a 12-acre
park and recreation area in the heart of
downtown. The view is beautiful, and so's the
interior of soaring ceilings, walls of plate glass,
and an innovative, elemental design that
stimulates conversation. This has helped keep it
a viable destination despite having lost the
attention of the city's gourmands. There have
been noticeable efforts to rein in the once-
ambitious kitchen and just play it safe—the
signature move of the Schiller Del Grande
Group, which rules The Grove with a bland fist.

Nevertheless, there's a mass appeal here that
begins with refreshing and fun cocktails and
sexy setting. You might still find a few
interesting wines left over from the time when
the selection was noteworthy—but the list's
new direction matches that of the kitchen. The
pre-theater crowd will be charmed by deviled
farm-eggs with chorizo that isn't spicy enough
to disrupt the evening. A daily changing Gulf
fish cooked in parchment is reliably moist, as is
local rotisserie chicken, but platings are
uninspired and rarely change. Filling a menu
with words describing the provenance of its
bounty only thrills a diner so much; the flavors
we once experienced here, particularly those
that took the biggest risks, have been
dampened somewhat. Still, if you're downtown
and like a scene, you won't be disappointed.

Modern
Upmarket restaurant

Downtown
1611 Lamar St.
(713) 337-7321

Hours
Mon–Thu
11:00am–10:00pm
Fri–Sat
11:00am–11:00pm
Sun
11:00am–9:00pm

Bar
Beer, wine, liquor

Credit cards
Visa, MC, AmEx

Reservations
Accepted

Features
Date-friendly
Outdoor dining

7.1 | 7.5
Food | Feel

$35 | 8.0
Price | Margs

Guadalajara Hacienda

Despite the goofy font and neon lights, this is some serious stuff

www.guadalajarahacienda.com

Mexican
Casual restaurant

Greenway Plaza
2925 Southwest Fwy.
(713) 942-0772

Downtown
1201 San Jacinto
(713) 650-0101

Memorial
9799 Katy Fwy.
(713) 461-5300

North Houston
27885 IH-45 N.
(281) 362-0774

Hours
Sun–Thu
11:00am–10:00pm
Fri–Sat
11:00am–11:00pm

Bar
Beer, wine, liquor

Credit cards
Visa, MC, AmEx

Reservations
Not accepted

Features
Brunch
Kid-friendly
Outdoor dining

The people behind Guadalajara take Tex-Mex quite seriously. Few places in town execute this cuisine so comfortably and consistently, with many unexpected winners among a broad range of dishes (and the weekend crowds know it—expect a wait). Refried beans become platforms for pork fat, and even chips and salsa are better-textured and more complex than you expect. The marinade for fajitas is so intense with fruity complexity that it's almost too much. "Guadalajara Enchiladas" are delicious, with a roasted corn salsa whose buttery, creamy goodness has an inexplicably deep appeal. The dryish shredded chicken within—normally a recipe for disaster—is wonderfully smoky. Queso, tamales, and tortillas perform as well as or better than expected, too.

We're befuddled by the aesthetic: why has Guadalajara adopted over-the-top, Disneyish fonts and a menu with the graphic-design look of a Chili's, creating the illusion that it's a huge chain when it's really just a three-branch Houston institution? (Four, if you count the spiffier, more pretentious Guadalajara del Centro, where, although you can get better margaritas and beer, the high-flying dishes fall flat.) At least the Hacienda spaces are fun when full of people; the Greenway Plaza branch even features a pleasant patio to take you away from the constant swish and zoom of the nearby highway.

Guy's Meat Market

One half-pound smoked burger, hold the
fuss and flair, for a limited time only

7.8 Food
7.5 Feel

$5 Price

You can smell smoldering wood and meat the
moment you pull into the parking lot of Guy's.
For a long time, this place was known as a good
ol' Texas barbecue joint, but the barbecue's not
so much the point these days. The lunchtime
crowds are here for the smoked burger, one of
the greatest treasures you can find in a humble
meat market—there are no tables here;
everything is take-out. Burgers are a half-pound
of dense, well-done, thick meat with a pretty
smoke ring. Unsurprisingly, they tend to run out
by about noon. (The creation of artificial
shortage is a great marketing gimmick.) Given
the demand and shortage, it's surprising that
the price is still only $4.92. The toppings aren't
anything to write home about, but do add
cheese and jalapeños, and forget the fries—
there aren't any.

The barbecue (brisket, ribs, sausage, and
chicken) is more hit-or-miss, but jalapeño
sausage, with a pleasantly burning flavor in the
back of your mouth, is seasoned well and
smoked beautifully. Upon walking in, the faint
haze of smoke deludes you into thinking that
either this is hamburger heaven or the depths of
Hell. We'll take Hell if it smells and tastes like
this.

**Barbecue
Burgers**
Counter service

Medical Center
3106 Old Spanish Trail
(713) 747-6800

Hours
Tue–Fri
9:00am–5:30pm
Sat
9:00am–4:00pm

Bar
None

Credit cards
Visa, MC, AmEx

Hank's Ice Cream

A hot city needs a cool man like Hank

www.hanksicecream.com

Ice cream
Counter service

Medical Center
9291 S. Main St.
(713) 665-5103

Hours
Tue–Sun
noon–9:00pm

Bar
None

Credit cards
Visa, MC, AmEx

Features
Kid-friendly
Veg-friendly

A Houston institution for 20+ years, Hank's has always produced ice cream the old-fashioned way: slowly, by hand, using fresh ingredients. The man himself even scoops the ice cream most nights, with a captivating smile. While the wondrous ice cream attracts diverse crowds from all walks of the city, Hank's outgoing manner and quick wit also have a hand in customer retention; testimonials paper the walls in the forms of framed autographed photos. So numerous are these 8x10 accolades, that one assumes Hank must be the most well-loved man in Houston.

The brightly lit, humble parlor showcases 18 delicious flavors each day and night, rotating from a list of nearly 100. Devotees swear by the butter pecan—but really, you can't go wrong with any flavor. Dulce de leche, cake batter, and chocolate chip…we can't decide what we like best (so we get a triple scoop). Even the offbeat ones like sweet potato and creamed corn have garnered loyal followings. And rumor has it that Beyoncé always gets banana pudding when she's in town.

Bluebell is good, yes, Amy's is, first and foremost, Austin's sweetheart. But Hank's is and always has been Houston's own ice cream man.

Haven

Philosophy and execution meet up in small plates and a lovely beverage program

8.2	8.5
Food	Feel

$70	9.0
Price	Wine

www.havenhouston.com

Haven claims to be Houston's first certified-green restaurant. We could stop there and still respect it substantially, but fortunately, we don't have to.

Start with buttery, crusty Parker House rolls spiked with Gulf sea salt; or end with them, in the form of what must be Houston's best bread pudding. Deviled farm-fresh eggs are even better with the $1 extra bowfin caviar on top. Generally, sides and starters seem to be the most reliable orders: exquisite al dente peas, slow-cooked grits, and a bacon spätzle teeming with hallucinogenic flavor. People rave about corndog shrimp with Tabasco rémoulade, and for good reason. Mains tend to be weaker, sometimes with tougher meats and flatter flavors.

Greenness aside, the cavernous room represents a chic and humorless genre of modern fine dining, although the prodigious use of reclaimed wood gives it an elemental sense of benevolence. That benevolence extends to the unbelievably well-priced wine list, which features several food-friendly, terroir-driven bottles (choose after you've ordered your food; there are some potential trouncers here). Beware the glass selections, culled from the weaker bottles on the list. As any self-respecting restaurant in Houston would, Haven has employed Anvil's help in creating its cocktail program, and many of these make great food pairings for the wine-weary. Haven's good attitude, meanwhile, provides respite for the world-weary.

Modern
Upmarket restaurant

Upper Kirby
2502 Algerian Way
(713) 581-6101

Hours
Mon–Thu
11:00am–10:00pm
Fri
11:00am–11:00pm
Sat
5:00pm–11:00pm

Bar
Beer, wine, liquor

Credit cards
Visa, MC, AmEx

Reservations
Accepted

Features
Date-friendly
Good cocktails
Outdoor dining
Veg-friendly
Wi-Fi

9.5 8.0
Food Feel

$15
Price

Himalaya

The absolute best in its class, now with even more class

Pakistani Indian
Casual restaurant

Southwest Houston
6652 Southwest Fwy.
(713) 532-2837

Hours
Tue–Thu
11:30am–9:30pm
Fri–Sun
11:30am–10:30pm

Bar
BYO

Credit cards
Visa, MC, AmEx

Reservations
Accepted

Features
Veg-friendly

Himalaya, despite its recent updates and gussying-up, continues to bask in the sort of achingly authentic excellence you'd expect from a hole-in-the-wall ethnic joint. The walls are a cheery adobe red, the tables are glossy, and we can now recommend bringing a first date (or, shudder, in-laws) about whose aesthetics you're not yet certain.

We love the relaxed BYO policy, but bring stemware, and order one main per person to avoid a (small) corkage fee. You can order takeout up to a half-hour later than the posted dining-room hours. The glorious Indo-Pak fare is an object lesson in spices: fennel seed, fenugreek, cardamom, and anise. Try aloo tikka, a complex, meaty sauce topping potato croquettes so lush they'd make Joël Robuchon blush. Coriander and chili-spiked chicken hara masala, which was already outstanding, has somehow even improved over the years. Green curries out-blaze even vindaloos from other restaurants, and the perfumed biryani and gently crisped, impossibly fluffy naan are heads and shoulders above those of the competition. Vegetarian dishes like malai kofta (a potato dumpling with a creamy, spicy sauce) make carnivores forget about meat. There isn't a dud on the menu; do ask Chef Kaiser for his recommendations—his oil-stained shirt proves that he knows what's best from his kitchen that day. Plus, you shouldn't miss the chance to engage with his generous personality.

Hobbit Café

5.6	8.0
Food	Feel

A surprisingly non-gimmicky vegetarian fantasy that's all heart and ale

$20	8.5
Price	Beer

www.myhobbitcafe.com

Okay, look. You need to go here. Just once. Then decide if you really love *Lord of the Rings* enough to ever come back. We grew up on the stuff, so we can't help but love Hobbit Café, which, despite the recent Hollywood-fueled resurgence (the owners must have been *thrilled*), has been an institution since the '70s, a decade of young idealists who relished—among houseplants, macramé, and shag carpeting—the fantasy world created by J.R.R. Tolkien.

Past the jarring life-sized figurine of the film version of Gollum standing in the foyer, colorful lights keep the atmosphere kitschy and fun, rather than scary and obsessive. The health-conscious fare does its best work as all-day brunch; most plates include either a low-fat this or a whole-wheat that. Avocado and alfalfa sprouts appear on many dishes; an avocado omelette is fantastic for the first half, but a struggle for the second half, as it seems like it's made with at least two whole avocados. Spinach-and-mushroom enchiladas have a nutritious, nutty taste, and are, thankfully, covered in cheese.

Given how much hobbits love their drink, there's an appropriately extensive selection of ales, stouts, Belgians, U.S. microbrews, and more. Opt for these over the grocery-aisle wines. And resist asking for a bit of "pipe-weed" to smoke afterward. They're probably sick of this one.

Vegefusion American
Casual restaurant

Upper Kirby
2243 Richmond Ave.
(713) 526-5460

Hours
Mon–Thu
11:00am–9:30pm
Fri
11:00am–10:30pm
Sat
10:30am–10:30pm
Sun
10:30am–9:00pm

Bar
Beer, wine

Credit cards
Visa, MC, AmEx

Reservations
Not accepted

Features
Brunch
Date-friendly
Good beers
Kid-friendly
Outdoor dining
Veg-friendly

Hong Kong Dim Sum

Skip the so-so Malaysian menu and order
freshly made dim sum, any time of day

Chinese Dim Sum

Casual restaurant

Bellaire Chinatown
9889 Bellaire Blvd.
(713) 777-7029

Hours
Mon
10:00am–5:00pm
Tue
10:00am–10:00pm
Wed
10:00am–5:00pm
Thu–Fri
10:00am–10:00pm
Sat–Sun
9:00am–10:00pm

Bar
None

Credit cards
Visa, MC

Reservations
Not accepted

Features
Brunch
Kid-friendly

Ah dim sum, that great divider. Everyone has a
favorite, and this is it for a few of our panelists
(the others declare Dim Sum King's the best).
There's a hefty Malaysian menu as well, but we
recommend saving that meal for Banana Leaf.
Dim sum devotees will be delightfully surprised
that there are no carts here—you order by
checklist, so you'll at least learn the Chinese
names of those items you always had nicknames
for (slimy pork bits = pai gwat; fluffy pig buns =
char siu bao). This also means you have to flag
down a server, which is actually a nice reprieve
from being interrupted every ten seconds by an
upsell wizard. In a shockingly rare move that we
are quite fond of, tea is free of charge.

Har gao, whose dough-wrapped shrimp can
get quite sticky as they cool on a cart, are
especially good here. Chicken feet, too, benefit
from coming piping hot, and stuffed eggplant is
wonderful. Egg custard tarts aren't a strong
point here—these ones have a stale-hard pastry
shell (stop by ECK Bakery for spectacular egg
custard after your meal here). It's nice that you
can get dim sum any time of day or night, but
come too close to closing and you'll be
unceremoniously rushed out, and gagging on
the smell of cleaning fluids all the while.

Hong Kong Food Street

8.5
Food

8.0
Feel

Make the best of the pricey late-night
Cantonese menu by sticking close to the sea

$20
Price

www.hongkong-foodstreet.com

Goat, Dungeness crab, and sea cucumber. This
unlikely *Incredible Journey* remake takes place
on the menu at Hong Kong Food Street, one of
those classic Bellaire Chinatown palaces of live
seafood, hot pot, and congee; of sizzling
platters, Singapore noodles, and fried rice.
Deciding what to order here can be daunting,
but we'll narrow it down for you: Cantonese.
Go ahead and bypass anything with
"Szechuan" in the name; it won't be as
peppercorny and chili-oil-spiked as the better
Szechuan in town. Of course, Cantonese isn't
renowned for its love of salt and spice, and
many dishes here attempt to adjust for
American palates, but with mixed success.

Stick with the live seafood from the tanks:
Hong Kong-style baked lobster and crab are
reliable, as are their steamed preparations,
served with glass noodles. Salted fish and pork
with spinach is also a wonderful combination of
briny, earthy, and lightly sweet—a subtle cruise
to the many ports of the tongue. Fried rice with
crab and fish roe is even more palate-pleasing, if
more one-dimensional. Congee is great,
warming comfort food for a post-drinking
resuscitation, and HK Food Street has a rare gift
for abalone. As for the goat? Leave it to the
Mexicans and Indians and look simply to the
sea.

Chinese
Casual restaurant

Bellaire Chinatown
9750 Bellaire Blvd.
(713) 981-8888

Hours
Daily
11:00am–2:00am

Bar
Beer, wine

Credit cards
Visa, MC

Reservations
Accepted

Features
Kid-friendly
Veg-friendly

Hot Breads Bakery

Hot, sweet, creamy, flaky: the best of both
the French and Indian worlds

www.houstonhotbreads.com

Baked goods
Indian
Counter service

Bellaire Chinatown
5700 Hillcroft St.
(713) 785-1212

Hours
Daily
9:00am–9:00pm

Bar
None

Credit cards
Visa, MC, AmEx

Features
Veg-friendly

Hot Breads's claim to fame is not so much straight-ahead Indian sweets as it is French-style baking with a South Asian twist. The "hot" refers to the spice level of the breads. Spicy bread? Believe it. The regular breads aren't all that remarkable, but Hot Breads shouldn't be used for normal bakery purposes...except for the cheap little cakes that are far superior to the much more expensive, boutique-y versions around town.

Mango cake is fruity and delicious; nougat cake layers caramelized crunch with capable buttercream; black forest cake is light on chocolate and cherries, not quite the classical interpretation of this dessert, but a white forest cake (using white chocolate, of course) is better than your average cream cake. Chocolate éclairs are a surprise—although whimsically decorated with superfluous candy sprinkles, the crunchy choux shell is filled with generous amounts of barely sweetened whipped cream and coated with a good dark-chocolate ganache. We can't think of a better way to soothe a mouth burning from spicy bread.

For savories, we like the croissants stuffed with chicken tikka, paneer, and spinach and potatoes, as well as laminated puff pastries topped with various cheeses. The staff offers to warm up pastries in the microwave, but go home at heat them in the oven, lest they go all soggy on you. You can wait with some cake.

House of Pies

The secret to this beloved 24-hour diner is to stick to breakfast and *only* breakfast

4.0	8.0
Food	Feel

$10
Price

www.houseofpies.com

American
Casual restaurant

Upper Kirby
3112 Kirby Dr.
(713) 528-3816

Galleria
6142 Westheimer Rd.
(713) 782-1290

Hours
24 hours

Bar
None

Credit cards
Visa, MC, AmEx

Reservations
Not accepted

Features
Brunch
Kid-friendly

House of Pies has long been our diner-breakfast favorite—we prefer its honest simplicity to the overpriced, overhyped Breakfast Klub any day. Plop yourself next to the pie cases at a counter that feels like a middle-of-nowhere truck-stop. If you're lucky, a big-haired waitress will call you "hon." Ask her for the corned-beef hash and eggs. The corned beef isn't freshly shaved or anything, nor is it mealy and gross—and it's crisped slightly on the grill. Why is this so hard to find at other breakfast joints in Texas? Order your eggs poached so you can break them over the top, forming a delicious pile of meat, potatoes, and runny yolk. Sop up the rest with toast, and you have one of the finest, most satisfying meals in town.

The pancakes, while not fluffy, are still a decent choice; stay away, though, from flimsy waffles. Really, the lunch and dinner options should be ripped out of the menu: steaks and burgers come out looking steamed, and salt is clearly not taken seriously. And those "famous" pies look and taste like something a group of 12-year-old girls made during a slumber party. They could rename the place "House of Hash," but that would just make the midnight crowds even bigger.

7.7	8.0
Food	Feel

$60	7.0
Price	Drinks

Houston's

A classy, contemporary chain that manages to avoid a chain's usual weak links

www.hillstone.com

American
Upmarket restaurant

Upper Kirby
4848 Kirby Dr.
(713) 529-2386

Galleria
5888 Westheimer Rd.
(713) 975-1947

Hours
Sun–Thu
11:00am–10:00pm
Fri–Sat
11:00am–11:00pm

Bar
Beer, wine, liquor

Credit cards
Visa, MC, AmEx

Reservations
Accepted

Houston's, with locations from OC to DC, enjoys a legendary success wherever it is. The décor, which was cutting-edge in the '90s, manages to evade that datedness from which contemporary interiors from that period often suffer. Instead, it's more of a classic and clubby feel that integrates elements that seem almost Art-Deco-Navajo. The shiny red banquettes are comfy, but you'll have to negotiate some ghastly downward lighting. As the waitstaff can be disturbingly attentive, it's a slightly better group spot than a date one. If there's a long wait, sidle up to the bar and enjoy a stuffed-olive martini

We love to start with cedar-smoked salmon, whose followers are legion. It's flaky and topped with a dollop of dilly crème fraîche. Filet mignon is unusually flavorful, although we prefer the fattier ribeye. Here it's dolled up annoyingly as "Hawaiian," with a sweetish marinade. Still, this is top-steakhouse quality in a less pretentious atmosphere, at a price that undersells the big names. As expected, there's a delicious burger that comes in several configurations, all tasting of a good smokehouse grill. Get it medium-rare, and don't miss the exemplary thin fries.

The wine list has a few pleasant surprises at much lower markups than usual, and cocktails are of the sort that come in martini glasses the size of Texas, but they're solidly crafted—like this enduring and still lovable chain.

Hubcap Grill

A tiny lunchtime grill serving up the best basic burger in town—and a few novelties

9.2 Food

7.5 Feel

$10 Price

www.hubcapgrill.com

Some of Houston's best burgers are grilled up at lunchtime in this downtown nutshell decorated with—naturally—hubcaps. Inside the peacock-blue cinderblock, there's only room for a couple of tables, a long counter against one wall, and an ATM (Hubcap is cash-only). A covered patio runs alongside the building to the garbage containers in the back, which can get downright fetid in the summer. Humble plastic tables out front make for better ventilation.

Hand-cut fries (sweet potato and regular) are fried and salted just right. The grill has even won over the medium-rare purists with hand-formed patties cooked to well done with a nice charred flavor and cheese that melts right into the little meaty grooves. It's a beefy, juicy, gooey thing of beauty. A "Hubcap Decker" doubles that pleasure with two 1/3-pound patties and a single toasted, homemade bun between them that sponges up all the juice while remaining just crunchy enough. A "Philly Cheese Steak Burger" is a regular hamburger topped with thinly shaved ribeye, fresh grilled peppers and onions, and lots of melty Swiss cheese; and a "Sticky Burger" is like Elvis's dream, with peanut butter, bacon, and American cheese. It's really too much for one person—split this and a zippier, tangier "Greek" with a willing friend. At the truck by the Liberty Station bar on Washington, such friends should be easy to come by.

Burgers
Counter service

Washington
2101 Washington Ave.
No phone

Downtown
1111 Prairie St.
(713) 223-5885

Hours
Mon–Sat
11:00am–3:00pm

Bar
None

Credit cards
None

Features
Outdoor dining

Hugo's

Modern, chef-driven Mexican served in a romantic, Montrose-driven space

www.hugosrestaurant.net

Mexican
Upmarket restaurant

Montrose
1600 Westheimer Rd.
(713) 524-7744

Hours
Mon–Thu
11:00am–10:00pm
Fri–Sat
11:00am–11:00pm
Sun
10:00am–9:00pm

Bar
Beer, wine, liquor

Credit cards
Visa, MC, AmEx

Reservations
Accepted

Features
Brunch
Date-friendly
Good cocktails
Live music
Outdoor dining
Wi-Fi

Hugo's fits in beautifully to the restaurant row of ever-hip Montrose, with a décor that is as Spanish colonial as it is contemporary: lofty ceilings, exposed brick, and a gorgeous wood bar where you can enjoy a flight of mezcals or refreshing sangría.

Start with a bright, zesty ceviche. You could easily make a meal out of small plates (just don't fall for the novelty of chapulines, crickets that are made more mushy and salty here than is traditional), but don't miss one of the deeply flavorful and complex mains, like a take on cochinita pibil in which pork is slowly roasted in banana leaves with tart pickled onions and a sneaky red salsa. Moles are rich and layered, and seafood is generally stronger than less-flavorful cabrito and carnitas platings. The Saturday to-order brunch is, naturally, slightly better than the Sunday steam-table buffet. While flan is pleasantly creamy, the real dessert winner is a plate of crunchy churros filled with dulce de leche and served with spiced Mexican hot chocolate.

The wine list is loaded with Mexican-food-friendly wines from around the world, from big, spice-loving Syrahs to seafood-smitten Albariños. The tequila selection's fine, but better are the Del Maguey mezcals, whose smoky medicinal aspects are as sensual a pleasure as much of Hugo's food.

Huynh

Vietnamese that's date friendly and
accessible, in every sense of the word

8.5	8.5
Food	Feel

$20
Price

www.huynhrestauranthouston.com

Where some places are famous for pho and
others best for banh mi, Huynh is a more
comprehensive Vietnamese experience,
conveniently located right on the edge of
downtown. We think the execution's seen
better days, but even having slipped from being
in the top five of its cuisine, it's still very solid
and delightful. The spacious, sparse interior is
prettier than that of other Vietnamese
restaurants, making it ideal for dates and
business lunches. The low lighting, avocado-
green walls, and smattering of Southeast Asian
art translates to a contemporary coolness that,
thankfully, doesn't reflect upon the staff: they're
warm and helpful as ever.

   We order pork spring rolls, served in opaque
white rice paper that's much more toothsome
than the translucent, thin kind found in ordinary
spring rolls; plus, the char-grilled pork is more
flavorful and less dry than elsewhere. A cha gio
roll's wrapper appears to have been shredded
before it was fried, resulting in an intriguing
crunchiness and cleaner taste. Bun bo Hue is
authentic and deeply flavorful, with homemade
noodles. We also love goi vit (duck salad), and
grilled beef short ribs, cross-cut so each slice is
marbled beautifully and charred to a crisp on
the edges.

   Best of all, prices are still in line with those of
its inferiors, and a $2 per drinking person
corkage is, like Huynh, abundantly hospitable.

Vietnamese
Casual restaurant

Downtown
912 St. Emanuel St.
(713) 224-8964

Hours
Mon–Sat
10:30am–9:00pm

Bar
BYO

Credit cards
Visa, MC, AmEx

Reservations
Accepted

Features
Date-friendly

7.1	8.5
Food	Feel

$70	9.5
Price	Wine

Ibiza

Decent food and a much better wine list,
for geeks and goombas alike

www.ibizafoodandwinebar.com

**Spanish
Modern**
Wine bar

Midtown
2450 Louisiana St.
(713) 524-0004

Hours
Tue–Thu
11:00am–10:00pm
Fri
11:00am–11:00pm
Sat
5:00pm–11:00pm
Sun
5:00pm–9:00pm

Bar
Beer, wine, liquor

Credit cards
Visa, MC, AmEx

Reservations
Accepted

Features
Date-friendly
Outdoor dining
Wi-Fi

Ibiza's Midtown parking lot, on a warm weekend evening, is an unlikely mixer of H3s and Toyotas; of goombas and wine geeks drawn by the generous range of barely marked-up wines. The candlelit indoors, if slightly pretentious, can be noisy and distracting on busy nights. It's tempting to write off Ibiza as a trendy singles scene, but the kitchen is surprisingly competent. To be clear, it's spotty, but not as bad as the high-gloss scene would suggest. We've had brilliant fried oysters with spicy tasso cream sauce, some of the better truffled french fries in town, and spectacular locally produced goat cheese with morcilla (blood sausage) and roasted beets. Aside from those small plates, the rest of the menu feels somewhat phoned in. Stuffed piquillo peppers have a tinny taste, and larger plates are ill executed. Braising is uneven, cuts are tough, and overcooking pork is a reliable occurrence. Crispy, personal-sized pizzas are fine, like one that incorporates the local goat cheese with oven-dried tomato, Portobello, and apple-smoked bacon.

Like its sister restaurant Catalan, Ibiza's wine list is great—better when the more obscure French, Spanish, and Italian bottles from classic vintages show up at prices often a smidge above retail. There's even some geekiness in the domestics, if quite a bit more prestige-minded choices. Like we said, something for everyone.

Indika

Fabulousness and fusions that stay, thankfully, close to the subcontinent

9.0	8.0
Food	Feel

$60	8.5
Price	Drinks

www.indikausa.com

We have to admit, we were worried there for a while: as much as we were enamored with Indika's creative approach to Indian cuisine, the kitchen seemed to start taking its cues from the demands of the mass market, playing into some trendy gimmicks that somewhat undermined the once-vibrant flavors we loved. It was still great, but the overbearing, gloopy sauces suggested Beaumont more than Bombay.

Happily, it seems Indika's been restored to its former glory. Recently, a lusty-pink beet soup expertly melded sweet earthiness with coconut milk, while stuffed karela (bitter melon) crowned with green masala sauce flaunted flavors of the spice route, layering tones that worked wonderfully with the sharp gourdiness. Proteins continue to be consistently overcooked, but flavor pairings hug the subcontinent more tightly than before, like Gulf-caught grouper paired with khichri, a familiarly informal stew of rice and lentils. Goat brain masala is, as always, a spectacular treat for anyone willing to dare.

The airy space is decorated in subtle colors and flowing curtains. It's a great atmosphere for cocktails, which, for once, we appreciate erring on the sweet side. (Sweet beverages best complement Indian spices. Unfortunately, few wines on this list fit the bill.) A "Kama Sutra" (passion fruit, gin, cranberry, and black salt) makes a refreshing palate cleanser for the creative—and once again inspiring—meal ahead.

Indian
Upmarket restaurant

Montrose
516 Westheimer Rd.
(713) 524-2170

Hours
Tue–Fri
11:30am–2:30pm
6:00pm–10:30pm
Sat
6:00pm–10:30pm
Sun
11:00am–3:00pm

Bar
Beer, wine, liquor

Credit cards
Visa, MC, AmEx

Reservations
Accepted

Features
Brunch
Date-friendly
Outdoor dining
Veg-friendly

6.3	6.5
Food	Feel

$30
Price

Istanbul Grill

Turkish pizza and beer—Houston: what a country!

www.istanbulgrill.com

Turkish
Casual restaurant

Rice Area
5613 Morningside Dr.
(713) 526-2800

Hours
Tue–Sun
11:00am–10:00pm

Bar
Beer, wine, BYO

Credit cards
Visa, MC, AmEx

Reservations
Not accepted

Features
Outdoor dining

Houston is blessed with several Turkish restaurants, all with pretty comparable kitchens. Istanbul Grill's the only one with such an extensive selection of Turkish wines and beers (the virtue lies more in the novelty than in the enjoyability, although some of these beers are decent); and the décor, while simple, is pleasant enough. The whites and deep blues evoke a Mediterranean scene, and the nazar (the lapis-colored evil eye) is ever-present, doing its job of warding off malicious spirits. Other than that, a big brick oven and a vertical turning spit roast are the most eye-catching things in the room.

The big deal here is döner kebab—strongly seasoned beef and lamb turned on a self-basting spit over an open fire, and then sliced to order. We also love smoky charbroiled adana kebab, made with chopped lamb and seasoned with Aleppo red pepper. Where Istanbul stands above the others is in its freshly made breads and excellent, doughy Turkish pizza. Almost everything is served with pilaf rice and cabbage, and the cold salads and appetizers here are refreshing and delicious. It all manages to leave you feeling full, but quite healthy—hey, a cuisine this old surely knows what it's doing.

Jarro Café and Trailer

Pleasure and pain, inside or out

7.0 Food
6.5 Feel

$10 Price

www.jarrocafe.com

Jarro is a great jumping-off point for the taco-truck uninitiated. For one thing, you won't be faced with anything challenging like lengua or tripe, and if you chicken out (or the weather sucks), you can head inside to the café it opened. It's a little pricier in there, but it's also air conditioned, and the Beatles posters and mustard-and-ketchup-colored walls are cheery. There's also an expanded menu inside, including slightly mushy tortas, your average enchiladas and quesadillas, and much more importantly, chilaquiles con carne asada. The tortilla strips stay crisp even under all the fresh crema and cheese, and get a bang from salsa verde and thinly sliced grilled steak. Cheesy creamy meaty spicy crispy goodness.

On the taco front, both in the truck and the café, you can't go wrong with slow-roasted pork cochinita pibil tacos with pickled oregano-scented onions. Bistec is grilled to tender sirloiny bliss. Al pastor has a great spicy-pineappley contrast, the pork slightly crispy. While the tacos are good, they're mostly a vehicle for six different homemade salsas: a roasted tomatillo salsa verde with nuclear-hot serranos; a dense, smoky, brick-red ancho salsa; chopped and pickled onions with white-hot heat lurking within; for the masochistic, there's a lurid green killer and a fiery orange salsa, both of which hurt so good.

Mexican
Counter service

Spring Branch
1521 Gessner Dr.
(713) 365-0373

Hours
Mon–Fri
8:00am–10:00pm
Sat–Sun
8:00am–11:00pm

Bar
Beer, wine

Credit cards
Visa, MC, AmEx

Features
Brunch
Outdoor dining

6.4 6.0
Food Feel

$10
Price

Jerusalem Halal Deli

Superb hummus and lamb chops in the back
of a Middle Eastern meat market

www.jhmeats.com

Middle Eastern
Counter service

Hillcroft Area
3330 Hillcroft St.
(713) 784-2525

Hours
Mon–Sat
10:00am–9:00pm
Sun
10:00am–6:00pm

Bar
None

Credit cards
Visa, MC

Features
Veg-friendly

This deli's in the back corner of a grocery that is
about as organized as a freshman-year locker
before final exams. With enough time and
patience, however, you will probably be able to
find just about any canned or jarred item that
exists in the Middle East. The center of the store
is a working meat market where sub-primal cuts
are broken down by a team of five men. The
smell is one you must get used to, but if you
want authentic, it's a small price to pay.

During lunch, you'll find Middle Eastern
businessmen lined up for the daily specials,
kebabs, and salads. You'll have to ask for the
menu—most people who eat there know
exactly what they want. The hummus is the
stand-out here, as well as rice dishes, long-
cooked with meat (a different one is featured
every day). If you don't mind the wait, lamb
chops are spectacular when prepared to order,
and don't dry out like most everything else
sitting in the steam-table buffet. But even
among those, lamb shawarma is hard to argue
with at under $5.

There are few tables, and it's not the most
blissful atmosphere, but the food transports you
miles away from the strip mall, and from
Houston.

Jonathan's the Rub

A lunch spot with a good burger and some decent other items—no more or less

7.8 Food | **6.5** Feel

$35 Price

"Best burger" contests aside, and after attempting to ignore both sides of the infamous incident in which a critic was asked to leave (it's less punk rock than it might sound), and despite the extreme opinions people have about Jonathan's the Rub, our repeated visits confirm that the truth lies—hardly shocking— somewhere in the middle of it all.

That burger is thick and drippy—half that juice is a chile-seasoned mayonnaise—with a sweetish bun that holds in the ooze and quality toppings rather well. (For the record, our entire panel agrees that it's not the best in town, and this panel rarely agrees unanimously on anything.) Fries are fresh cut, properly salted, but not exactly crispy if that's your obsession. Other than that, it's hard to take things too seriously: it's an add-grilled-chicken-to-your-Caesar-salad sort of place. A mango-salmon sort of place. Shrimp is plump and healthy, if a little overcooked; it's also better prepared on creamy polenta than as "scampi," although the accompanying seafood broth can be off-puttingly astringent. A steak sandwich is fine, but owes its excellent moments to the lightly toasted bread.

We love the BYO option ($5). Lunch is busy here, and it's small (at the moment), so everyone serves everybody's tables. It's a bit haphazard, but polite and gracious. Well, if you're not a critic.

Burgers
American
Casual restaurant

Memorial
9061 Gaylord St.
(713) 465-8200

Hours
Mon–Fri
11:00am–5:00pm

Bar
BYO

Credit cards
Visa, MC, AmEx

Reservations
Not accepted

Features
Outdoor dining

Jungle Café

A stylish pâtisserie that's dialed down the sugar and turned up the art

Baked goods
Counter service

Bellaire Chinatown
9110 Bellaire Blvd.
(713) 272-6633

Hours
Sun–Thu
10:00am–8:00pm
Fri–Sat
10:00am–9:00pm

Bar
None

Credit cards
Visa, MC

Features
Date-friendly
Veg-friendly

This Chinatown pâtisserie looks nothing like the rest of Chinatown. The space is all exposed brick, natural wood, and glass—as modern and chilly as any high-end jewelry store. And those cases glow with some pretty baubles. People stream in and out of Jungle Café with space-agey boxes full of exquisitely decorated cakes, truffles, macarons, and tarts. But wait! There's more: have an out-of-this-world milk tea—in an actual glass!—with lovely tapioca pearls. Pastry chefs trained in the French tradition find the treats here a little…restrained. Jungle Café began as an operation catering to the more sugar-sensitive palates of Asian shoppers, but has won fans among the less-is-more set.

Sometimes cakes come adorned with decorations like Japanese cartoons. Flavors are interesting (dark chocolate, Madagascar, and lemon), but our absolute favorite is Black Forest. Alhough it also comes in a mini-plated size, you'll probably want to pre-order a large one for yourself and hide in the corner eating it. It's hard to believe that one thing can be so light while so decadent, with layers of chocolate sponge, buttercream, and rum-soaked cherries. Mango mousse cake is another signature of the shop, with impossibly airy layers of cake sandwiching a mousse made of fresh sweet-and-sour mangoes. Taro cake is an acquired taste, with earthy woodiness cutting through the sweet flavor. Chocolate and mocha desserts are weaker; a chocolate-hazelnut pyramid lacks definitive bold flavor. But then, there's a call for that, too.

Kaneyama

No-frills, consistently executed Japanese
that doesn't require you feeling lucky

6.8	7.5
Food	Feel

$35
Price

www.kaneyama-houston.us

Kaneyama is as good as when it first opened
about two decades ago, with its straightforward
menu that's low on the frills and never fails to
deliver. If chef-owner Keeper Lin was a movie
star, he'd be Clint Eastwood, with his straight-
shooting, hard-charging, gruff attitude and
unwavering enthusiasm for hard work. While
many other sushi bars in Houston cater to a
crowd that's there to throw back sake bombs
and go gaga over complicated rolls that end up
tasting like nothing but mayo, cream cheese, or
avocado, Keeper has cultivated sushi that's
simple and high quality; totally worthy of its
following.

Little touches show how much these sushi
chefs care; yellowtail and yellowtail belly are
served separately, the belly a gorgeous, fatty cut
that melts in your mouth. Flounder is cut thin to
display the white fish's unique texture; another
treat is the sea trout, as oily as salmon but with
smaller, sweeter flakes. Hot food is not an
afterthought, either. Tempura is, for the most
part, beautifully fried, with the flavor and
texture of its innards beautifully preserved.
Onigiri, or grilled rice balls, are a rare treat in
town; they're firm and a touch charry. Agedashi
tofu is also outstanding—the pinnacle of
Japanese comfort food from the capable hands
who know its simple pleasures best.

Japanese
Casual restaurant

Westchase
9527 Westheimer Rd.
(713) 784-5168

Hours
Sun–Thu
11:30am–10:00pm
Fri–Sat
11:30am–10:30pm

Bar
Beer, wine, liquor

Credit cards
Visa, MC, AmEx

Reservations
Accepted

Features
Kid-friendly

Kanomwan

Strong Thai that's a little overrated, and a little less fun without its resident grouch

Thai
Casual restaurant

East Houston
736 1/2 Telephone Rd.
(713) 923-4230

Hours
Mon–Fri
11:30am–2:00pm
5:30pm–9:00pm
Sat
5:30pm–9:00pm

Bar
BYO

Credit cards
Visa, MC

Reservations
Not accepted

Features
Kid-friendly

Kanomwan (popularly known as "Telephone Thai" because of its location on gritty Telephone Street, near the University of Houston) acquired cult status among fans who deemed it some of the most vividly flavored Thai food in the city. Its critics, on the other hand, pointed out that it was more expensive and less authentic than Vieng Thai. But there's one thing everyone agreed on: the owner, affectionately referred to as the "Thai Nazi," who took (and gave) orders and worked the cash register, had to be the surliest dude in the Houston restaurant business. When he passed away in 2010, Houston found itself grieving at the loss of one of the world's great colors.

But fear not, the back of house continues unscathed by the loss of its front-of-house personality. Cashew chicken is more commonly known as "crack chicken" because, apparently, when you combine shrimp paste, red chilies, and sugar, it makes people go crazy. The ubiquitous tom kha gai soup and shrimp soup have more flavor than at most Thai-American joints. But curries are where Kanomwan really kicks ass: green chicken curry is one of the hottest dishes in Houston. Ask for it spicy, and get ready for tears. (Sadly, they're no longer caused by the lovably gruff Thai Nazi.)

Kata Robata

Domo arigato, Kata Robata

9.5 **8.0**
Food · Feel

$70
Price

www.katarobata.com

Although it belongs to a restaurant group (that also owns sushi hotspots Soma and Azuma), Kata Robata behaves as if it were a chef-owned venture. It is, after all, helmed by one of Houston's most respected Japanese masters. But it's the contributions of the inspired and talented kitchen as a whole that's rocketed Kata Robata into a world-class ranking. To get the real point, order omakase; each dish in the chef's tasting menu is a study in balance. Even if a description flirts with disaster, the components are deftly reined in to the surprise and delight of even jaded diners. Lately, the traditional oak-burning robata grill has featured more authentic meats than it did in its chickeny beginnings: mackerel and squid are standouts.

On and on the pleasures come: slow-poached eggs with smoked gnocchi and black garlic sausage; oak-grilled yellowtail with Brussels sprouts and grapefruit emulsion. Nigiri garnishes are intended to bring out each fish's unique flavor, and the rice is shorter grained and well seasoned. Don't touch the soy sauce—you're paying for art; art, incidentally, goes superbly with some of the cold sakes on this list. The space here is far too minimalist-chic to be confused with a trashy sake-bomb circus, and the brown-focused décor allows you to concentrate on the carefully made and brilliantly conceived food. It's a confident move you won't find in many other restaurants—this group's or otherwise.

Japanese Modern
Upmarket restaurant

Upper Kirby
3600 Kirby Dr.
(713) 526-8858

Hours
Mon–Thu
11:30am–3:00pm
4:00pm–10:30pm
Fri
11:30am–3:00pm
4:00pm–11:00pm
Sat
noon–11:00pm
Sun
noon–10:00pm

Bar
Beer, wine, liquor

Credit cards
Visa, MC, AmEx

Reservations
Accepted

Features
Date-friendly
Outdoor dining
Wi-Fi

6.1 | 8.0
Food | Feel

$25
Price

Kenny & Ziggy's

The closest thing Houston has to a New York deli

www.kennyandziggys.com

Jewish-style Deli Sandwiches
Casual restaurant

Galleria
2327 Post Oak Blvd.
(713) 871-8883

Hours
Mon–Fri
7:00am–9:00pm
Sat–Sun
8:00am–9:00pm

Bar
Beer, wine

Credit cards
Visa, MC, AmEx

Reservations
Not accepted

Features
Brunch
Kid-friendly

A great pastrami, corned beef, or tongue sandwich is hard to come by in Houston, and many people have accepted that fact. Still, many still lavish upon Kenny & Ziggy's an unfettered rhapsodizing; perhaps those fans will be thrilled to learn that, while it may be the best in this city, this is nowhere close to how good a New York-style deli can get.

The paper bag-brown space is airy, and everything from the layout to the dishware to the Manhattan-fetishizing décor is actually pretty spot-on. Add the noise level at lunchtime, and it successfully evokes the feeling that you're in a Lower East Side institution. But the pastrami and corned beef, reportedly flown in from New York, aren't as convincing. Why can't we get that thick, fatty corned beef that we lust after? (It's brisket, after all, and we're the brisket state.) There are wonderful successes, including onion rings, matzoh ball soup, pickled green tomatoes, and mocha milkshakes. As well as giant, pricy sandwiches, there's plenty of typically Jewish food like whitefish salad and chopped liver (both are pretty good). Corned beef hash is some of the best in town, and if you need a fix of sable or lox—accompanied by red onion, capers, tomatoes, and schmear—at least it's here. Many cities can't even claim so much.

Killen's Steakhouse

For steak devotees, this is a worthy trek to the hinterlands

8.9	7.0
Food	Feel

$105	6.0
Price	Wine

www.killenssteakhouse.com

Even die-hard Inner Loopers will make the pilgrimage to Pearland for Killen's steaks. This kitchen turns out some of the best grilled meat in the Greater Houston area. The inside reminds us of a West Texas country club, with low ceilings giving a cozy vibe; still, it's not exactly casual enough to ditch the cuff links and loosen up the belt. The polite, knowledgeable staff and expertly made martinis provide the polish that takes the edge off the astronomical bill.

Steaks here are a cut above—literally. A glorious long-bone Kobe ribeye is a sweeping piece of architecture whose each bite releases a mouthful of unctuous, beefy flavor. It stays with you the way a great book does (at $98, it had better). An aggressively seasoned dry-aged New York strip is best ordered medium-rare, expertly seared with a crusty edge and warm, ruby-red center. Sides follow suit, like the sweetly grassy haricots verts with shallots, restrained creamed corn, and luscious mac and cheese.

Don't waste room on overdressed salads and oversauced starters. Save it instead for dessert, which includes an exalted crème brûlée bread pudding, a brick of buttery, eggy indulgence invigorated by apple chutney. The wine list offers very little stylistic variation; but then, all this char and fat and beef really loves a big, blousy New World juice. Nothing goes better with excess than excess.

Steakhouse
Upmarket restaurant

Pearland
2804 S. Main St.
(281) 485-0844

Hours
Mon–Thu
5:00pm–9:00pm
Fri–Sat
5:00pm–10:00pm

Bar
Beer, wine, liquor

Credit cards
Visa, MC, AmEx

Reservations
Accepted

Features
Date-friendly

Kim Chau

A sexy bun bo Hue that presents a problem
we like having

www.kimchaurestaurant.com

Vietnamese
Casual restaurant

Spring Branch
6806 Long Point Rd.
(713) 683-8277

Bellaire Chinatown
11210 Bellaire Blvd.
(281) 498-9888

Hours
Daily
10:00am–7:00pm

Bar
BYO

Credit cards
Visa, MC

Reservations
Not accepted

Features
Kid-friendly
Veg-friendly

Sometimes you're presented with a glut of options. A Las Vegas buffet, bottomless mimosa specials, a harem—all are pretty universally thought to be good problems to have. Houstonians encounter this conundrum with quality Vietnamese noodle joints. Kim Chau, from both of its non-descript locations, throws another wrench into the decision machine with what might be the best bun bo Hue in a town teeming with great noodles.

Bun bo Hue, like its cousin pho, is an anytime meal that envelops all the senses with its broth, whose deep livestockiness, luxurious noodles, and pig debris are dangerously arousing. First-timers may stumble upon this like a surprise fetish. This bun bo Hue is redolent with slowly simmered bones, and beads of marrow glisten on its surface, which is piqued with spices and lemongrass. Tender morsels of pork shank and gelatinous, velvety cubes of blood are the textural equivalent of a deep kiss, the kind where a little tinniness lingers long after and excites the heart.

Having so many other quality items on the menu may make life hard for you, like bun rieu oc, in which noodles ensnare snails and seafood in a broth spiked with funky shrimp paste, or divine rice-flour cakes topped with crushed shrimp. But hey, life in the big city will throw a lot of challenges at you: a noodle problem, you can handle.

Kim Tai

Salty, strong duck noodle soup and a banh bot chien worth hunting for

8.6 Food
6.0 Feel
$10 Price

Vietnamese
Casual restaurant

Midtown
2602 Fannin St.
(713) 652-0644

Hours
Mon–Fri
8:30am–9:00pm
Sat–Sun
11:00am–9:00pm

Bar
Beer, wine

Credit cards
Visa, MC

Reservations
Not accepted

Look for the green awning that says "Luong Ky Mi Gia"—no, Kim Tai's not next door. This is Kim Tai. Signage can be expensive, you know. Besides, isn't there something of an allure to those restaurants claiming to be one thing, but secretly being another, like an illicit speakeasy trucking in duck noodle soup? There's something charming about this shabby, plain place—perhaps it's those dangling old lanterns over the counter, or the ornate wood chairs that appear to have been culled from some failed Cantonese banquet hall.

And Kim is a real person—a character, in fact. She runs the whole show, from door to kitchen to table, so when it's busy, you might wait…and wait. Come during off hours and you can watch TV together. While you watch, enjoy the main draw here, terrific roast-duck noodle soup; the meat falls right off the bone, but the salt sensitive should opt instead for the good pho or bun bo Hue. Either way, you must also try the other star attraction, banh bot chien, a fried rice flour cake scrambled with egg and scallions. It's slippery, chewy, and slightly crisp in places—absolutely a textural wonderland. We still think Tam Tam's assembly-lined, popular version is more viscerally pleasurable, but Kim's are made fresh to order, and you can taste that difference.

9.1
Food

7.5
Feel

$10
Price

Korean Noodle House

Noodles made by hand and served in a
happy little house of love

Korean
Casual restaurant

Spring Branch
1415 Murray Bay St.
(713) 463-8870

Hours
Tue–Sat
11:00am–9:00pm
Sun
noon–9:00pm

Bar
None

Credit cards
Visa, MC

Reservations
Not accepted

Features
Outdoor dining

Korean Noodle House won't play games with
you. It won't hold your hand, pretend to love
you, and then leave you high and dry. It's pretty
upfront about who it is and what you can
expect—it's in the name, after all: a house. A
house that serves handmade Korean noodles. In
fact, "homey" doesn't begin to describe the
atmosphere at this Spring Branch-area
bungalow. What so many modern restaurants
attempt to capture in their décor—the feeling
that you're over to a friend's house for dinner—
is almost uncomfortably authentic here, at first.
You may want to apologize, for intruding, to
the fatherly figure reading a newspaper near the
kitchen, but once you sit down to an
earthenware pot of zingy, funky kimchi—the
best in the city—you'll feel right at home.

You may flirt around the menu of Korean
classics, but the reason you're really here is to
ravish the noodles. Each strand has its own
personality. Some are rustic, but have a
sensational bite, like the noodles in the jjam
pong, a spicy seafood soup with a broth that
sets your tongue and heart on fire. A loving
beef kalguksu is down to earth, and full of nutty
buckwheat noodles. And when it's hot outside,
cold noodles don't give a cold shoulder—so go
on, let go and love.

Kubo's

Up or down, the average at this lively second-story sushi bar is pretty high

6.7	7.5
Food	Feel

$45	5.0
Price	Wine

www.kubos-sushi.com

Kubo's is one of Houston's best-loved Japanese restaurants, but there seems to be little regulation in its execution, and so as chefs come and go the quality at this chic and lively little second-floor joint dips and soars. But lately, the daily specials often include Tsukiji-market-fresh fish, and their platings don't read all that differently from those at laudable places like Kata Robata and Sushi Raku. The difference is more noticeable on the palate, often missing a bright-acidity component; still, it's quite enjoyable for the price. At press time, there was a chef there specializing in pricy kaiseki meals (think Japanese haute cuisine, incorporating several different cooking methods) that you need to reserve in advance. Aside from that, however, the hot menu really doesn't change.

As ever, if you sit at the sushi bar and ask for omakase, you can get some surprising stuff. Nothing as authentic and adventurous as, say, Nippon (but then, you really have to work those chefs to get the real deal, anyway). Now and then, the nigiri includes springy sea bass; great sweet shrimp; delicate seared white tuna; and soft, mild mackerel. The rice seasoning is pretty spot on lately, and they'll often invent new rolls for you on the fly. That is, until things change again. (Get while the gettin's good.)

Japanese
Casual restaurant

Rice Area
2414 University Blvd.
(713) 528-7878

Hours
Mon–Thu
11:30am–10:00pm
Fri
11:30am–11:00pm
Sat
noon–10:30pm
Sun
noon–9:00pm

Bar
Beer, wine, liquor

Credit cards
Visa, MC, AmEx

Reservations
Accepted

Features
Live music
Outdoor dining

7.0	6.5
Food	Feel

La Guadalupana

Excellent pastries and authentic Mexican in—where else?—a colorful hole in the wall

$10
Price

**Mexican
Baked goods**
Casual restaurant

Montrose
2109 Dunlavy St.
(713) 522-2301

Hours
Mon–Tue
7:00am–3:00pm
Wed–Sat
7:00am–9:00pm

Bar
BYO

Credit cards
Visa, MC, AmEx

Reservations
Not accepted

Features
Brunch
Outdoor dining

La Guadalupana is more than just a shabby bakery in a flamingo-pink-and-yellow strip mall—it's also a popular, homey Mexican restaurant. The small, haphazardly decorated space suggests authenticity in all its downmarket glory. You're first greeted by the case of cakes and cookies, and croissants that are used on Mexican hybrid breakfast sandwiches. Take-out is common, but there are about ten tables squeezed into another room, where you might start your morning with chilaquiles, breakfast tacos, or spot-on huevos rancheros with a spicy salsa ranchera.

For lunch and dinner, try torta sandwiches with a choice of pork, chicken milanesa, or carnitas, piled with beans, jalapeños, onion, lettuce, tomato, and avocado. Considering the bakery, the torta bread is delicious, a bit sweet and spongy. Even slightly overcooked, a chicken breast with mole poblano (a dark, bittersweet dry-roasted chile sauce integrating pumpkin seeds and chocolate) is nutty and complex. Authentic soups like caldo de mariscos (seafood soup) and pozole (soup with hominy) are comforting and delicious.

As you can imagine, these prices are unbeatable. And there's a surprise treat in daily changing juices, like carrot, orange, or "Vampire" (carrot, orange, and beet). Cinnamon-spiced Mexican coffee is terrific with a pastry, even a not-so-Mexican almond croissant.

La Moreliana

Past the sides of beef and heaps of tripe, a hidden gem of authentic Mexican cooking

8.0 Food

4.0 Feel

$5 Price

Mexican
Counter service

Bellaire
6225 Southwest Fwy.
(713) 272-0227

Northwest Houston
2012 W. 34th St.
(713) 263-9509

Southeast Houston
3401 Broadway St.
(713) 644-5323

Hours
Daily
6:00am–10:00pm

Bar
None

Credit cards
Visa, MC, AmEx

La Moreliana's no ordinary store. First off, they sell giant slabs of carcass—every part of the cow but the moo—at crazy low prices (not for the locavores, however, and no one can answer for the ethics). More importantly, the kitchen, which is really just one or two squat ladies maneuvering behind the counter, turns out excellent tacos and daily specials to a few day laborers and local Mexican businessmen at breakfast and lunchtime.

An order of three tacos—a totally filling lunch—rings in at around three bucks; it would be hard to argue that there's a better deal in this city, anytime, anywhere, beginning with mind-blowing tacos al pastor, which favor the marinated pork flavor over that of sweet pineapple. Tender, gamey tacos de lengua are terrific with fiery house-made red and green salsas, the traditional onions and cilantro, and, of course, a squeeze of lime. Fajita tacos are fine, but not as make-your-eyes-roll-back good.

Don't miss the daily stew, once a spectacular, authentic version of mole coloradito, a treat from the Oaxaca province, rich in dried chile flavor. It's a general rule that the dingiest dives often make the best Mexican food of all—La Moreliana is one of the foremost examples.

La Pupusa Alegre

$2 pockets of oozing cheesy goodness—
yeah, we're pretty happy, too

Latin American
Casual restaurant

Bellaire
6209 Bellaire Blvd.
(713) 778-9222

Hours
Daily
11:00am–9:30pm

Bar
None

Credit cards
None

Reservations
Not accepted

The world loves its hot pockets: pasties, empanadas, dumplings, samosas. In this genre, El Salvador wins the Best Name prize with its pupusas. And a happy pupusa this is indeed at La Pupusa Alegre: the masa's corny sweet and soft, with a little bit of blackened goodness that reminds us of what we love in a pizza crust. Inside is a filling that might include any combination of shredded pork, cheese, refried beans, or loroco (an herbaceous flower indigenous to El Salvador). The standard order on the streets of San Salvador is a revuelta, with chicharrones and cheese oozing out at each bite. Sure, they're a little greasy, but not overly so, and anyway you're supposed to cut it with the runny salsa and curtido (pickled cabbage) that comes in a little heap on the side.

In this neighborhood, there are pupusas aplenty, but we like this place best for its dressed-down simplicity—it's definitely a hole in the wall, complete with checked tablecloths, Spanish soaps on the TV, and scarcely English-speaking (but patient) service. And each pupusa is less than $2, so even though it's cash only here, you can probably scrounge up enough change in your car to give you a mighty good snack.

La Sani

It may be a rough neighborhood, but inside, a welcoming spice market awaits

7.8 Food
7.0 Feel

$30 Price

Pakistani cuisine is, like Northern Indian, pretty meat forward. Goat, mutton, and lamb simmer for hours in spiced sauces and are then served on sizzling plates with tomatoes and ginger. They pass through the dining room, perfuming the air like intoxicating, carnal hashish. Relax all control—besides, the menu is little help; a dish might be described as having "selected mild spices," but then arrives with tons of mouth-searing (but seductive) garam masala. If you don't recognize a morsel, don't bite into it too confidently—whole peppers are everywhere.

But La Sani's perfected the art of balance. Hot fried papadum (flatbread) are served with sour-sweet plum chutney and soothing, thin raita. Beginners will like chicken handi, with its lightly creamy sauce scented with cardamom and ginger. Scoop it up with fresh ghee-slicked naan and have some palak paneer and fried onion bhaji, and you'll get a good sense of the flavors without breaking a sweat. Don't miss shahi kheer rice pudding for dessert, with cardamom, chopped pistachios, and a whisper of rosewater.

It's common knowledge that lunch buffets are never as strong as made-to-order dinners, and La Sani's no exception. Also, it's totally halal, so BYOB isn't an option, but there's a house sparkling beverage of chopped fruit, Perrier, and apple juice. Just the thing for the excellent sting.

Pakistani
Casual restaurant

Southwest Houston
9621 Bissonnet St.
(713) 270-4040

Hours
Mon–Thu
10:00am–10:00pm
Fri–Sat
10:00am–11:00pm

Bar
None

Credit cards
Visa, MC, AmEx

Reservations
Accepted

Features
Live music

Lankford Grocery

A camera-ready old-timey spot cooking up hot-as-hell burgers and good CFS

www.lankfordgrocery.com

Burgers
American
Casual restaurant

Midtown
88 Dennis St.
(713) 522-9555

Hours
Mon–Sat
7:00am–3:00pm

Bar
Beer, wine

Credit cards
None

Reservations
Not accepted

Features
Kid-friendly
Outdoor dining

Guy Fieri's like the Pied Piper of Hamburger; wherever his fluffy head travels, people follow, saucer-eyed and drooling, visions of grease traps and checkered wax paper dancing in their heads. And Lankford's ramshackle old mom-and-pop grocery—or rather, its vintage Coca-Cola sign—would be just the thing to send "Diners, Drive-Ins, and Dives" scouts into a tizzy. Its garage full of Texas memorabilia could've been conceived by a production team, and the regular cast of old men who seem to all know each other—with their Southern colloquialisms and nicknames—is TV gold.

Fortunately, the time-warpiness and vibe are roughly the same as ever, if now a little more…famous. And the burgers are still course-ground, hand-formed, half-pound monsters, charred to a (if you ask for it) juicy medium-rare. It's oozy and messy. Gluttons for punishment love the "Firehouse Burger," studded with home-grown habaneros before grilling, and slathered in a vicious sauce. Chicken-fried steak, crispy and succulent, is another favorite here, and you must have some cobbler, whether cherry, peach, blackberry, or chocolate. Everything else, including the fries, is just so-so (opt for thick, not-too-greasy onion rings), and forget the enchiladas. You're here for a burger. Listen to the Pied Piper, y'all—even if he does look like Corey Feldman doing an impression of Andrew Zimmern.

Last Concert Café

3.7 Food

9.0 Feel

$35 Price

We'll happily endure middling Tex-Mex for this nighttime hippie scene

www.lastconcert.com

Last Concert Café started out as a humble Mexican restaurant, but it was slowly taken over by the dreadlocked set (or those who wore dreadlocks in their youth). These days, people don't go so much for the just-serviceable Tex-Mex, but to partake in a drum circle or psychedelic hula hoop show. Call it a contact high, but it's hard to stay grumpy inside this compound hidden on the edges of downtown. Under its spell, it's easy to fall in love with the botana platter, with its quesadillas, jalapeños, chicken flautas, and guacamole. Or you might declare potato with green chile soup "the best thing in the world," with its chunks of potatoes simmering in chicken broth full of poblanos, cheese, and pico de gallo. Maybe you'll construct epic poems about "Apolinar's Enchiladas," two roast-beef-stuffed enchiladas with chili gravy and rice and beans.

Then again, maybe it's all just an illusion, man. In the harsh light of day, this food is actually pretty greasy and underwhelming. Does the flavor come from the sauce, or from the wisps of patchouli that linger as women dance by? Maybe from the delicious memories of Grateful Dead show parking lots, in which vendors hawked beads and handmade jewelry, as they do here, in this strangely bordello-like yard where the squares have to knock to be let in.

Mexican Vegefusion
Casual restaurant

Downtown
1403 Nance St.
(713) 226-8563

Hours
Mon
11:00am–9:00pm
Tue–Thu
11:00am–10:30pm
Fri
11:00am–midnight
Sat
5:00pm–midnight
Sun
10:30am–9:00pm

Bar
Beer, wine, liquor

Credit cards
Visa, MC, AmEx

Reservations
Accepted

Features
Brunch
Live music
Outdoor dining
Veg-friendly
Wi-Fi

Laurier Café and Wine

Simple and well-made food that goes unnoticed in these daring times

www.lauriercafe.com

Modern French
Upmarket restaurant

Greenway Plaza
3139 Richmond Ave.
(713) 807-1632

Hours
Mon–Fri
11:00am–10:00pm
Sat
5:30pm–10:00pm

Bar
Beer, wine, liquor

Credit cards
Visa, MC, AmEx

Reservations
Accepted

Features
Date-friendly
Outdoor dining

Laurier Café keeps things refreshingly simple, considering its cuisine—classic-French-meets-modern-Texas—is so often capable of mucking things up with cumbersome ingredients. The décor sort of hints at the minimalism to come; it's colorful, but contemporary and simple, with abstract art and down-tempo club music played at a conversation-friendly softness. Most of the clientele is over 50; leave the young to their experiments with bar food and shiny new openings, oui?

Dishes rarely feature more than four main components, and portions are on the smaller side—quality over quantity. Salads are splendidly spartan, allowing the natural beauty of their ingredients to shine. We've had remarkably light cassoulet, although still rich with duck and pork sausage flavor. While biting into the expert flakiness of a thin pastry, revealing neatly julienned vegetables and silky goat cheese within, you can't help but feel that this kitchen understands that its job is to choose well and then get out of the way. There is, still, some innovation. Seared sea scallops are served on a bed of roasted, matchstick-cut beets—a classic French preparation—yet with a smear of Thai chili paste.

The wine list is similarly modest; most bottles are priced between $30 and $60 and broadly represent the most commonly sought-after varietals. There are few rare, small-production wines, but many are well-suited to the subtle success on the plate.

Le Mistral

Provence by way of the Energy Corridor

8.3	8.5
Food	Feel

$75	8.5
Price	Wine

www.lemistralhouston.com

Le Mistral's in a location that seems puzzling—flanked between gas stations in the Energy Corridor—until you consider that many Western Europeans are brought here by oil business. And then it makes sense, even if its move to the larger, more contemporary space next door makes the food taste somehow less Provençal and more suburban. While it's gorgeous and the kitchen is state-of-the-art, everything seemed a little more authentic, a little more careful at the intimate original.

Still, you'll hear the co-owner/sommelier conversing with customers in French while his brother cooks in the back, and the bright yellow curtains keep the world of parking lots and refineries a safe distance away. And the food is as soul-warming as ever. French onion soup is addictive, its beef stock deep and rich, its onions adding a brown, caramelized taste that's exactly as it should be, the Gruyère melting in an exemplary fashion. A Provençal lamb stew comes laced with the unexpected brightness of preserved lemons, and a duo of duck leg confit and pan-seared duck breast is gorgeous. For brunch, the béchamel-rich croque madame is a flawless meld of ham, cheese, egg, and crusty bread. Pass up the obligatory Napa heavy-hitters on the wine list—you wanted to be transported to France, otherwise you wouldn't be here.

French
Upmarket restaurant

West Houston
1420 Eldridge Pkwy.
(832) 379-8322

Hours
Mon–Thu
11:00am–2:00pm
5:30pm–10:00pm
Fri
11:00am–2:00pm
5:30pm–11:00pm
Sat
5:30pm–11:00pm
Sun
11:00am–2:00pm
5:00pm–10:00pm

Bar
Beer, wine, liquor

Credit cards
Visa, MC, AmEx

Reservations
Accepted

Features
Brunch
Date-friendly
Live music
Outdoor dining
Wi-Fi

7.2 Food
5.5 Feel
$10 Price

Les Givral's

All Les Givral's are created equal? Now that's a tall tale

Vietnamese Sandwiches
Counter service

Midtown
2704 Milam St.
(713) 529-1736

Hours
Daily
10:00am–8:00pm

Bar
None

Credit cards
Visa, MC

Features
Veg-friendly

A story:

Once upon a time, a Vietnamese family owned Les Givral's in Midtown. Then there was a rift of some sort—you can use your imagination, or go ahead and ask and then let us know if you get a sexier answer than we did. Some disgruntled family members opened up the Les Givral's Kahve locations, tricking them out with abstract art and capitalizing on the original's well-earned reputation. Then a bunch of people got confused and declared that the food at all three was equal. But you did comparison visits and found this location far superior: the pho broth, while not on the same level as Pho Danh or Pho Binh, was much more clean and layered; the banh mi ingredients stood out as being of much better quality. You thought you might like to taste more lard spread here—its butter was a little skimpy—but at around $3 for a sandwich with chargrilled pork and pâté, who was complaining? Then a big mean ogre came and said you have to meet the $10 minimum to use your card, so you bought a few more, and there was much rejoicing back at your office and now you run the place and have a harem or whatever.

The End

Les Givral's Kahve

Sandwiches are really the key here—for more, step out of the Kahve

6.0 Food

7.0 Feel

$10 Price

www.lesgivrals.com

There are two Les Givral's (spelled this way on the signage) Kahves, and one Les Givral's Sandwich and Café, on Milam. Although owned by different relatives, the three menus and prices are nearly identical, but with distinct atmospheres. But the critical distinction is in the execution. Although the Kahve offers bun, pho, and com tam, what you should order here is a banh mi sandwich. Period. If it's good rice plates and soup you seek, head to Midtown for the original.

As for these locations, they're small and modern, with a wall of wooden stakes making a sort of organic art backdrop. There's a generous BYO option at the Downtown location, but we're just here for the sandwich, remember? It comes on an ideal, lightly toasted French roll, filled with marinated meat, pickled carrots, onion, and cilantro, with just enough julienned jalapeño for a punch. These are extra tasty when you add the double-secret fried egg option. Always add pâté: its funky iron flavor makes sweet music with the pickled veggies and herbs. The tofu sandwich, with its spongy texture and tangy sauce, is also surprisingly tasty. And by the way, these sandwiches will set you back less than will a beer at most restaurants, making this the perfect cuisine de la récession.

Vietnamese Sandwiches
Counter service

Heights
4601 Washington Ave.
(832) 582-7671

Downtown
801 Congress St.
(713) 547-0444

Hours
Mon–Thu
10:00am–6:00pm
Fri
10:00am–10:00pm
Sat
11:00am–10:00pm
Sun
11:00am–9:00pm
Hours vary by location

Bar
BYO

Credit cards
Visa, MC, AmEx

Features
Wi-Fi

<table>
<tr><td>**6.0**
Food</td><td>**7.5**
Feel</td></tr>
<tr><td>**$15**
Price</td><td>**4.0**
Wine</td></tr>
</table>

Little Big's

Ignore the business plan and stick to
chicken sliders, fries, and shakes

www.littlebigshouston.com

Burgers
Counter service

Montrose
2703 Montrose Blvd.
(713) 521-2447

Hours
Sun–Wed
11:00am–10:00pm
Thu
11:00am–11:00pm
Fri–Sat
11:00am–3:00am

Bar
Beer, wine

Credit cards
Visa, MC, AmEx

Features
Kid-friendly
Outdoor dining
Veg-friendly
Wi-Fi

We had high hopes for this slider place,
considering that the exceedingly capable Reef
people opened it. The outdoor deck dotted with
picnic tables is nice on warm nights; you can
just make out the downtown skyline behind the
Phone Pole Wasteland. The menu's short and
sweet, but we'll make it even easier: skip the
dry, overcooked beef sliders and too-rich fried
crimini mushrooms. Order a trio of good all-
natural chicken sliders with homemade
breading; it's deliciously moist, even if it could
stand a little more spice. Then get those "four-
minute" hand-cut french fries, but make sure
they don't sit in the window forever. Add
Sriracha rèmoulade from the well-stocked
condiment bar. Done.

As for that boast about "really, really good
wine"? Hardly. This list is best summed up by its
Sutter Home White Zinfandel and oily-sweet
Shiraz (there is one good Chablis lurking about,
but demand a freshly opened bottle). The
selection is cheap, but amateurish—the same
goes for the beer and sweet frozen (non-
distilled-spirit) cocktails, although we'd rather
have a "White Russian milkshake" than Bud on
draft any day. But hey, if you really want to
blow people's minds, make a great burger, and
then serve it with its secret soul mate, crazy-
affordable cru Beaujolais. After all, people pay
you to turn them on to things they couldn't
have just experienced at a drunk neighbor's
cook-out.

Little Bitty Burger Barn

This little place is bigger than Little Big's on slider (and burger, tot, and chicken) success

6.6	7.0
Food	Feel

$10
Price

www.littlebittyburgerbarn.com

Listen up, self-touted slider joint with a strikingly similar name: this is how to make a slider. The ones at the shabby, hokey Little Bitty Burger Barn are juicy flavor bombs that are miles above Little Big's, with buttery grilled buns. There's not a whole lot of money poured into this venture, which looks like a bland doublewide trailer mated with a small town's elk lodge painted with whatever colors were lying around. The walls are filled with customer photos, sponsored little league teams, and write-ups; look for the shelves of hot sauces ranging from mildly zingy to masochistically murderous.

Most of the focus here is, as it should be, on the burgers (plus other sandwiches, wings, and various Southern favorites like fried catfish and Frito pie). The burgers are attired as usual, with blue cheese and feta being the fanciest among the options. For vegetarians, there are serviceable grain-based and black-bean patties; and you can substitute fries or onion rings for (drumroll) tots! What a simple joy are crispy, well-seasoned tots. The burger's of the unabashedly sloppy and huge variety—and it gets sloppier, if you want it to; patties come in third, half, and full-pound sizes, and may be studded with jalapeños. Patties and fries are from fresh, never frozen, and few elements don't work (one of them being a runny guacamole). But at some point, do yourself a favor and try the chicken-fried pork tenderloin sandwich—it's crispy, thick, and even better than the chicken-fried steak. Now sub tots. Done deal.

Burgers
American
Counter service

Northwest Houston
5503 Pinemont Dr.
(713) 683-6700

Hours
Mon–Fri
10:00am–9:00pm
Sat
11:00am–9:00pm
Sun
11:00am–7:00pm

Bar
None

Credit cards
Visa, MC

Features
Kid-friendly
Outdoor dining
Veg-friendly

8.0	8.5
Food	Feel

$30	7.5
Price	Beer

London Sizzler

Sizzling meat platters and Brit-style curries light up this jolly, pubby place all the more

www.londonsizzler.com

Indian
Casual restaurant

Southwest Houston
6690 Southwest Fwy.
(713) 783-2754

Hours
Tue–Thu
5:00pm–11:00pm
Fri–Sun
noon–11:00pm

Bar
Beer, wine, liquor

Credit cards
Visa, MC, AmEx

Reservations
Accepted

Features
Date-friendly
Good beers
Veg-friendly
Wi-Fi

London Sizzler is the most authentic rendition of a British-style Indian restaurant around. We love the vibe here even more than at Himalaya—ranked our favorite on food alone—which is caddy-corner from it in the same hidden strip mall. It's dark and gregarious, with a friendly staff, a full bar (the well-stocked British beer selection is recommended over the cocktails), and flatscreen TVs playing whatever footie game's on. Modern Indian club music makes a cool backdrop, and long tables beckon large groups.

The kitchen's focus is classic Brit-Indian dishes like deep, creamy chicken masala, and, of course, grand, sizzling platters of meat. Surprisingly for a grilled-meat restaurant, vegetarians love it just as much as carnivores do. Although some descriptions seem senseless ("California blend vegetables," and "Manchurian sauce"), these can't be denied in the mouth—dumplings, which may seem out of place here, are actually toothsome, savory delights. Also non-Indian but still great are East African-inspired dishes like well-cooked, pretty tender lamb in pili pili, a sauce that's spicier than almost anything else here.

Go to Himalaya for the biryani and tikka masala, but here, you should confidently order buttery vindaloos and vegetable curries, like they would on Brick Lane. Happy hour from 5–7pm Tue–Thurs, and nearly all day on Friday, is a great time to come—or any time United is playing Liverpool.

Los Guanacos

Salvadoran homestyle cooking that's worth the drive

7.4 Food

7.0 Feel

$10 Price

Latin American
Casual restaurant

Northwest Houston
16282 Loch Katrine Ln.
(281) 550-3467

Hours
Tue–Fri
11:00am–9:00pm
Sat–Sun
9:00am–10:00pm

Bar
Beer

Credit cards
Visa, MC

Reservations
Not accepted

You'll likely have to drive a fair distance to Los Guanacos, but trust us, it's worth it. (A warning: we have trouble pinning them down about hours of operation, so call before you go and ask "¿Cuándo se cierra?") The word "guanaco" is slang for a person from El Salvador, and this humble little place is all about Salvadoran street foods, namely pupusas, tamales, and pasteles. Its Northwest shack is clean and respectable, and the food's totally cheap, which is good, considering the gas money it takes to get out here. The spacious dining room is often packed with regulars.

Pupusas, a mainstay of Salvadoran cuisine, are good here; the small discs of hand-patted masa (corn flour) are stuffed with a choice of cheese, chicharrones (fried pork skins), or loroco (a green, mild flower indigenous to the area). They're fluffy, and surprisingly, not greasy. Curtido—pickled cabbage and carrots—is an essential condiment that adds a much-needed crunch of salty acidity. Tamales are good, too. Not to be confused with the denser Mexican version, the Salvadoran tamal is made from a light, fluffy masa. Simple elote, chicken, or poblano are good filling options. Ask for Salvadoran crema; it's thick and somewhat like sour cream, and completes whichever little pocket of masa joy you choose.

Lucky Pot

Authentic Northern Chinese cooking that's best from, well, a pot

Chinese
Casual restaurant

Bellaire Chinatown
9888 Bellaire Blvd.
(713) 995-9982

Hours
Daily
11:00am–9:30pm

Bar
BYO

Credit cards
Visa, MC

Reservations
Not accepted

Don't walk into Lucky Pot looking for a $3.99 special of General Tso's chicken, fried rice, and an egg roll; if you do, you may elicit stares of contempt, or possibly have the waitstaff pretend not to speak English just so they can ignore you. Lucky Pot serves an authentic style of Northern Chinese cuisine—one which emphasizes crispiness and crunchiness in texture, as well as heartiness in taste. It's not for everyone: service will be curt and won't hold your hand while you figure out the menu. It's best to do some research (which we'll help you with) and just dive in.

For hot days, there are fantastic cold dishes, like sliced beef shank that's marinated, slow-cooked, then chilled to an odd, but addictive, gelatinous texture from the tendons. Steamed pork, lamb, and vegetable dumplings have thicker-than-normal skins, but they're still light and delicious. For colder days, tofu casserole with a steaming, mushroomy broth warms you up; better are the savory, crunchy, appropriately greasy pan-fried green-onion cakes. But make the darkly rich beef noodle soup your centerpiece. The noodles are toothsome and the broth marrowy and soothing. Peking duck's fine here, but better at Peking Cuisine. (Most of the time, we find the name of the restaurant's a good guide to ordering.)

Lupe Tortilla

Decent Tex-Mex, good tortillas, and some goofy stereotypes even Disney won't touch

7.7	7.0
Food	Feel

$35	5.5
Price	Margs

www.lupetortilla.com

Lupe Tortilla is everywhere, and its popularity transcends the generations: the playscape-sandbox areas are always active; children run about and throw sand, while inside, their parents try vainly to buzz from the weak margaritas. Service ranges from distracted to just plain rude: requests are shrugged off, food can take forever to come out, and few apologies are offered. What's more, the menu has an annoying, patronizing, borderline offensive habit of writing some things as a non-native speaker of English would say them—chicken becomes "cheekin," fish is "feech," and mixed fajitas are "meexed." It'll make you cringe, especially given that the restaurant's founders, according to the restaurant, spoke no Spanish when they launched Lupe in the '80s.

Still, they know their way around the parrilla. Carne asada and "3-Pepper" flank steak are best; the latter is marinated in lime, habanero, jalapeño, and serrano. But we've had it come quite tough. Chicken has a nice smoky sear, but is of the spongy, dry breast variety. For starters, share the pepper shrimp (would that be "shreemps"?), which are gargantuan—stuffed with Monterey Jack and chilies, then wrapped in bacon and grilled to creamy, crunchy goodness.

In the end, this Tex-Mex is merely serviceable to Houstonians, who laugh when we tell them that we've heard pasty-white oil executives from the UK in a neighboring booth exclaim "this is the *best* Mexican food I've ever had."

Mexican
Casual restaurant

Greenway Plaza
2414 Southwest Fwy.
(713) 522-4420

Heights
1511 Shepherd Dr.
(713) 231-9040

Spring Branch
9313 Katy Fwy.
(713) 491-6165

More locations
and features at
fearlesscritic.com

Hours
Sun–Thu
11:00am–9:00pm
Fri–Sat
11:00am–10:00pm
Hours vary by location

Bar
Beer, wine, liquor

Credit cards
Visa, MC, AmEx

Reservations
Accepted

Features
Kid-friendly
Outdoor dining

6.5 Food   6.0 Feel

$20 Price

Madras Pavilion

Good health and good prices at this Kosher vegetarian Indian restaurant

www.madraspavilion.us

Indian
Casual restaurant

Upper Kirby
3910 Kirby Dr.
(713) 521-2617

Sugar Land
16260 Kensington Dr.
(281) 491-3672

Hours
Mon–Thu
11:30am–3:00pm
5:30pm–9:30pm
Fri
11:30am–3:00pm
5:30pm–10:00pm
Sat–Sun
11:30am–10:00pm

Bar
Beer, wine, liquor

Credit cards
Visa, MC, AmEx

Reservations
Not accepted

Features
Veg-friendly
Wi-Fi

Madras used to be the strongest Southern Indian game in town—whichever town it was in—but recent visits have found it slipping a bit beneath one or two of its competitors (although we shrink from the notion of competition as a bad thing; there's room for plenty of Southern Indian restaurants in any city of any size). Some of its handful of Texas locations feel, even the older ones, like a work in progress—often, a buffet steam table takes up a good amount of space, and the rest is mostly unadorned, save for some distinctly 1980s touches. Service can be a bit gruff, and English speakers difficult to find (which inspires confidence).

Most notable are the tremendous dosai—at a foot and a half long, these rice-and-lentil-flour crêpes might be the biggest around, even if they haven't been nearly as crisp and hot as they used to be. Best of these is still a buttery masala dosa, filled with curried potatoes, onions, and nigella seeds. Curries are also a good choice—palak paneer has an unusual nutty flavor to its spinach, and the cheese comes in nice big cubes. Spicy malai kofta has sliced almonds and is so rich that you might not even realize that the "meatballs" are vegetarian.

There's a good-sized and cheap daily lunch buffet, which, by the way, is totally Kosher. L'Chaim!

Mandarin Café

If it sounds gross in English, it's precisely
what you should be ordering

7.6 Food

4.5 Feel

$15 Price

For the best Chinese food in the Long Point area
(and a few astounding Korean dishes), look to a
barely noticeable strip mall containing several
Spanish-speaking businesses. It's predictably
small, dingy, and somewhat depressing, but less
so once you convince the staff you want real
Chinese food (a needless hassle that will scare
away Americanized customers, not win their
loyalty). There's a lot of Korean overlap here, so
you'll be offered several okay banchan sides—
kimchi's really wimpy and watery—and you can
pick around some good, quite spicy Korean
stews. Jellyfish salad has a great toothiness and
fresh, gingery flavor; fried dumplings are
ambrosial and tons of fun to chew. Stir-fry
dishes are all executed superbly, with careful
cuts as impressively uniform as a culinary
student's midterm exam.

But if you look around, the tables around you
are all having "Chinese spaghetti," and so
should you (its Korean name is jjajang myeon).
This majorly comforting dish full of scallops,
shrimp, and jellyfish is in a thick black bean
sauce that's pure umami heaven. Just look to
the inky splatters on everyone's shirts as
testament to its irresistibility.

Do your part to improve Chinese-American
relations: fearlessly order whatever sounds
strangest on the menu—it's just a translation
hiccup—and repeat as needed, until you are no
longer offered sweet and sour pork.

**Chinese
Korean**
Casual restaurant

Spring Branch
9486 Long Point Rd.
(713) 461-1857

Bar
None

Credit cards
Visa, MC

Reservations
Accepted

7.9	8.5
Food	Feel

$110	4.5
Price	Wine

Mark's

A good meal lies within these elegant walls,
somewhere beneath these elegant prices

www.marks1658.com

Modern
Upmarket restaurant

Montrose
1658 Westheimer Rd.
(713) 523-3800

Hours
Mon–Thu
11:30am–11:00pm
Fri
11:30am–midnight
Sat
5:00pm–midnight
Sun
5:00pm–10:00pm

Bar
Beer, wine, liquor

Credit cards
Visa, MC, AmEx

Reservations
Accepted

Features
Date-friendly

Mark's is set in a 1920s brick church, and boasts seasonal and often local ingredients—this description alone suggests the sort of DIY, repurpose-obsessed sincerity that characterizes so many newer, hipper restaurants. But instead of untreated pine tables sanded by bearded twentysomethings with visions of Brooklyn, there's a more (ahem) seasoned and conservative approach. Graceful lines gently balance deco with Protestantism, and muted orange walls envelope you with warmth and calm—a remarkable feat given the high ceilings.

In the past, we've found the menu peppered with adjectives and boasts that did little for us on the palate, but recent visits have yielded expertly cooked and artfully layered dishes that we'd return for. Pork has been especially masterful, in any preparation, and ingredients taste fresh and high quality. Some dishes (lobster tail and nearly anything crab-related) deliver a scarcity of experience that's almost exponential to its soaring cost; others are surprising and aptly priced, layering flavors cleanly and creatively.

The only abject failure is an outdated, showboating wine list. It's nearly impossible to drink well here for less than $120. At least the glass of Veuve Clicquot Yellow Label has been knocked down from a heinous $28 to a merely criminal $26. Well, look around the award-crusted anteroom: obviously *Wine Spectator* is impressed. (Then again, with just $250 and a SASE, we won that award, too.)

Masraff's

World fusion's alive and (fairly) well in this cool, contemporary space

www.masraffs.com

7.1	8.0
Food	Feel
$85	7.0
Price	Wine

Masraff's embodies the upmarket experience of the booming late '80s through mid '90s, when Asian fusion was hot, seasonality wasn't a concern, and Dadaist platings were often more impressive than the balance of flavors within. That's not to say it doesn't enjoy its merits—in fact, we've had a few pretty enjoyable dishes here, and there are private meeting rooms that make it ideal for business functions when you want (or need) dispirited execs to feel like Gordon Gekko.

The space is a little chilly with its high ceilings and contemporary décor; we appreciate when a place takes itself seriously if it amounts to service this professional and a capable kitchen. But even it struggles with this many cross-continental influences: soy glaze is like corn syrup; seared tuna is a little overcooked; and anything advertising truffle comes reeking of the more concentrated oil, rather than the subtler fresh shavings. Your best bet is to order a tasting menu at the chef's table, where you can get dishes the kitchen's more excited about making; or enjoy discounted apps like caramelized lamb lollipops in the bar, with nectar-sweet cocktails.

Like the menu, the wine list is a perfunctory study in the varietals and regions that are historically well regarded by diners; as such, it's pretty négociant-heavy, but you can find some good values in there—just not much personality or a sense of philosophy.

Modern
Upmarket restaurant

Memorial
1753 Post Oak Blvd.
(713) 355-1975

Hours
Mon–Thu
11:00am–10:00pm
Fri
11:00am–11:00pm
Sat
6:00pm–11:00pm

Bar
Beer, wine, liquor

Credit cards
Visa, MC, AmEx

Reservations
Accepted

Features
Brunch
Date-friendly
Live music
Outdoor dining
Wi-Fi

Max's Wine Dive

The wine's improving, but the calculated feel and overpriced food drive us elsewhere

www.maxswinedive.com

Modern
Wine bar

Washington
4720 Washington Ave.
(713) 880-8737

Hours

Sun
9:00am–11:00pm

Mon
4:00pm–11:00pm

Tue–Wed
4:00pm–midnight

Thu
4:00pm–2:00am

Fri
11:00am–2:00am

Sat
10:00am–2:00am

Bar
Beer, wine

Credit cards
Visa, MC, AmEx

Reservations
Accepted

Features
Brunch
Date-friendly
Outdoor dining
Wi-Fi

A good rule of thumb is that if you want to know where the best wine bars are, go where the wine industry goes. Max's Wine Dive is not that place, even for its pseudo-irreverent crowing about "Fried chicken and Champagne? Why the hell not?!"

Although catalog-ish and plastered with corporate posters, the décor isn't what deters us. The food is sometimes quite good, but often grossly overpriced. That fried chicken, when fried too long, tastes burnt from over-caramelized buttermilk marinade; on one visit, it even came with watery greens dumped on the top of it—imagine how that turned out. "Pan Borracho" is basically soggy bread with congealed cheese. But big and juicy burgers are great, "Nacho Mama's Oysters" (sigh) are a delicious twist on an old classic, and it's hard to argue with the "Max 'n Cheese" unless it's been primed with too much pungent truffle oil.

The wine program has a few moments of redemption (a grower Champagne here, a culty Rhône producer there), but is mostly populated with boring, unbalanced wines that are served either too warm by the glass or way too cold from the Cruvinet. There's no coherent train of thought in the selection here other than *Wine Spectator* scores—and perhaps the occasional coup by someone who cares—which is a glaring neon sign that a wine bar has no idea what it's doing but desperately needs you to think it does.

Mélange Crêperie

France's mad crêpe skills collide deliciously
with Houston's mélange of cultures

7.3 Food
6.5 Feel

$10 Price

melangecreperie.wordpress.com

All the world loves a crêpe, but, believe it or
not, they can be screwed up pretty badly. You
have to get the consistency just right—that
resilient, but delicate thinness, the whisper-
crisped edges. Traditionally, one uses lightly
sweetened wheat flour for crêpes sucrées, and
buckwheat for savory salées. Happily for
Houston, the fedora'd man behind griddle-on-
wheels Mélange Crêperie has a knack for this
precise craft that has so far eluded even the
Frenchest kitchens in town. That doesn't mean
his crêpes by any means escape cross-
culturalization: some specials have included
palak paneer, outstanding fig and feta, and
ajvar (the Slavic roasted pepper and eggplant
sauce that's been gripping the city's kitchens
lately). The usual ham, egg, and cheddar easily
unseats the breakfast taco as our favorite
morning meal on the go, wrapped for
portability in a cone shape (add fresh spinach
for a healthy tinge of depth). As a snack or post-
lunch treat, the simple lemon and sugar is divine
and restrained. When available, don't miss
creamy, tart lime curd.

We suggest transporting the seductively
gooey Nutella and banana to your destination
before digging in. But quickly—the lifespan of a
crêpe is mere seconds from the pan. The cart's
often at the downtown farmer's market—good
news for fans of fresh produce.

French
Food cart

Montrose
403 Westheimer Rd.
(713) 291-9933

Hours
Mon
7:00am–1:00pm
Thu–Fri
7:00am–1:00pm
Sat–Sun
10:00am–2:00pm
Check website for
current hours and
location

Bar
None

Credit cards
None

Features
Kid-friendly
Outdoor dining
Veg-friendly

Mikki's Soul Food

Forget how it looks—the Deep South
flavor's all on the plate

Southern
Counter service

Southwest Houston
10500 W. Bellfort St.
(281) 568-5115

Hours
Mon–Sat
11:00am–8:00pm
Sun
11:00am–7:30pm

Bar
None

Credit cards
Visa, MC, AmEx

Features
Kid-friendly

One of the best soul-food experiences we ever
had was years ago in Athens, GA, at Weaver
D's. Two people stirred giant cauldrons in the
semi-open kitchen, and barked out your two
choices of meat that day: stewed pork or fried
chicken. Then you chose your sides from a
selection of five, which were plopped
unceremoniously on your Styrofoam plate. No
one asked if you wanted sweet tea—it was just
handed to you, all 42 ounces of it. We are
heartsick with this memory as we stand in line in
Mikki's off-puttingly newish and bland strip-mall
suite. The steam-table buffet looks squeaky
clean and unseasoned, the black-and-mauve
chairs are of the Chinese-restaurant variety, and
the carpet and tile—industrial they may be—are
hardly hallmarks of great Southern dining. (No
wonder most business is take-out.)

Yet there it is, exactly one second after taking
our first forkful: that same swampy, Deep
South-terroired taste of Weaver D's. Oxtail
draws you into its murky depths, mixing with
pork-laced collard greens and allspiced sweet
potatoes to make what has to be among
America's best contribution to humanity. Pork
chops smothered in rich, salty gravy are also
terrific, and fried catfish has just the right
whisper of muddy riparian fishiness under a
gently cayenned crust. Of course, as it sits in the
tray, it gets mushier. On weekends, Mikki's sells
chitterlings to go. Now *that's* Deep South
terroir.

Mockingbird Bistro

A great deal and some very good meals
(better, if you like truffle oil)

8.3	8.5
Food	Feel

$70	8.0
Price	Beer

www.mockingbirdbistro.com

Mockingbird Bistro still rocks the "country-French-meets-American-market" ethos that won it acclaim in the early '00s. Since then, the fickle young crowd has moved on, but the kitchen tries to re-energize, and often produces some of the best deals in the city. Its bar menu has a wealth of these, like a $9 juicy Kobe burger with sharp Stilton and delicious bacon-onion marmalade. Kobe short ribs are also terrific, braised to tender with a tangy tomato polenta and good asparagus. Fish is always strong, like impeccably fresh rainbow trout, or maple-basted salmon that's so restrained that it surpasses expectations. But lately we've detected beleaguered truffle oil smells wafting up from several dishes. Was this the result of a comment card left by someone wearing a "fun" embroidered cat vest? Come on.

The modern interior has moments of Old-World class: large, medieval-looking chandeliers lording over tables of crisp white linens, and sill-to-ceiling windows bring an airiness to the red brick walls and exposed ceiling pipes. The unpretentious and homey feeling is buffeted with terrifically low mark-ups at the bar ($10 for 10-year Ardbeg? Here?). There's a good showing of local and imported beers, and cocktails are made from small-batch spirits. The broadly appealing wine list is sometimes curious (since when is California Cabernet Franc an "Exciting Alternative"?). But mostly, the bistro sings right on key.

Modern
Upmarket restaurant

River Oaks
1985 Welch St.
(713) 533-0200

Hours
Mon–Fri
11:30am–2:00pm
5:30pm–10:00pm
Sat
5:30pm–10:00pm
Sun
11:00am–3:00pm
5:30pm–10:00pm

Bar
Beer, wine, liquor

Credit cards
Visa, MC, AmEx

Reservations
Accepted

Features
Brunch
Date-friendly
Good beers
Good cocktails
Outdoor dining

7.6 Food 8.0 Feel

$30 Price

Nam Gang

As auntie tells you: charcoal-grilled quality meat doesn't cost nothing, you know

Korean
Casual restaurant

Spring Branch
1411 Gessner Dr.
(713) 467-8801

Hours
Daily
11:00am–10:00pm

Bar
Beer, wine, liquor

Credit cards
Visa, MC, AmEx

Reservations
Accepted

Features
Veg-friendly

Nam Gang is best on weekdays when it's slower and you can get better service; during those calmer times, the staff is more than happy to help you cook your well-marinated meats at your table.

In fact, on those nights, there's something inherently homey about it, like you just walked into your aunt's house, where the air is filled with cooking smells, and you're fussed over with cheek pinching and comments about how skinny you've become. When they're swamped (usually on weekends), all that goes out the window and it becomes everyone for themselves.

While anything that's been soaked in soy, sugar, and spice probably won't taste bad, there's something about Nam Gang's galbi (beef shortribs) and bulgogi (ribeye) that has that extra kick. Flavor penetrates every protein cell and sinew of the beef, putting the intensity of Nam Gang's Korean barbecue a notch above the rest. It also uses heated pieces of charcoal in a town where gas grills are almost exclusive. It's not all roses: kimchi pancakes are flimsy, and that quality meat costs a little more than you're used to. But much of the banchan is better and spicier than elsewhere. Soju and Hite beer will help quell the fire (and up your already voluminous tab, so be careful).

Nelore Churrascaria

It matches Fogo gaucho-for-gaucho, but wins by a thin slice of rump

7.0	8.0
Food	Feel

$75	8.0
Price	Wine

www.nelorechurrascaria.com

Fogo de Chão is emulated at the smaller, locally owned Nelore in every possible fashion, from the unbelievably appealing cheesy popovers that start the meal to the extensive salad bar and the overwhelming array of meats shaved by roaming waiters dressed as gauchos. But Nelore is cheaper than Fogo, and most importantly, the consistency of the meat is better.

Rump roast is our favorite, served in thin, tender slices and cooked medium-rare with a slightly charred outer crust. Garlic beef, also a rump cut, comes close in its moist and juicy decadence, but adds a welcome and unmistakable wave of garlicky potency. No need to waste space on sausage; it's nothing special. Bacon-wrapped filet too often arrives dry and overcooked, but most other cuts—like top and bottom sirloin, flank steak, lamb, and more— sing with flavor and juice. We can't resist the tiny chicken hearts, which we pop like pills. Since you're already paying for the whole shebang, you may as well try it all. The keys to success here are pace and resisting most of the salad bar—although the not-very-filling hearts of palm are a welcome treat.

The wine list has several excellent bottles from South America and Spain, and even a few obscure, culty Italians. Try finding that at a nationwide chain.

Steakhouse
Brazilian
Upmarket restaurant

Montrose
4412 Montrose Blvd.
(713) 395-1050

Hours
Mon–Fri
11:00am–2:00pm
5:00pm–10:00pm
Sat
11:00am–3:00pm
5:00pm–10:00pm
Sun
11:00am–9:00pm

Bar
Beer, wine, liquor

Credit cards
Visa, MC, AmEx

Reservations
Accepted

Features
Brunch
Date-friendly
Kid-friendly
Outdoor dining

8.0 6.0
Food   Feel

$10
Price

Nga Restaurant

This old Midtown favorite's improved its pho, but by no means is that its only virtue

Vietnamese
Casual restaurant

Midtown
2929 Milam St.
(713) 528-6055

Hours
Daily
9:00am–9:00pm

Bar
Beer, wine

Credit cards
Visa, MC, AmEx

Reservations
Not accepted

This recently improved old standby is a favorite of some of our panelists, because it does so much so well, across the board. While its pho was forgettable back when it was called "Pho Nga," it's now frolicking among the top ten, especially the spicy and subtle chicken version. But it's rare that you can get good pho *and* much else, like mindboggling "Phoenix"—half a roast chicken, the meat mixed with the thin, crispy skin. The kicker is the dark sauce that comes with it, bursting with salty soy and spicy ginger. Minced duck with mint and sautéed onions is transcendent and light; and bo luc lac is tender, beefy and seasoned well—a delight with its mint and nuoc mam companions. And there's a vermicelli here that's higher in gluten, stickier, and better able to take on the flavors of pickled vegetables than any other.

Nga is pretty big and well known, even in Midtown circles, but it still has some hole-in-the-wall qualities, like a dingy, worn feel, almost glowing yellow from a lack of upkeep. But the service is accommodating and gracious—as long as you make sure they get your order right. As always, it's a good sign that most of the people that frequent the place are Vietnamese.

Nguyen Ngo

Banh mi on a buttery croissant—who needs the bread pudding? (We do)

7.8 Food
4.5 Feel

$5 Price

Nguyen Ngo (pronounced "nuWHEN no") has a well-deserved reputation for excellent banh mi. If you just want a snack, the smallest size really is quite small, and the basic ham with pâté is the best order. Bread can be somewhat chewy here, but you can order your banh mi on a buttery croissant—which, if not traditional, is absolutely delicious. Regardless, the pâté is nice and salty and livery, and the crunchy vegetables properly spicy; all the elements inside are totally working better than just about anywhere else.

Most of the business here is take-out; not surprising, given its bland strip-mall location. Service can be alarmingly slow, so don't try to cram in other lunchtime errands. The shredded chicken is also great—better when lubricated with mayonnaise. You won't find grilled pork on this menu, which we know is a popular order in the banh mi world, but if you usually get it as a substitute for the flavor missing from the cold cuts and pâté, you won't miss it here.

There are also French-inspired desserts here, like creamy and rich crème caramel and an excellent banana bread pudding. And since everything costs between two and three bucks, you should go ahead and get one to eat while you wait interminably for your sandwich. After all, lunch is short: eat dessert first.

Sandwiches
Vietnamese
Counter service

Bellaire Chinatown
11210 Bellaire Blvd.
(281) 495-2528

Hours
Sun–Tue
8:00am–7:00pm
Thu–Sat
8:00am–7:00pm

Bar
None

Credit cards
None

Niko Niko's

A crowded Greek counter that can be quite good, if you order right

www.nikonikos.com

Greek
Counter service

Montrose
2520 Montrose Blvd.
(713) 528-4976

Downtown
301 Milam St.
(713) 224-4976

Hours
Mon–Thu
10:00am–10:00pm
Fri–Sat
10:00am–11:00pm
Sun
11:00am–9:00pm
Hours vary by location

Bar
Beer, wine

Credit cards
Visa, MC, AmEx

Features
Brunch
Kid-friendly
Outdoor dining
Veg-friendly

People love Niko Niko's, as evidenced by the unbearable crowds that pack the inside; sit outside, if you can—or better yet, head to the open-air Market Square location, which cuts to the chase with the best of the Niko's menu.

Its popularity is—like most extremely popular things—strongly earned by a few appealing facets, while the rest is sort of blithely accepted. Roasted potatoes are great. Pork chops are generous and delicious. Fries are good, but order them extra crispy, and they're even better. Lamb shank is tender. Desserts—especially galaktoboureko and loukoumades—are fitting ends to a meal. And then, of course, there's the classic gyro, with its warm, soft pita bread that's worthy of eating by itself. It's wrapped around complex, richly flavored meat.

The rest of the menu, we have to warn you, is terrible. Salad vegetables taste like tap water, or nothing at all. Souvlaki meat is overcooked and challenging to chew. Moussaka wants for seasoning, and fish is cardboardy. "Greek lasagna" tastes like Chef Boyardee, and falafel is dry. So stick to the good stuff and don't even think about ordering a Greek wine (not even remotely the best Greek wine you can get in Texas anymore); and definitely not a margarita. But then, we didn't need to tell you that, right?

Ninfa's on Navigation

8.0 Food
8.0 Feel
$30 Price
9.5 Margs

Forget the rest—the original Ninfa's (and its Anvil-perfected 'rita) is still the best

www.mamaninfas.com

Anvil is taking over the city—a situation we're thrilled with. It's just that you wouldn't expect one of the nation's strongest bar programs to inform the margarita of a humble, longtime Tex-Mex establishment. But then, this branch of Ninfa's—the original and the only one we recommend (the others are owned by totally different groups)—is no ordinary Tex-Mex restaurant. In fact, it's supposedly where fajitas were invented.

The run-down neighborhood's mostly Hispanic, and the shack-like exterior suggests rural Mexico, but the interior looks more polished and put together. A new outdoor bar area is the ideal place to taste Anvil's spectacular Mex-inspired cocktails, as well as a menu of Ninfa'd-up bar classics like spicy chicken wings and ribs. About those fajitas: high-quality skirt steak is brushed with soy sauce, salt, and pepper while on the grill, so it comes tender and savory. But they're even better mixed into ground beef and sandwiched into a Slow Dough bun as an outrageous, juicy "Fajita Burger." When it's available, soft-shell crab is also showstopping, the gently marine, lightly spicy meat fried to a golden brown atop a tangy bed of jicama-cucumber slaw. Skip subpar chiles rellenos and enchiladas, but do start with sopapillas, a puffy razor-thin tortilla drizzled with some of the best chile-laden queso in town. Now served with the best margarita in town.

Mexican
Casual restaurant

Downtown
2704 Navigation Blvd.
(713) 228-1175

Hours
Mon–Thu
11:00am–10:00pm
Fri
11:00am–11:00pm
Sat
10:00am–11:00pm
Sun
10:00am–10:00pm

Bar
Beer, wine, liquor

Credit cards
Visa, MC, AmEx

Reservations
Accepted

Features
Brunch
Good cocktails
Kid-friendly
Outdoor dining

Nippon

Repair the broken trust between sushi chef and diner, and you will be rewarded

Japanese
Casual restaurant

Montrose
4464 Montrose Blvd.
(713) 523-3939

Hours
Tue–Sat
11:30am–10:30pm
Sun
11:30am–10:00pm

Bar
Beer, wine, liquor

Credit cards
Visa, MC, AmEx

Reservations
Accepted

Features
Kid-friendly
Outdoor dining

Nippon, even after twenty years, is still family owned, family run, and family friendly. One look around the often-full dining room reveals an eclectic look into Houston's diverse demographics: older Japanese businessmen flanked by swinging singles alongside families with young children and representatives from all ages and ethnicities.

Servers here are actually Japanese, but they seem to be playing to their experience with hakujin preferences, suggesting things like tempura (slightly overcooked and sometimes chewy). Instead, concentrate on the fish, which is some of the freshest in town. All of the basics—maguro, sake, hamachi, and more—are textbook delicious. Ask for aji tataki, lightly seared horse mackerel dressed ever so gently with fresh ginger, spring onions, and sesame seeds.

Better: run the gauntlet. Sit at the sushi bar and order omakase. At first, they might commend you for ordering in the proper way, but they'll be hesitant to break outside the boundaries of rolls and nigiri. They've been burned by those who claim to be adventurous, but aren't. Teach them how to trust again. Chastise them until they agree. Thump your chest a little, even—they love it.

With enough assurances (maybe learn basic Japanese? Tell them you miss the izakaya bars of Tokyo?), you can score yourself some fantastic delicacies, raw and cooked—and they'll definitely remember you next time.

Ocean Palace

A mega-Chinese resaurant that's not the standard-bearer people make it out to be

4.5 Food
6.0 Feel

$30 Price

www.oceanpalacerest.com

Ocean Palace needs to be much better than it is, given the responsibility it carries as an introduction of Chinese cuisine to so many Westerners. At least the setting is legit, if you can brave the blue fountains without losing your appetite: the place has two stories of glorified banquet rooms (fish tank here, obligatory golden dragon there). If you can brave the dim-sum hordes, you'll be seated upstairs, where a holistic-feeling dome allows beautiful sunlight to shine onto the non-stop movement below. It may all evoke the hustle and bustle of Hong Kong, but the food isn't even close.

How do you control food quality at a place that seats more than two hundred people? You don't. It's hard to believe some of the swill that comes out of this kitchen. During its city-famous dim sum—now available on weekdays, as well—dishes come out lukewarm in both temperature and quality. Chong fun (meat or shrimp wrapped in a flat-rice-noodle envelope) is flimsy and lacks even subtle flavor. Barbecued pork buns are stuffed with honey-sweet pork with no savory balance. Almost nothing else coming off the carts has that flavor-forward, punch-you-in-the-mouth taste to it that you expect from Chinese cuisine. For dinner, ordering anything live out of the tank is a good idea. Simple preparations of fish, like flounder steamed just with soy sauce, make for a light, if pricey, meal. Still, you can get a cheaper, better Chinese dinner somewhere else.

Chinese
Dim Sum
Seafood
Casual restaurant

Bellaire Chinatown
11215 Bellaire Blvd.
(281) 988-8898

Hours
Sun–Thu
10:00am–10:00pm
Fri–Sat
9:00am–11:00pm

Bar
Beer, wine

Credit cards
Visa, MC, AmEx

Reservations
Accepted

Features
Brunch

7.8	7.0
Food	Feel

$10	7.0
Price	Margs

100% Taquito

Surprisingly authentic Mexican street food for the West U set

www.100taquito.com

Mexican
Counter service

Greenway Plaza
3245 Southwest Fwy.
(713) 665-2900

Hours
Sun–Thu
11:00am–10:00pm
Fri–Sat
11:00am–11:00pm

Bar
Beer, wine, liquor

Credit cards
Visa, MC, AmEx

Features
Kid-friendly
Outdoor dining

100% Taquito aptly fills a need for authentic Mex-Mex in this area. The place is full of quirks, from its location in a homogenized strip along I-59, to the Mexico City taxicab that's parked inside the restaurant, to the trompe l'oeil of dingy Mexican storefronts on the walls.

An extensive menu features sopes, quesadillas, and tortilla soup, but the appropriately tiny, delightfully cheap tacos are the headliners. Tinga (soft, gentle brisket) earns well-deserved praise, but our favorite is carne asada, whose meaty, sensationally seasoned singe epitomizes the genre. Watch for bones, which sometimes appear in the hunks of steaming, pulled meat—a sign of authenticity. But it's in the torta—not the taquito—that the carne asada shows best. The meat's juices, opaque from a smear of mayonnaise, fill the fluffy cavities of fresh-baked bread. Add to this a slice of ripe avocado, shredded lettuce and tomato, tangy chile, melted cheese, and optional spicy pickled carrots, and you have a sandwich that is an everyday miracle of balanced flavors and satisfying textures.

Skip the puny, underwhelming shrimp in any form, and don't buy into the tres leches hype. For something sweet, we prefer the underappreciated cucumbers, jicamas, and oranges with chile, lime, and salt—yet another welcome dose of unexpected authenticity.

Oporto Café

Perhaps the closest thing to a proper tapas bar in Houston

www.oporto.us

7.1	7.5
Food	Feel

$50	8.0
Price	Wine

Portuguese Modern
Wine bar

Greenway Plaza
3833 Richmond Ave.
(713) 621-1114

Hours
Mon–Wed
11:00am–11:00pm
Thu–Fri
11:00am–midnight
Sat–Sun
4:00pm–midnight

Bar
Beer, wine, liquor

Credit cards
Visa, MC, AmEx

Reservations
Accepted

Features
Date-friendly
Outdoor dining
Wi-Fi

Tapas are bar food, yet in Houston, most are sold in large, fussy restaurants. Oporto is the exception: it's more of a wine bar. A Portuguese one, at that. Below waist level, the narrow room looks European—there's an old, sturdy wood bar with stools, and tables with white cloths. Above, the atmosphere goes awry; the upper halves of two walls are garishly colored and covered with equally garish contemporary art. It's a good thing it's so dark in there.

The lunch menu focuses on salads, pizzette, and panini, but it's the nightly Portuguese tapas menu that's most interesting: steamed mussels in tangy white wine broth; salt cod—a Portuguese and Spanish staple rarely found in Houston—served in a salad of potatoes, chickpeas, olives, and egg; and canja, a chicken-and-rice soup with a rich broth and lemony-mint exotic edge. Also interesting is homemade sausage served with spicy piri-piri oil.

The focus is on wine, so ignore those pandering "-tinis." Not including dessert Ports, there are about ten different Portuguese wines—not a lot, but probably Houston's largest showing. There are also smaller-production wines from Spain and Italy, as well as some South and North Americans. Nightly specials make this place an even better bet—on Tuesdays, bottles are half-off, and Sunday paella is only $12 per person.

6.4 Food 7.5 Feel

$35 Price

Osaka

Decent-quality fish in risky-sized bites—a low-cost thrill of the most primitive kind?

Japanese
Casual restaurant

Montrose
515 Westheimer Rd.
(713) 533-9098

Hours
Mon–Thu
10:30am–10:30pm
Fri
10:30am–12:30am
Sat
noon–12:30am

Bar
Beer, wine, liquor

Credit cards
Visa, MC, AmEx

Reservations
Accepted

Features
Date-friendly

Osaka's draw is its huge portions and relatively low prices. Counter to popular tastes, bigger sushi is not necessarily a good thing. Not only will it destroy the balance between sweet-sour-sticky sushi rice and fish—balance that world-class sushi chefs are intent on creating—but it's potentially dangerous. Even when a fish looks healthy, it's harder to detect parasites in such thick cuts. What's more, careful slicing means even amounts of fat, and thus better flavor and texture.

That's not to say that Osaka's sushi doesn't taste fine—in fact, that's all it is: fine. If you get the chirashi, a bento box of rice and huge cuts of varying fish, you can balance textures yourself. Several renditions of udon and not-so-crispy tempura are serviceable. Meals begin with a complementary amuse bouche (one time an okay tempura shrimp paste on shiso leaf) and end with a lovely bit of ice cream.

The atmosphere is the essence of Japanese culture, serene and controlled. This is not a sake-bomb kind of place; instead, it's pretty uniformly dark-wood colored—a stark contrast to some of the circuses that call themselves sushi bars in this town. If the goal is to tap into your inner Gollum and gnaw a huge chunk of pretty tasty fish for not much money, then this is the best place to do it.

Ouisie's Table

5.6	9.0
Food	Feel

For brunches, elegant Southern munches,
and "ladies who lunch"-es

$60	6.0
Price	Wine

www.ouisiestable.com

Ouisie's Table looks like something out of *Southern Living* magazine: elegant in its white tablecloths, but not uptight; classy yet quaint, with a rustic chalkboard for specials. Though the décor is not overtly feminine or anything, this spot draws mostly groups of gals, who convene in the airy "sun room," with its summertime piano player, or on the lovely outdoor patio.

Aside from some gorgeous salads, the food's mostly of the heavy Southern ilk. A capable chicken-fried steak with a luxurious (but not too thick) black pepper-milk gravy comes with mashed potatoes, corn pudding, bacony black-eyed peas, and greens—all of which are delicious. An ill-conceived venison version is tougher and a bit gamey. Expertly fried Gulf oysters pair brilliantly with Maytag blue cheese slaw and tomato salad. Shrimp and grits are fantastic, but a mac and cheese that separates from its béchamel base isn't worth the price; neither, for that matter, is the unmemorable brunch or the recently offered breakfast service.

The wine list is dominated by prestigious names and generic-tasting biggies, but for anyone who actually minds, there are some respectable Italian and French bottles at fairer prices. Or get drunk on Ouisie's tempting desserts, like dense old-fashioned chocolate layer cake, creamy pots de crème, and a superb key lime tart. After all, a waist is a terrible thing to mind.

Southern
Upmarket restaurant

River Oaks
3939 San Felipe St.
(713) 528-2264

Hours
Mon–Thu
7:00am–10:00pm
Fri
7:00am–11:00pm
Sat
8:00am–11:00pm
Sun
8:00am–10:00pm

Bar
Beer, wine, liquor

Credit cards
Visa, MC, AmEx

Reservations
Accepted

Features
Brunch
Kid-friendly
Live music
Outdoor dining

7.1 Food | 8.0 Feel

Pappadeaux

A kitschy Cajun good time that we sort of
enjoy in spite of ourselves

$45
Price

www.pappadeaux.com

**Seafood
Southern**
Casual restaurant

Upper Kirby
2410 Richmond Ave.
(713) 527-9137

Galleria
6015 Westheimer Rd.
(713) 782-6310

Southwest Houston
2525 S. Loop W.
(713) 665-3155

More locations
and features at
fearlesscritic.com

Hours
Sun–Thu
11:00am–10:00pm
Fri–Sat
11:00am–11:00pm
Hours vary by location

Bar
Beer, wine, liquor

Credit cards
Visa, MC, AmEx

Reservations
Accepted

Features
Kid-friendly
Live music
Outdoor dining

It feels like there's a nightly party at
Pappadeaux, with the perpetual floods of
people clamoring to pay pretty high prices for
pretty huge portions of generally pretty good
seafood. The staff is well trained, if at times
young and awkward, and the restaurant always
seems to be brimming with excitement; a quiet
night is out of the question.

With Dixie blasting in the background, this
restaurant might not appear to be Greek-
owned—until you see the streams of orders for
the special tableside-prepared Greek salad,
which would probably give Paul Prudhomme a
heart attack if he saw it. If *you* get a heart
attack here, though, it'll likely be from the
reliable, tasty fried seafood and cream-laden
bisques.

Precious little on the menu—aside from
decent raw oysters—is allowed to retain its
natural flavor (and cocktails will taste like
anything but liquor, if you like that sort of
thing). The appetizer section of the menu reads
like a bypass-surgery sampler of everything from
gator to shrimp, and you can opt for all of it
fried or blackened. Gumbo's lukewarm and
tasteless. Shrimp or oyster po' boys are your
best bet, as they're the lightest of all the fried
foods. They're also the best value on the menu.
Whatever you get, though, the food is what it
is: salty, crunchy, creamy, sometimes tasty, and
hell-bent on destroying your waistband.

Pappas Bros.

As stuffy as a powdered wig, but the dry-aging and wine list we dig

www.pappasbros.com

8.5	7.5
Food	Feel

$105	8.5
Price	Wine

Steakhouse
Upmarket restaurant

Galleria
5839 Westheimer Rd.
(713) 780-7352

Hours
Mon–Thu
5:00pm–10:00pm
Fri–Sat
5:00pm–11:00pm

Bar
Beer, wine, liquor

Credit cards
Visa, MC, AmEx

Reservations
Accepted

Features
Date-friendly

We still think this a hoax
Whose tab would make even sheiks choke.
But lately we find a slight change of mind:
This steak's gotten better, no joke.

The Prime beef is in-house dry aged,
The well-marbled ribeye's the rage.
Wagyu's quite pricey; the taste difference is dicey
But you probably won't care at this stage.

The kitchen's still somewhat impaired—
Oversalted and creamed everything, squared—
But they cook a good meat, medium-rare's no small feat.
Still, the mark-up is grossly unfair.

The wine list deserves our redress
You can drink well for considerably less.
Better's not darker; ignore Robert Parker!
Ask which bottle the som would suggest.

The service is kind and attentive
It should be: this place is expensive!
We're still somewhat jaded, but can be persuaded.
(If you're paying we won't be so plaintive.)

Pappas Burger

Those Pappas Bros. make a mighty good burger

www.pappasburger.com

Burgers
Counter service

Galleria
5815 Westheimer Rd.
(713) 975-6082

Southeast Houston
7088 Airport Blvd.
(281) 657-6168

Hours
Sun–Thu
11:00am–10:00pm
Fri–Sat
11:00am–11:00pm

Bar
Beer, wine, liquor

Credit cards
Visa, MC, AmEx

Features
Kid-friendly

We struggled with whether or not to include Pappas Burger as one of our recommended restaurants. On one hand, there are far better burgers in town; on the other, the Pappas Bros. restaurants are homegrown institutions. And, come to think of it, this is a really good burger.

There's a rumor that the patties incorporate Prime beef from their steakhouse. Whatever the case, this fresh-ground meat comes seasoned and cooked to your liking. You can add bacon, blue cheese, chili, or a number of other condiments, but the beef flavor's so good on its own, you don't really need to. French fries, on the other hand, look homemade, but are limp. There's also fried shrimp and catfish, but it's not as good as it is at the soul-food restaurants in town. Salads and vegetarian sandwiches will fulfill the non-meat-eaters in your party, if not as well.

There's a confused retro theme to both locations. You got your counter seating; red, white, and blue colors; and creamy milkshakes that all sell the 1950s concept—but the giant televisions, goofy staff uniforms, and high prices snap you right back to present-day. Then again, the present's where you find the burger fetish that means plump, juicy patties like these.

Pappas Seafood

Less shuck 'n' suck, and more upscale seafood for your buck

www.pappasseafood.com

6.2	7.0
Food	Feel
$50	7.5
Price	Drinks

Seafood
Casual restaurant

Upper Kirby
3101 S. Shepherd Dr.
(713) 522-4595

Southeast Houston
6945 I-45 S.
(713) 641-0318

North Houston
11301 I-45 N.
(281) 999-9928

More locations
and features at
fearlesscritic.com

Hours
Sun–Thu
11:00am–10:00pm
Fri–Sat
11:00am–11:00pm

Bar
Beer, wine, liquor

Credit cards
Visa, MC, AmEx

Reservations
Accepted

Features
Kid-friendly

At Pappas Seafood, the emphasis is more on the seafood—not so much the Cajun—and the vibe aims for something more upmarket than Pappadeaux's raging bar scene. You won't find people sucking the heads of crawfish here; but you will, happily, find that same awesome tableside Greek salad.

The décor's remarkably genuine for a chain; it's not over-the-top nautical, nor does it go out of its way to feign a downmarket feel. Rather, with its high-backed booths and bow-tied servers, you might say it's trying to be the seafood equivalent of a steakhouse. As at Pappadeaux, the treatment is more hands-on than hands-off, but that's not always a bad thing: the balance of its lemon-garlic-butter sauce is admirable. Jambalaya, though, is boring; even the sauce can't revive it. Fish is cooked expertly, and the daily specials are generally a good bet; still, think cream sauce and zucchini ribbons. Not exactly highbrow stuff.

Margaritas avoid being sickly sweet or too tart, and their strength will creep up on you. We can't give the wine program a rating—only the Little Pappas on Shepherd has a shockingly astute list of well-made wines that pair beautifully with seafood; oddly, the other branches don't seem to have a clue. Even an average number wouldn't make sense. Suffice it to say: oenophiles, head to the Little Pap.

5.4	7.5
Food	Feel

$35	7.5
Price	Margs

Pappasito's

As this Tex-Mex empire grows, order fajitas and 'ritas with caution

www.pappasitos.com

Mexican
Casual restaurant

Upper Kirby
2536 Richmond Ave.
(713) 520-5066

Downtown
2515 S. Loop W.
(713) 668-5756

Galleria
6445 Richmond Ave.
(713) 784-5253

More locations
and features at
fearlesscritic.com

Hours
Mon–Thu
11:00am–10:00pm
Fri–Sat
11:00am–11:00pm
Sun
10:30am–10:00pm
Hours vary by location

Bar
Beer, wine, liquor

Credit cards
Visa, MC, AmEx

Reservations
Accepted

Features
Kid-friendly
Outdoor dining

Pappasito's liquor-endowed margaritas and tender beef fajitas have a well-earned place in the hearts of Houstinites. So what if their char doesn't have much of the wood smoke flavor we so cherish? Grilled quail comes out with a lot of flavor—it's a great way to impress the out-of-towners with the sophistication of our Tex-Mex scene. Cheese enchiladas with chili gravy are just about flawless, spinning certain unwitting customers off into a nostalgic euphoria that takes them straight back to childhood outings with the family.

Generally, Pappasito's also does the little things well, like charro beans that burst with pork-fat flavor from cubes of bacon, or chile con queso with more tomato-and-pepper texture to stand up to the creamy cheese than most versions have. It can be obnoxiously corporate, however, with peppy servers uttering cheeseball phrases like "Anyone save room for a delicious dessert?" and an over-studied Tex-Mex atmosphere.

Yet it's exactly this sort of chain—with the culinary rigor required to execute one regional cuisine faithfully—that fails to produce anything truly sublime. Shrimp fajitas are only memorable because of their lemon butter; dry-rubbed baby back ribs are fine, but far from barbecue-joint excellence; soft tacos are relatively bland. We've also found troublesome consistency issues, like dry fajitas and soapy-sweet 'ritas, at certain branches. Upper Kirby seems to be the most reliable.

Pasha

A delicious and affordable meal, whether as
a casual lunch or a nice dinner

www.epasha.com

7.5	8.0
Food	Feel

$35
Price

Don't be intimidated by Pasha's white-
tableclothness; it's fairly cheap and casual. Deep
red walls and dark wood chairs make it
something of a safe haven for Rice Village
lunchgoers, as well as a nice date-night
prospect. Cold starters such as ezme (chopped
tomatoes, onions, parsley, and crushed
walnuts), imam bayildi (stuffed eggplant cooked
in olive oil), and labneh (yogurt curd, walnuts,
dill, and garlic), are refreshing, flavorful
introductions and palate cleansers. All mains
come with Turkish rice, grilled tomato, and
cabbage, and yogurts and hummus are made
in-house. Like Istanbul Grill, Pasha serves Turkish
pizzas, and they're nearly as good; their thick
crusts are piled high with specialty toppings,
which can include lamb, feta, dill, egg, or
Turkish sausage. There's a hospitable BYOB—
we'd like to recommend one of the Turkish
wines here, but they're not among some of the
better Turkish wines out there; bring some of
Lebanon's outstanding and pretty affordable
Château Musar for real fireworks.

For dessert, baklava is a solid staple—not too
dry nor too honeyed—but baked rice pudding is
rich and dreamy. Lunch will run you less than
$10 and includes some soup or salad, which is a
good deal for a filling, quite healthy meal. That's
somewhat worth the hassle of parking in the
Village.

Turkish
Casual restaurant

Rice Area
2325 University Blvd.
(713) 592-0020

Hours
Tue–Thu
11:00am–10:00pm
Fri–Sat
11:00am–11:00pm
Sun
11:00am–10:00pm

Bar
Beer, wine, BYO

Credit cards
Visa, MC, AmEx

Reservations
Accepted

Features
Date-friendly
Outdoor dining
Veg-friendly

8.0	8.0
Food	Feel

$20	8.0
Price	Wine

Paulie's

More than just a neighborhood Italian sandwich shop—thanks to the details

www.pauliesrestaurant.com

Italian Sandwiches
Counter service

Montrose
1834 Westheimer Rd.
(713) 807-7271

Hours
Mon–Sat
11:00am–9:00pm

Bar
Beer, wine, BYO

Credit cards
Visa, MC, AmEx

Features
Outdoor dining
Veg-friendly

Paulie's quaint flagship in the 'Trose wins loyal followers with its artsy feel and sweet, relaxed service. Large windows face the street, while a low ceiling and low noise level lends an intimacy. There's a good selection of Italian wine, which best complements the easy and recognizable Italian-American fare here, and for only $10 you can bring something of your own.

Of course, one of the first things you'll notice is a bakery case of artful and cheap cookies, of which the raspberry sandwich is terrific (the sugar cookies are pretty, but not as good). And we're happy to report that the food—which was never bad—is improving quite a bit. Weekly specials are some of the best orders here: eggplant parmesan is good, but avoid anything sounding suspiciously American-influenced, like a bland spinach pasta with prosciutto and peas. Osso buco is marrowy and tender, and pizzas are passable. Sandwiches are still the favorite here, and the shrimp BLT, while it has its detractors (who say it's briny and messy), is lauded by many—its delicious bun helps. In fact, all of Paulie's breads are delicious; also, fries are crisp and taste clean, while potato salad is fresh and flavorful. To further prove that the details are everything, Paulie's has commissioned the Greenway Coffee geniuses to train its baristas. Now that's community service.

Peking Cuisine

If you don't call far enough in advance, no duck for you!

8.2	6.0
Food	Feel

$15
Price

This is just about our top place for Peking duck in the city. But you *must* call several hours in advance for it (one feeds about 3 people comfortably). It's worth the extra trouble: this duck deconstruction team is deeply in tune with the process—which, when executed properly, as it is here, includes air-drying and slow roasting that produces extra-crispy, fatty skin ready to be sandwiched between somewhat stiff pancakes, with umami-sweet hoisin sauce, Napa cabbage, scallions, and bok choy. Bringing along a Chinese acquaintance helps; while the staff means well, nobody in the dining room tends to be fluent in English. Pointing at a menu probably won't work either, as many of the descriptions are either spelled wrong or are missing important verbs or adjectives.

The duck is the be-all of the rather plain, tidy restaurant, but it's not the end-all. Discreet flavors are not a forte of northern Chinese cuisine, and the flavors in soft, spicy marinated beef aren't either, but its gelatinous, rendered tendons get just the right amount of spice and oiliness. Stir-fried spicy eggplant's flecks of red pepper make it look hot, but a surprising sweetness balances the dish. And la pi (broad glass noodles) are some of the best around. Get some to distract your friends while you eat their share of duck.

Chinese
Casual restaurant

Bellaire Chinatown
8332 Southwest Fwy.
(713) 988-5838

Hours
Daily
11:00am–3:00pm
4:30pm–9:30pm

Bar
Beer, wine

Credit cards
Visa, MC, AmEx

Reservations
Accepted

Features
Kid-friendly
Veg-friendly
Wi-Fi

Perry's Steakhouse

This shameless, showy steakhouse serves the mother of all pork chops

www.perryssteakhouse.com

Steakhouse
Upmarket restaurant

Memorial
9827 Katy Fwy.
(832) 358-9000

Sugar Land
2115 Town Square Place
(281) 565-2727

Northwest Houston
9730 Cypresswood Dr
(281) 970-5999

More locations
and features at
fearlesscritic.com

Hours
Mon–Thu
4:00pm–10:00pm
Fri
11:00am–11:00pm
Sat
4:00pm–11:00pm
Sun
11:00am–9:00pm
Hours vary by location

Bar
Beer, wine, liquor

Credit cards
Visa, MC, AmEx

Reservations
Accepted

You might wonder how a glitzy steakhouse chain landed among our top places to eat— many of our favorite steaks these days are made in modern, farm-to-table-aiming kitchens that are nowhere near as extravagantly priced as Perry's. And while the steaks here are quite convincing, we'll cut to the chase: Pork Chop. Even when your server holds up seven fingers indicating its thickness, it does not prepare you for the mammoth hunk of swine that appears (and is deftly carved) tableside. It is a revelation; a succulent symphony sung by the sweet caramelization of pork, right down to the crisp "eyelash" where the juices accumulated during its four-day smoke.

Otherwise, the selection is a little Love-Boat-Meets-Dynasty: gigantic shrimp cocktails, jumbo lump crab cakes, and turtle soup. As usual, the latter is done little justice (it tastes alarmingly like canned chili). Steaks are expertly cooked, with a good crust and all the greatness of a month-long dry aging. Sides don't measure up: runny potatoes au gratin, overbroiled crabmeat atop asparagus, and so on.

Provided you're on someone else's expense account, there is something admittedly fun about this over-the-top show. Each location varies slightly, but they all feature a Frank Lloyd Wright-inspired décor and Vegas carpeting. If you pad around the wine list, you might even find some character-driven bottles worth the (sizeable) dent in your wallet.

Petrol Station

An homage to microbrews with a burger that earns its own cred

8.8	8.0
Food	Feel

$25	9.0
Price	Beer

Take a decommissioned antique gas station, add deeply colored paint and a trip to Restoration Hardware, several rustic wooden tables and benches, and an enormous collection of taps siphoning the more venerable and exciting American microbrews—and you have a recipe for guaranteed success. But then Petrol Station really shoots the moon by making a best-in-class burger, and even giving more thought than is usual to the coffee. (Wine is still relegated to the back of the bus—why have it at all, then?) The vibe is way less focus-group deliberate than it is simply conceived of good taste and an obsession with beer. Although there are few kids here, they do get their own menu—including a scaled-down version of the burger, which is a popular option among adults with petite appetites.

The full-sized version is sloppy, huge, and delicious, with a glossy bun whose eggy fluffiness supports a half-pound Angus patty that, when cooked medium and below, is a celebration of grain-fed beefiness. There's also a burger with a whisper of lamb that needs a rare to medium-rare order to really show itself (and its tzatziki, cucumber, and tomato will convince you it's really just a gorgeous gyro on a bun). "The Rancor," with a near-vinyl layer of cheese, thick bacon, and fried egg, delivers a wallop directly to the brain's pleasure center. Fries have that wonderful earthy ugliness of real, actual potato—they're killer with bacon crumbles and feta cheese. It's all ample support for a beer education.

Burgers
Counter service

Northwest Houston
985 Wakefield Dr.
(713) 957-2875

Hours
Mon
5:00pm–midnight
Tue–Fri
2:00pm–midnight
Sat
11:00am–1:00am
Sun
noon–10:00pm

Bar
Beer, wine

Credit cards
Visa, MC

Features
Good beers
Live music
Outdoor dining
Wi-Fi

7.8	8.0
Food	Feel

$80	8.5
Price	Wine

Phillippe

An over-the-top circus of pretense with some legitimate highlights

www.phillippehouston.com

Modern
Upmarket restaurant

Galleria
1800 Post Oak Blvd.
(713) 439-1000

Hours
Mon–Thu
11:00am–3:00pm
5:30pm–10:30pm
Fri
11:00am–3:00pm
5:30pm–11:30pm
Sat
noon–3:00pm
5:30pm–11:30pm

Bar
Beer, wine, liquor

Credit cards
Visa, MC, AmEx

Reservations
Accepted

Features
Date-friendly
Outdoor dining

Oozing with pretense seems to be a lease requirement in the Galleria's BLVD Place (which also houses that overpriced opera buffa RDG), as exemplified by Phillipe's menu of annoying, unhelpful doublespeak like "Contained Decadence" (pots of brioche spreads), "Satisfaction…Guaranteed" (this one baffles us: are the other items on the menu not guaranteed?), and "Unrestrained" (again, the suggestion is unnerving). The absolute limit, however, is the "art menu," which provides information on the (albeit lovely) art on the walls. The minimalist, striking décor works another gallery of sorts, one that showcases the gussied-up clientele.

If you enjoy such charades (it does feel like a real night out), you're in luck: the food can be quite good. A "contained" venison pâté with bright mustard and house-pickled vegetables is terrific; "Au Naturel" (doubly pomped as "naked") tuna is a fun edible margarita with a bath in tequila, Cointreau, and orange zest; and classic, comforting French dishes like beef cheeks invoke a brisketey Texan essence. Mac and cheese is drowning in truffle oil, though; time to retire that old culinary mare. A Southwestern spin on the Caesar, with skirt steak and cactus, is nice, but avoid a po' boy (here a "rich boy"—sigh) with over-battered shrimp. While the wine list offers some of the world's best under-hyped bottles, the inclusion of stylistically generic "familiar" wine is distracting, and the staff's not much help. Perhaps some Orwellian subtitles will help.

Pho Binh

In a city of pho, Binh is still the king

www.phobinh.com

9.2	5.0
Food	Feel

$10
Price

In Houston, which boasts the third largest Vietnamese population in the country, you can find noodle shops so good they run out of pho before lunch. Pho Binh is—just ahead of Pho Danh II—our panel's favorite, especially from the trailer location. You heard us right: That trailer on Beamer slightly bests the other four locations (although the Beechnut location has better rice plates); Pho Binh by Night provides a welcome 2am option in Bellaire Chinatown, but its pho is just really, really good instead of stupendously, eye-rollingly good. Oh well. Typically, they're situated in rather plain and beaten-down shopping centers with a non-descript mess of tables and chairs inside.

This pho is a penetrating potion of profoundly developed flavors of beef bones intertwined with twists of sweet onion, ratcheted up with slips of hard spices like star anise and clove. We like to order ours with fatty brisket, crunchy tripe for extra texture, and rare eye-round on the side. The noodles are ideally toothsome and not overcooked, like seemingly everywhere else.

Other items aren't bad, either, like plates of fluffy crushed rice and aggressively flavored, but overcooked meat (again, not as much on Beechnut). You can skip the starters such as unexceptional fried Vietnamese egg rolls. In fact, skip it all and go right for the pho.

Vietnamese
Casual restaurant

Spring Branch
2021 Mangum Rd.
(713) 686-6408

Bellaire Chinatown
10827 Bellaire Blvd.
(281) 568-7333

Bellaire Chinatown
10815 Beechnut St.
(281) 568-7333

More locations
and features at
fearlesscritic.com

Hours
Mon–Fri
9:00am–4:00pm
Hours vary by location

Bar
None

Credit cards
Visa, MC, AmEx

Reservations
Not accepted

Pho Danh II

Great pho and bun bo Hue from the cleanest corner of Hong Kong Mall 4

Vietnamese
Casual restaurant

Bellaire Chinatown
11209 Bellaire Blvd.
(281) 879-9940

Hours
Daily
8:00am–8:00pm

Bar
None

Credit cards
Visa, MC

Reservations
Not accepted

Pho Danh II is buried in the side of Hong Kong Mall 4, which houses several of the city's most underwhelming pho houses. But this restaurant stands out so much from the rest of the mall, it's shocking. And not just because of the pho— if it weren't mostly liquid, you could probably eat it off the floor it's so clean in here. Even the kitchen looks like it's swept and buffed hourly.

Whereas most pho places have rice plates, spring rolls, and egg rolls, the Danh doesn't deviate much from its eponymous achievement. You can actually distinguish each flavor in this broth. It has a strong beefiness, with a base built on onions, yet a licoricey, bright anise shows up, too. We admit we find Pho Binh's just a bit more sublime, but Danh has got its meat beat. These ones come freshly sliced, and only slightly cooked before broth immersion. The accoutrements are vastly improved, as well, each leaf looking hand-picked, the basil a vivid green.

Pho Danh II also does a wonderful bun bo Hue, flavored with lemongrass and shrimp paste, so that the broth transports you from the garden to the sea and back again. It's teeming with flavor-importing pigs' feet and cooked blood, congealed into tofu-textured, mildly ferrous cubes to comfort and energize, in the good old-fashioned Hue.

Pho Ga Dakao

A chicken noodle soup that'll make you say "pho bo *who*?"

8.8 Food

5.5 Feel

$10 Price

We all love beefy pho bo, and given that Houston's got the third-largest Vietnamese population in America, we have no shortage of great options in that territory. But what about the pre-French Colonial tradition of pho ga; that is, what about chicken soup? The world loves its chicken soup—nearly every culture has its own version (and this being America, we're blessed with all of them). To try the best of Houston's Vietnamese entry, hearken to the restaurant with it right in the name. Pho Ga Dakao is a bright, modern, clean space in a strip mall with "Chicken Noodle Soup" lit up right beneath its Vietnamese name—happily, few other concessions are made to English speakers (and don't expect gratuitous service or anything).

The eponymous soup may not get a richness from marrowy beef bones, but if you order the one "with everything," you get a developed, intoxicating depth from the inclusion of gizzard, heart, liver, chicken tripe, and fatty skin, as well as the hard-boiled yolk of a fertilized chicken egg. The soup's best with just a little pepper and fresh jalapeño—too much else will mask the subtle flavors that crescendo with each slurp until you are left with a resonant and complete harmony that you won't be able to get out of your head. There are other items—like a salad with shredded chicken, sprouts, cabbage, fried crispy shallots, and rice noodles that's outstanding with a little nuoc mam—but honestly, we rarely get past the soup.

Vietnamese
Casual restaurant

Bellaire Chinatown
11778 Bellaire Blvd.
(281) 879-5899

Hours
Daily
8:00am–10:00am

Bar
None

Credit cards
Visa, MC

Reservations
Not accepted

Features
Brunch

Pho Saigon

Reliable pho, pretty much wherever you are

www.phosaigonnoodlehouse.com

Vietnamese
Casual restaurant

Midtown
2808 Milam St.
(713) 524-3734

North Houston
7400 W. Tidwell Rd.
(713) 462-4935

Westchase
2553 N. Gessner Dr.
(713) 329-9242

More locations
and features at
fearlesscritic.com

Hours
Daily
9:00am–9:00pm

Bar
None

Credit cards
Visa, MC, AmEx

Reservations
Not accepted

Features
Kid-friendly

Given the reach of the Pho Saigon chain (which extends up to Austin), the quality here remains pretty high. People swear that the broth varies somewhat from location to location, but we generally find it deep and beefy, intensely flavored and nourishing. It's not as redolent of clove and star anise as the excellent and venerable Pho Binh's, but it's still good. Just ask the hordes of people who swarm this place at lunch and on weekends.

Small bowls are big, and large bowls are gargantuan. Fatty brisket is either tough and crumbly or rubbery and inedible—but you should totally get it, just to flavor the broth further. Ask for eye-round rare on the side so you can dunk it just before eating. Chicken-based pho is lighter, but salty and flavorful, with those same magical healing powers. Vermicelli dishes are less oily than some other versions around town, with nicely crisped pork, a refreshing fish sauce, and sweet, charred shrimp. Soft spring rolls are just okay, but bereft of enough mint or cilantro to make them worthwhile, and unaided by a saccharine-sweet peanut sauce.

Most locations have a mass-produced, clean and nonspecific feel to them. It's an impressive turn-and-burn operation—more good news, if you're in a hurry.

Pico's Mex-Mex

Want some amazing mole and cochinita pibil? Just follow your nose...

8.5	8.0
Food	Feel

$35	8.5
Price	Margs

www.picos.net

Mexican
Casual restaurant

Southwest Houston
5941 Bellaire Blvd.
(713) 662-8383

Hours
Sun–Thu
9:00am–10:00pm
Fri–Sat
9:00am–11:00pm

Bar
Beer, wine, liquor

Credit cards
Visa, MC, AmEx

Reservations
Not accepted

Features
Good cocktails
Live music
Outdoor dining
Wi-Fi

From Froot Loops to Pico's Mex-Mex, toucans are always showing us the way to something delicious. This unassuming restaurant surprises with its chef-driven chalkboard specials and adherence to authenticity. Even with specious phrases like "traditional and contemporary," Pico's manages to stay on track. There's much better Tex-Mex around; you're best sticking to straight-up Mexican here, from the Yucatán (red snapper seasoned with achiote seed and wrapped in banana leaves) to Oaxaca (chicken served in black mole).

The thatched-roof patio and fountain are cute, and festive when there's mariachi music and happy hour specials. Margaritas keep it real with good tequila, Cointreau, and fresh lime, but tell them to go easy on the agave nectar unless you like 'em sweet. Queso flameado, packed with chorizo and peppers will have you wondering where queso has been all your life. Cochinita pibil and chile en nogada are some of the best of their kinds in the city. Charcoal-broiled meats, on the other hand, are inconsistent—sometimes they taste of carbon and are underseasoned; sometimes, they're tender, juicy, and well-singed. But this kitchen turns out three incredible moles—complex and flavorful, they have been hiding right under Houston diners' noses for years.

What is it with these toucans? They know where *all* the good stuff is.

Pierson and Company

A hospitable house of excellent brisket, good ribs, and homemade sides

Barbecue
Counter service

Northwest Houston
5110 T.C. Jester Blvd.
(713) 683-6997

Hours
Tue–Sat
11:00am–7:00pm

Bar
None

Credit cards
Visa, MC

Pierson and Company has built a loyal following. The family is as welcoming and hospitable as Southern law dictates; new customers can get full on the free samples alone. The red-and-white house sits on stilts at the crossroads of Manfield and TC Jester, and has that allure that only hidden gems can hold.

The brisket's the best thing here. Otherwise, we'd hesitate to rave about Pierson, as brisket is more important to Texas barbecue than anything. All meats here are smoked with mesquite, with the brisket benefiting the most. It's tender, smoky, and with a nice seasoned crust. Ribs are nearly as good, but sausage is eerily similar to the one served at Burn's just down the road, which has a regrettable processed flavor and texture. Other meats include chicken (Fridays and Saturdays only) and turkey, pulled pork, and smoked boudin. The sauce is excessively sweet but has a nice tang to it—but this is Texas, so you leave it off of a good brisket, anyway.

Unlike at other barbecue establishments that tend to just phone in this important detail, homemade sides are terrific. Beans are smoky and spicy, and potato salad is creamy and a little sweet. Peach cobbler, although served in tiny portions, is a must. The dining room is precious, but we take ours to go. (For the beer, you know.)

Pink's Pizza

The politics of pizza

www.pinkspizza.com

6.2 Food

5.5 Feel

$20 Price

Never bring up religion, politics, or pizza in polite conversation. Not only does it invite bad blood, but you're as likely to bring others to your camp as you are to forge peace among all nations. Pizza's no stranger to being loosely interpreted, and each variation has its own rabid defenders of the faith. Where in the pizza spectrum does culty, love-it-or-hate-it Pink's fall? Pink's, with its shabby seating and bubbly menu font from 1981? Pink's, which also runs the dubious Asian fusion "bistro" Dragon Bowl? Its wimpy convection oven won't draw the occultists who worship a 900-degree fire, nor the coal-burning defectors. Perhaps it will attract the atheists, who declare that no one knows how to use either properly, anyway.

Regardless, Pink's seems perfectly happy to stay out of these arguments with a crust that is doughy and pretty bland, but that supports often delicious ingredients. Tomato sauce is on the sweet side, but cheese is, refreshingly, restrained. A "Classic" will come with feta, Pecorino Romano, fresh mozzarella, Roma tomatoes, sun-dried tomatoes, and plenty of garlic; all evenly dispersed in an egalitarian jubilee of flavors. The "Santa Monica" (Gorgonzola, prosciutto, eggplant, artichoke, cranberries, and an olive oil base) is fun and carefree, like its namesake city. In fact, maybe Pink's is that guy who roller-skates up and down Venice Beach in a gold lamé thong, with a winged helmet and a boom box, amusing some and disgusting others as he blissfully does his own thing, unaware of any discord.

Pizza
Counter service

West U
2726 Bissonnet St.
(713) 528-7465

Montrose
710 W. Gray St.
(713) 521-7465

Heights
1403 Heights Blvd.
(713) 864-7465

North Houston
3404 N. Shepherd Dr.
(713) 861-7465

Hours
Sun–Thu
11:00am–10:00pm
Fri–Sat
11:00am–11:00pm

Bar
None

Credit cards
Visa, MC, AmEx

Features
Veg-friendly

8.2 Food   8.0 Feel

$30
Price

Piola

A scritchy, blistered pizza that evokes the Italian cultural centers of the world

www.piola.it

Pizza
Casual restaurant

Midtown
3201 Louisiana St.
(713) 524-8222

Hours
Sun–Thu
11:00am–11:00pm
Fri–Sat
11:00am–1:00am

Bar
Beer, wine, liquor

Credit cards
Visa, MC, AmEx

Reservations
Accepted

Features
Date-friendly
Kid-friendly
Outdoor dining
Veg-friendly

Pizza's like sex—everyone has a position, and it's upsetting when it's not yours. For many, only Neapolitan is acceptable (where crust blisters are concerned, once you go black, you never go back?), while New Englanders fight among themselves over whose interpretation is best (never mind Chicago's deep-dish proclivities; large swaths of the country think the best pizza has a doughy, bland crust and "gourmet" canned ingredients (thanks, CPK).

But *everyone* agrees that Houston suffers a dearth of good pizza. Along comes Piola, a small chain with cred-inspiring success in Italy, Brazil, and Argentina. The oversexed advertising and rainbow-colored pendant lamps remind us of the endearingly gaudy Buenos Aires clubs, as does the happy hour where free food keeps coming so long as you're drinking. But nothing speaks to the pizza's relative proximity to Italy (if not quite Naples) more loudly than the crust, which "scritches" when folded, showing off its lightly salty black beauty marks. The middle of a margherita oozes with firm bufala balanced by fresh-tasting tomato sauce and basil; artichoke hearts and hearts of palm are wonderful with the Brazilian cream cheese Catupiry; eggs, beef carpaccio, prosciutto, and Kalamata olives allow for great combinations that still stick to the point.

Forget the pasta—it's mediocre, and gnocchi are smooshy. At the bar, skip the few dull iterations of South American and Italian wines for beer; Italians prefer beer with their pizza, anyway—a position we can get behind.

Polonia

Old-World-priced, delicious food served
with Old-World warmth and generosity

7.0 Food
7.0 Feel

$30 Price

www.poloniarestaurant.com

Polish
Casual restaurant

Spring Branch
1900 Blalock Rd.
(713) 464-9900

Hours
Tue–Fri
11:00am–9:00pm
Sat
11:00am–10:00pm
Sun
11:00am–8:00pm

Bar
Beer, wine, liquor

Credit cards
Visa, MC, AmEx

Reservations
Accepted

Features
Date-friendly

Polonia's run-down exterior is no indication of
the coziness you'll find inside. It's so charming:
dark wood wainscoting, textured mauve
wallpaper, antique-looking Polish relics, and
flags. The romance is killed somewhat by five
television sets, even if they're usually tuned to
Polish shows. Forget the plonk wines; the only
beer you should bother with here is the Pilsner
Urquell on draft. Or, when in Poland, drink
vodka.

The crispy potato pancakes, served with sour
cream and apple sauce, are worlds away from
the mushy messes you get at IHOP. (Just don't
let them get cold, as they lose much of their
appeal.) The brothy beet barszcz filled with
fluffy meat-filled dumplings tastes like liquid
health. We also like the sour rye soup with
sausage and egg. Try a little of everything with
the combination plate for two (bigos (a.k.a.
hunters' stew), pierogi, kielbasa, cabbage rolls,
meatloaf, duck legs, and cold carrot and beet
salads). Veal schnitzel, accompanied by delicious
mounds of sauerkraut and mashed potatoes, is
another winner, but the unanimous favorite is
the golonka. Stewed in an enticingly rich sauce,
the fatty, flavorful pork shank slides off the
bone at the smallest provocation, and the sauce
makes a dipping medium for other dishes.

On Sundays, a post-mass crowd from Our
Lady of Czestochowa adds to the ambience
(and the wait).

8.2 Food 8.5 Feel

$40
Price

Pondicheri Café

East sort of meets West in this simple, chic little space

www.pondichericafe.com

Indian
Casual restaurant

Upper Kirby
2800 Kirby Dr.
(713) 522-2022

Hours
Mon–Sat
6:00am–10:00pm

Bar
Beer, wine

Credit cards
Visa, MC, AmEx

Reservations
Not accepted

Features
Brunch
Date-friendly
Veg-friendly

Pondicherry the city is a gorgeous seaside jewel in what used to be French India's crown. The prospect of a namesake café is understandably thrilling, given that French-Indian fusion has had some beautiful cultural results, but Pondicheri the café (brought to you by the folks behind Indika) is actually pretty straight-ahead Indian. Its only telling French influence is, perhaps, that vegetables aren't simmered to a stewy sameness, and flavors—which might seem, at first glance, too mild to some—are subtle and layered into a sometimes revelatory complexity.

The design of the small space has the charm of a reclaimed industrial space made chic with orange translucent curtains, artfully distressed light fixtures, and shimmering brocaded booths. There are responsibly raised meats and eggs (breakfast will be a big focus here soon), wild-yeasted homemade breads, and accessible prices. Assemble a tableful of plates from a list of mild pickled vegetables (turmeric root's a standout), vegetable dishes (each with its unique flavor preserved), and tender, delicious meats. Proceed with caution to a fish in banana leaf that is undercooked in its thickest parts.

A decent beer selection also offers a few fun "cocktails" made with herbs and peppers; the wine list, however, is surprisingly uninformed (not at all a French attribute). There are none of the floral, residual-sugared whites that so ideally pair with this cuisine. But there *are* gooey oatmeal chocolate chip cookies with cardamom and fleur de sel. That's a pairing we can live with.

QQ Cuisine

All hail this tiny den of porky bliss

6.5	6.0
Food	Feel

$10
Price

Pork belly. It's the root of all evil and the essence of everything good. It breaks waistlines and brings us bacon, the Texan fruit of life. QQ Cuisine in the Dun Huang Plaza makes it into one of the most delicious bites in town, a soft, steamed bun filled with succulent braised pork belly.

Aside from that, almost everything is unapologetically greasy, and some items—such as stir-fried spicy eggplant—are oily enough to slip out of your chopsticks. The kitchen specializes in all things wrapped and pan-fried. Pan-fried pork buns have a crispy bottom, fluffy bun, and juicy pork-and-chive filling; pan-seared dumplings are also great, with uniformly browned bottoms and a touch of fire inside. Scallion pancakes could use more scallions, but it's rolled thin and pan-fried to an ideal crispness.

At first glance, QQ doesn't look like much, more of dent than a hole in a wall. The industrial design seems built for speed, with tight-knit corners and openings just wide enough for a waiter to zoom back and forth between picking up orders and dropping off plates. The staff doesn't spend much time on you, but with $3–$10 plates, it's more about turning tables than building any sort of customer rapport. Besides, there's pork belly; why wouldn't you come back?

Chinese
Casual restaurant

Bellaire Chinatown
9889 Bellaire Blvd.
(713) 776-0553

Hours
Sat–Sun
10:00am–10:00pm
Mon–Fri
10:30am–10:00pm

Bar
BYO

Credit cards
Visa, MC

Reservations
Not accepted

9.0
Food

7.0
Feel

$10
Price

Que Huong

Inside a run-down Chinatown dive lies a
one-way ticket to Vietnam

Vietnamese
Casual restaurant

Bellaire Chinatown
8200 Wilcrest Dr.
(281) 495-2814

Hours
Mon–Fri
9:00am–10:00pm
Sat–Sun
8:00am–10:00pm

Bar
None

Credit cards
Visa, MC

Reservations
Not accepted

This cuisine is capable of so much sensory
stimulation, so many aromatic peaks and
succulent, complex valleys, that even the least
mind-blowing renditions tend to turn people on
for life. In that case, Que Huong may well
convince you to just sell the store and move to
Vietnam for good. At first glance, it seems like
any other Chinatown restaurant, beaten down
and caked with dust and grease. But this eatery
is in fact superlative. Order by numbers, or
better yet, bring a Vietnamese friend and tell
them you'll eat anything their grandmother
would eat.

The usual suspects like pho and banh mi are
passable but not special. Start with goi ngo sen
tom thit, a cold salad of julienned crunchy lotus
stems, plump shrimp, and tender sliced pork
laced with cilantro and a punchy vinaigrette. For
less-adventurous eaters, banh hoi bo lui nuong
is a good introduction, with assertively grilled
beef that's meant to be rolled into the
accompanying rice paper with carrots, radish,
basil, and mint, then dipped in fish sauce, giving
the entire package a strikingly sweet-umami
finish. Quails simmered in honey and soy
balance sweetness with light gaminess.
Lemongrass and chilies do a sprightly dance in a
dish of tender squid that transports you to the
other side of the world...but you may find
yourself booking a ticket anyway.

The Queen Vic Pub

Pretty much London's Brick Lane, but with more heat and good Texas beers

8.9	8.5
Food	Feel

$40	8.5
Price	Beer

www.thequeenvicpub.com

India and England—there are books and films exploring the complicated centuries-old colonial relationship between these two…but we'd rather eat about it. Here, The Queen Vic represents the best of both worlds, starting with the singular cozy and welcoming British pub aesthetic (too welcoming: it's often jam-packed with young, pretty people, so think twice before you valet, just in case you have to jam). Of course, the dozen or so beers on tap are carefully chosen from standard UK favorites to (mostly) the local greats. There are beer dinners and cask tappings, too. The bar stocks some great liquors and mixers and so on, but nimbly navigate the list if you want savory or bitter flavors. But if British Indian food is notorious for being of the sweeter, creamier, less spicy rendition, the stuff here's surprising. A special of whole roasted branzino rubbed with spicy curry paste was fantastic—look for it. The vibrant lamb vindaloo is borrowed from The Vic's sister restaurant Oporto, and naan glistens with ghee. Best to skip the skewered kabobs, which can be tough; saag pizza isn't better than the sum of its parts, either.

Of the British fare, fish and chips are controversial—some say it's too greasy, but hey, it's greasy there, too. Scotch eggs are great, but the prosciutto and egg biscuit is too marmaladey and meat-skimpy to recommend. But no worries; there's oodles more to love.

Indian
British
Casual restaurant

Upper Kirby
2712 Richmond Ave.
(713) 533-0022

Hours
Tue–Fri
11:00am–midnight
Sat
4:00pm–midnight
Sun
4:00pm–11:00pm

Bar
Beer, wine, liquor

Credit cards
Visa, MC, AmEx

Reservations
Accepted

Features
Date-friendly
Good beers
Good cocktails
Outdoor dining

7.9	7.5
Food	Feel

$100	8.0
Price	Drinks

RDG

Mo' money, mo' pomp, mo' circumstance—
trendiness over culinary greatness

www.rdgbarannie.com

Modern
Upmarket restaurant

Galleria
1800 Post Oak Blvd.
(713) 840-1111

Hours
Mon–Fri
11:30am–2:00pm
6:00pm–10:00pm
Sat
6:00pm–10:00pm
Sun
noon–3:00pm
5:00pm–9:00pm

Bar
Beer, wine, liquor

Credit cards
Visa, MC, AmEx

Reservations
Essential

Features
Brunch
Date-friendly
Good cocktails

If you thought it impossible for the flagship restaurant of the Schiller/Del Grande empire to reinvent itself as something even flashier, more upmarket, and more of an "it" restaurant than Café Annie, its previous incarnation, then you'd be wrong. Even more pomp and circumstance and showy interior design attend this entry into the most elite of Houston social spheres.

Still, at its best, this restaurant turns out some fascinating flavors, spiking a martini with smoked tea, or adorning maple-cured quail with a wild-mushroom chili, venison sausage, and cornbread dressing—a sort of homage to Texas Hill Country that's impossible not to stop eating. But turbulence plagues the menu. The simplest dishes are often the worst: "wood-grilled king salmon," for instance, is little more than a puny, uninteresting sockeye cooked appropriately rare. A $42 wood-grilled ribeye comes out with little of the marbling we associate with that cut or a Prime grade, and its fries come with a radioactive-orange dipping sauce that's a dead ringer for that Chinese take-out "duck sauce."

However high the high points may be, and however consistent the execution—cooking meats properly to temperature, expertly frying oysters—these recipes are too clunky, their ingredients too often inferior. It may be great business, but the food, even at its best, is further diminished by the rip-off prices. Do indulge in the bar's delicious burger.

Red Lion

The standard British-style pub made unique with its above-average food

6.0	8.0
Food	Feel

$25	8.5
Price	Beer

www.redlionhouston.com

As the old joke goes, in Hell the policemen are German, the mechanics are French, and the cooks are English. But unlike there (and unlike at our other favorite British-style pub, Black Labrador), the British fare here is quite good. Check the chalkboards for weekly specials, like Wednesday's $18 curry and a pint. Those British curries are decent, if you like the style, which is a bit rich and spice-poor. Burgers are oversized, and you can opt for delectable roasted Brussels sprouts instead of fries; steaks are cooked expertly. Fish and chips have come pretty soggy, but the homemade malt vinegar is kickin'. For dessert, there's a show-stopping bread pudding. Avoid anything far beyond the realm of the crown: Thai and Mexican-influenced dishes are disastrous.

This is an ideal place to stop by after work for the outstanding beer selection, both on draft and in bottle; there's also a pretty good single-malt Scotch selection. You can also watch a game on the telly without the oversexed, fratty feeling of other pub-style bars. Large, wooden doors lead into a dimly lit dining room with small lamps on each table. There's a fire burning away in a hearth at the end of the dining room, and the patio's full of chatty people and their dogs. Hey, if this is Hell, sign us up.

American British
Bar

Upper Kirby
2316 S. Shepherd Dr.
(713) 782-3030

Hours
Thu–Sat
11:30am–1:00am
Mon–Wed
11:30am–11:00pm
Sun
11:30am–10:00pm

Bar
Beer, wine, liquor

Credit cards
Visa, MC, AmEx

Features
Date-friendly
Good beers
Outdoor dining
Wi-Fi

Reef

Some of the best raw and cooked local-fish dishes in the city, with wine to match

www.reefhouston.com

Modern Seafood
Upmarket restaurant

Midtown
2600 Travis St.
(713) 526-8282

Hours
Mon–Thu
11:00am–10:00pm
Fri
11:00am–11:00pm
Sat
5:00pm–11:00pm

Bar
Beer, wine, liquor

Credit cards
Visa, MC, AmEx

Reservations
Accepted

Features
Date-friendly
Outdoor dining

At Reef, the city's most diverse selection of Gulf fish is selected carefully, cleaned in-house, and astutely prepared. Much of the menu is static, but with seasonally changing twists and daily specials; raw dishes excel almost as much as the cooked. We still find the crispy-skinned snapper one of the best dishes in Houston, served with sweet and sour chard; we've also loved roasted grouper and spectacular dry-aged steak. Meats and fish are cooked with equal expertise, and dishes are artfully plated, but without venturing much into molecular-gastronomy territory; homemade rolls dusted with coarse salt sop up delicious sauces, old-school style. Blackfin tuna bacon can be unbearably salty at times, lunacy-inducing at others; mac and cheese, fried into a cute cube, tends to be dry and mealy inside, but these low points are rare (and not really all that low).

The dining room appears aquatic in its spare, wavy lines and lagoon shades; an open kitchen, city view, and high ceilings make for a vibrant—often very noisy—scene, and happy hour specials are a terrific draw. Still, service is some of the most professional and efficient around. Cocktails are largely of the fruity and clear-liquored variety; we'd take advantage, instead, of the outstanding wine list of small-production vineyards, marked up barely over retail. Now that's Southern hospitality.

Rioja

A decent introduction to Spanish wine and food in a charming, romantic space

www.riojarestaurant.com

8.0	9.0
Food	Feel

$65	8.0
Price	Wine

Spain has found itself at the butt end of the joke that is the so-called "New World" (or, on this menu, "modern") winemaking style, made popular in the past couple of decades. It's the school of inky, ultra-concentrated fruit, aggressive new oak (despite the misinformation on Rioja's menu about modern meaning *less* oaky), more residual sugar, and lower acidity than most of the wines that had been historically produced there.

We mention this because, like Spanish wine, tapas are terribly misunderstood in America. Like Rioja's wine list, which could much better represent the typicity that set the region apart in the first place, its food menu offers the well-known classics, but executes them somewhat haphazardly (fish fillets have come rather ragged and sad, but stuffed piquillo peppers are fine). The paella's serviceable, but not winning over any Spanish natives; its slightly disjointed taste suggests the components were cooked separately, rather than together, so that seafood and sausage can infuse each rice grain. The warm-toned walls and lovely patio make this place a beloved date destination—best if your date is a sommelier, and even better if neither of you has eaten tapas in Spain, so you don't know what you're missing.

Spanish
Upmarket restaurant

West Houston
11920 Westheimer Rd.
(281) 531-5569

Hours
Tue–Fri
11:00am–2:00pm
5:30pm–11:00pm
Sat
5:30pm–11:00pm
Sun
11:00am–9:00pm

Bar
Beer, wine, liquor

Credit cards
Visa, MC, AmEx

Reservations
Accepted

Features
Brunch
Date-friendly
Live music
Outdoor dining
Wi-Fi

5.7	8.5
Food	Feel

$30	8.5
Price	Beer

Rudi Lechner's

Kitsch and comfort food at Houston's best
German restaurant (also just about its only)

www.rudilechners.com

German
Casual restaurant

Southwest Houston
2503 S. Gessner St.
(713) 782-1180

Hours
Mon–Sat
11:30am–10:00pm

Bar
Beer, wine, liquor

Credit cards
Visa, MC, AmEx

Reservations
Accepted

Features
Date-friendly
Good beers
Kid-friendly
Live music
Wi-Fi

Before you double-check our lukewarm food
rating, keep in mind Houston's best German
restaurant is also one of its *only* German
restaurants. As a result, this place is often
packed, and at lunch, Rudi might even seat you
himself. Oktoberfest is a blast, of course, with
live music on many nights.

The décor's totally Epcot Center "Germany:"
the waitstaff wears the closest thing to
lederhosen you've probably seen since
Wurstfest, and the restaurant is adorned with
three decades of Bavarian décor, imported beer
empties, and enough animal heads to make any
Texan feel at home. The regulars have been
coming for a long, long time; if you prefer to
hang out with the under-80 set, grab a table in
the bar area and dig into the extensive beer
list—sip a Warsteiner or go the wine route with
an Austrian Grüner Veltliner.

Rudi's has some of the best Wiener schnitzel
around. Hot and crispy, straight from the fryer,
and served with a mound of homemade
sauerkraut, it is a thing of beauty. Throw in
Polish sausage, roasted pork loin, red cabbage,
and mounds of Austrian potatoes, and you've
got a steal of a 14-dollar lunch sampler that's
plenty for two. Good, too, are braised pork
shank and goulash. That said, it's all uniformly
undersalted; season your palate accordingly
with Spaten and some hard-to-find German
digestifs.

Saigon Pagolac

Beef seven ways and a killer baked catfish make for a long, entertaining evening

8.6 Food

6.5 Feel

$25 Price

Vietnamese
Casual restaurant

Bellaire Chinatown
9600 Bellaire Blvd.
(713) 988-6106

Hours
Tue–Sun
11:00am–11:00pm

Bar
Beer, wine, BYO

Credit cards
Visa, MC, AmEx

Reservations
Not accepted

Beef Fest. That's why you come to Saigon Pagolac when there are easily a dozen terrific Vietnamese places on every side of you. You bring a few people and get seven courses of beef: sliced eye round served with a bit of hot vinegary broth for you to flash-cook it in; ground beef wrapped in a fragrant leaf and lemongrass-marinated beef that you grill over charcoal at the table; bite-sized meatballs; and even alphabet soup with beef. It's an event unto itself, so be patient, and then dip and get your fingers all coated in nuoc man, and add the accompanying veggies—we need more interactive meals like this in town.

But balance your beef with fish; whether we're in Vietnam, Italy, or Mexico, there are few things we love more than a good whole-fish preparation. The bones keep all the moisture in the meat while it's being grilled, steamed, or fried. Here, it's a huge baked catfish, glistening with sweet-lemony sauce and coated in garlic chips and scallions. The atmosphere's not much to look at—it's too bright and cold, with a painted mural not doing much to warm it up— but with what's happening on your table, we doubt you'll even notice.

8.6 Food	**8.5** Feel
$75 Price	**8.0** Wine

Samba Grille

A handsome, excellent churrascaria fit for even pre-theater and lunch crowds

www.sambagrillehouston.com

Steakhouse
Brazilian
Upmarket restaurant

Downtown
530 Texas Ave.
(713) 343-1180

Hours
Mon
11:00am–2:00pm
Tue–Thu
11:00am–2:00pm
4:30pm–10:00pm
Fri
11:00am–2:00pm
4:30pm–midnight
Sat
4:30pm–midnight
Sun
noon–9:00pm

Bar
Beer, wine, liquor

Credit cards
Visa, MC, AmEx

Reservations
Accepted

Features
Date-friendly
Outdoor dining

Samba Grille, perhaps more than any other churrascaria in Houston, deserves to prevail. If we sound slightly nervous about its prospects, it's because this location seems to be cursed, and there are already a jillion equally vibey, modern, and dimly lit steakhouses around it that are competing, too, for the lunchtime and pre-theater hordes. The service seems to bear this slight patina of desperation, and patrons are often directed towards the more expensive bottles on the wine list—which aren't hard to find, given the outrageous mark-ups. The selection is great, if curiously all-inclusive: grocery-store Torrontés sits (at five times retail) next to fantastic South American, French, and American wines. These are available by the glass from Enomatic-style preservers that keep them alive and fresh; good news, if you've just plunked down $25 for a glass.

The meats often outdo their chain-y competitors; even filet mignon has come with a slight ring of fat, adding flavor to this otherwise bland cut. New York strip is dry aged, a rare delight, and rarer still at $39 for 14 ounces. Lamb chops are absolutely outstanding, and fat, juicy burgers are divine. In lieu of a nasty, congealing salad bar, you can choose from a few excellent all-you-can-eat options, like jade soup (spinach and broccoli cream with crabmeat) and zesty gazpacho. A lunchtime 3-course prix fixe is hospitable and quick, and when there's a show on, Samba extends its hours to lunch Saturday and dinner on Monday.

Sam's Deli Diner

The greasy-spoon burger made better than the sum of its parts

8.5 Food

6.5 Feel

$10 Price

Here's the deal about Sam's burger: it's not a thick, from-fresh patty. It's from frozen, which, these days, is like saying it kicks kittens. And the bread's not very good at all. But if too many places these days are jumping on the "quality ingredients" bandwagon only to produce underwhelming dishes, Sam's does the opposite. It takes those thinnish patties and char-grills the everloving blah right out of them. Then it butters, batters, and grills that bun until you have no choice but to love it, and the way the copious cheese melts and seeps into folds of exquisitely crisp bacon. (It's especially great when teeming with sautéed mushrooms.) Beware: the jalapeño burger is not for the light of stomach. French fries and onion rings are okay on a good day, inedible on a bad one. Save your calories instead for hand-dipped Blue Bell milkshakes and ice cream.

Incidentally, this place doesn't have anything to do with a deli or a diner. The walls, which are painted with the mascots of the neighboring high schools, say a lot about Sam's clientele: you'll even see Memorial and Stratford High School students—sworn enemies—rubbing elbows. This is a downmarket atmosphere deeply evocative of the heart-to-heart, family-to-customer restaurants that are more common up in Philadelphia, Chicago, and New York, but scarce here in Houston. That's yet another reason to love Sam's, frozen burger patty and all.

Burgers
American
Counter service

West Houston
11637 Katy Fwy.
(281) 497-8088

Hours
Mon–Sat
7:00am–9:00pm
Sun
10:00am–9:00pm

Bar
None

Credit cards
Visa, MC, AmEx

Features
Kid-friendly
Live music

San Dong Noodle House

The secret at this tiny shop is to only order food with outerwear

Chinese
Counter service

Bellaire Chinatown
9938 Bellaire Blvd.
(713) 271-3945

Hours
Tue–Sun
11:00am–9:00pm

Bar
None

Credit cards
None

Features
Kid-friendly
Veg-friendly

When the dreary Santong Snacks, which developed a feverish horde of followers for its exemplary dumplings, moved into brighter, shinier digs and became San Dong Noodle House, there was a severe drop in the near-perfect quality of its prized preparations. Not enough to completely eradicate it from our radar, but it was certainly no longer in the upper echelon of Chinese eateries. But we've since seen steady improvement, and things are almost as excellent as they were before the move. We're not sure what it is about grimy, tiny places—we think of those things as "seasoning"—but they're usually primo spots for finding the city's best Chinese food (whatever city, really). That said, San Dong's nicer, cleaner—but still modest—digs produce pan-seared pork dumplings with that elusive crispy bottom; they're juicy and bursting with flavor on the inside. Really, they're some of the best in town. Leeks are assertively funky in that wonderful Chinese leek way. Pan-fried pork with rice is also reliably good, with the flattened, panko-coated pork like an Asian chicken-fried steak; its tangy pickled cabbage brightens it considerably.

Other dishes are serviceable, but not among the best in their class. The key to success here is to order it only if it's wearing some kind of dough or bread-crumb jacket.

Seco's Latin Cuisine

Who knew Mexican food without lard could be so good?

7.8 Food
7.0 Feel

$30 Price

Mexican
Casual restaurant

Rice Area
2536 Nottingham
(713) 942-0001

Hours
Mon–Thu
11:00am–10:00pm
Fri–Sat
11:00am–11:00pm
Sun
10:30am–10:00pm

Bar
Beer, wine, liquor

Credit cards
Visa, MC, AmEx

Reservations
Accepted

Features
Brunch
Outdoor dining

Seco's advertised fusion of Mexican and "Continental" cuisine would normally have us speeding away from the scene, spurred on by nightmarish visions of quail in a pico de gallo aspic. But dishes are surprisingly—shockingly, sometimes—judicious and successful. A starter of calamari al ajillo, which typically consists of squid in a thick slick of garlicky butter or oil, is here much lighter and more ethereal, served with red onions, cilantro, and spicy peppers. Veracruz is channeled strongly in a "Snapper Seco," a fillet of fish topped with a mound of red onions, jalapeño, garlic, cilantro, and capers.

Even the creamier dishes taste balanced and healthy: spinach enchiladas in a light cream sauce are delicious. A dull-sounding "Pollo Moran," grilled chicken breast topped with sautéed mushrooms, onions, and poblanos, is actually intriguing in its own, slightly different cream sauce. On Sundays, the cute little café draws a crowd for its best buffet spreads in town, with more traditional Tex-Mex and Tex-Tex dishes like tamales, enchiladas, crab-stuffed jalapeños, and an omelette bar.

As opposed to other "Latin" restaurants, the ultimate appeal here isn't authenticity or liquor-soaked festivity, but rather the freshness of the ingredients and the healthy cooking style (olive oil instead of lard). It tastes good, but we hesitate to even call this Mexican, or European, for that matter. It's just…Seco's.

7.9	8.5
Food	Feel

$60	8.0
Price	Wine

Shade

Membership has its privileges, like drinking good wine in a lovely neighborhood

www.shadeheights.com

Modern
Upmarket restaurant

Heights
250 W. 19th St.
(713) 863-7500

Hours
Mon
11:00am–2:30pm
5:00pm–9:00pm

Tue–Thu
11:00am–2:30pm
5:00pm–10:00pm

Fri
11:00am–2:30pm
5:00pm–10:30pm

Sat
10:00am–3:00pm
5:00pm–10:30pm

Sun
10:00am–3:00pm
5:00pm–9:00pm

Bar
Beer, wine, liquor

Credit cards
Visa, MC, AmEx

Reservations
Accepted

Features
Brunch
Date-friendly
Outdoor dining

Shade's the sort of neighborhood restaurant that you want to be at, and you'll forgive most offenses to do it. Fortunately, those offenses are relatively few, especially if you stick to small plates. The sage-green space is perfectly amenable to a casual meal—it's effortlessly stylish, and we love hanging out at either the chilled-out bar or in the somewhat intimate alley seating. If you want to drink wine (the mostly New World list is well priced and well chosen), you'll first need to join Shade's "private club," an amusing way of getting around the dry-neighborhood restrictions. There's no membership fee, and the unstuffy staff will explain it all to you.

The menu does a little globe-trotting from the American South to the Middle East to Southeast Asia, but its preparations are intuitive and mostly successful. We didn't expect to like the wasabi-and-cucumber-crusted red snapper, but it's tender and harmonizes nicely with its coconut milk-based red curry broth. We've also liked Panko-fried shrimp with spectacular smoky bacon grits and Frank's Hot Sauce. Duck breast with corn-poblano polenta reaches towards West Texas, but a side of collard greens braised with bacon brings it back to the South while staying on pitch.

Most dishes here fall into the "passable" designation. But it's an affordable and perfectly lovely evening if you aren't looking for fireworks.

Shanghai Restaurant

The family who runs this Cantonese gem is practically restaurant royalty

9.2 Food **7.0** Feel

$15 Price

Chinese
Casual restaurant

Bellaire Chinatown
9116 Bellaire Blvd.
(713) 988-7288

Hours
Sun–Thu
11:00am–midnight
Fri–Sat
11:00am–1:00am

Bar
BYO

Credit cards
Visa, MC

Reservations
Accepted

Features
Kid-friendly

It's hard not to perk up when you hear that Chinese families have followed the career of a certain restaurant family for about 25 years. Such is the case with our longtime favorite Shanghai, whose owners have won and kept fans as they traversed Bellaire Chinatown in a series of small and larger operations. Having finally settled into the Welcome Supermarket center as Shanghai, they consistently serve the best, most down-to-earth Cantonese cuisine in the city. (Amusingly, it's not the least bit Shanghainese—they just didn't bother to change the name when they took over the lease.)

The place makes the requisite stabs at decoration but is totally low-key, and the family members are the ones serving, managing, and cooking. Their collective culinary experience results in feats of balance and elegance in dish after comforting dish: from the intensely flavored broth that serves as a sort of amuse bouche, to superlative shrimp and pork dumplings in soup, to vegetables balanced and brought out in style with garlic and shrimp paste. Salt fish and salt-and-pepper pork ribs both have a terrific crunch in the outer crust that unlocks the delectable meat inside.

While other places are good for one or two particulars, Shanghai's an all-round masterpiece.

6.2 Food | 6.5 Feel

$10 Price

Shawarma King

Reliable and friendly Middle Eastern eating that won't cost you a king's ransom

www.shawarmakingonline.com

**Middle Eastern
Greek**
Counter service

Hillcroft Area
3121 Hillcroft St.
(713) 784-8882

Hours
Mon–Thu
11:00am–10:00pm
Fri
11:00am–11:00pm
Sat
noon–11:00pm
Sun
noon–10:00pm

Bar
None

Credit cards
Visa, MC, AmEx

Features
Outdoor dining
Veg-friendly

Much of Shawarma King's continued success has to do with its owners being just about the nicest people in the city. Even if it's not mind-blowingly good or anything, it's solidly enjoyable, and cheap. In addition to shawarma, there are kebabs, kofta, dolmeh, falafel, and much, much more. But heed the sign: the point's the shawarma—spiced beef, chicken, or lamb, stuffed with tomato, lettuce, and tzatziki in a thin, soft pita. The kitchen tends to spice heavily, but the seasoning doesn't overpower the meat. Kebabs are especially aggressive—a plus, given how well heavy seasoning works in this cuisine. It's beautifully balanced by fluffy saffron rice, or cool, minty salads.

Like most Middle Eastern restaurants, there's plenty of vegetarianism allowed in this kingdom. The falafel's one of the best in town, fried to ideal crispiness, and the option is yours to make it a plate or wrap it up in a sandwich (we recommend the latter, for both price and taste reasons). Douse them with plenty of acidic yogurt sauce for their fullest potential. At lunch, there are several combos all costing around $7 that will stuff you like a shawarma pita, yet somehow leave you feeling light and healthy. Long live the King.

Shiv Sagar

Among the cheapest and best vegetarian meals in the city—even on Tuesdays

8.9 Food

6.5 Feel

$10 Price

Indian
Counter service

Hillcroft Area
6662 Southwest Fwy.
(713) 977-0150

Hours
Daily
11:00am–9:30pm

Bar
None

Credit cards
Visa, MC, AmEx

Features
Veg-friendly

In the shopping center with our favorite Indo-Pak restaurant, Himalaya, and the sporty good time of London Sizzler, Shiv Sagar presents a worthy stop for cheap and easy chaat lunches; most specifically, wonderful dosai and dahi puri. On Hindu-holy Tuesdays, many other Indian restaurants are closed, but this one's open, and often crowded. Take someone who can scope out a table while you stand in line to order (and tell your cashier which table number you're at—be prepared or you'll annoy them and everyone in line behind you).

The crowd's here for daily changing thali, filling platters of various bites that ring in around $8 with tax. Or order à la carte and focus your digestion. While we prefer the fried, savory-donut vada and idli steamed lentil cakes at Krishna Chaat House, the dosai here are, again, sublime—crispy, crêpey, and tender-bellied. Samosas are also very strong, but better are dahi puri, flaky little shells filled with chickpeas, potatoes, zingy sweet onions, and spices. They're too light on yogurt, but otherwise terrific. Chutneys aren't as world-rockingly vibrant as elsewhere, and raita's properly cooling, but not particularly strong in cilantro, mint, and/or cucumber. Still, you can't beat this place for made-to-order, cheap, delicious lunches and a TV screen filled with mood-inducing Bollywood films.

8.0 Food   7.0 Feel

$15 Price

Sichuan Cuisine

Find a couple of other fiends, order the hot pot, and bubble away

Chinese
Casual restaurant

Bellaire Chinatown
9114 Bellaire Blvd.
(713) 771-6868

Hours
Daily
11:00am–10:00pm

Bar
BYO

Credit cards
Visa, MC

Reservations
Not accepted

Our drug of choice is Szechuan peppercorn, and Sichuan Cuisine's hot pots are a terrific source of it. We fiends sit around bubbling cauldrons of fiery broth, heaping plates of raw flesh into it for about an hour and a half. (Show up much later than 8:30pm, and you may not get to indulge in this communal ritual.)

The menu is rife with other mouth-watering, authentic dishes like ma la, crispy intestine, and a tea-smoked duck that's sometimes exceptional and sometimes oversalted and dry, but if you've got 3 or more, go hot pot. You first must specify yuanyang (divided into half spicy and half mild), all spicy, or all mild broth. "Spicy" is an ass-kicker, but yuanyang will give you all the clove-anise flavor you want. While you wait for your broth to boil, head to the back table for a cold snack of garlic cucumbers, sliced beef, and jerky; or mix your own sauce from sa tsa (Chinese barbecue sauce), raw egg, cilantro, chilis, and soy sauce.

When you choose your vegetables, noodles, and meat, consider that head-on shrimp or thinly sliced beef or lamb must be fished out quickly or they'll overcook. You can opt to have a live fish brought from the tank to boil to death in your cauldron. But dude, some things you should never see while high on Szechuan.

Sinh Sinh

Live nude fish every night into the wee hours

8.0 Food

7.0 Feel

$30 Price

www.sinhsinh.net

Sinh Sinh's seafood tanks are the best in the city, and you can even indulge at one or two in the morning. Don't let the briny smell deter you: it's the glorious byproduct of one tank full of huge geoduck clams (the only thing here that gets consistently overcooked) and another of Maine lobster; sweet shrimp here (spectacular), and live soft-shell crabs there. The Vietnamese side of the menu isn't much better than average—skip it in favor of the barbecue (pork can sell out early in the night), or better yet, the seafood tanks. Sinh Sinh's responsible for what must be Houston's best preparation of soft shell crab, as well as great sizzling oysters, salt crusted shrimp, and fish maw soup.

True, the bright, modern décor has all the class of shoddy plastic surgery. The ceiling is painted a textured blue to look like clouds. Even more bizarre is the temperature-controlled wine-storage area amidst the scramble of tables and hanging roasted ducks. Château Margaux? Silver Oak? With shellfish?

Service is weird too, when it's not just plain rude or pushy; if you go down the path of live seafood—as you should—you'll be encouraged to spend your month's salary in one go. (Live seafood is pricey; Dungeness crab, for instance is $33.95 per pound. Always ask for a cost estimate when ordering.)

Chinese Seafood
Casual restaurant

Bellaire Chinatown
9788 Bellaire Blvd.
(713) 541-0888

Hours
Sun–Thu
10:00am–2:00am
Fri–Sat
10:00am–3:00am

Bar
Beer, wine

Credit cards
Visa, MC, AmEx

Reservations
Not accepted

Features
Kid-friendly

7.1	7.5
Food	Feel

$105	7.0
Price	Wine

Smith & Wollensky

Splurge on a midnight dry-aged meat mass

www.smithandwollensky.com

Steakhouse
Upmarket restaurant

River Oaks
4007 Westheimer Rd.
(713) 621-7555

Hours
Mon–Wed
11:30am–11:00pm
Thu–Sat
11:30am–1:00am
Sun
11:30am–10:00pm

Bar
Beer, wine, liquor

Credit cards
Visa, MC, AmEx

Reservations
Accepted

Features
Date-friendly
Outdoor dining

None of the latest branches of Smith & Wollensky boast the nostalgic patina of the Midtown Manhattan branch, which dates back to 1977.

And while Houston's got plenty of wonderful homegrown options, this is a rare worthy inclusion…mainly for its late-night hours. It's hard to find anything decent to eat outside of Bellaire Chinatown at midnight. Here, you have good dry-aged Prime steak, for about the highest price in town. (Did we mention you can order them at midnight?) They're well marbled and well prepared—even the filet mignon, which can so often be flavorless and chewy— and come drowned in butter, a good cheap trick. We think they're best with a dreamy-textured creamed spinach. The out-of-the-oven pan of bread that you start with—another good cheap trick—is deliciously doughy. Butter and beef are the best choices here; salads aren't so great, and fish is just so-so compared with that of our superlative seafood houses.

The environment is refined, but some touches are amusing (vintage clocks and copper-shaded lamps) or Disneyish (plaques bearing names of wealthy patrons above a sort of marble frieze). A heavily California-cabbed wine list is pricey, and a classic gin martini comes beautifully rendered, if huge. For some reason, Thursdays seem to be popular with gorgeous ladies of a certain age…in case a tasty steak's not all you like in a steakhouse.

Soma

Innovation and noise and sex-appeal, but also some quiet moments of excellence

www.somasushi.com

7.2	8.0
Food	Feel

$75	7.5
Price	Wine

Japanese Modern
Casual restaurant

Washington
4820 Washington Ave.
(713) 861-2726

Hours
Mon–Wed
11:30am–11:00pm
Thu–Fri
11:30am–midnight
Sat
noon–midnight
Sun
noon–10:00pm

Bar
Beer, wine, liquor

Credit cards
Visa, MC, AmEx

Reservations
Accepted

Features
Outdoor dining

Soma captures the exposed-pipe vibe of the Washington Avenue scene with Japanese-fetishist reds and blacks, woven seats, picture-window-sized screens depicting austere woods and tattooed body parts. Loud music competes with the shrieking laughter of attention-starved twentysomethings, while an elevated dining area lets diners gawk at each other. This is far from a romantic dinner; then again, jealousy is a powerful aphrodisiac. And the trouble isn't that the food isn't good—occasionally it's even great—it's just that the pretense speaks louder than any dish.

Recipes will seem flashy to some, derivative to others—which wouldn't be so bad if the execution were consistently there. We've been told that fish shipments are on Tuesdays and Fridays; on those days, we've had much better sushi, although the rice is often packed a bit too cold and tight. If the sashimi seems stringy and off-tasting that night, ask for hamachi or sake kama, where tender, succulent yellowtail or salmon cheek (or collar) meat is grilled to perfection. In fact, we've more often enjoyed Soma's cooked dishes, especially those off the menu: handmade ramen noodles in excellent broth, outstanding short ribs, and smoked pork with Fuji apple.

Eschew the silly, candyish cocktails for the thorough sake list, despite its high mark-ups. Or ask your server for a good Riesling…if they can hear you above all the noise.

7.2 Food | 6.0 Feel

$10
Price

Stanton's City Bites

A divey market with some unlikely specials and a killer old-school burger

Burgers
American
Take-out

Washington
1420 Edwards St.
(713) 227-4893

Hours
Mon–Fri
10:00am–6:30pm
Sat
11:00am–5:00pm

Bar
None

Credit cards
Visa, MC

Stanton's is the kind of sketchy hole in the wall that has gourmands all atwitter—especially burger aficionados. It's hard to find at first, because the signage is really a sloppy hand-painted job on the bottom floor of an off-white clapboard building. Inside, this old convenience mart is a friendly little time warp, with the meat counter still operating, and rows of chips and sodas. The only place to sit is at a dingy little four-top—most business is take-out anyway.

Despite its weekly lunch specials, which are broadcast on Twitter and include middle-Americana favorites like fettucine alfredo, meatloaf, and Southern-fried pork chops (even, eep, egg rolls), this place is known for one thing above all: the burger, of which there are over a dozen different preps. Its patty is thick, juicy, hand-formed, and cooked only one way: medium-well to well. We especially love a "Truck Stop," with a thick onion ring tucked inside. There's also an old-school patty melt, although it comes on wheat bread instead of rye; rye does appear on an occasional pastrami sandwich special, though, so you could ask for it. Sweet potato fries are better than the regular (from frozen), but onion rings beat them all, crispy and with a moderate breading.

You might want to call ahead, as Stanton's claims to close one unspecified Saturday a month.

Stella Sola

Northern Italian cuisine speaks with a sexy Texas twang in this temple of temptation

9.2	8.0
Food	Feel

$55	9.0
Price	Wine

www.stellasolahouston.com

Brillat-Savarin wrote of the virtues of an "impassioned, reasoned, and habitual preference for everything which gratifies the organ of taste"—virtues often curated by the sort of people who opened Stella Sola, a restaurant that invites hyperbole not because it is flawless or particularly cutting-edge, but because it does something that few restaurants anywhere do: it pays tribute.

The menu is a seasonal portrait of Texan ingredients, employed in mostly Northern Italian preparations. Handmade pastas and charcuterie intertwine with local produce, Gulf seafood appears in Ligurian-style stews, and so forth. In these expert hands, the results are sensual delights: poached quail eggs, ravioli, and meatballs all burst with a warm filling. A brown butter gnocchi prep skips the sage in favor of a surprising peppery arugula, and ideally al dente house-made pappardelle is topped with velvety, baking-spicy wild boar ragù.

The mostly Italian wine list features several obscure winners among some bigger names. It skimps somewhat on the crazy Friuli reds, Pinot Nero blends, and lower-priced Nebbiolos that Northern Italy is known for, but everything's just a fraction above retail. The restaurant can get unbearably loud at peak hours, given its sparse décor (save for some hanging house-cured salumi, which is fantastic on a pizza with peperone, lardo, duck prosciutto, and ricotta). An outdoor spot on a warm evening should let you better focus the organ of taste.

Modern Pizza
Upmarket restaurant

Heights
1001 Studewood St.
(713) 880-1001

Hours
Tue–Thu
5:00pm–10:00pm
Fri–Sat
5:00pm–11:00pm
Sun
11:00am–3:00pm
5:00pm–9:00pm

Bar
Beer, wine, liquor

Credit cards
Visa, MC, AmEx

Reservations
Accepted

Features
Brunch
Date-friendly
Good cocktails
Outdoor dining
Veg-friendly

7.6 | 8.0
Food | Feel

$45
Price

Sushi Jin

This low-key, authentic place has one of the better omakase experiences in town

Japanese
Casual restaurant

West Houston
14670 Memorial Dr.
(281) 493-2932

Hours
Mon–Thu
11:00am–10:00pm
Fri–Sat
11:00am–11:00pm

Bar
Beer, wine, liquor

Credit cards
Visa, MC, AmEx

Reservations
Accepted

Features
Date-friendly

Sushi Jin suffered under the weight of its opening rave reviews, but has since found solid footing. Of course, it's better if you sit at the sushi bar and engage the Japanese sushi chef—they're less gregarious than the Nippon chefs, but their omakase usually involves not only the freshest, but some of the most exciting and traditional dishes in town. The nice vibe, minus the least bit of pomposity or arrogance, is a welcome respite from the noisy poseurs.

Tuna belly dependably melts in the mouth, and hamachi is silky and slightly buttery, served at the appropriate not-icy temperature. When available, grilled hamachi collar (same as cheek) is moist and succulent as ever; never toss away your fish heads, by the way—face meat's where the magic is. Ask for uni seared atop a raw scallop—it's mind-blowing; the uni's buttermilky softness plays off the smooth, sweet scallop, and the two dissolve into one.

You'll also find a rare treat here in the pressed sushi: fish (usually saba—horse mackerel) is pressed between well-seasoned rice and sweet kelp, then sliced into intensely flavored cubes. As ever, hands off the soy sauce, and the chef smears on as much wasabi as he feels is needed to balance with the well-seasoned rice. Your job is just to trust and enjoy; and, of course, offer some sake to your gracious host.

Sushi Miyagi

A friendly, familial sushi bar that's as authentic as you need it to be

7.3 Food
7.5 Feel

$35 Price

Japanese
Casual restaurant

Bellaire Chinatown
10600 Bellaire Blvd.
(281) 933-9112

Hours
Mon–Sat
11:30am–10:00pm

Bar
Beer, wine, BYO

Credit cards
Visa, MC

Reservations
Not accepted

Features
Veg-friendly

The mom-and-pop operation is very much alive—in a Bellaire Chinatown sushi joint, of all places. Mrs. Miyagi warmly greets and seats you on simple wood chairs amid white walls hung with her cheerful art (which is for sale). Her husband, Chef Miyagi, calls out a welcome from behind what looks like a sushi bar torn straight from old Edo, with a shoji screen softening the overhead lights and a large fish-shaped flag of the sort hung outside many Tokyo sushi places.

At busier times, it can get a little chaotic, and your order may run behind. Also, unless you stress familiarity with traditional Japanese cuisine, you might be steered towards the cheesier rolls and baked-mayonnaisey dishes. Just say "agedashi tofu," whose curls of bonito shavings wriggle upon crisp-exteriored, velvety cubes. The dashi sauce is a touch too sweet and could use more fresh ginger, but it's a lovely opener. Further establish your cred by asking for battera (pressed sushi boxes) and an ume shiso roll (Japanese plum—actually more of an apricot—and basil-minty shiso leaf). Sashimi is cut on the thick side, but the fish is great quality—perhaps because they don't carry a wide selection, so they can run through it all much faster. Don't expect a great sake list or anything—it's all perfunctory. But you can bring your own, for a little upcharge. (Don't forget to offer some to your gracious hosts.)

Sushi Raku

A flashy place where the cooked classics yield the best results

www.sushi-raku.com

Japanese
Upmarket restaurant

Midtown
3201 Louisiana St.
(713) 526-8885

Hours
Mon–Thu
11:30am–10:00pm
Fri
11:30am–midnight
Sat
noon–midnight
Sun
noon–10:00pm

Bar
Beer, wine, liquor

Credit cards
Visa, MC, AmEx

Reservations
Accepted

Features
Date-friendly

From the two-syllable, four-letter name right down to the lower-case font and hanko stamp, Raku's logo bears an uncanny likeness to that of a certain famed Austin restaurant. And like it, Raku sells modernized Japanese to well-dressed folks looking for dim lighting and artful platings. Resemblances beyond that grow blurrier; for one thing, the interior's expensively designed, but to good effect? The color scheme and furnishings borrow smartly from a Kubrickian vision of space, but with diaphanous curtains and red ropes flung about with the artless melodrama of a *Project Runway* challenge. The best place to sit, as ever, is at the sushi bar, where you can ask for the goods of the day. Mostly, however, the sushi's unremarkable, suffering from average-quality fish and underseasoned rice that's served much too cool.

The beverage program is oddly more like that of a careless dive than a swanky hot spot, with cheap, nameless sake (available in "hot," "cold," and "flavored") and sugary, poorly made cocktails using standard liquors. If anything, we like Raku for its hot small plates. We've had killer tontoro (Berkshire pork belly roasted for 12 hours to tender, and served not too sweet) and delicious buttered mushrooms en papillote. A robata grill special of snapper head has also been terrific. But unlike the better modern-Japanese kitchens, whose unlikeliest-sounding dishes often reveal delightful surprises, dishes here that sound poorly conceived—like yellowtail over greens with truffle oil—also taste it.

Sweet n Namkin/Salaam

8.4 Food
7.0 Feel
$15 Price

Explore both the masculine and feminine sides of these lovely Indo-Pak twins

Indian
Counter service

Southwest Houston
10736 West Bellfort St.
(281) 988-9598

Hours
Tue–Sat
9:00am–2:00am

Sun
9:00am–midnight

Bar
None

Credit cards
Visa, MC, AmEx

Features
Veg-friendly

Sweet n Namkin and Salaam Namaste are side-by-side polar opposites. The former's brightly colored, specializes in vegetarian chaat, and is overseen by a clucking motherly figure. The latter, on the other hand, sells a meaty menu, is colored in masculine darks, and offers pool tables, flatscreen TVs broadcasting cricket matches, and coin-operated massage chairs. The sibling places are linked by a swinging door, so one can freely order from either counter, sit in either dining area, and order either menu.

On the Sweet n Namkin side, the daily chaat specials rotate and present inexpensive, filling options. Get dahi puri to share; these are impressively constructed crispy shells filled with yogurt and chutney. The bhel puri is a riot of flavors and textures, and vegetarian sandwiches pop with hidden pomegranate seeds. Dhokla is baked into little muffins for easy service. The only weak link are pani puri—they're perfectly acceptable until you compare them to the better executions here.

At Salaam Namaste, halal meats come redolent of spices, from kebabs to amazingly moist chicken to expert lamb chops. Fish katakat is like a relish that dances flavorfully on your tongue. Eat it up with some of the best naan in the city: warm, crisp, and fluffy at the same time. Afterward, soothe your excited senses with fresh juices and lassis from next door.

<table>
<tr><td>**7.3**
Food</td><td>**7.5**
Feel</td></tr>
<tr><td>**$20**
Price</td><td>**7.0**
Margs</td></tr>
</table>

Sylvia's Enchilada Kitchen

Good enchiladas and a whole lot more, now even more within reach

www.sylviasenchiladakitchen.com

Mexican
Casual restaurant

Montrose
Truck: W. Alabama and Mandell
(713) 213-2409

Memorial
6401 Woodway Dr.
(713) 334-7295

West Houston
12637 Westheimer Rd.
(281) 679-8300

Hours
Mon–Thu
11:00am–9:00pm
Fri
11:00am–10:00pm
Sat
11:00am–9:00pm
Hours vary by location

Bar
Beer, wine, liquor

Credit cards
Visa, MC, AmEx

Reservations
Accepted

Features
Outdoor dining

The original Sylvia's on Westheimer features enhanced wood archways, bright hues, blue-and-white colored tiles, and open, airy rooms; the newer Memorial branch—like Sylvia herself—is as warm and welcoming as any Texican-ranch kitchen. There's even a bright blue truck parked in the Menil Museum parking lot during lunch Wed–Fri.

Margaritas are not quite the bright spot they once were. Skip the bland tortilla soup, and instead try the guacamole served with piles of diced tomatoes, onion, and jalapeños on the side so you can flavor it up to your liking (instead of watching a waiter do so, as is the pretentious trend at upscale joints). But get to the enchiladas without further delay. Not only is a standard cheese enchilada the paragon of its category, but even testy variations like crab are excellent, balancing the sweetish meat with a judicious sauce. Virtually all enchiladas are well executed, if uncreative. Also, Sylvia actually employs an arrocero who is responsible for nothing other than making the rice, which is fantastic. Anything mesquite-grilled is also great, like beef fajitas, shrimp, and tilapia. These arrive with delicious picante poblano rajas in a creamy cheese sauce. And cabrito is intoxicating, served as a tender guisada with vegetables silky from a long, slow braise. If you can stand to order anything but enchiladas, that is.

t'afia

A pleasant locavore restaurant whose best dishes are its smallest

7.1	9.0
Food	Feel

$65	8.5
Price	Wine

www.tafia.com

It's true that t'afia is among the most fanatical of the locavore restaurants; this doesn't necessarily translate to excellent execution, despite being the brainchild of one of the city's most acclaimed chefs. It's a reliable and pleasing experience if you stick to small plates and drinks on the lovely patio. Creole cocktails made with ratafia (fortified wine infused with seasonal fruits, vegetables, and and/or herbs)—the restaurant's namesake—are often refreshingly tart, and the wine list showcases small producers from around the world whose wines are both affordable and loaded with personality. Even the Texas wines are carefully selected.

Irreproachable, too, is the flowing Midtown space, an object lesson in resourceful postindustrial-chic-meets-IKEA design. The concept of free, tasty, all-you-can-eat snacks during happy hour—have a drink, and they're all yours—is glorious. Tasting menus are relentlessly probing, sensationally seasonal, fearlessly local, reasonably priced. At their best, the creations can materialize miracles in your mouth, like medjool dates stuffed with chorizo and wrapped in bacon; or a sashimi-and-tempura roll, which is surprisingly accomplished in its lightness and heat. White anchovies are served simply, with plump, tart caper berries. But with larger dishes, you're more exposed to rampant seasoning issues and meats that tend to come overcooked to flavorlessness. Just keep it small and simple, and you'll do fine.

Modern
Upmarket restaurant

Midtown
3701 Travis St.
(713) 524-6922

Hours
Tue–Thu
4:00pm–10:00pm
Fri
11:30am–1:00pm
4:00pm–10:00pm
Sat
4:00pm–11:00pm

Bar
Beer, wine, liquor

Credit cards
Visa, MC, AmEx

Reservations
Accepted

Features
Date-friendly
Good cocktails
Live music
Outdoor dining
Veg-friendly

3.9	3.5
Food	Feel
$10	**2.0**
Price	Margs

Taco Cabana

Tex-Mex fast food that isn't all that bad—
and is made from actual food

www.tacocabana.com

Mexican
Counter service

Upper Kirby
3905 Kirby Dr.
(713) 528-6933

Greenway Plaza
5 Greenway Plaza
(713) 621-2017

Medical Center
8101 Main St.
(713) 668-4863

More locations
and features at
fearlesscritic.com

Hours
24 hours

Bar
Beer, wine

Credit cards
Visa, MC, AmEx

Features
Kid-friendly
Outdoor dining

Taco Cabana, a San Antonio-based 24-hour fast-food joint, does a surprising number of things right. The ingredients are fresh and simple, the flavors spicy and limey, and the salsa bar seals the deal: this place takes Taco Bell's beef-ish fare and stuffs it right up its bell.

This food is cheap, fast, and sorta good—what more do you need? For something impressive, try this: flour tortillas are freshly pressed on-site at each restaurant, all day long. What's more, nothing is reconstituted or defrosted, and along with the variety of salsas (pico de gallo, verde, mild, and en fuego), there are plenty of pickled jalapeños, fresh cilantro, and lime and lemon wedges on offer. At 3am, we like to get some queso (a very respectable version, and the only respectable fast-food version) and roasted chicken "flameante"—it has a spicy, tangy skin and juicy, smoky meat. With borracho beans and fresh tortillas, that's some tasty fast food. Otherwise, lightly crisp quesadillas and chicken fajitas are pretty good (beef can be tough). Skip the oily burritos, enchiladas, and horrific pupusas entirely.

The branches are generally clean and bright, with hand-painted Mexican tiles and metal tables made out of bent beer signs adding that faux-old-Mexico touch. Avoid the sticky-sweet frozen margaritas. But a fast-food joint that serves cold beer? Respect.

Tacos Tierra Caliente

Someone tie this terrific taco truck down

7.4 Food

4.5 Feel

$10 Price

This taco truck can't sit still. It's moved under the West Alabama Ice House sign, and we can't promise it will still be there when you read this. You might want to check online, but of course, a place like this doesn't have a Twitter feed or Facebook page or anything. The menu's handwritten on the side of the truck, for crying out loud. That list is a mouthwatering array of meats available in either a taco on a corn tortilla with cilantro y cebolla, or in a torta sandwich.

Barbacoa is fatty and juicy with a touch of lime for brightness; top it off with the tangy and spicy salsa verde. Bistec is all right, but a less savory version of barbacoa. Pastor is our top choice here, hot and sweet from pineapple. Delicious lengua (tongue) is sliced thin and grilled after boiling to tender, then tossed with a subtly spicy red sauce. Add a little kicking fiery red salsa for extra heat, but be careful—it's muy picante. Both salsas are available in a ketchup squeeze bottle on the counter, so you can apply with abandon. A refreshing toronja (grapefruit) soda will cool it down, and it goes great with the tequila in your hip flask.

Mexican
Food cart

Montrose
1919 W. Alabama St.
No phone

Hours
Mon–Sat
7:00am–7:00pm
Check website for current hours and location

Bar
None

Credit cards
None

Features
Outdoor dining

7.5 Food
4.5 Feel

$20 Price

Tampico Seafood

No bells and whistles, just a totally authentic Mexican seafood experience

www.tampicoseafood.net

**Seafood
Mexican**
Casual restaurant

Heights
2115 Airline Dr.
(713) 862-8425

North Houston
10125 I-45 N.
(281) 445-2525

Hours
Mon–Thu
10:30am–10:00pm
Fri–Sat
10:30am–midnight

Bar
Beer, wine, liquor

Credit cards
Visa, MC, AmEx

Reservations
Accepted

Features
Kid-friendly
Outdoor dining

Tampico Seafood transports us south of the border, from the saltine crackers that come with the mediocre, fruit-punchy, but enjoyable seafood cocktails to the ice-cold bottles of Sol. Very little is put into the décor; bright fluorescent lighting dominates, and the walls are dotted with random Mexican memorabilia, from soccer posters to beer advertisements. Christmas lights adorn the exterior, and as you walk in, you pass a glass case from which they're selling fish.

Seafood, clearly, is the way to go here; camarones al ajillo—shrimp sautéed in lots of garlic and even more butter—are just as they should be, cooked not a second too long. Use the irresistible buttered-and-griddled bread that comes with it to sop up the garlicky sauce. Order whole fish grilled; its frying is just a bit too heavy-handed. When grilled, its skin gets wonderfully crispy, with moist and tasty meat. The juices will make the other side of the fish's skin soggy, but they also flavor the onions underneath. Perhaps one of the most interesting things about Tampico is the Chinese fried rice. Its origins baffle us, but it actually hits the spot, and it makes sense: fried rice pairs nicely with fish. Margaritas tend to be weak, so order a floater and sip slowly while waiting the 20 minutes for your fish to grill.

Tan Tan

The original's our favorite for people-
watching, hot pots, and banh bot chien

8.6	7.5
Food	Feel

$15
Price

www.tantanrestaurant.com

We love the Bellaire Tan Tan, which keeps
Christmas lights eternally running all over the
restaurant, while moving-picture waterfalls and
stuffed monkeys perched on top of fake palm
trees complete the bewildering, but memorable,
scene. Best of all, you can eat some pretty good
pan-Asian (an oxymoron, usually) until the wee
hours of morning. The newer Westchase
location is decidedly more sterile—or fancy,
depending on how you look at it (and closes
much earlier). We swear the food's somehow
not quite as transcendent at that one, either,
but it must be the monkeys.

Waiters at Bellaire try to take your order even
before you crack your menu, then never show
up again except to deliver your food and bill—
it's hard to complain, however, because the
diverse crowd is like a free dinner show.

The menu takes a bit of maneuvering: pass on
greasy Americanized dishes (kung pao chicken,
beef with broccoli). Some of the best choices
here are steaming hot pots with outstanding
broth; delicious congee; and banh bot chien
(pan-fried rice cakes fused with eggs and
liberally sprinkled with green onion, fried
shallots, and fried radish). This is definitely one
of the city's best late-night dishes, especially
while being entertained by the odd late-night
crowd.

Chinese
Vietnamese
Casual restaurant

Westchase
8066 Westheimer Rd.
(713) 977-6682

Bellaire Chinatown
6816 Ranchester Rd.
(713) 771-1268

Hours
Sun–Fri
10:00am–midnight
Sat
10:00am–3:00am
Hours vary by location

Bar
Beer, wine, liquor

Credit cards
Visa, MC, AmEx

Reservations
Not accepted

Features
Date-friendly
Kid-friendly

8.4	6.0
Food	Feel

$20
Price

Tandoori Nite

Outstanding tandoori delights under the twinkling glow of...a gas station?

Indian
Food cart

Sugar Land
7821 Hwy 6 S.
(713) 852-7642

Hours
Wed–Mon
5:30pm–midnight
Check website for
current hours and
location

Bar
BYO

Credit cards
Visa, MC

Features
Outdoor dining
Veg-friendly

Atmosphere's a tough thing to pull off when you're a food trailer, but it helps to be open only at night, like Tandoori Nite is (naturally). Aided by strings of little white lights—the ultimate cheap-n-easy ambience-maker—the parking lot of the Phillips 66 gas station actually looks inviting, especially on balmy evenings. The few wooden benches scattered alongside the truck are somewhat hidden from the unromantic view (and smell) of people gassing up their cars, and the convenience store makes grabbing a six-pack of Shiner very, well, convenient. Bring your own wine; we wouldn't trust the mart's selection of demi-sec Vouvray or anything.

The tandoor oven is the star here, sending wisps of gray, meaty smoke across the night sky. Intense heat (always nice in a little Texan trailer, no?) quickly sears chicken so it stays succulent and moist; it's served with grilled jalapeños and onions, and a great coriander chutney. Chana masala is spicy and delicious, and capsicum-phobes will love butter chicken in a creamy sauce with surprising depth. Mattar paneer's cheese cubes are substantial and mutton korma is intensely flavorful and tender (all meat here is halal). The naan varies from fine to terrific. In fact, the only real bummer about this charming, delicious little trailer is the upcharge for rice. Ah well, the drinks are cheap.

Taquería Del Sol

A Mexican trek where the rewards surpass
the slight distance

8.6 Food

8.0 Feel

$10 Price

This hidden festive, old-school Mexican
restaurant way out by Hobby Airport reminds us
of an abuela's kitchen, if abuela were just trying
to make a few bucks while she was at it. The
simple meal you have here—on floral oilcloths
and cheap plastic plates—will easily blow away
those at more centrally located, yup-tacular
Mexican joints. The lunch rush starts near
breakfast time (which should tell you how early
the breakfast rush starts). And these wonderful
huevos rancheros could make us into early
risers.

The lunch menu's outrageous superstar is the
torta, the best we've had in Houston. No lie.
The magic is mostly in the bread, which is baked
here daily with some kind of double secret anti-
sog agent, and also in the tender meats bursting
with flavor. Ask for the torta de barbacoa, a
Mexican sandwich of melting barbecued meat
atop a soft bun stuffed with lettuce, tomato,
guacamole, and sour cream. It's got the holy
trinity going on: it's delicious, it's huge, and it's
dirt-cheap.

Taquería Del Sol will also ply you full of
dinner, right up into the wee hours on
weekends. Quesadillas and enchiladas are fine,
but stuffed gorditas are better, especially with
pillowy chicharrones or golden nopales. Service
is absolutely good-mood-inducing; and there's a
bakery attached if you need a little postprandial
pan dulce.

Mexican
Casual restaurant

Southeast Houston
8114 Park Place Blvd.
(713) 644-0535

Hours
Sun–Thu
7:00am–11:45pm
Fri–Sat
7:00am–2:45am

Bar
None

Credit cards
Visa, MC, AmEx

Reservations
Not accepted

Features
Kid-friendly

Taquería Tacambaro

These sweetbread and tripe tacos will turn you into an offal fan

Mexican
Food cart

Heights
2520 Airline Dr.
No phone

Hours
Daily
7:00am–3:00pm
Check website for
current hours and
location

Bar
None

Credit cards
None

Features
Brunch
Outdoor dining
Veg-friendly

In the parking lot of the Airline Farmer's Market, Taquería Tacambaro's truck is the next step for anyone looking to advance his or her taco experience beyond the basic al pastor and barbacoa. There's no better place to start trying organ meats than here, as evidenced by the number of local Mexican produce vendors and shoppers lined up to sample the Michoacán regional offerings.

They're having tacos de mollejas (sweetbreads), and so should you. They can be crispy on the outside, and wonderfully creamy in the middle. They might also come mixed with intestine and tripe for a more extreme, and chewier, offal experience. Either way, they're ideal with simple onion and cilantro, a dab of the smoky red salsa in a molcajete bowl on the counter, and a squeeze of fresh lime.

But should you still feel squeamish, fear not: al pastor is also exemplary, crispy and spicy. Deliciously fatty chicharrones are griddle fried to a light crunchiness. There are even concessions for the health-conscious: savory, juicy nopales and calabacitas (zucchini). Thick-masa gorditas, or tortas on soft telera bread are good, too. But if any taco could convince you that organ meats are underappreciated, this one should.

The Tasting Room

The lively vibe, good pizza, and accessible
pricing make wine less daunting for many

8.0	8.5
Food	Feel

$35	8.0
Price	Wine

www.tastingroomwines.com

This small collection of wine bars is awesomely
useful for girls' nights, date nights, or for last-
minute dinner party accessories. Bottles are
priced for retail, with just a small charge for
consuming on the premises (we've never
understood why this is disagreeable to some
people: glassware costs money, and so do
servers). At any rate, you'll still be spending less
than at most restaurants. The selection, which
appears impressive stacked along the exposed
brick walls, is ideal for those recently graduated
from grocery store wines but who may not be
able to fully appreciate a wild deviation from
that style. In other words, it's a great study
companion to a beginner's guide to wine. The
slogan is entirely accurate: "A comfortable place
to get serious about wine."

The simple and chic locations are great fun
for gatherings, especially Memorial's large,
buzzing patio and frequent live music. But the
Town and Country location is where it's at for
pizza, with its wood-burning oven; the
margherita is mighty convincing. The changing
selection of small plates is more impressive than
ever, as well. Brunch is pretty solid, and the first
mimosa of the morning is free, which is a win-
win, considering a daytime buzz loosens the
wallet like nothing else.

Pizza
Wine bar

Upper Kirby
2409 W. Alabama St.
(713) 526-2242

Memorial
1101 Uptown Park Blvd.
(713) 993-9800

Town and Country
818 Town and Country
(281) 822-1505

Hours
Mon–Fri
2:00pm–midnight
Sat
2:00pm–1:00am
Sun
2:00pm–10:00pm
Hours vary by location

Bar
Beer, wine

Credit cards
Visa, MC, AmEx

Reservations
Accepted

Features
Brunch
Date-friendly
Live music
Outdoor dining
Veg-friendly
Wi-Fi

Tau Bay

Good pho and an even better rice plate—if you're willing to brave the grunge

Vietnamese
Casual restaurant

Bellaire Chinatown
8282 Bellaire Blvd.
(713) 272-8755

Bellaire Chinatown
8150 Southwest Fwy.
(713) 771-8485

Hours
Daily
10:00am–10:00pm

Bar
None

Credit cards
Visa, MC

Reservations
Not accepted

Judging by its old, chipped tables and torn-covered seats, you can bet Tau Bay has seen a lot of action over the years. There's a nicer location nearer the hospital, but there are more menu options at that sketchier, grimier Bellaire Boulevard spot. It's often dubbed the "Airplane Restaurant" for the odd Microsoft clip-artish airplane on the cover of its menu.

The pho's been better on recent visits, richer and more deeply beefy—we can finally recommend it, but we still think the best order here is a plate of crispy egg rolls, a char-grilled beef rice plate, and Vietnamese coffee. The freshly fried egg rolls come in orders of eight, so your office snacks are covered for the day (so long as your coworkers don't mind onion breath). That rice plate is wonderfully comforting, with its slices of char-flavored meat, shredded pork (texturally generous, if not flavorfully so), and egg cake that's like a crustless quiche with dried mushrooms and rice noodles, delivering a rich savoriness. With a bit of accompanying sweet-salty nuoc cham, it's a well-rounded and delicious meal. It's not quite as good as Thien Thanh or Thuan Kieu Com Tam, but it will definitely do in a pinch.

Tel-Wink Grill

A good old-school breakfast diner with freshly ground coffee

6.6 Food

7.0 Feel

$10 Price

This sweet old diner on a forlorn section of Telephone Road packs loyalists in every morning. It's nothing novel or thrilling, but still, it's not unusual to see a queue around the restaurant, usually composed of a thorough sampling of the entire city of Houston. Duct-taped beaters sit alongside luxury imports in the potholed, unpaved parking lot. The interior is bright, but has the overly decorated wood-paneled warmth of an elementary school classroom. Sit at the great old-school counter if you can.

Tel-Wink really only serves breakfast, so it's carved a nice niche for itself in that scene. Firm waffles and standard short-order egg dishes are the best bet, with the usual sides. We suggest ordering hash browns and biscuits with pretty much everything: hash browns are served in a giant mound with an attractive skillet-fried crunch on the outside, while biscuits are super fluffy and the size of your fist. An order of bacon gets you several slices the size of your plate. Other breakfast meats are hit or miss: overcooked pork chops are puny and chicken-fried steak is a little flaccid and crunchless. But behold the freshly ground coffee—a rare move for a greasy spoon. We imagine some splatter-aproned Mel-type character in the back grumbling about kids these days and their gourmet demands.

American
Casual restaurant

Southeast Houston
4318 Telephone Rd.
(713) 644-4933

Hours
Daily
6:00am–3:30pm

Bar
None

Credit cards
Visa, MC, AmEx

Reservations
Not accepted

Features
Brunch
Kid-friendly

Teotihuacán

Amazing tortillas, charro beans, and
parrilladas on the cheap

www.teotihuacanmexicancafe.com

Mexican
Casual restaurant

Heights
1511 Airline Dr.
(713) 426-4420

North Houston
4624 Irvington Blvd.
(713) 695-8757

Southwest Houston
6579 W. Bellfort St.
(713) 726-9858

Hours
Daily
8:00am–10:00pm

Bar
Beer, wine, liquor

Credit cards
Visa, MC, AmEx

Reservations
Accepted

Features
Brunch
Live music
Outdoor dining

This reliable little place manages to do great business while keeping standards and quality high. It's not creative or anything, but some specials, like pollo mostaza and pollo corral will surprise you—the first, chicken in mustard cream sauce, is a bit heavy, but undeniably good; the latter is half a delicious roasted chicken covered in spicy red sauce.

Aztec-ish murals cover the walls; their dark and relaxing colors are warm and comforting. Sit at the wooden tables, and you'll be greeted by Teotihuacán's sweet, razor-thin chips and famous salsa. Neither the warm red nor the cold green is particularly spicy, but both are delicious, brandishing sharp, clear, smoky chile and tomatillo flavors. Chicken flautas are delicious, crispy on the outside with steamy, spicy goods inside. Shrimp is juicy and garlicky, and the parrillada is one of the best in town. Agujas (beef short ribs) are sometimes chewy, as are fajitas.

Accompanying charro beans are some of the best in town, like a well-developed, spicy soup with lots of pork buried inside. Even rice is beautifully textured and flavored, and homemade tortillas are unparalleled, whether the sweet, angular corn version or the wonderfully rich wheat-flour version; they're translucent with fat, like Malaysian roti. We don't know what it is, but we swear the North Houston branch is the best.

Teppay

An authentic experience can be yours, if you play your cards right

8.9 Food
7.5 Feel

$60 Price

You can have a ho-hum experience at even an authentic and high-quality sushi place like this; it entirely depends on what and how you order. If you opt for a table over the bar, for instance, and order Sushi Combination B, you might as well go to Azuma. You came to Teppay, presumably, for the real deal, so sit at the bar and order the omakase tasting menu. (Call the day before for a more expensive and elaborate omakase.)

Also, ask if the uni is good that day, or if there's any live scallop, and you'll be treated to the better stuff on offer, the delicacies that they hate seeing go unappreciated, wasted, and returned by American diners looking perhaps for a more flavorless, generic, and safe sushi experience. But that's not you, so ask for ankimo (monkfish liver, creamy-dreamy and not as rich as foie gras). The freshest fish here is often flown in directly from Japan several times per week. When available, order the aji (a milder mackerel), filleted right in front of you, then its skeleton deep-fried so you can eat it, too. And don't stop at fish; on a rainy day, the ramen and udon here goes from good to superlative, and crispy-fried pork katsu is comforting and delicious. Leave the rolls to the lesser places.

Japanese
Casual restaurant

Galleria
6516 Westheimer Rd.
(713) 789-4506

Hours
Mon–Sat
6:00pm–10:30pm

Bar
Beer, wine, liquor

Credit cards
Visa, MC, AmEx

Reservations
Accepted

Features
Date-friendly

6.9 Food

7.5 Feel

$25 Price

Thai Gourmet

Good Thai that's even better when it's kicking your butt

www.thaigourmethouston.com

Thai
Casual restaurant

Galleria
6324 Richmond Ave.
(713) 780-7955

Hours
Mon–Thu
11:00am–2:30pm
5:00pm–9:30pm
Fri
11:00am–2:30pm
5:00pm–10:30pm
Sat
11:00am–10:30pm

Bar
Beer, wine

Credit cards
Visa, MC, AmEx

Reservations
Not accepted

Features
Date-friendly
Veg-friendly

The owners of Thai Gourmet also run a very popular kickboxing studio next door. Kru Pong (Kru means "teacher" in Thai) and his wife Toon lord over this set of strip-mall digs made somewhat nicer with tropical plants. There are unique touches inside as well: a beautiful chalk landscape, wood carvings, and random artifacts that are classy and not overdone. You're not underdressed in shorts and a T-shirt, but this could also make for a nice evening out.

Fried okra is a favorite around here, deep fried with no batter and seasoned with sugar, lemongrass, garlic, and spices. Also try flash-fried and silken "Triple Spicy Tofu," with crispy casing and chilies. The contrasting textures and flavors will jump and dance in your mouth—but eat the dish quickly or it gets soggy. Seafood is a strong suit, like briny and plump aromatic basil shrimp, or chu chee tilapia, slowly simmered with a delicious red curry.

Dishes ordered "Hot" and "Thai-Hot" cannot be returned for a refund. Does that clue you in? But at medium-spicy or less, you might wind up with icky, candied renditions of Thai classics (and a few not-so-Thai classics): pad kee mao may seem bland, Massaman curry much too peanut-buttery, and crab fried rice almost dessert. For a fun Thai ass-kicking experience, go "Hot"…or go next door.

Thai Spice

Thai eateries with consistently good deals
and varying authenticity

www.thaispice.com

6.9	6.0
Food	Feel

$10
Price

Thai
Casual restaurant

Rice Area
5117 Kelvin Dr.
(713) 522-5100

Downtown
777 Walker St.
(713) 222-8883

Westchase
2520 S. Voss Rd.
(713) 782-1100

More locations
and features at
fearlesscritic.com

Hours
Daily
11:00am–10:00pm
Hours vary by location

Bar
Beer, wine

Credit cards
Visa, MC, AmEx

Reservations
Accepted

Features
Kid-friendly
Live music
Veg-friendly
Wi-Fi

Thai Spice has nine restaurants, each with a distinct feel tailored to its particular clientele. Thai Spice Express on Bellaire near Gessner seems to be the one most frequented by Thais, and the one with the most authentic menu. If we were rating this location separately, it might be in the top three Thai restaurants in town.

If you go there, stray from the usual curries and satays to try the mussels and Thai fried rice; the latter incorporates chunks of lime, peel and all, to bring pops of freshness to the heat. Red curry with chicken and tons of chilies is spicy, sweet, and flavorful. Shrimp are tempura-fried with the shells and heads still on, but they're often served too cold. Pad ka praw is stir-fried with chili and basil, a fiery yet mellow meal. Som tam (green papaya salad) and spicy bamboo salad are ways to eat light and stay refreshed.

All locations boast contemporary colors and lighting that make them look like showrooms at a fast-Asian restaurant expo. Still, they deliver consistently good food with the right balance between heat and other flavors, unlike the overly sweet concoctions that other, more Americanized restaurants provide—but Thai Gourmet's got 'em beat in the heat category. Some locations have buffets (where quality obviously suffers somewhat), and most offer weekly discounts and kid specials.

Thien An Sandwiches

Get in, get your belly full of hot noodle soup, and get out

Vietnamese Sandwiches
Counter service

Midtown
2905 Travis St.
(713) 522-7007

Hours
Sun–Fri
8:00am–6:00pm

Bar
None

Credit cards
Visa, MC

The lunchtime service at this busy chow factory is all about turn 'n' burn, but asking for help with the menu isn't out of the question; the staff will happily give suggestions. You may not even much mind the assembly-line feel, noisy clatter, and communal seating, once you dig into your good, cheap meal.

Although the name advertises sandwiches, these don't compete with the best banh mi on Bellaire; baguettes are, by comparison, rather smooshy and the grilled pork within is wimpy. But the cilantro, jalapeño, and pickled carrots are all right on, so considering they cost $3 a pop, it's not a terrible idea. Vermicelli dishes tend to be better, especially with a char-grilled, fragrant beef referred to as "Hanoi-style," as it's flecked with bright lemongrass and piqued with chilies. Soups are also strong, the broths complex with marrowy meatiness, spicy jalapeño, tangy lemongrass and the exotic undertones of star anise, cinnamon, and cloves. We like the pho, but if you've never experienced the tofu-like consistency and savory, gently metallic flavor of pig's blood, this bun bo Hue is a safe and delicious way to start. And—dare we say?—it's a terrific, quick hangover cure before work.

Thien Thanh

You're here for one reason: otherworldly banh cuon

8.8 Food

6.5 Feel

$10 Price

Vietnamese
Casual restaurant

Bellaire Chinatown
11210 Bellaire Blvd.
(281) 564-0419

Hours
Daily
7:00am–8:00pm

Bar
BYO

Credit cards
None

Reservations
Not accepted

Features
Kid-friendly
Outdoor dining
Veg-friendly

Read enough restaurant websites and you'll see the phrase "…will transport you to a different place" tossed around like a vermicelli noodle in a bowl. Many claim such dramatic otherworldly experiences, but few deliver; those that do, like Thien Thanh, seem to do it effortlessly and humbly. This dilapidated shop is convincing despite (or perhaps due to) being bereft of bells and whistles: its fading green tables are barely lit, and lingering scents of its house-blended nuoc cham (fish sauce) really do transport us off of the streets of Bellaire Chinatown into a dining district of Saigon.

Many Vietnamese restaurants focus their excellence into one singular, spectacular dish, and Thien Thanh's is banh cuon, a multitude of intensely flavored fillings wrapped in a thin steamed rice crêpe. There are serviceable soups and vermicelli bowls, but these are beside the point. English is a challenge here, so order by number. Shrimp and crab are good, but we favor #11, banh cuon thit nuong, with delicate slices of heavily charred pork inside a diaphanous warm rice wrapper. It's got that wonderful aroma of fresh mint and cilantro; dip it in nuoc cham, with its sharp umami kick, and alternate between bites of crunchy bean sprouts, and you may as well have purchased a plane ticket to Vietnam. Except, happily, without the pat-downs and leg cramps.

13 Celsius

The main course here is the exciting, ambitious wine program

www.13celsius.com

Modern
Wine bar

Midtown
3000 Caroline St.
(713) 529-8466

Hours
Sun–Wed
4:00pm–midnight
Thu–Sat
4:00pm–2:00am

Bar
Beer, wine

Credit cards
Visa, MC, AmEx

Reservations
Accepted

Features
Date-friendly
Good beers
Live music
Outdoor dining
Veg-friendly
Wi-Fi

The run-down-warehouse look of 13 Celsius is handsome and genuine; the point—often missed by other, flashier wine bars—is to not steal focus from the wine (or the few good craft beers). It's still cozy, with some plush leather couches and a small courtyard usually filled with industry folks. Don't know anything about these wines? No worries—the bartender will set you up with something interesting and accessible, and (depending upon the night) might be able to tell you something about it. If, however, you are well traveled through winedom, you'll revel in the selection of small-production, terroir-driven bottles. It's a playground of Zweigelt, Gaglioppo, and Refosco.

The eponymous temperature at which the wine is stored and served is a refreshing change from the irresponsibly warm pours at wannabe wine bars, and if it suggests that the people behind this operation truly love wine, it's even more evident in the criminally low markups that allow the masses to try something better than the mass-produced, chemically engineered stuff their pocketbooks force them to drink.

There's a succinct menu of wine-friendly bites, but even these are carefully chosen: charcuterie and cheese, marcona almonds, and serviceable panini. And if you've ever wanted to experience Jerez in the South of Spain, just close your eyes, inhale some Fino sherry, and pop a nut. We just did.

III Forks

A Texan vibe and good Prime steaks even a little later at night

7.7	8.5
Food	Feel

$95	6.5
Price	Wine

www.iiiforks.com

Of the pricey chain steakhouses, III Forks feels more fun and Texan than the rest. It's lively, with an elegant, almost Art Deco clubbiness. Of course, the service is of the expected bumbling-over-the-top ilk; it's endearing at times, when not awkward. You'll find a few too many designated "sommeliers," the opposite problem most modern restaurants have, but there's such little variation between its big, oaky wines that it obliterates the need for guidance. The bar's list of "Modern Classics" comprises sugared-up cocktails that are neither modern nor classic, and Scotch is egregiously marked up.

The steaks are wet-aged, so they don't get that tangy funk a good dry-aging can accomplish, but they are cooked expertly to their correct temperatures. A Porterhouse for two has good texture, the ribeye is well marbled, and an order of medium-rare will result in a nice, if faint, crust. Although peppery enough, they often need help from the table saltshaker. As for sides, which we find less than enchanting at other steakhouses, these are all quite good: "off-the-cob cream corn" is beguiling and sweet, while creamed spinach and onion rings are correct. We're not over the moon about our dining choices downtown at 10pm on a Saturday, but you could do worse than this.

Steakhouse
Upmarket restaurant

Downtown
1201 San Jacinto St.
(713) 658-9457

Hours
Mon–Thu
11:00am–10:00pm
Fri
11:00am–11:00pm
Sat
4:00pm–11:00pm

Bar
Beer, wine, liquor

Credit cards
Visa, MC, AmEx

Reservations
Accepted

Features
Date-friendly

Thuan Kieu Com Tan

Bring a group and sample everything—or
don't...and still eat some terrific broken rice

Vietnamese
Casual restaurant

Bellaire Chinatown
10792 Bellaire Blvd.
(281) 988-8865

Hours
Daily
8:00am–10:00pm

Bar
BYO

Credit cards
None

Reservations
Not accepted

Features
Kid-friendly
Veg-friendly

Ruggedly wholesome, slightly sloppy, and generally delicious Thuan Kieu Com Tam stands out in the dizzying Houston Vietnamese restaurant scene (the gargantuan lettering on its strip-mall storefront certainly helps). The large hall and community tables make family-style dining totally attractive.

There are many options on the menu—really, every possible permutation of soup, noodle, rice, pork, chicken, beef, and seafood. But stay calm: at dinner, you need only order one of the set menus, which will get your per-person average to as low as eight bucks. Tableside hotpots are strong, particularly one teeming with fish chunks, taro leaf, and tomatoes; its spritely lemongrass-and-basil-perfumed broth wakes up the senses and readies you for more. Hainan chicken isn't the best, filled with annoying bones, and yet somehow lacking the juiciness that bone-in cooking usually preserves. But the catfish clay pot, steeped in a savory caramel is possibly the best rendition in town, an indulgent balance of sweet and savory. Each bite of this normally bland and muddy fish is studded with crispy bits of pork fat.

If you do find yourself dining alone, go for the eponymous com tam (broken rice) dishes. While their varying grilled-meat-and-egg toppings are welcome additions, the expertly cooked, fluffy rice could be good enough on its own. But you really should bring people for more dishes and more flavors to sample.

Tintos

Pricey twists on traditional tapas, but at least you can stay still for the night

7.6	7.5
Food	Feel

$55	8.5
Price	Wine

www.tintosrestaurant.com

Tintos refers to its food as "Spanish influenced." Meaning that, while the menu is pretty faithful to Spain's various dialects of tapas, there are some fruity Caribbean accessories and modern American twists. Indeed, the gridded black exterior looks decidedly (1980s) American, and the inside's polished, catalog-ish décor is hardly reminiscent of Madrid's intimate tapas bars. On sweltering evenings, it's nice to sit outside and listen to live flamenco with a terrific trio of gazpachos that are quite refreshing. Beyond that, stick with traditional tapas.

We've enjoyed some great caracoles (snails) here, as well as plump mussels in addictive broth, and albondigas (meatballs) in a spicy almond-tomato sauce. Paella is reliable, with enough saffrony depth. Homemade chorizo is good and not greasy, but piquillo peppers lack bite, and shrimp have sometimes come mealy and not so fresh smelling. Octopus tends to be tough, if well integrated with its flavors. The menu is priced for River Oaks, so go with a group if you want to try many different things, or risk leaving hungry and broke.

The wine selection is extensive, which means you can find a sensuous, rustic, terroir-driven wine, if you pad around the menu a bit. Or stick to the sherries, which grew up with much of this food and, in many cases, can actually improve it.

Spanish
Upmarket restaurant

River Oaks
2015 W. Gray St.
(713) 522-1330

Hours
Sun–Wed
11:00am–10:00pm
Thu–Sat
11:00am–midnight

Bar
Beer, wine, liquor

Credit cards
Visa, MC, AmEx

Reservations
Accepted

Features
Brunch
Date-friendly
Live music
Outdoor dining

Tiny Boxwood's

Are you a lady? Do you like to lunch?

www.tinyboxwoods.com

American
Pizza
Casual restaurant

Greenway Plaza
3614 W. Alabama St.
(713) 622-4224

Hours
Tue–Sat
7:00am–10:00pm
Sun
9:00am–2:00pm

Bar
Beer, wine

Credit cards
Visa, MC, AmEx

Reservations
Not accepted

Features
Brunch
Outdoor dining
Veg-friendly

Tiny Boxwood's, how cruel and kind you are!

Cruel:
You must stand in an interminable line to order, but no one can hold your table.
The chocolate-chip cookie. Evil incarnate.
The pastries are not that good.
Service is pretty rude.
Pizza crusts are whiter than the clientele.
The ho-hum wine list panders to whatever's appeared recently on "Desperate Housewives:" Malbec, Shiraz, Cakebread, watery Pinot Grigio, and buttery Chardonnay.
The prices. We must be paying for the adorable topiaries and posh wicker furnishings.

Kind:
The adorable topiaries and posh wicker furnishings.
The secluded, lovely garden of the Thompson + Hansen Nursery actually convinces us there's no ugly concrete jungle out there.
The salads are nice.
Giant lattes and homemade mint lemonade are good.
Breakfast pizzas get an egg on top.
Fluffy quiche.
Again, the atmosphere. It's like a visual positive affirmation for achieving wealth.

Tofu Village

Comforting tofu stews and a wonderful
plethora of free sides

6.8	7.0
Food	Feel

$20
Price

www.tofuvillage.net

The specialty here's apparent in the name:
piping-hot bowls of traditional Korean tofu
stews, a perfect match for the many rainy days
in Houston.

The interior's prettier and more modern than
usual, if a little bit silly: ever-changing colored
lights lining the walls and cheesy pictures of
Korean pop star Rain plastered everywhere. But
who doesn't love a little giggle while they slurp?
The stew comes in different varieties—with
meat, seafood, kimchi, or a combination of all
three—and in varying amounts of spiciness. The
tofu is always the star, though, silky and subtle,
softening the caustic spices.

As successful as the specialty tofu is, Tofu
Village should stop while it's ahead, because
some of the other Korean dishes suffer horribly,
like the rendition of the Korean seafood
pancake, pajeon—it's flimsy and filled with
seafood that doesn't taste the freshest. And
then there's Korean barbecue, flavorful, but
greasy and totally overcooked. Jap chae noodles
are overwhelmed with sauce, but are
toothsome. Regardless, it's a totally generous
meal for little lucre, as everything comes with a
fried whole sardine, copious and delicious
banchan, and a little iceberg salad for good
measure. Just remember, if you want the best of
Tofu Village, go tofu stew.

Korean
Casual restaurant

Bellaire Chinatown
9889 Bellaire Blvd.
(713) 777-9889

Hours
Sun–Thu
10:00am–10:00pm
Fri–Sat
10:00am–11:00pm

Bar
Beer, wine

Credit cards
Visa, MC

Reservations
Accepted

Features
Veg-friendly

7.1	8.0
Food	Feel

$70	7.0
Price	Drinks

Tony Mandola's

White-clothed Cajun cuisine that's a
Houston icon wherever it goes

www.tonymandolas.com

Seafood Southern
Upmarket restaurant

Upper Kirby
2810 Westheimer Rd.
(713) 528-3474

Hours
Mon–Thu
11:00am–10:00pm
Fri–Sat
11:00am–11:00pm
Sun
5:00pm–9:00pm

Bar
Beer, wine, liquor

Credit cards
Visa, MC, AmEx

Reservations
Accepted

Features
Date-friendly

Tony Mandola's is currently in its "Miracle
Location" on Westheimer, but (as of press time)
plans to move to a new, permanent space later
in 2011. The temporary space is actually quite
nice, with all the vibrancy and class of a smallish
New Orleans restaurant, even if it does get quite
crammed at busy times with longtime loyal
supporters.

On any given night, the crowd of oil execs,
former mayors, financiers, and anchorwomen
dines on white tablecloths littered now and then
with oyster shells. They adore the variety of
terrific snapper dishes; our favorite is "Snapper
Martha," grilled to golden and topped with
shrimp, crawfish, and crabmeat. Most sinful is
the appropriately named "Snapper Decadent,"
topped with blackened shrimp, oysters, lump
crabmeat, and brown butter. Although pasta
dishes are overtly creamy and a bit mushy, we
just can't quit the crawfish ravioli. Fried dishes
are good, but nothing special.

While there's plenty of recognizable Cajun
fare on the menu, there are places around town
where you can find better po' boys, gumbo, and
étouffée for much less money. The wine list is a
perfunctory, showing of recognizable names
from here and abroad. It's totally boring but
competitively priced. But we'll take a "Cajun
Martini," because it's the ideal marriage of spice
and class, just like Tony Mandola's is, always has
been, and—we bet—will continue to be,
"Miracle Location" or no.

Tony Thai

Pretty good Thai served in a dizzying kaleidoscope of contemporary colors

5.9	7.0
Food	Feel

$30
Price

www.tonythairestaurant.com

Tony's décor is best described as "tacky modern." Think multi-colored pendant lamps; flowing waterfalls; curvy ceiling panels with recessed lighting; and, most amusingly, a giant, mechanized menu scroll that's constantly cycling through the various menu items, with spectacularly unattractive photos. It's little touches like these that make the place feel appropriate for neither an elaborate dinner nor a light, relaxing lunch.

Still, certain parts of the menu are more authentic than most. It's one of the best som tam in town, that classic, refreshing green-papaya salad that's a staple all over Thailand. Here, the salad's laced with plenty of hot chili and the trademark tang of fermented shrimp. Lime, peanuts, and underripe tomato slices—the only inauthentic touch—complete the picture.

Tom yum goong soup's appropriately salty and spicy, with fresh shrimp—even if it is missing the aromatic oomph of kaffir lime leaves. Seafood mains are the way to go, especially the live Dungeness crab. Various versions of crispy whole fish can be successful, and sautéed catfish in chili sauce is another safe bet; the flavor's there, even if the deep-fried fish texture is unremarkable.

Pay no attention to the awful gas-station wines in the ultra-modern wine racks, nor to the perfunctory sushi; there's too much authentic Thai scattered on this menu for that nonsense.

Thai
Casual restaurant

Bellaire Chinatown
10613 Bellaire Blvd.
(281) 495-1711

Northwest Houston
17513 Gessner Dr.
(281) 469-3188

Hours
Daily
11:00am–10:30pm
Hours vary by location

Bar
Beer, wine

Credit cards
Visa, MC, AmEx

Reservations
Accepted

Features
Veg-friendly

Tony's

Amid much grandiosity and noise, a simplicity quietly succeeds on the plate

www.tonyshouston.com

Italian
Upmarket restaurant

Greenway Plaza
3755 Richmond Ave.
(713) 622-6778

Hours
Mon–Thu
11:00am–10:00pm

Fri
11:00am–midnight

Sat
6:00pm–midnight

Bar
Beer, wine, liquor

Credit cards
Visa, MC, AmEx

Reservations
Essential

Features
Date-friendly
Live music

Tony Vallone's name has, in Houston, become synonymous with success (although we don't think his middling Café Bello and Ciao Bello ventures qualify). His eponymous Italian restaurant turned a corner in 2009, finally trading in much of its fussy, creamy American-pleasers for more authentic, simple preparations. The modesty just makes the bright, soaring dining room all the more obscene; while the redesign reduced the sleaze factor considerably, the color palette of burnt-peach and brown is merely a bland backdrop for fake tans and bizarre modern art.

The kitchen's makeover is better. There's still some seared-ahi silliness, but it's done reasonably well. You really ought to focus on homemade delicate pasta dumplings, like pansotti and cappelletti. Carbonara is done properly, with poached egg and Parmigiano-Reggiano emulsifying into sauce, and plenty of black pepper. Fish is superbly cooked, although we prefer the chef, not the customer, decide which sauce to put on it. Nevertheless, the range of successes is great, and some dishes even rival Da Marco for excellence.

Most of the 23-page wine list is sheer gobbledygook—flagrant expense-account Californians and an admirable but out-of-place French selection. Spend those hundreds instead on Sagrantino de Montefalco or Barbaresco. Or, for much less, match the décor with an Umbrian blend that's elegantly matured and nearly orange.

ToreOre

Chicken and joy in a modern Korean mega-mart

8.2	5.5
Food	Feel

$10
Price

This Korean fast food chain, whose sole Houston location is tucked into the food court of the giant Super H-Mart, has got a bit of a cultish following that is singularly focused; the only thing you'll get there besides some of the greatest fried chicken in town is a side of pickled radish (which offsets the chicken grease nicely) and a soda. This makes ordering simple, wherein you only have to choose which kind of chicken you want, and if you want 7 or 14 pieces.

The most basic version involves marinated, juicy chicken pieces sealed inside savory, crispy skin. "Garlic tasty" offers the same great flavor as the original, but is tossed with a lightly toasted chopped-garlic coating. Thrill-seekers will love the "sweet & spicy," where the sweetness of the immediate bite is hijacked by a sneaky heat on the finish. The fearless chile-head should move directly to the "hot sweet & spicy" chicken, which is a full frontal assault on the senses—and on the skin around your mouth.

This is meant to be eaten right out of the fryer for the most sublime results—the to-go boxes, although cute, will steam it soggy. Super H's food court is as clean, contemporary, and dull as any American mall's, so go for it.

Korean
Counter service

Memorial
1302 Blalock Rd.
(713) 468-3838

Hours
Daily
11:00am–9:00pm

Bar
None

Credit cards
Visa, MC

Features
Kid-friendly

7.4	7.0
Food	Feel

$10
Price

Tornado Burger

One of the best fast-food-style burgers in—
or out of—Houston

Burgers
Counter service

Stafford
505 FM 1092
(281) 403-3278

Hours
Mon–Sat
11:00am–10:00pm
Sun
11:00am–9:00pm

Bar
None

Credit cards
Visa, MC, AmEx

Stafford, you lucky dogs! Tornado Burger is housed in an old fast food drive-thru joint on a strip center outparcel. The inside's spare and kitschy, with corrugated-metal-paneled walls, vinyl booths, and a handful of small tables with rickety chairs. The drop ceiling has been removed, and old bicycles and sleds and such hang from the rafters. Maybe a tornado dropped them there.

Burgers come with single, double, and triple patties, which come in either regular or "spicy," with jalapeños and garlic mixed in. Despite being thin and cooked to well done, they're quite flavorful—but you really need to order a spicy double (at least) for the bread-to-meat ratio to work. You'll also need to ask for easy lettuce and maybe do a little repositioning, or the stuff will fly out after a bite. The french fries here are thin, hand-cut beauties that are crisp on the outside and slightly mealy on the inside. They come rather old school in a Styrofoam soft-drink cup (dump them out to keep them crisp or they'll steam themselves).

Be prepared for a bit of a wait after ordering—these puppies aren't pre-made. You might want to avoid the drive-thru, or else risk waiting in your car for 10 minutes. After sitting in traffic to get here, you probably don't want that.

Turquoise Grill

7.1 Food **7.5** Feel

$35 Price

The décor may be no frills, but the Turkish food's all the stimulus you need

www.turquoisegrill.info

The extended Turkish family who operates this small restaurant embraces customers with stories about food and life in Turkey. When the restaurant isn't too busy (on weekends you must make reservations), they may invite younger customers to help make their own pizza. And at the end of some evenings, it is not uncommon for the whole family to gather around the television to eat and watch Turkish movies or soccer matches as you finish your meal. Such warmth makes it easy to forget the colorless surroundings. Furnishings are mostly utilitarian, and white walls are lined with souvenirs from Turkey that are cheaply framed and educational.

The focus then is on the food. "Shepherd's Bread," cooked in the brick oven, is fluffy and complements everything else in the meal. Tabbouleh is bracing and bright with more parsley and lemon than bulghur, while baba ghanoush is appropriately light on tahini and full of smoky eggplant with chives. Traditional grilled items are best here, like Inegöl köfte meatballs, redolent of onions and cumin; Adana kebab's minced lamb is alluringly smoky; even chicken becomes intriguing on this grill.

The couple of Turkish wines on offer aren't some of the country's best work; the pilsner's a far better option, but really, you should bring a wine that will better suit the complex and amazing flavors here.

Turkish
Casual restaurant

Upper Kirby
3701 Kirby Dr.
(713) 526-3800

Hours
Mon–Thu
8:00am–9:00pm
Fri
8:00am–10:00pm
Sat
11:00am–10:00pm
Sun
11:00am–4:00pm

Bar
Beer, wine, BYO

Credit cards
Visa, MC, AmEx

Reservations
Accepted

Features
Brunch
Date-friendly
Outdoor dining
Wi-Fi

9.1 Food 7.5 Feel

Udipi Café

$10 Price

Southern Indian dishes that edify vegetables, lentils, and grains

www.udipicafeusa.com

Indian
Casual restaurant

Hillcroft Area
5959 Hillcroft St.
(713) 334-5555

Sugar Land
3554 Hwy. 6 S.
(281) 313-2700

West Houston
4632 FM 1960
(281) 397-7200

Katy
557 S. Mason Rd.
(281) 829-6100

Hours
Sun–Thu
11:00am–10:00pm
Fri–Sat
11:00am–11:00pm
Hours vary by location

Bar
None

Credit cards
Visa, MC, AmEx

Reservations
Accepted

Features
Kid-friendly
Veg-friendly

Each location in this small chain is humble yet cheerful, serving a vegetarian cuisine built around centuries-old recipes from south India's Karnataka region, birthplace of the masala dosa, one of the world's gastronomical treasures. Dosai, of which there are about 20 at Udipi, are big, thin rice crêpes characterized in their finest form—as they are here—by an ineffable lightness, a precise interplay between crispy and spongy. (These are even available with the lunch buffet; you need only ask.) You must have them with sambar, a lentil-and-vegetable stew in a tamarind broth—another backbone of Southern Indian cuisine. Other staple starches from the area include sauce-absorbing idli (steamed rice-lentil cakes) and medhu vada (deep-fried lentil-flour doughnuts).

Regardless, Udipi's not to be demoted to strictly being a vegetarian's restaurant. Even hardcore carnivores find that the kitchen's faithful renditions of centuries-old recipes employ enough complex spice combinations and textural variation between starches, legumes, fruits, greens, and dairies to burrow straight into the pleasure centers of the brain. Sample silky and complex paneer makhani; smooth, subtle yellow dal; flawless coconut chutney and "pickle" with the deep pucker of preserved lemon; and world-class versions of yogurt rice, rich vegetable korma, and sweet sheera. Bombay-style chaat (snack-sized street foods) served next door to Udipi's Hillcroft location, at Krishna Chaat House, are equally delicious and unbelievably cheap.

Vic & Anthony's

9.1	8.5
Food	Feel

$90	7.5
Price	Wine

Head and shoulders above the rest, this steakhouse is one of Houston's own

www.vicandanthonys.com

Vic & Anthony's maintains the very best of its genre (warm, dark-wooded décor; high-class clubby feeling; and pervasive sizzling-beef aroma) while finding admirable motivation to not rest on its laurels. Its crab cakes have to be the best in Texas, full of sweet lump crabmeat with virtually no filler, and accompanied brilliantly by a chive beurre blanc. Sides are simple but extremely well prepared, and often with a little something extra to distinguish them from their ilk (why, is that nutmeg in the creamed spinach?).

Steaks are Prime and wet-aged, but somehow manage the concentrated beefiness and tanginess associated with dry-ageing. Bone-in ribeye (when available) is marbled beautifully, melting in the mouth at medium-rare. Larger cuts, like a Porterhouse for two, can be more unevenly cooked, but the flavor is there—helped, no doubt, by a pool of bubbling butter. Have a thick, juicy burger in the lounge, or in the dining room on Fridays; the bloom-rinded blue cheese on the "Anthony" is surprisingly complemented by a touch of balsamic vinaigrette coating the lettuce leaves. Crispy and endless onion strings fare better than mealy fries.

There are craft-brewery tastings now and then—another rarity among steakhouses; not so rare is an epic wine list of status-symbol names. Still, you can find a memorable and personality-driven bottle for around $70, especially if you venture beyond our borders. Ask the knowledgeable staff for guidance.

Steakhouse
Upmarket restaurant

Downtown
1510 Texas St.
(713) 228-1111

Hours
Sun–Thu
5:00pm–10:00pm
Fri
11:00am–11:00pm
Sat
5:00pm–11:00pm

Bar
Beer, wine, liquor

Credit cards
Visa, MC, AmEx

Reservations
Accepted

Features
Date-friendly
Live music

Vieng Thai

Houston's best renditions of the cuisine
from Thailand's greatest culinary region

www.viengthaihouston.com

Thai
Casual restaurant

Spring Branch
6929 Long Point Dr.
(713) 688-9910

Hours
Mon–Fri
11:00am–9:30pm
Sat–Sun
noon–9:30pm

Bar
BYO

Credit cards
Visa, MC

Reservations
Accepted

Features
Veg-friendly

Isan (or Isaan, or E-Sarn) is the northeastern
portion of Thailand, bordering Cambodia on the
south and Laos in the east and north. It is one of
Thailand's poorest, most rural regions, and
arguably its greatest culinary district.

Here, you'll be fed som tam, a salad of crisp
and sour green papaya, fiery chilies, palm sugar,
salt, garlic, dried shrimp, peanuts, fish sauce,
lime, and often other ingredients, ground
together with a mortar and pestle. It's unique,
delicious, and virtually impossible to find done
right in Texas. Vieng Thai does a faithful version,
but ask for it "very spicy," if you can handle it.
There's also a Laotian version here involving
ground crab shells, but it's just okay, and like
eating gravel. The cardinal sin here is ordering
food-court Thai dishes. Just say no to spring
rolls, Massaman curry (a dish from the south), or
pad Thai. None of it's bad, but it's dullsville next
to the gamey regional "E-Sarn Sausage;" fried
pilot fish; or, perhaps, pla pad ped (crispy catfish
sautéed in curry paste). Try anything with kaffir
lime leaves, a unique, authentic Thai flavor
scarce elsewhere.

Meats are sometimes overcooked and
flavorless, the room's small and dingy, and
service is perfunctory and unhelpful—but, given
the opportunity to taste authentic Isan food in
Houston, we hardly notice.

Viet Hoa

Delicious roast pork and some incredibly cheap dishes to eat now or save for later

7.6 Food
5.0 Feel
$10 Price

www.viethoa.com

Chinese
Counter service

Southwest Houston
8300 W. Sam Houston Pkwy.
(832) 448-8828

Hours
Daily
9:00am–10:00pm

Bar
None

Credit cards
Visa, MC

This Asian megamart's lain out cleanly, with ample parking, fresh and exotic produce, whole fish that are cleaned and filleted as you watch, and an entire aisle dedicated to the various incarnations of fermented fish sauce. In the back, of course, is a rotating selection of pretty good and really cheap Chinese dishes on a steam table.

The sheer variety of the rotating selection ensures something for everyone: stir-fried bok choy; fried fish; meatballs; stewed pork belly with garlic, anise, and whole hard-boiled eggs; sweet and sour spare ribs; and several versions of stir-fried noodles often occupy the steam table. Don't miss the tart, spicy, and crunchy Asian chicken salad—a far cry from the saccharine-sweet versions in American restaurants. Most of the dishes are unlabeled, but pointing to things that look good is a great way to expand your horizons—it's all better than the neighboring Kingsway Buffet, where everything's made in such bulk that quality often suffers.

Also visit the barbecue corner, featuring whole-roasted pig, whole-barbecued duck, and crisp-skinned, succulent char siu pork. Tip: wait until after 8pm, when the steam table crew packages up the remaining food and marks it down dramatically. Meat dishes seldom cost more than $3 a tray; vegetables, rice, and noodles go for $1.50. Time appropriately, and whole families can be fed well for a pittance.

6.8
Food

5.5
Feel

$10
Price

Vinh Hoa

You can still see your food with its fins, but not everything on this menu wins

**Chinese
Vietnamese
Seafood**
Casual restaurant

Bellaire Chinatown
9600 Bellaire Blvd.
(713) 271-3122

Hours
Sun–Thu
11:00am–10:00pm
Fri–Sat
11:00am–11:00pm

Bar
Beer

Credit cards
Visa, MC, AmEx

Reservations
Accepted

For cuisine where freshness is chief
(Have you ever smelled dead coral reef?),
Vinh Hoa's the king of oceanic things
Like Dungeness crab lotus leaf.

The atmosphere's filled with the jive
Of bounty that's still quite alive.
Lobster tanks brimming and fishes are swimming
To be lunch that costs just over five.

Fans of the General be damned;
And kung pao ought to be banned.
Heed the fried-sole call, eat it up, fins and all—
Don't bother with meat from the land.

But not every dish hits the spot—
Black bean squid may be the worst of the lot;
The flavor has no power and you'll be chewing for hours
(But the salt-toasted version is hot).

Slow service is part of the deal
When the prices are such a big steal.
The place isn't purty, but it's fine and not dirty,
And one hell of a fresh seafood meal.

Vinoteca Poscol

Still life with Sagrantino and pig face

9.3	8.0
Food	Feel

$40	9.0
Price	Wine

Vinoteca Poscol performs several roles admirably and convincingly. (No wonder, given that the venerable powers behind Da Marco and Dolce Vita are responsible for it.) The room is simple and classic, and natural light pours in through the front windows. Really, the most dramatic decoration is a leg of prosciutto, poised on a gleaming slicer, awaiting another order.

We find this place ideal for dates: it's romantic, with relaxed yet knowledgeable service. And its desserts—often among the best in town—are nothing short of aphrodisiac. What's more, you can control the amount of food you order (and money you spend), either by ordering the always-wonderful specials on the chalkboard, or a selection of the usual small plates. Either way, you'll hardly eat anything more sensually, truly Italian: grilled whole sardines, braised cardoons, garlicky bagna cauda. Some things, like fried spaghetti, are utterly enjoyable for their novelty. But don't miss Vinoteca's cured meats: veal tongue, porchetta di testa, pork cheek, and so on. If it's got a face, you can probably eat it here, and it will be delicious.

The spectacularly well-priced list of smaller-production Italian wines, often using rare and indigenous varietals from the North, encourages better drinking than you might otherwise afford—and if you have no problem dropping a bill or more, there are several bottles here that will change your life.

Italian
Wine bar

Montrose
1609 Westheimer Rd.
(713) 529-2797

Hours
Tue–Thu
5:00pm–10:00pm
Fri–Sat
5:00pm–11:00pm

Bar
Beer, wine

Credit cards
Visa, MC, AmEx

Features
Date-friendly

Virgie's

The friendlies here manage to nail brisket, ribs, *and* sausage

www.virgiesbbq.com

Barbecue
Counter service

Northwest Houston
5535 N. Gessner Rd.
(713) 466-6525

Hours
Wed–Fri
11:00am–6:30pm
Sat
11:00am–5:30pm

Bar
None

Credit cards
Visa, MC, AmEx

Some blame Houston's clean-air laws (we have those?) as the reason why the city's barbecue doesn't stack up to that of the Hill Country. Aside from the Chinese version, of which we can be enormously proud, our city's self-proclaimed barbecue barons dish up mushy brisket and meats with nary a hint of smoke. However, on the outskirts, in its modest little house, Virgie's nails it. This may be a bold statement, but the brisket will back us up, aggressively smoked as it is and tearing apart with ease. Pork ribs have a vigorous pepper coating, mild smoke flavor, and are moderately tender without being mealy. The sausage is a surprise here, juicy and delectable, and of the loose-packed style from Central Texas, as opposed to the finely ground, yammy stuff we find out here.

Sides are harmless, but they don't stand out either, and the sauce is much too sweet; we prefer the sweetness of the welcoming staff, anyhow. There are some quirks: apparently, sometimes meat's zapped in the micro for a sec to reheat it for off-hours visitors, and everything's served in styrofoam, whether you're dining in or not. But even a cardinal barbecue sin like nuking doesn't reveal itself in the flavor or texture somehow. Who struck this devil's deal?

Voice

What a good boutique-hotel restaurant ought to be: elegant and accessible

www.hotelicon.com

7.3 Food

7.5 Feel

$70 Price

8.0 Wine

Modern
Upmarket restaurant

Downtown
Hotel Icon, 220 Main St.
(832) 667-4470

Hours
Mon–Thu
7:00am–10:00am
2:30pm–midnight
Fri–Sat
7:00am–10:00am
2:30pm–1:00am
Sun
7:00am–noon
2:30pm–10:00pm

Bar
Beer, wine, liquor

Credit cards
Visa, MC, AmEx

Reservations
Accepted

Features
Brunch
Date-friendly
Wi-Fi

Strikingly set in an old bank, Voice is a seamless blend of straightforward American modernism and elegant European antiquity, both in menu and design. The lounge is done up in gleaming marble and dark wood, but flat-screen TVs and rustic cowhide chairs keep it from being stuffy. The main dining room is spacious, with soaring ceilings and large picture windows letting in natural light.

The food's much better than the traditional overpriced, underwhelming fare you find at most hotel restaurants—especially at breakfast. The kitchen was, until recently, known for its outstanding charcuterie; in general, the overall level of confidence waxes and wanes (and the menu names are revolting: "A Study in Beets" is a beet salad with sea beans and coffee oil, and is much more interesting and serious than its silly name suggests). Shoestring fries lightly tossed in truffle oil, parmesan, salt, and herbs are worth every penny. We find ourselves dining most often in the lounge on good small plates, like miniature crab cakes served with a sort of refined Sriracha.

The wine list is a studied and careful selection in which regional typicity is preferred to bankable varietals. What's more, these mark ups are just above retail. It would be just as easy to enjoy a three-digit Vosne-Romanée here as it would a terrific $40 Italian white. Well, depends who's paying.

5.2 | 5.0
Food | Feel

$10
Price

Whataburger

These burgers aren't *that* great, but we all like them in a nostalgic kind of way

www.whataburger.com

Burgers
American
Counter service

Upper Kirby
3712 S. Shepherd Dr.
(713) 529-0216

Spring Branch
1718 W. Loop N.
(713) 868-8988

Heights
905 North Loop W.
(713) 880-8840

More locations
and features at
fearlesscritic.com

Hours
24 hours

Bar
None

Credit cards
Visa, MC, AmEx

Features
Kid-friendly

People that move away from Texas still talk about Whataburger with such awe, endowing it with the hallowed status of a last meal on death row. Why? We suspect that it's only wonderful whenever Mr. Jack Daniels is leading the way at two-thirty in the morning. But Whataburger's standard burgers are only slightly above average for fast food. Ditto for the chicken sandwiches, chicken tenders, and so on.

Around lunchtime, it's also not so fast. Not that that's necessarily a bad thing; Whataburger prides itself on fresh food that isn't made until you order it. A thin, tasteless patty, often gray and dull, comes seasoned with a blend of spices and topped with fresh and crispy lettuce, tomato, pickles, and onions. You can add cheese, bacon, or pickled jalapeños; we recommend all three. Better than the burgers is the breakfast taquito, served daily from 11pm to 11am. It's filled with eggs and your choice of bacon, potato, or sausage.

There are plenty of other burger joints that are ten times better than Whataburger, and at two in the morning, there are many taquerías that have better food, too. But Whataburger cravings are intense; when you get one, it stays with you until you satisfy it—or at least drunkenly start to, possibly passing out mid-burger.

Zabak's

Cheap and decent sumac-sprinkled comfort food

6.4 Food **7.0** Feel

$15 Price

www.zabaks.com

First, let's dispel a myth: Zabak's is not the best Middle Eastern/Eastern Mediterranean food in town. Not by a long shot. It's easy to be convinced now and then, especially on a good day, when the falafel is properly crisp on the outside and fluffy green inside from jalapeños—but sometimes, it's got a reheated, tough texture. Its generous coating of sumac is definitely appealing, and the pita's terrific; on a gyro, zippy tzatziki's lively and fresh-tasting, but the meat's just okay (it's the flat, dryish standard stuff). Chicken shawarma has had a grayish look the last few visits, and its tahini comes regrettably watery.

Baba ghanoush and hummus are reliable, though, and the price and vibe are totally lovable—like, ridiculously cheap. Especially if you bring your own wine (you're allowed, for a small upcharge); we would steer clear of the wine and beer on offer here—it's a little counter café, so that hardly counts against them.

And it's slightly modern inside, and clean and bright, but we honestly have much better experiences in this cuisine type from the backs of dingy markets and in fluorescent-lit dives. Still, it's hard to find a good, filling, casual stop in the Galleria, and this is certainly one of them. Especially on that falafel's good days.

Middle Eastern Greek
Counter service

Galleria
5901 Westheimer Rd.
(713) 977-7676

Hours
Mon–Sat
11:00am–8:00pm

Bar
Beer, wine, BYO

Credit cards
Visa, MC

Features
Veg-friendly

8.9	8.5
Food	Feel

$40	8.5
Price	Wine

Zelko Bistro

This teeny spot is one huge move in the right direction for restaurants

www.zelkobistro.com

American Modern
Casual restaurant

Heights
705 E. 11th St.
(713) 880-8691

Hours
Tue–Sat
11:00am–10:00pm
Sun
10:00am–9:00pm

Bar
Beer, wine

Credit cards
Visa, MC, AmEx

Reservations
Not accepted

Features
Brunch
Date-friendly
Outdoor dining

Zelko Bistro exudes a humble sincerity, not only in service and food, but décor: natural light fills the wee space by day, and by night, Mason jar lanterns with green bulbs gently light the bar. The wine list of newer vintages and less-traversed terroirs is imaginative, sensible, and hospitable, with little over $40—precisely the food-friendly, small-production wines that flashier restaurants utterly ignore. Also unlike those restaurants, Zelko takes no reservations, and ingredients are farm fresh (so menus seasonally change).

Comfort food here is either modernized with a seamless marriage to French traditions—exemplified by fried gherkins served with homemade ranch—or borrowed from other cultures entirely (like much-lauded bruschetta with feta, roasted red peppers, and hummus: better than the sum of its parts). Fish tacos with caramelized plantains seem puzzling on the menu, but their wonderful flavor and texture are beyond convincing. Fried chicken is wonderfully crisp and juicy, its playful Cap'n Crunch batter spiced profusely. More inconsistent is "Homeless Joe" meatloaf, cooked—in true hobo fashion—inside of a can. It's dense, but at best is still moist; sometimes it has come a little dry, but the sweet and tangy ketchup makes amends. Do finish up with an icebox pie or other nostalgic dessert that evokes the truck stop or county fair (thankfully in name, not execution).

INDEX

Index

NOTES